16.74
525
Bib

10642899

"*Beyond Homelessness* is a passionate call to move from being tourists in the world to active agents of God's shalom. Bouma-Prediger and Walsh point out that the housing crisis for the most vulnerable among us is also a cultural crisis. The solution to both is a recovery of the God of hope and overflowing love. Pastors, students, theologians, and Christians in every vocation should read *Beyond Homelessness* — a truly visionary book for our times."

— MARK R. GORNIK
author of *To Live in Peace: Biblical Faith and the Changing Inner City*

"This astutely timely book deserves an extensive audience — environmentalists, pastors, low-income housing advocates, students, those who forecast doom, good citizens eager to make changes, *all* Christians! Just to whet your appetite, you'll learn such things as nine kinds of homelessness, eight characteristics of 'home,' many imaginative ways to ponder Scripture, ten drivers of environmental deterioration, and one colossal hope. Broadly researched and splendidly written, this book is essential reading for anyone who wants truly to comprehend and mend our culture!"

— MARVA J. DAWN
author of *Truly the Community* and *Unfettered Hope*

San Diego Christian College
2100 Greenfield Drive
El Cajon, CA 92019

261.8
B764b

BEYOND HOMELESSNESS

Christian Faith in a Culture of Displacement

Steven Bouma-Prediger *&* Brian J. Walsh

WILLIAM B. EERDMANS PUBLISHING COMPANY
GRAND RAPIDS, MICHIGAN / CAMBRIDGE, U.K.

© 2008 Steven Bouma-Prediger and Brian J. Walsh
All rights reserved

Published 2008 by
Wm. B. Eerdmans Publishing Co.
2140 Oak Industrial Drive N.E., Grand Rapids, Michigan 49505 /
P.O. Box 163, Cambridge CB3 9PU U.K.

Printed in the United States of America

15 14 13 12 11 10   7 6 5 4 3 2

Library of Congress Cataloging-in-Publication Data

Bouma-Prediger, Steven.
Beyond homelessness: Christian faith in a culture of displacement /
Steven Bouma-Prediger & Brian J. Walsh.
p.   cm.
Includes bibliographical references.
ISBN 978-0-8028-4692-1 (pbk.: alk. paper)
1. Home — Religious aspects — Christianity. 2. Homelessness —
Religious aspects — Christianity. I. Walsh, Brian J. II. Title.

BR115.H56B67   2008

261.8 — dc22

2007045769

www.eerdmans.com

For
Crossroad Chapel/La Capilla de Crucijada,
Holland, Michigan

and

Russet House Farm,
Cameron, Ontario

Contents

Contents

Preface

Have you ever had a time when you were "home alone"? You know, when the people you live with are all away and you've got the house to yourself. And you are thinking, "Finally, some peace and quiet. Finally a time to just be by myself, follow my own routines, my own schedule, my own whims." It's great, isn't it? To have the house to yourself, to be home alone. But after a while, maybe a day or two, don't you get lonely? Sure, it's great to have the quiet, but don't you start to miss the noise of everyday life at home — the clanking of the pots in the kitchen, the giggling from the children, the music coming from the living room. Being home alone might be nice for a while, but as a lifestyle, it can be pretty empty, kind of isolating.

We think that "home alone" is actually an oxymoron. There is no such thing as being home alone. Home is a matter of community. Home is about belonging, connectedness, and shared memory. Home involves relationships of trust. While we may live alone, we can never be home alone. To be at home in the world, indeed to be at home within ourselves, we must be in a home that is shared. Home is a matter of community.

What is true of home is also true of books on home. For a number of years we had both been thinking about themes of home, mostly in relation to a rethinking of a Christian view of creation in the context of what has been described as postmodern homelessness. Brian was also thinking about homelessness in terms of folks who live on the streets, and Steve was following these themes through from the perspective of the ecological crisis. While we had been friends for a long time and both vaguely knew of each other's work in this area, it wasn't until we started hearing each other's papers presented at conferences that it became clear that we were working on the same project. We were reading the same books, struggling with the same questions, and formulating the same response to the crisis of homelessness in our time. We both knew that homelessness was a culture-wide phenomenon, that it wore many faces, and that a deeply biblical worldview had the resources to respond to this crisis with a vision of redemptive homecoming. So it became clear that we should work together to envision a Christian response to our culture of displacement.

Displacement. To be displaced. To be disconnected from place. To "diss" place. That's our current place. We in North America live in a culture of displacement. "This world is not my home, I'm just a passing through" is no longer the sentiment of a certain kind of dualistic pietism; it is a culture-wide attitude. Whether we are talking about the upwardly mobile who view each place as a rung in the ladder that goes up to who knows where, or the postmodern nomad with no roots in any place or any tradition of place, or the average consumer who doesn't know anything about the place where she lives or the places her food comes from, the reality is the same — we are a culture of displacement.

Christian faith is a faith that is always placed. Placed in a good creation. Placed in time. An incarnational faith. A faith rooted in one who took flesh in a particular place. And it continues to be a faith of embodied presence. The church is the body of Christ, and bodies can only exist in place. Moreover, this is a faith with a placed hope — a new heavens and a (re)new(ed) earth. This is not a faith about passing through this world, but a faith that declares this world — this blue-green planet so battered and bruised, yet lovely — as our home.

This book is an extended essay on homecoming. And one of the things we say is that home is always rooted in memory. Indeed, there is no vision, no future-directed hope, apart from memory. Future homecoming, in the face of present homebreaking, requires a memory of past homemaking. Our argument is that the scriptures of Israel and the Church provide us with a powerful vision of home, a devastatingly truthful picture of homebreaking, and an empowering hope for homecoming.

The scriptures, therefore, are at the heart of our analysis. And while we hope that such a biblical vision breathes through the text whether we are talking about socioeconomic homelessness, ecological despoliation of home, or the displaced nature of the postmodern condition, we also want to bring specific attention to the scriptures through a series of interludes that run between each chapter of this book. As you read these interludes (and you can do them all together, or let them arise for you as you proceed through the book), we suggest that you also read the biblical texts that are under consideration in each interlude. There are nuances in the interludes that will likely be missed if you do not also read these biblical texts.

Home, we have said, is a matter of community. And so is the writing of books that attempt to lead us beyond homelessness. We have written in community with each other, but also with a host of fellow homemakers. Analysis of socio-economic homelessness lacks vitality and integrity if it is divorced from life on the street and in substandard housing. We are, therefore, indebted to friends who are at the forefront of ministry amongst the homeless in Toronto for much of our analysis in chapters three and four. Dion Oxford, Greg Paul, Michael Blaire, Carmel Hili, Phil Nazar, Joe Mihevc, and Murray MacAdam read all or part of these chapters and provided invaluable advice. And Chris Gousmette from Wellington, New Zealand, facilitated an invitation for Brian to present much of chapter four to the policy analysts at Housing New Zealand. That interaction was most helpful.

For constructive criticism on chapters five and six we thank Barry Bandstra, Steve Hoogerwerf, Lynn Japinga, Phil Munoa, Jenny Powers, Jeff Tyler, Kent VanTil, Allen Verhey, and Boyd Wilson. Of the many people to thank for kind invitations to present some of these chapters in public, we are especially grateful to Roy Berkenbosch for the opportunity to try out the ideas in chapter six at the King's University College in Edmonton, Alberta. With regard to chapters seven and eight, we thank (in addition to most of the above) Jim Olthuis, a teacher and friend who we hope will find the seeds from his own scholarship growing and flourishing in this the work of his former students. Finally, a word of thanks to Merold Westphal, whose insights in a summer research seminar a decade ago first started Steve thinking about the core ideas of this book.

Other friends read the whole manuscript and offered their comments and encouragement. We thank Ryan Atwell, Byron Borger, Norman Wirzba, and Loren Wilkinson for their generosity. One person, however, read the entire manuscript and provided an indispensable editorial service to us. With a sharp and critical eye Sylvia Keesmaat read this book so closely that we are confident in saying that in the very few places where we did not take her editorial advice, we take full responsibility. Any other errors in the book are wholly hers.

Institutions can also be places of home. Brian thanks the Toronto Christian Resource Centre in Regent Park, Toronto, for hosting him as their "theologian in residence" in 2003. Researching, writing, and reflecting in the context of this inner-city ministry gave Brian's work a groundedness — a sense of place in the midst of placelessness — that would not have been possible sitting in an office at the university. Nonetheless, the academy is also a home in its own way. Brian serves as a Christian Reformed campus minister at the University of Toronto and as Adjunct Professor of Theology of Culture at Wycliffe College. Both contexts have proven to be very conducive to the kind of reflection necessary for a book of this magnitude.

Steve is on the board of the Macatawa Greenway Partnership, a local environmental organization in southwestern Michigan, and thanks all the good people of that grassroots organization, most especially Greg Holcombe and Derk Walkotten, for their support of this project. Steve also thanks those in his academic home who have generously supported this endeavor: Dean William Reynolds, Provost James Boelkins, and President James Bultman. President Bultman and the Hope Board of Trustees deserve special thanks for the sabbatical that allowed Steve to complete the final work on this book. Friends at Western Theological Seminary, most notably Leanne VanDyke and Dennis Voskuil, are also deserving of thanks for providing Steve an office on the seventh floor of the Cook Center for Theological Research. Such a perch not only provided easy access to needed books and a quiet place to work but also a bird's-eye view of blue herons and brown houses, strolling people and steadfast white pines.

The Stanford and Priscilla Reid Trust showed faith in the project at its earliest stages. Through a grant to the Christian Reformed Campus Ministry at the University of Toronto, they enabled Brian to hire an assistant to take some of Brian's ministry load in order to release him for writing. That funding not only encouraged Brian at a crucial stage of his research, it also proved to be the seed for an expansion of the campus ministry through the introduction of Geoff Wichert as Brian's colleague. In a similar way, the John H. and Jeanne M. Jacobson Chair in Religion, which Steve held for a four-year term, greatly facilitated this project by providing needed funding for various book-related tasks, most notably travel for face-to-face meetings. To all those who have contributed financially, we thank you.

We are also grateful to Michael Iafrate for his work compiling the subject index. Michael's passion for justice, and for a church that makes a difference in the world, combined with his own interdisciplinary curiosity in scholarship, made him a natural for doing our index. Thank you.

A life of teaching is a life with students. Our students at Hope College, Wycliffe College, and the University of Toronto, and with the Creation Care Studies Program in Belize and New Zealand have walked this path of homemaking with us. They have heard our ideas, challenged them, corrected them, and sometimes sent us down different paths. Their voices are heard in various sections of this book. We hope that this book will enable them to be homemakers in an academic world that seems to specialize in homelessness.

Of course, the notion of home usually conjures up the image of family in our imaginations. Steve's life of homemaking with Celaine includes Anna Meredythe, Chara Kristine, and Sophia Calvert. Brian's life of homemaking with Sylvia encompasses Jubal (now out of the house, but still in the home), Madeleine, and Lydia. There is no home without our families, and we hope that what we have written bears witness, if only in part, to the depth of home that we experience together.

Finally, if we are striving to shape Christian faith in a culture of displacement, then it is appropriate that we begin with places that have been sites of home for us. So Brian dedicates this book to Russet House Farm and the community that shares this experiment in sustainable living near Cameron, Ontario. And Steve dedicates this book to Crossroad Chapel/La Capilla de Crucijada, and all those who have over the years been a part of this experiment in church in the core city of Holland, Michigan.

The Bible begins and ends with places — a garden and a gardened city. Both are places of inhabitation, places of homemaking, precisely because God is at home in both places. Our prayer is that this book might make a contribution to the redemption of place, the restoration of home in a culture of displacement.

Christmas 2007

There's No Place
Like Home

There's no place like home.
There's no place like home.
There's no place like home.

Dorothy in *The Wizard of Oz*

If you ever met them, you wouldn't think that Kenneth and Kenny share much more than their names. But even their names are different. No one would ever call Kenneth Kenny, and Kenneth doesn't even appear on Kenny's birth certificate. No, Kenny was Kenny from the beginning.

There are, however, a few things they have in common. They are both male, white, and of English descent. And we could also say that they are neighbors, although they've never met. If Kenneth ever saw the face and body of this particular neighbor, Kenny, it certainly didn't register. Kenneth was probably on his way to a meeting when he passed Kenny on the street.

Kenny lives in the ravine with a couple of his brothers. They have a squat down there with a couple of tents and some furniture they picked up on garbage day. It might have come from in front of Kenneth's place. Kenny and the boys live close to nature. Real close. In fact, when a flash flood came down the river, they almost drowned. They lost everything, and they had to cobble together tents, sleeping bags, and some cast-off furniture to start all over again. One of the local street outreach organizations helped out, though the cops seemed pretty angry about having to save these guys.

Kenneth, however, enjoyed watching that violent thunderstorm from

1

the vantage point of his twentieth-floor condominium because he happened to be in town that day. He actually has two other "homes" in other parts of North America. Kenneth's business activities require him to work out of three cities, so his wife, Julie, suggested that they should have three places to live; that way Kenneth would not be stuck in boring hotels, and she could accompany him regardless of which office he was working out of at any particular time. This particular condo is certainly comfortable: one bedroom, two baths, living room, dining room, den, patio, and a very well-equipped kitchen. All of their kitchens are well equipped: the latest in time-saving devices, the best in china and cutlery, a constantly well-stocked pantry and refrigerator, and, of course, a wine cabinet with choice vintages.

Kenneth and Kenny are neighbors, but they don't have that much in common. Kenny panhandles at a busy intersection, one that Kenneth drives by in his BMW with some frequency. Kenny likes cars but could never afford one. Actually, in his earlier days he had a bit of a problem with drinking and driving. Of course, Kenneth also drank and drove — but always carefully. Perhaps that's something that Kenneth and Kenny share: they both like cars, and they both enjoy a drink once in a while. Kenneth drinks better stuff than Kenny does, but the inebriating effects are similar. Of course, Kenny is also a crack cocaine addict. Not that Kenneth doesn't often require a little bit of a sedative to get to sleep at night, which he usually chases with a single-malt scotch. But he isn't an addict or anything. Not unless you count his walk-in closet that holds twenty-five suits, fifty shirts, twenty pairs of shoes, and more ties than you can imagine.

Kenny is poor and homeless; Kenneth is rich and has three homes. Kenny is down and out and essentially voiceless in our society; Kenneth is among the rich and powerful, and when he speaks, people listen. Kenny is dirty and can be a little foul-mouthed; Kenneth showers every day, shaves twice, has impeccable teeth and speaks with an educated eloquence. Kenny likes the heavy metal bands of his youth; Kenneth frequents the opera.

There are other things that are different about Kenny and Kenneth. Because Kenny lives in the ravine, he knows that white-tailed deer and coyotes are becoming plentiful in the city again. He has seen the odd salmon and trout make their way up the river. And though he is sometimes too strung out or hung-over to notice, there are some days when Kenny notices migrating magnolia warblers and Baltimore orioles flying past his squat. Warblers and orioles don't fly past Kenneth's place, and he could never notice deer or coyote from way up there. Kenneth and Julie's place (thanks to Julie and the condo staff) is beautiful, and the interior design consultant did a wonderful job. But the only plants up there, of course, are potted. Very nice, but a little limited.

Kenneth doesn't know Kenny, of course, but he doesn't really know any of his neighbors at the condo either. With two units per floor, he has been in the elevator with the other twentieth-floor couple only once in the last three years. And since he is only at this "home" for about one week per month, there isn't really time to make friends with the neighbors. Kenny, however, knows a lot of folks in the neighborhood. Every morning that he can get up (often in pretty bad shape), he makes his way to the local street outreach ministry and helps cook for other homeless people. Kenny likes to cook, and he especially likes to cook for people like himself, people who have no money and nowhere else to eat. He can get really excited when some fresh greens are available from the local community garden because he knows that a diet of starch and fat isn't all that good for his street friends. He also knows that Alice — his sometimes on, most times off, Aboriginal girlfriend — loves salad.

So here's the question: Who is homeless here? Kenneth or Kenny? Kenny is a local statistic of homelessness: he isn't simply underhoused; he has no house at all. On the other hand, Kenneth is, if anything, over-housed. Three distinct homes in three different parts of the country. But Kenny knows something about the ecosystem in which he lives and is deeply committed to the community of the homeless, the drug addicts, and the prostitutes that he counts as his friends. Kenneth and Julie have a lot of business acquaintances, but they don't even know their neighbors.

Kenny has lived in that ravine for three years. Kenneth has split his time between the condo, the other two places, and innumerable business trips and vacations over the last three years. Kenny is a man of one place; Kenneth is a man of numerous places. Kenny walks the streets, while Kenneth has a car in each of his three garages across the continent.

There is no denying that Kenny is homeless, and there is no virtue in esteeming his impoverished, drug-addicted life. But again, we do need to ask the question: Who is homeless here? Do Kenneth and Julie really experience any place in the world as "home" to them? In their wealth, their mobility, their power, are they any less homeless than Kenny is? Or perhaps that's the wrong way to put the question. Perhaps we need to ask whether Kenny and Kenneth are both deeply homeless, albeit in different ways.

Home is, among other things, a matter of place. Edward Casey has written that

> . . . to lack a primal place is to be "homeless" indeed, not only in the literal sense of having no permanently sheltering structure but also as being without any effective means of orientation in a complex and confusing world. By late modern times, this world has become increasingly placeless, a matter of mere sites instead of lived places, of sudden displacements rather than of perduring implacements.[1]

To be "home" is to experience some place as "primal," as first, as a place to which one has a profound sense of connection, identity, and even love. To be "emplaced" is to have a point of orientation. Homelessness, then, is a matter of profound and all-pervasive displacement. Homelessness is a matter of "placelessness."

If homelessness is a matter of *displacement,* who in the parallel of Kenneth and Kenny is the homeless one? Who has a "place," and who is "placeless"? In some respects, both Kenneth and Kenny have a place. And by this we don't just mean that they both have a place to sleep each night — very different places, but a place nonetheless. They also have a "place" in their respective worlds. Kenny is the guy who makes breakfast at the local outreach center. He is known as being a little loud, and sometimes he needs to be calmed down; but in this community of homeless folks, Kenny clearly has a place. He is respected and admired for his concern for his neighbors. He is also a little feared by those who have been on the receiving end of his anger. Also, at that busy intersection, Kenny or one of his boys can be clearly seen at their "place," asking for change from drivers stopped at the red light.

In his very different world, Kenneth also has his place. He's an executive: many people work "under" him, and his place is on top. He is a well-respected member of his church and is appreciated for the largesse of his donations. He has a place as Julie's husband, and together they cut a fine form as an established couple. And Kenneth seems to be "at home" in board rooms, executive lounges at airports, and flying business class.

Both Kenny and Kenneth are at home in their respective worlds, and yet they are both, in important respects, homeless, because they both expe-

---

1. Edward Casey, *Getting Back into Place: Toward a Renewed Understanding of the Place-World* (Bloomington, IN: Indiana University Press, 1993), p. xv.

rience deep displacement in their lives. Though Kenny has his place volunteering at the local center, his drug addiction, emotional outbursts, foul language, and poorly developed social skills make it impossible for him to ever find a place in regular employment. As one of the homeless underclass of our society, Kenny is certainly economically displaced: he exists at best on the very margins of normal economic life. And while his tenure in the ravine is as long as Kenneth's has been in the condo, and Kenny is more acclimated and attuned to his place in that ravine than Kenneth is in the condo, there is still something deeply precarious about Kenny's squat in the ravine that leaves him displaced in ways that Kenneth clearly is not. Though Kenny lives in the ravine 365 days a year, he is outside the bounds of "normal" society: he is subject to the threat of weather, is illegally squatting on city land, is constantly dependent on the charity of others, and is always living on the edge of violence. Kenny's place provides only a semblance of the kind of security that is necessary for a place to be home. He never knows when the next flash flood is going to wipe out his squat, or when the police are going to clear them out, or when he's going to end up in the emergency room from an overdose of bad crack.

As a homeless, poor, drug-addicted man living in a squat on someone else's land, Kenny is socially, economically, psychologically, legally, and geographically displaced. And we could also say that Kenny, as a visible member of the homeless underclass, functions as a symbol of displacement as he walks through the neighborhood with his shopping cart full of other people's junk or sits at the corner asking for change. Odd, isn't it? Kenny's "place" in our society is as a symbol of displacement.

What about Kenneth? Kenneth's social, economic, and legal place in the world is secure. He has a very clear social place in both business and church; his economic place is clearly established as a very successful businessman; and he has clear title on all three of his places of residence, with a lawyer in each city to tend to his legal affairs. And if you were looking for the very picture of success, the symbol of having arrived, you couldn't do better than Kenneth in a business suit driving his BMW past Kenny at the side of the road.

But Kenneth doesn't really "live" anywhere, because in the condo, with all of its opulence and fine taste, Kenneth is still displaced. Like his other residences, it is more the product of a highly paid interior designer than anything that gives Kenneth and Julie's life together an identity. Like the mansions and monster homes of the suburbs, this tasteful place lacks any sense of permanence. Because Kenneth is on the move in his career, he needs a place that "can be conveniently marketed" anytime he needs to move on to the next job. The condo is a utilitarian place "to inhabit, leave, and recirculate."[2]

Though Kenny's tenure in the ravine is precarious, at least he lives there, while Kenneth "stays" in his various places but never has time to become connected to any one of them. Wendell Berry has an explanation for this, but not one that Kenneth would like: "Our present leaders — people of wealth and power — do not know what it means to take place seriously: to think it worthy, for its own sake, of love and careful work. They cannot take any place seriously because they must be ready at any moment, by the terms of power and wealth in the modern world, to destroy any place."[3] Here's the contradiction: Kenneth's social, economic, and legal place in the world not only requires that he be geographically "displaced" (with no real home) and that he have a willingness to leave any place in order to facilitate his upwardly mobile climb; it also requires him to have the willingness to sacrifice any place — his own or someone else's — for the sake of power and wealth.

Berry argues that "a rootless and placeless monoculture of commercial expectations and products" is inherently a culture of displacement, of homelessness (p. 151). Kenneth's life moves in precisely such a rootless and placeless monoculture. He sinks no roots down in the cities where he lives, knows nothing of the social history of any of the neighborhoods, is unaware of the unique ecosystem that exists within a few blocks of his condo, and drinks coffee at the same chain of specialty coffee shops in every city to which his travels take him. Kenneth is placeless, and his business depends on his willingness to exploit any place and render any people placeless if it serves the interests of power and wealth.

But at least Kenneth has power and wealth, something that Kenny clearly lacks; and surely power and wealth can make his social, economic, and legal place secure. Or can it? Ever since September 11, 2001, Kenneth has been anxious when he gets on a plane. And it isn't just his own personal travel security that has him worried; he also knows that a world of

---

2. William Leach, *The Country of Exiles: The Destruction of Place in American Life* (New York: Vintage, 2000), pp. 76-77.

3. Wendell Berry, *Sex, Economy, Freedom and Community* (New York: Pantheon Books, 1993), p. 22.

international terrorism is a world of economic insecurity for all but those who deal in weapons, surveillance, and private security (business areas Kenneth never entered). Furthermore, he seems to spend an inordinate amount of time worrying about the stock market these days. During the few occasions that he and Julie actually eat a meal at the condo, the television is on and the stock reports scroll across the bottom of the screen, making for a rather distracted meal. If the market crashes, there goes the twentieth-floor condo, the BMW, the business-class seats on airplanes, and all the suits. Kenneth's distraction worries Julie, and sometimes she feels emotionally very alone, as though she has no real place in Kenneth's world of finance. Displacement migrates from an overly mobile life to a sense of monocultural placelessness, to economic anxiety, to distraction, to Julie feeling emotionally displaced, and so on. Who knows where all of this will end up for Kenneth and Julie?

A Culture of Displacement, Amnesia, and Homelessness

There is in our time a "creeping dread of homelessness."[4] Elie Wiesel once described the twentieth century as "the age of the expatriate, the refugee, the stateless and the wanderer." "Never before," he says, "have so many human beings fled from so many homes."[5] It is interesting that the Palestinian writer Edward Said agrees: "Our age, with its modern warfare, imperialism and quasi-theological ambitions of totalitarian rulers . . . is indeed the age of the refugee, the displaced person, mass immigration."[6] In our time there is "the unhealable rift forced between a human being and a native place, between the self and its true home." The "essential sadness" of such exile "can never be surmounted" (Said, p. 357).

It is thus not surprising that Iain Chambers argues that diaspora, the stranger, and migrancy are the dominant metaphors of our time. "The chronicles of diasporas," he says, "constitute the ground swell of moder-

---

4. John Della Costa, "Outsourcing, Downsizing, Mergers and Cutbacks: Folks Are Living with a Creeping Sense of Homelessness," *Catholic New Times* (May 3, 1998): 10.

5. Wiesel, "Longing for Home," in Leroy S. Rouner, ed., *The Longing for Home* (Notre Dame, IN: University of Notre Dame Press, 1996), p. 19.

6. Edward Said, "Reflections on Exile," in R. Ferguson, M. Gever, Trinh T. Minh-ha, Cornel West, eds., *Out There: Marginalization and Contemporary Cultures* (Cambridge, MA: MIT Press, 1990), p. 357.

nity. These historical testimonies interrogate and undermine any simple or uncomplicated sense of origins, traditions and linear movement."[7] This complicates and deepens our understanding of displacement precisely because the experience of diaspora peoples often entails a forgetting of the very place from which they have been displaced. No wonder, Chambers says, that "to be a stranger in a strange land, to be lost . . . is perhaps the condition most typical of contemporary life" (p. 18). Whether we examine the forced migrations of people who have been chased out of their homelands by ethnic violence, waves of immigrants seeking economic security, the marginality of the poor in the inner city, or the placeless and lonely anonymity of the elite business class, there is a profound sense that we are all strangers. And that estrangement, Chambers argues, that culture-wide sense of displacement, is fundamentally a feature of our *migrancy*. "The migrant's sense of being rootless, of living between worlds, between a lost past and a non-integrated present, is perhaps the most fitting metaphor of this (post)modern condition" (p. 27). Wanderer, expatriate, exile, diaspora, stranger, migrancy, displacement — all ways to describe the homelessness of the late twentieth century and early twenty-first century.

The novelist Barbara Kingsolver describes America as a culture of amnesiacs. In her novel *Animal Dreams* we meet Codi Noline, whom Kingsolver describes as the opposite of a "homemaker." She is a "home ignorer."[8] And as "a good citizen of the nation in love with forgetting," Codi has lost some very important and identity-shaping memories (p. 149). Her name is *Noline*, and her story is that of a young woman with "no line," with no sense of who she is, or of her lineage, her genealogy, her "place." But she is striving to find home. At one point she says, "I'd like to find a place that feels like it *wants* to take me in" (p. 183). And she learns that no such place of belonging can exist without embraced memory.

There is something nostalgic about Kingsolver's novels, but it is not a sentimental nostalgia. Rather, Kingsolver's nostalgia is that of imaginatively re-visioning and re-placing both memory and home. This is a reparative kind of nostalgia because it is a remembering that refuses to cover up the brokenness of the past, the painful and even home-destroying memories. Roberta Rubenstein suggests that, for Kingsolver, "home matters not

7. Iain Chambers, *Migrancy, Culture, Identity* (London and New York: Routledge, 1994), pp. 16-17.

8. Barbara Kingsolver, *Animal Dreams* (New York: HarperCollins, 1990), p. 77.

simply as a place but as the imagination's place marker for a vision of personal (and cultural) reunion, encompassing both what actually may have been experienced in the vanished past and what never could have been. The remembered/imagined vision of home is a construction, but it also constructs — and stokes and sometimes heals — the longing for belonging."[9] Memories may well be constructions, and thus never objectively neutral; but without memory, present homemaking and a vision of future homecoming is impossible. Kingsolver's novels assume that there is this longing for belonging, this ineluctable desire for homecoming, in the human heart.[10] The nostalgia in her fiction is rooted in what Rubenstein calls a cultural mourning, which "results from cultural dislocation and loss of ways of life from which an individual feels historically severed or exiled."[11]

Elie Wiesel would agree. The antidote to exilic dislocation is memory. Speaking from the context of the Jewish Diaspora, and especially in a post-Holocaust world, Wiesel says that forgetfulness is the devastating temptation of such an exilic and homeless condition: "Forgetfulness by definition is never creative; nor is it instructive. The one who forgets to come back has forgotten the home he or she came from and where he or she is going."[12] Forgetfulness closes down both the past and the future, thereby paralyzing the present. Exile is perpetuated by a cultural amnesia because "one who forgets forgets everything, including the roads leading homeward. Forgetting marks the end of human experience, and of longing too" (Wiesel, p. 25). Without memory there can be no vision, and without memory of home, there can be no longing for homecoming.

In Wendell Berry's novel *Remembering*, Andy Catlett is a prophetic opponent of the monocultural placelessness of contemporary agribusiness, an industry and culture that lives under "a great black cloud of forgetfulness."[13] Soon farmers who succumb to this forgetfulness will no lon-

9. Roberta Rubenstein, *Home Matters: Longing and Belonging, Nostalgia and Mourning in Women's Fiction* (New York: Palgrave, 2001), p. 164.

10. Charles Winquist has a similar perspective: "Homecoming is a re-collection of experience. Our remembrance is an interpretation. . . . To come home to the self we must be able to tell the story of our lives with a memory for reality." *Homecoming: Interpretation, Transformation and Individuation*, AAR Studies in Religion 18 (Missoula, MT: Scholars Press, 1978), p. 108.

11. Rubenstein, *Home Matters*, p. 38.

12. Wiesel, "Longing for Home," pp. 24-25.

13. Wendell Berry, *Remembering* (San Francisco: North Point Press, 1988), p. 38.

ger remember who or where they are, "their future drawn up into the Future of the American Food System to be seen no more, forever destroyed by schemes, by numbers, by deadly means, all its springs poisoned" (p. 38). In his early years as an agricultural journalist Andy learned

> ... that bigger was better and biggest was best; that people coming into a place to use it need ask only what they wanted, not what was there; that whatever in humanity or nature failed before the advance of mechanical ambition deserved to fail; and that the answers were in the universities and the corporate government offices, not in the land or the people. (p. 72)

But Andy could believe this ideology of displacement only if he was also capable "of forgetting all that his own people had been" (p. 72). Andy becomes a prophet of remembering in this story while also falling into the distrust of forgetting in his own life. The path to redemption, the path back home, back to his geographical, emotional, moral, and familial "place" is a path of remembering.

It is not surprising that themes of memory and homecoming are so prevalent in the writings of Kingsolver, Wiesel, and Berry, because they are, one could argue, the prevalent themes of all literature. The exiled Somalian writer Nuruddin Farah makes this observation with some eloquence:

> What is the topic of literature? It began with the expulsion of Adam from Paradise. What, in fact, writers do is to play around either with the myth of creation or the myth of return. And in between, in parentheses, there is that promise, the promise of return. While awaiting the return, we tell stories, create literature, recite poetry, remember the past and experience the present. Basically, we writers are telling the story of that return — either in the form of a New Testament or an Old Testament variation on the creation myth. It's a return to innocence, to childhood, to our sources.[14]

Whether or not we agree with Farah that all writers are telling the story of return in the form of Old or New Testament variations, it seems that there

---

14. William Gass, "The Philosophical Significance of Exile" (interview with Nuruddin Farah, Han Vladislave, and Jorge Edwards), in John Gladd, ed., *Literature in Exile* (Durham, NC: Duke University Press, 1990), p. 4. Cited by Rubenstein, *Home Matters*, p. 167, n. 4.

is indeed something universal about narratives of exile and return, of homelessness and the perilous journey back home. Humans are incurable storytellers, and our stories seem to be preoccupied with home.

Nuruddin Farah would likely concur with Roberta Rubenstein that nostalgia and homesickness are not necessarily sentimental and regressive modes of feeling precisely because "both may have compensatory and even liberating dimensions within the frame of narrative."[15] The question is, of course, which narrative? While it may be true that a legitimate nostalgia for home characterizes much literature and storytelling, not all narratives are created equal. Indeed, some memories or myths serve to legitimate genocidal homelessness, while others are too broken ever to provide enough vision and hope for restorative homemaking.

To return to Kenny and Kenneth for a moment, we might surmise that Kenny's memories are too full of violence, family dysfunction, and crippling poverty to ever give him the resources for restorative homemaking in his life. These are homebreaking memories. And without wishing to push it too far, we wonder whether Kenneth's grounding narrative of upward mobility, status, economic progress, and corporate power might be a story rooted in memories of conquest that continue to render much of the world's population impoverished and homeless. These are the same memories that legitimate the wanton destruction of ecosystems around the world, thereby deepening a widespread sense of displacement.

Similarly, Kingsolver, Wiesel, and Berry are not interested in remembering just any story. Barbara Kingsolver would certainly not want a renewed memory of America's Manifest Destiny to set a people on its path home again: that might be a homemaking memory for some, but only at the expense of the homelessness of others.[16] Elie Wiesel and Edward Said would agree that, as we live in a diaspora context and time of exile, memory and a longing for homecoming is necessary. But they happen to long to come home to the same place, Palestine, and they live out of often violently opposed memories. Wendell Berry may extol the virtues of a Jeffersonian, agrarian vision of life, but that is in clear conflict with the narratives of

---

15. Rubenstein, *Home Matters*, p. 5.

16. For Kingsolver's response to the renewed nationalism in America after September 11, 2001, see her essays "Small Wonder," "Saying Grace," and "And Our Flag Was Still There," in Barbara Kingsolver, *Small Wonder* (New York: HarperCollins, 2002).

technological progress and global capitalism that legitimate the home-destroying forces of monocrop agribusiness.[17]

So where do we begin? Which narrative will dominate our memory?

Which Memories, What Home?

Elie Wiesel tells us that the temptation of exile is forgetfulness. In fact, in the biblical tradition there is nothing that the forces of imperial exile want more than that those exiled will forget. If the Israelites forget their story of liberation from a previous imperial regime (Egypt) and forget that their story is rooted in a God who sets captives free, then they might become convinced that resistance to the empire is futile and become comfortable in their homeless exile. Amnesia breeds apathy; forgetfulness renders a people numb to their homelessness. But it is not just exile that tempts people to forgetfulness. In the Mosaic tradition, a secure sense of being at home can also be a temptation to an exile-producing forgetfulness. That's why Torah is a document of remembering. In the wilderness, in that place on the boundary between slavery and homecoming, Israel is admonished to be a people of memory:

> When the Lord your God has brought you into the land that he swore to your ancestors, to Abraham, to Isaac, and to Jacob, to give you — a land with fine, large cities that you did not build, houses filled with all sorts of

---

17. See Wendell Berry, *Citizenship Papers* (Washington, DC: Shoemaker & Hoard, 2003), especially the essays, "A Citizen's Response," "Thoughts in the Presence of Fear," "The Total Economy," and "The Agrarian Standard."

Norman Wirzba offers this exposition of Berry's agenda: "Berry believes that it is time for us to take full responsibility for the life-denying character of our histories and see in our damaged and exhausted landscapes the effects of a perverted desire. It is time too for us to recognize that disembodied desire, desire cut off from the natural and social webs of inter-dependence, eventually leads to our own homelessness." "Introduction: The Challenge of Berry's Agrarian Vision," in Norman Wirzba, ed., *The Art of the Commonplace: The Agrarian Essays of Wendell Berry* (Washington, DC: Counterpoint, 2002), p. xiii.

To describe our "histories" as having a "life-denying character," rooted in "perverted desire" and resulting in "homelessness," is to say that the memories of this history and this narrative make for homelessness, not homecoming. Berry counters this industrial vision with an agrarian vision. Conflicting memories and conflicting visions result in conflicting understandings of home and what it means to have a "place" in the world.

goods that you did not fill, hewn cisterns that you did not hew, vineyards and olive groves that you did not plant — and when you have eaten your fill, take care that you do not forget the Lord who brought you out of the land of Egypt, out of the house of slavery. (Deut. 6:10-12)[18]

Do not forget. "Guaranteed security dulls the memory," says Walter Brueggemann.[19] The temptation was to forget that they were a people rescued from slavery, to be so in control of the land that they took home for granted as eternally secure, their achievement and not a gift from the God who freed them.

Ancient Israel was a community constituted by memory. When that community suffered amnesia and no longer remembered the Exodus — the liberating, homemaking God — the result was invariably homeless and placeless exile all over again. But this isn't really about having memory or no memory. As in Kingsolver, Wiesel, and Berry, the question that faced ancient Israel, and continues to face us all, is *which* memory? The tradition of both Torah and the prophets makes it clear that, if Israel should forget Yahweh, then the necessary implication is that they have embraced idolatry. Deuteronomy couples "do not forget the Lord who brought you out of slavery" with "do not follow other gods" (Deut. 6:12, 14). Jeremiah says that, because the people forgot the God who liberated them from Egyptian bondage, led them in the wilderness, sustained them in a place of desolation, and brought them to a plentiful land of homecoming, they "went after worthless things and became worthless themselves," they "defiled the land," their "prophets prophesied by Baal," and they followed gods that "do not profit" (Jer. 2:4-8). But embracing idolatry is not a matter of living without memory. Instead, embracing idolatry is to embrace the memory, the mythology, and the narratives of gods other than Yahweh.

This is a very important point: human life is narratively rooted. Humans construct their lives and shape their world into home in terms of grounding and ultimate memories.[20] The overwhelming testimony and

---

18. Cf. Deut. 8:11-20. The fact that Israel's homecoming is at the expense of someone else's homelessness is a problem that we will address in the biblical interlude "Much Depends on Dinner."

19. Walter Brueggemann, *The Land: Place as Gift and Challenge in Biblical Faith* (Philadelphia: Fortress, 1977), p. 54.

20. See Peter Berger, *The Sacred Canopy: Elements of a Sociological Theory of Religion* (Garden City, NY: Anchor Books, 1967), esp. chs. 1-2.

claim of Hebrew Scripture is that embracing the memories of idolatry will always result in homelessness. Covenantal amnesia — forgetting the story of the homemaking God — might afford the people a place, even a "home" in the midst of another vision of life, another narrative, but such a home is judged to be no home at all.

We write this book from a perspective that shares this biblical vision of life. Humans today live in a culture of displacement, and homecoming is not possible without memory. In the conflict of memories, the conflict of narratives that characterizes our postmodern context, we are prepared to stake our lives on a biblical memory, a vision of life rooted in the narrative of the Old and New Testaments. Throughout this book we will offer biblical interludes between each chapter. In these meditations we will attempt to evoke themes of home, homelessness, and homecoming throughout the biblical narrative. In this introductory chapter it is appropriate to sketch out that story in broad strokes.

Biblical Homecoming[21]

The story begins with a homemaking God who creates a world for inhabitation. This God is a primordial homemaker, and creation is a home for all creatures. For the human creature, however, the divine homemaker plants a garden. This is a God with perpetually dirty fingernails, a God who is always playing in the mud. The human creature is created out of the earth (human from the *humus*) in the image and likeness of this homemaking and

21. We acknowledge our indebtedness in this retelling of the biblical narrative to Walter Brueggemann. Beyond his book *The Land*, already cited, see also *The Prophetic Imagination* (Philadelphia: Fortress, 1978); *Hopeful Imagination: Prophetic Voices in Exile* (Philadelphia: Fortress, 1986); *Cadences of Home: Preaching Among Exiles* (Louisville: Westminster/John Knox Press, 1997); and *Ichabod Toward Home: The Journey of God's Glory* (Grand Rapids: Eerdmans, 2002).

Also helpful are: Bruce Birch, *Let Justice Roll Down: The Old Testament, Ethics, and Christian Life* (Louisville: Westminster/John Knox, 1991); Paul Hanson, *The People Called: The Growth of Community in the Bible* (San Francisco: Harper and Row, 1986); William P. Brown, *The Ethos of the Cosmos: The Genesis of Moral Imagination in the Bible* (Grand Rapids: Eerdmans, 1999); Theodore Hiebert, *The Yahwist's Landscape: Nature and Religion in Early Israel* (New York: Oxford, 1996); J. Richard Middleton, *The Liberating Image* (Grand Rapids: Brazos, 2005); and N. T. Wright, *The New Testament and the People of God* (Minneapolis: Fortress, 1992) and *Jesus and the Victory of God* (Minneapolis: Fortress, 2002).

garden-planting God, and thus a creature called to be a homemaking gardener. Humans are "placed" in a garden home that they receive as a gift; they are called to tend and keep this home, to continue to construct this world as home in such a way that cares for all creatures and provides a place of secure habitation for all of its inhabitants. Creation is home, and humans are stewardly caretakers of this creational home.[22] This is the most foundational and (literally) grounding memory of biblical faith (Gen. 1–2). Without this memory, there could be no going home, there could be no vision of homemaking, no way beyond our present homelessness.

The biblical story does not get very far before we have an account of the defilement and despoliation of home. In the story of human disobedience in the garden and the consequent expulsion from Eden, the narrative takes the shape of a tragedy (Gen. 3). No longer responding to the call to tend and keep the creational home, Cain murders Abel and in so doing refuses to be his brother's keeper (Gen. 4:1-16; cf. Gen. 2:15). This is a story that moves quickly from home to homelessness, from a call to stewardly homemaking to disruptive homebreaking, from a vision of the home's harmony to a narrative of family violence. Eventually the gardened home becomes a tower of imperial aspirations. Alienated from God, from themselves, from other humans, and from the earth, humanity misuses its God-given power by fabricating a tower to storm heaven and take God's place (Gen. 11:1-9).[23] If home is a matter of imaging the homemaking and

---

22. The term "stewardship" has come under some criticism in the environmental movement of late for its overly managerial overtones. For some environmentalists, the notion of stewardship still smacks of anthropocentrism. And it is certainly the case that the term has been co-opted in various ways by government and business interests that are perhaps less concerned with environmental care than they profess to be. In Christian environmentalism, Paul Santmire has been the most eloquent critic of the notion of stewardship. See his "Partnership with Nature According to the Scriptures, Beyond the Theology of Stewardship," *Christian Scholar's Review* 32, no. 4 (Summer 2003): 381-412; and his book, *Nature Reborn: The Ecological and Cosmic Promise of Christian Theology* (Minneapolis: Fortress, 2000). We acknowledge the force of this argument but do not find it compelling enough to abandon the term. We trust that our language of stewardly "caretaking" and "homemaking," together with our theology of creation as articulated in this book, will convey a notion of stewardship that embraces human kinship and partnership with all of creation and goes beyond a narrowly managerial understanding of the term.

23. There is a tragic irony here: without a loving and caring embrace of our "place" within creation, humans reach beyond themselves, beyond their "place," and strive to take the very "place" of God.

garden-planting God, and of being stewards of the gift of our creational home, the story of the fall into sin is a story of broken stewardship and autonomous home construction. As image-bearers of the homemaking God, humans are incurably homemakers. But now, alienated from this God and striving to construct home outside of a relationship of grateful stewardship, humans construct homes of violence and idolatrous self-protective arrogance. Without grateful stewardship, humans face the fate of homelessness.

The homemaking Creator is not prepared to give up on this creational home and its homebreaking inhabitants. So God makes covenant. God is so committed to homemaking that after the flood God enters into covenant with the image-bearers and with all of creation. And God does so with the full recognition that his partner in this covenant is a violent homebreaker (Gen. 8:20–9:17).

If humans are to realize a renewal of home, they must abandon old cultural patterns of home construction. Thus God calls Abraham and Sarah to leave the home of their ancestors and sojourn with the homemaking God toward a new home, a promised land, that they will receive as they received the first home — as a gift (Gen. 12:1-2). The story of the patriarchs can then be read as the torturous journey toward this promised home. The promise seems to get stuck in Egypt. Rather than receiving the inheritance of a promised land, a site of homecoming for a sojourning people, the descendents of Abraham find themselves in the homelessness of imperial bondage (Exod. 1). The sojourner becomes the slave who is going nowhere, a being who is definitely not at home. It's hard to have a sense of home when you are subject to the impossible brick quotas of Pharaoh and you are spending your strength and your life building the hegemonic home of someone else's empire.

In the face of imperial homelessness, however, the homemaking Creator becomes the God of liberation who insists that the people be set free. God hears the cries of his people, remembers his covenant, and acts to set his people free (Exod. 2). The anti-creational, home-destroying, and enslaving forces of empire cannot thwart the Creator's homemaking intentions for his people and his creation (Exod. 11–15). The story of the Exodus, then, is a story of liberation from homeless slavery in order to be at home again with the covenant-making God, even if that requires being at home in the uninhabitable place of wilderness. This story takes strange turns. This is no garden into which Yahweh has led his people, but it is a place where they can be at home only because the sustaining and liberating Creator dwells with them (Exod. 16). For some, this is too risky and too tenuous an experience of home, and they conspire to return to the imperial security of Egypt (Num. 14; Exod. 16:1-3). For those people there will be no inheritance. By refusing to be at home with God on God's terms, and by insisting on the authoritatively controlled and managed home of the empire over the more precarious and risky home of promised gift, they have rejected the covenantal home, forfeited their inheritance, and abandoned hope of any covenantal homecoming.

This story has a wonderful irony. Wilderness is Israel's most radical memory of landlessness. The wilderness is a site of chaos reminiscent of the "formless void" before the dawn of creation, before this world was created as home. Wilderness is "land without promise, without hope, where no newness can come" because wilderness does not provide the necessary resources for homemaking.[24] And yet it is in the wilderness that Israel learns anew that they must receive home first as a gift before they can ever manage or construct it. In the wilderness, Israel forges new memories with Yahweh, rooted in the old homemaking promises of covenant and creation and in conflict with recent memories of an imperial home.

Covenantal home is home constituted by covenantal word. Homemaking stewardship is predicated on covenantal listening. Thus Israel listens and becomes a people of Torah in the wilderness. Torah is God's charter for a homemaking people, a manual for covenantal home construction. Do this, says God, and you will flourish in the land. "Torah exists so that Israel will not forget whose land it is and how it was given to us."[25] Therefore, Torah is breathtakingly comprehensive in its scope: it addresses every dimension of communal life, every dimension of what it means to make this world into a cultural site of homemaking — agricultural practices, building regulations, gender roles, sanitation, ecology, and economic justice.

But it is justice that is at the heart of Torah: "Justice, and only justice, you shall pursue, so that you may live and occupy the land that the Lord your God is giving you" (Deut. 16:20). And Torah seems to be especially preoccupied with justice and protection for those with little or no standing in the community — the poor, the stranger, the widow, and the orphan. If

24. Brueggemann, *The Land,* p. 29; cf. George Williams, *Wilderness and Paradise in Christian Thought* (New York: Harper and Brothers, 1962).
25. Brueggemann, *The Land,* p. 61.

there is to be homemaking in Israel, it must be a homemaking of inclusion, not exclusion. The homeless, the vulnerable, the marginal — all must have the room to make home as well (Deut. 10:17-19).

That is why Sabbath and Jubilee are the climax of Torah: "Sabbath is a voice of gift in a frantic coercive self-serving world."[26] And to keep Sabbath is to free slaves, to rest the land, and to cancel debts (Exod. 21:1-11; Deut. 15:1-18; 22:1-4; Lev. 25:1-55). The year of Jubilee, the fiftieth year, is a Sabbath of Sabbaths in which the yoke of injustice is broken, institutionalized slavery and expropriation of land is overturned, and the homeless receive their inheritance back so that they will again have the resources of homemaking available to them and their families. In a world of homelessness, violence, injustice, and sin, Jubilee is rooted in atonement and forgiveness. In this covenantal vision of homemaking, debts are forgiven and the possibility of homemaking is renewed.

That was the vision, of course, but the reality was something quite different. Again, this story of homecoming gets lost in a morass of homebreaking violence. This is called the story of the Judges, a story where the two refrains are "the people did what was right in their own eyes" and "the people did what was evil in the sight of the Lord" (Judg. 21:25; 3:7). In the midst of such homebreaking, the story of faithful Ruth and covenant-keeping Boaz is a welcome alternative to the sexual violence of Judges. But since not all Israelites are as attuned to Torah as was Boaz, they look elsewhere for home-ordered security. If the judges are too loose of a system for a secure and safe home, then more effective homeland security measures will need to be established.

So the people ask for a king. More specifically, they demand a king — "like the nations" (1 Sam. 8:5). If there is a king, secure in his palace, and if that king should also establish a temple to be the home of God, then the political and religious structures will be in place for the rest of the nation to have the sociopolitical and mythic-sacral security to engage in homemaking. But there are at least two problems with this scheme. First, kings tend to provide only the illusion of security under the guise of an authoritarian regime; in fact, they are notorious not for what they give, but for what they take. They take your sons for their armies and for their imperial agricultural and building programs. They take your daughters to be palace servants and to keep the royal harem well stocked. They take your grain and your

26. Brueggemann, *The Land*, p. 63.

wine for the imperial household. They take your flocks and herds for their tables. They take your wealth for their treasury (1 Sam. 8:10-18).[27] Kings take, take, and take some more. And in the context of such taking, such expropriation and royal control, covenantal homemaking is not possible.

But there is another problem with the imperial vision of homemaking: it requires the domestication of God! If the king is to be secure in his home, and if the royal regime is to be a secure structure of imperial homemaking, then the system will require a god who will provide such sacral legitimacy to the royal vision. It will require a tamed god safely living next door to the palace in his temple (1 Kings 5–9). But that is not the God of Israel.[28] Thus the necessary and devastating implication of the monarchy in Israel is that the promised land of homecoming devolves into a cursed and idolatrous land of expropriation and homelessness.[29] Imperial homemaking that forgets the liberating memories of Israel necessarily ignores Torah, violates Sabbath, oppresses the poor, and follows idols. Such amnesia can only result in homelessness. So we are still in this dialectic of home/homelessness, land/loss of land, place/displacement. The prophets had a word for such sociocultural, geopolitical, and religio-economic displacement: *exile.*

Exile is a return to wilderness. It is an experience of radical land loss and hence a fundamental experience of homelessness. Not only are the elite of the land displaced as captives in the midst of the Babylonian Empire, but the religious and political foundations of a royal vision of homemaking are deconstructed. With both the palace and temple destroyed, and both the king and God gone into exile, Israel comes to new depths in its experience of homelessness. They mourn the loss of home. The city of shalom — Jerusalem, the city of the Great King, the very center of homemaking in a covenantal universe — is no longer a place of order and joy, but one of chaos and grief:

> The city of chaos is broken down,
> every house is shut up so that no one can enter.
> There is an outcry in the streets for lack of wine;

---

27. We can count the good kings of Israel on one hand.

28. Perhaps the most devastating attack on the legitimacy of the Temple comes from Jeremiah in Jer. 7. Jesus refers to Jeremiah's critique in his own action against the Temple in Matt. 21:13 (cf. Mark 11:17; Luke 19:46).

29. See Isa. 5:1-13; 24:1-13; see also 1 Kings 4:20-28; 5:13-18; 9:10-22.

all joy has reached its eventide;
the gladness of the earth is banished.

(Isa. 24:10-11)

In a world of chaos and violence, hospitality is impossible as people attempt to keep the chaos at bay through locked doors. And when joy has reached its eventide, when the history of royal homemaking is over and the very gladness of the earth is banished, it is no wonder that everyone is looking for some cheap wine to dull the pain. No wonder the prophets are singing the blues:

How lonely sits the city
    that once was full of people!
How like a widow she has become,
    she that was great among the nations!
She that was a princess among the provinces
    has become a vassal.

She weeps bitterly in the night,
    with tears on her cheeks;
among all her lovers
    she has no one to comfort her;
all her friends have dealt treacherously with her,
    they have become her enemies.

Judah has gone into exile with suffering
    and hard servitude;
she lives now among the nations,
    and finds no resting place. . . .

(Lam. 1:1-3)

If home is a resting place, a place of security and comfort, exile is the deepest and most devastating experience of homelessness.

The homemaking and homebreaking memory of Israel is one of radical reversals. The landed royal court will become landless exiles. Those who are securely at home in their fortress-like homes will be homeless. And yet those who are thrust into a barren homelessness will settle down and bear fruit. Jeremiah counsels the exiles in Babylon to make even that exilic situation into home, to "build houses and live in them; plant gardens and eat what they produce . . . multiply there and do not decrease" (Jer. 29:5-6). Walter Brueggemann observes:

> The assurance is that what had seemed homelessness is for now a legitimate home. What had seemed barren exile is fruitful garden. What seemed alienation is for now a place of binding interaction. His very word redefined a place for placeless Israel. The assurance is that the landless are not wordless. He speaks just when the silence of God seemed permanent. Exile is the place for a history-initiating word.[30]

Just as the creational home comes into being by the word of God that says, "let there be," and the wilderness of the Exodus journey becomes home by the sustaining presence and life-giving word (Torah) of Yahweh, so also is homemaking possible in exile. Where there is covenantal word and a listening to that word, human beings can experience life as home in creation. Home construction apart from that word will always result in homelessness; that was the painful lesson of exile. But listening to that word empowers us to build houses, to be at home, and to experience fruitfulness even in the barrenness and oppression of exile.

But exile is never the final word of the covenantal God. That is why the prophets envision a world beyond exile: landedness beyond landlessness.[31] They envision homecoming. Isaiah 40 to 55 is perhaps the most evocative literature of homecoming in the whole Bible. And again, it is all a matter of covenantal word. Believing that God himself sent his people into cruel exile, Isaiah proclaims that the word of God, rooted in memories of both exodus and creation, will do a new thing and will not return empty (Isa. 55:11):

> Thus says God, the Lord
>> who created the heavens and stretched them out,
>> who spread out the earth and what comes from it,
> who gives breath to the people upon it
>> and spirit to those who walk on it. . . .

Thus says the Creator God, the homemaking God, the God with dirty fingernails, the God of unspeakable intimacy, the God who is your very breath . . .

---

30. Brueggemann, *The Land*, pp. 125-26.

31. "The Bible never denies that there is landlessness or that it is deathly. But it rejects every suggestion that landlessness is finally the will of God." Brueggemann, *The Land*, p. 127.

I am the Lord, I have called you in righteousness,
    I have taken you by the hand and kept you. . . .

I am the God of covenant, the God who called your father Abraham. I am
the God who liberated you from slavery by my strong arm and took you by
the hand through the wilderness wanderings.

I have given you as a covenant to the people,
    a light to the nations,
        to open eyes that are blind,
    to bring out the prisoners from the dungeon,
        from the prison those who sit in darkness.

(Isa. 42:5-7)

Here is a most radical and subversive promise of homecoming. Yes, this
God promises that Israel will see the exiles "gather together" and "come to
you." And yes, there is a vision of unspeakable joy when "your sons will
come from far away, and your daughters will be carried on their nurses'
arms" (Isa. 60:4). But Isaiah's vision of homecoming is more profound
than just a return from exile.

Rather than simply present the exiles with the rhetoric of ultimate victory over their oppressors, this God promises that they will be a covenant to
the people and a light to the nations. After all, this is not a local deity but the
Creator God speaking here (cf. Isa. 40:28; 42:5; 45:18). This God is concerned
with all of creation and thus with all of the nations (Isa. 56:7). Homecoming, then, must not be yet another attempt to build a home with even
higher protective walls; rather, it is a matter of renewed covenant. It is significant that the text does not say that Yahweh will make a covenant *with* Israel; instead, Yahweh will *give* Israel to *be* a covenant to the peoples. The
very existence of the people of God — their return home — is to be of service to others. Such an open, hospitable home is the only kind worth having. Indeed, without such an understanding of covenantal homemaking, all
of our homebuilding efforts will result in homelessness.[32]

Against all of the evidence, the homemaking God continues to hold out
a vision and a promise of homecoming. And the evidence doesn't seem to

32. This discussion of Isa. 42 is dependent on J. Richard Middleton and Brian J. Walsh,
Truth Is Stranger Than It Used to Be: Biblical Faith in a Postmodern Age (Downers Grove:
InterVarsity, 1995), pp. 159-60.

get much better after the exile. Yes, there is a return, and a rebuilding project in Jerusalem will ensue,[33] but a comprehensive vision of covenantal home-making remains unattainable because Israel continues to live under the oppressive regimes of one empire after another. Once the Babylonians are gone, the Persians take over, and then the Greeks and then the Romans. Under imperial rule, Israel concludes that the promises of return, of an end to exile, and of homecoming, remain unfulfilled. By the time Jesus enters the story, the burning question in Israel is, when will God make good on his promises and bring our exile to an end? When can we really come home?[34]

Biblically speaking, we can put this question in various ways: When will the homemaking reign of God be realized on earth? When will we experience anew an exodus from our present homeless bondage to the freedom of homemaking? When will the poor and dispossessed hear good news and experience the homecoming reality of Jubilee in their lives? When will we be forgiven for our distorted, broken, and sinful home-breaking? When will the image-bearers of this homemaking God take up their calling to a homemaking stewardship of all of creation with faithfulness and integrity?

Sometimes the "Sunday school answer," in all of its wonderful simplicity, is correct: Jesus. "The time is fulfilled, and the kingdom of God has come near; repent and believe the good news," is Jesus' proclamation (Mark 1:15). The royal vision of Israel's failed monarchy was a home-breaking vision. Jesus brings a radically alternative vision of royal rule, a vision that will see him enthroned on an imperial cross. In this vision the homemaking reign of God is at hand.

Jesus manifests this new vision of homemaking rule in the healing of the sick, the casting out of demons, and the restoration of outcasts. He pays special attention to those who are ritually, symbolically, and socially unclean, and thereby have been rendered deeply homeless. Often he engages in activities that have unmistakable memories of Moses. A crowd is hungry in the wilderness, and he tells them to sit down in groups of fifties and hundreds. From a meager meal of five loaves and two fish, he feeds the whole crowd of five thousand people, with twelve baskets left over (Mark 6:30-40; Matt. 14:13-21; Luke 9:10-17; John 6:1-14). Sustenance in the wilder-

---

33. Recorded in the books of Ezra and Nehemiah.

34. See N. T. Wright, *The New Testament and the People of God,* pp. 268-71, 299-301; *Jesus and the Victory of God,* pp. 126-29.

ness? Could this be a new Moses? Could this be a new Exodus? A new pathway home? Might these twelve baskets suggest the reconstitution of Israel?[35]

When Jesus delivers his inaugural sermon in his hometown synagogue in Nazareth, he finds a Jubilee text in the prophecy of Isaiah:

> The Spirit of the Lord is upon me,
>> because he has anointed me
>> to bring good news to the poor.
> He has sent me to proclaim release to captives
>> and recovery of sight to the blind,
>> to let the oppressed go free,
> to proclaim the year of the Lord's favor.
>
> (Luke 4:18-19)

And then Jesus preached the shortest sermon of his career. "Today this scripture has been fulfilled in your hearing" (Luke 4:21). Today is Jubilee time, today is the year of the Lord's favor, today there is good news for the poor, release for captives, freedom for the oppressed. Jubilee homecoming and liberation is at hand. The folks in Nazareth might not have understood the radical scope of Jesus' proclamation of Jubilee. Indeed, when they got wind of the idea that this homecoming was not just for them but for all people, including their enemies, and that Jesus' vision of homecoming was as broad in scope as the covenantal vision of the homemaking Creator, they were prepared to disown him — even murder him (Luke 4:24-29). But there can be no mistaking that this is a Jubilee vision.

But Jubilee homecoming and return from exile is impossible if God remains in exile, that is, if God remains absent. God must come home if we are ever to come home. The homemaking word that called all of creation into being must be uttered anew if there is to be real homecoming. This is

---

35. The Moses allusions are also clear when Jesus chooses to give his most important sermon from a "mount." Indeed, Matthew weaves his whole narrative around five teachings (chs. 5-7, 10, 13, 18, 24-25), suggesting that Jesus is the new Moses bringing the new Torah and covenant. Moreover, just as Moses brings the Torah, the word of the covenant, from Mount Sinai, so Jesus brings his word of the new covenant from a mountain. No one present that day would have missed the allusion. Not surprisingly, Moses appears with Elijah and Jesus on the Mount of Transfiguration in Mark 9:2-13, Luke 9:28-36, and Matt. 17:1-8. It is also interesting that John's telling of the feeding of the five thousand brings together both the wilderness feeding tradition and the motif of the mountain.

clearly how John's Gospel understands the ministry of Jesus: "In the beginning was the Word, and the Word was with God, and the Word was God. . . . All things came into being through him, and without him not one thing came into being" (John 1:1-2). In an audacious move of breathtaking scope, John identifies Jesus with nothing less than the word that calls all of creation into being. John goes on: "And the Word became flesh and lived among us, and we have seen his glory, the glory of a father's only son, full of grace and truth" (John 1:14).[36] The homemaking glory of God has returned, "moved into the neighborhood,"[37] and taken up residence with us. Homecoming is possible again.

Because this divine presence, this glory of God embodied in Jesus, is "full of grace and truth," and because this homecoming reign of God proclaimed by Jesus is a Jubilee reign, there is forgiveness for our homebreaking past. "Forgive us our debts," Jesus teaches us to pray, "as we also have forgiven our debtors" (Matt. 6:12). Let the indebtedness that renders us homeless be no more; let it be swallowed up in forgiveness. When a woman is brought to Jesus charged with sexual homebreaking, a woman who is subject to the sentence of ultimate homelessness (i.e., death), he meets her sinfulness with his forgiveness. He refuses to condemn her, to isolate her from the love and protection of his homemaking kingdom, and he offers her forgiveness (John 8:2-11).[38] Jesus seems to repeat this pattern,

36. Literally, "the Word pitched his tent among us."

37. Eugene Peterson's wonderful paraphrase of John 1:14 in *The Message* (Navpress, 2005).

38. It is interesting to note that this story comes at the end of a passage about Jesus teaching and stirring up controversy in Jerusalem during the festival of booths. This was a festival of exodus remembrance that celebrated the time of God's sustaining presence in the wilderness when the people lived in the temporary and mobile structure of booths (or tabernacles). The passage ends: "Then each went home, while Jesus went to the Mount of Olives" (7:53). Everyone is back home — not in booths but in their permanent structures; this Moses figure also goes home — not to a house but to a mountain. Jesus, like Moses, is at home on a mountain, with his Father. The next day Jesus goes to the Temple, the place taken to be the proper domicile of God. And what does he find there but a crowd determined to make this homebreaking woman homeless once and for all. The home of God becomes the site of ultimate and final homelessness. And reminiscent of the God with dirty fingernails, Jesus is writing something in the loose dirt at his feet. Perhaps he is writing a new Torah in that dirt, but whatever he is writing, it is clear from what he does that Jesus will not tolerate this spirit of violent and self-righteous dispossession. Jesus is the image of a homemaking God who is rich in the kind of compassion and forgiveness that is essential if there is to be homecoming for broken and sinful people. As a result, he refuses to condemn this woman; rather, he gives her a new chance to become a homemaker in the kingdom of God.

especially with women, but also with other outcasts (e.g., Luke 7:1-10; 7:36-50; 8:40-50; 19:1-10). "Come unto me, all you that are weary and are carrying heavy burdens, and I will give you rest" (Matt. 11:28). Come to me, come home and experience sabbath.

Who can hear such an invitation? Who can recognize the homemaking one in our midst? Who can see that the end of exile is at hand, that the Creator's dream of homecoming is about to be fulfilled? And if people do recognize him, if they do begin to proclaim that Jesus is the homemaking king who comes in the name of the Lord, then what would the authorities say? They would say — they *did* say — "Shut up!" They tell Jesus to order his disciples to be quiet, to cease and desist from this blasphemy, this politically dangerous talk. And Jesus replies: "I tell you, if these were silent, the stones would shout out" (Luke 19:40). The stones themselves would recognize their Redeemer. The stones, which had been there from the beginning, which had borne witness to Israel's covenant making (Josh. 24:26), and which would cry out when they were used as construction materials for houses of oppression (Hab. 2:11) — those stones would sing out, "Hosannah!" St. Paul understood this when he said, "For the creation waits with eager longing for the revealing of the children of God" (Rom. 8:19). All of creation waits for the children of God to be revealed as the creational homemakers that they were always called to be, because then, and only then, will creation be released from its bondage and be set free to be the home that God created it to be. On that day the stones on the side of the road to Jerusalem recognize such a child of God, such a home-making steward of creation.[39]

When will the image-bearers of this homemaking God take up their calling with faithfulness and integrity? When they recognize that the resurrected one is the gardener of the new creation, the new Adam (John 20:15; 1 Cor. 15:45; Rom. 5:12-21). When they follow and confess this Jesus as Lord, the one who was rendered homeless on a Roman cross and resurrected with homemaking power on the third day (Matt. 28; Luke 24; Mark 16; John 20). When they recognize that this Jesus is the image of the invisible God and that in him all of creation is redeemed and humanity is called to be renewed

---

39. On the responsiveness of all of creation, see Brian J. Walsh, Marianne Karsh, and Nik Ansell, "Trees, Forestry and the Responsiveness of Creation," *Cross Currents* 44, no. 2 (Summer 1994): 149-62. Reprinted in Roger Gottlieb, ed., *This Sacred Earth: Religion, Nature, Environment* (New York: Routledge, 1995), pp. 420-45.

and restored as God's homemaking image-bearers, embodying in their lives the homemaking virtues of compassion, kindness, humility, meekness, patience, forgiveness, and love (Col. 1:15-20; 3:10, 12-14). When the peace of this Christ rules in their hearts and the word of this Christ dwells in them so richly and so deeply that they begin to shape dwellings (homes) of hospitality, justice, and shalom (Col. 3:15-16; Eph. 2:11-22).

When will all of this happen? If you take biblical faith seriously, it begins to happen now.[40] But we are still in that dialectic that we have discerned throughout the whole biblical narrative. We live in the tension of being rooted and uprooted, of being at home and yet a sojourning people (see Heb. 11:13-16; 1 Pet. 2:11). And we know that we are homebreakers, even when we long to be homemakers. So when will all of this happen? When there will be a new heaven and a new earth. When we receive the city of shalom as a gift, not an accomplishment. When we hear a loud voice from the throne of the homemaking God say:

> See, the home of God is among mortals.
> He will dwell with them as their God;
> they will be his people,
> and God himself will be with them;
> he will wipe every tear from their eyes.
> Death will be no more;
> mourning and crying will be no more,
> for the first things have passed away.
>
> (Rev. 21:3-4)

This is the ultimate hope of biblical homecoming. Here the Creator's intent finally comes to its full realization. A people rooted in liberating memories of creation, covenant, exodus, exile, return, and then Jesus' ministry, death, and resurrection, is a people animated by a vision of an eschatological homecoming, when God will dwell with us and be at home with us. No wonder every tear will be wiped from our eyes. That's the kind of thing that should happen at home.

40. Indeed, the earliest church immediately began practicing Jubilee homecoming in their communities. See Acts 2:43-47 and 4:32-37. We are indebted to Anthony Riciutti's master's thesis, "The Economics of the Way: Jubilee Practice Among the Early Christians According to the Acts of the Apostles" (M.Phil.F. thesis, Institute for Christian Studies, Toronto, 2001).

We could summarize the overall structure and shape of this biblical vision in terms of the narrative dynamic of creation/fall/redemption.[41] But we could describe it in other ways as well. We can see in the overall shape of the narrative a pattern of being rooted/uprooted/replanted, or of being placed/displaced/re-placed, or of a garden/wilderness/gardened city. The biblical telling of things contains a profound memory of home, the painful experience of homelessness, and the ineluctable longing for home-coming. In short, the biblical story we have traced tells the tale of home/homelessness/homecoming.

Kenneth and Kenny Again

Both Kenneth and Kenny are homeless, though in different ways: Kenny demonstrates the socioeconomic homelessness that plagues Western society; Kenneth embodies a cultural homelessness that is rampant in an affluent society. This book is about a future beyond homelessness. What would it take for both Kenneth and Kenny to be at home?

We have seen that homecoming is only possible with memory, but the question is still, which memory? We wish to dream big, so we are going to reach into a narrative and a memory that we find life-giving and home-restoring — the narrative of covenantal homemaking that we can find in Hebrew and Christian Scripture. That narrative — and, more importantly, the homemaking God we meet in that story — offers us a vision of home-coming that can redemptively address our socioeconomic, ecological, intellectual, and cultural homelessness. That story invites us home, and by living in that story we are shaped by the virtues of homemaking. That story offers us a place beyond our placelessness, a place in nothing less than a new creation, the home for which we so deeply long. Only such a God of overflowing love can nourish us for the journey. Only such a vision of God's indwelling of all creation, of God's coming home to us, can sustain us as a sojourning community in exile.

But what is a home? And how would we know one if we ever met one? That is the subject of our next chapter.

---

41. See Brian J. Walsh and J. Richard Middleton, *The Transforming Vision: Shaping a Christian World View* (Downers Grove, IL: InterVarsity Press, 1984), part 1.

Creation, Covenant, and the Homemaking God

Genesis 1–3, 6:5-21, 9:1-20

It all began with joy.

In the beginning was joy,
    pure, holy, ecstatic, life-giving, celebratory joy!

I mean, it's true that God spoke the world into being,
    it is true that the Creator said, "let there be"
    and the creation, in its very being,
    was a response to that word.

But this wasn't just any word,
    this wasn't just any speech,
    not even by God's standards.

We had heard the Holy One speak before;
    awesome, beautiful, sovereign and loving.
And this speech, this "let there be" had all of that
    and more.
In fact, this creational speech,
    this creating, calling, blessing, ordering,
        engendering word of God,
    was maybe more like a song than a speech,
        a song that can call the whole universe into being
        and set it to dancing.

29

That's it . . . or at least it's close to getting it.
    God, the cosmic song and dance artist
    performing and dancing in such a way
    that creation just couldn't help but come into being,
    creation just couldn't help but join in the singing
    and dancing with the Creator.

And what a dance it was!
    We had seen holy joy before,
    but this . . . this was holy ecstasy.
The Creator was almost beside himself with joy,
    as each new dimension of creation emerged,
    as each new kind of creature appeared.
As each movement of this cosmic art piece came to a conclusion
    the Creator would dance around and say,
"My, isn't this good!"
His song would collapse into a divine giggle
    as he would say, "This is delightful!"
And the joy of earth was matched by the joy of heaven.

We were so caught up in the sheer generative joy of it all,
    so taken by the wonderful array of creatures,
        all interrelated,
        all in their place,
        all so fitting
        in their blessed conviviality,
    that we didn't immediately get the big picture.
And then it became clear,
    then we saw:
        God had made a home.
        This was a place of dwelling,
          a place of belonging,
          a place of homecoming.

Yes, a home for all creatures he had called into being,
    but even more,
    this was a home for God!

A world for inhabitation,
    created for communion,
    created for dwelling,
    created for homemaking,
      a home for God!

A temple,
a sanctuary,
a royal building,
    with sure foundations,
    with a well-placed cornerstone.

A house of God,
    full of Love,
    full of the Spirit.

A house of God,
    a house of hospitality,
    a house for filling.

A house of God,
    a house for tending,
    a house for gardening.

But who would till the ground?
    Who would tend the house?
    Who would fill this house and make it fruitful?

But then . . . in the sixth movement,
    on the second half of the sixth day,
    the Holy One outdid himself
      and pretty much undid us.
    The Creator's homemaking song reached such a moment of
      unparalleled joy, creativity, and love,
    that he created a creature
      with whom none of the host of heaven could compare.
    God created humankind in his own image:
      his overflowing joy
      and overwhelming love

called forth a creature
who was as close to being like God as any creature could be
    and yet still be a creature,
        a creature of the soil,
            yet a creature in the very image of the soil-creating God.

    And we gasped!
Caught up in the wonder of it all,
we could scarcely breathe as we stood in a rejoicing awe,
    that here, in humankind,
        God had made a creature to bear his image,
to tend and keep this world of wonders
    that his song had created.
A creature who could mirror the Creator's love and his joy
    to the rest of the world,
    to us in the heavenly court,
    and even to God himself.

And now we could see that God's song had reached a crescendo in this
creature and that God's joy was complete.

In the extravagance of love,
    in an unspeakable generosity,
God had created a home,
    a world of homemaking,
    a world of care and affection.

And with a sense of deep satisfaction
    that none of us could ever fully grasp,
    the Creator said a final time,
"Oh, this is very, very good . . . most delightful!"
    And with the Creator we rested in that satisfied joy.

Yes, it was good — very, very good . . .
    but it didn't stay that way.

You know the story, and for me it is tedious to repeat at any length.
You know that joy was turned to grief,
    you know that this song,
    this creational dance of faithfulness and truth

dissolved into a morass of disobedience and lies;
you know that this world of blessed homemaking
 fell into a cursed homebreaking;
and you know that this creation of peace and love
 mutated into a site of violence and hate,
 and death overpowered life,
 and blessing gave way to curse,
 and home became homelessness . . .
you know all that.

But do you know what was going on inside of God through all of this?

Do you know what it's like to witness that kind of
 creative and joyful ecstasy
 only for it to turn out as such a terrible disappointment?
Do you know anything of the suffering of a broken home?
 of God's broken home?
Can you imagine what it is like to witness that kind of grief
 in the very heart of God?

You see, the brokenness of earth is the brokenness of God's home;
 the grief of sin not only distorts and defiles all of creation
 . . . that grief reaches the very throne of God.

Until one day something snapped,
 one day God's grief simply overflowed and knew no bounds.
And we were all there in the heavenly court when,
 with a heaviness that was unbearable,
God saw . . .
 that the wickedness of his image-bearers
 was great in the earth,
 that the whole earth
 was filled with violence,
 that the human heart,
 a heart created for God,
 a heart created to image nothing less than
 the creation-blessing, shalom-bearing heart of God,
 that heart was now full of evil continually
 and held captive by an imagination of violence.

33

And when the Creator looked into the heart
    of his image-bearing creature,
    it broke his heart,
    the grief of creation now reached right into his heart,
    and then,
        in a moment of the deepest despair,
        in a moment of grief that was as deep
            as any moment of creational joy,
        the Lord who had spoken and sung all of creation into being,
            quietly and through his tears said,
    "I am sorry that I ever made humankind on the earth."

And there was silence in heaven,
    a deathly silence.

And then the grieving Creator said it again,
    "I am sorry that I have made them."

This home was irreparably broken,
    homecoming was no longer possible.

Then God quietly announced that he was going to destroy them all,
    humans, animals, reptiles, birds,
    all the creatures on the face of the earth.
The God whose word creates
    can also be a God who uncreates.

There was no joy in heaven,
    but perhaps there was some relief.
You see, the heavenly host love and adore and worship the Holy One,
    and I don't think we could bear his grief any longer.
No one could blame the God who created in such joy
    if he should then,
    in his grief, decide to destroy.
It was over — it wasn't going any further!

But. . . but God saw something else.
But. . . God saw Noah.
    Noah, a man of the soil,
        who would bring relief from curse.

But . . . God saw Noah,
  a new Adam.

So Noah gets advance warning:
  there's a flood coming,
  everything will be destroyed,
  all will die,
  there will be no more breath,
  there will be no more home.

But there was more.
  The Creator said more:
"But I will establish my covenant with you . . ."

If the divine confession that God was sorry he had created humankind
on the earth was met by a deathly silence in the heavenly court,
their overhearing what God just said to Noah occasioned an audible gasp.

But unlike the gasp of joyful awe at the creation of humankind,
this was a painful gasp of unbelief.

We were shocked and confused, dumfounded and worried.

After a period of awkward quiet, one of the younger, brasher angels
finally spoke up.

  "Excuse me, Lord, but we are not sure we heard correctly. Did you
say, 'covenant'?"

  The Creator turned a knowing eye to the angel and replied, "Yes,
my friend, I said 'covenant.'"

  "Forgive my impudence, Most Holy One, but surely you can't mean
that. Surely you can't consider making covenant with a Son of Adam."

  "Oh, but I do, young angel, that is precisely my intention."

  "But my Sovereign Lord, you know in the grief of your own heart
that the human heart is full of nothing but evil continually. You know

how they have so distorted your image that they have imaginations of evil instead of good, of hate instead of love. Surely you can't consider uniting in covenant your already grieving heart with such hearts of evil!"

"Yes, my increasingly impudent friend, in the depths of my broken heart I long to make covenant with my image-bearers, in all of their distorted brokenness."

"I am sorry, my Lord. My protest only arises out of my worship, love, and honor of your holiness. But perhaps your grief is so deep that it is distorting your vision. Lord, you have seen clearly the evil that is in the human heart. But can you not see that, if you make covenant with that heart, if you enter into a marriage relationship with humankind, that violence will rebound onto your very self? Lord, they have already grieved you, they have already broken your heart; if you now marry them, if you enter into covenant with them, they will do violence to you. They will be an abusive partner and bring even deeper grief to you. O, homemaking God, you know that these are homebreaking creatures!"

"I understand all of that, my friend."

"No, no, I don't think you do! It's not just grief I am worried about, and it's not just abuse. . . . No, my fears are deeper than that. Lord God, if you make covenant with these creatures, then they will kill you for all of your covenantal efforts! Holy and loving God, I can see the future of this relationship, and it is murder!"

"Yes! It's all true. You have seen well! And now, my young angel, I invite you and all of the heavenly host to bear witness to this covenant that I freely make with this violent lover. I am the homemaking God, this creation is my home, and these creatures are the stewards of this home. We will build a home together based on covenant."

And so, after the flood, we gathered for the wedding, but we came with mixed emotions.

Some wanted to simply boycott the whole affair, to demonstrate their disapproval of this union through their absence. But when the Holy

One invites you to his wedding, when the Creator bids you to bear witness to his covenant-making, it is best not to be a no-show.

So we gathered and watched. And what we saw only deepened our emotional turmoil.

On the one hand, the whole thing gave us a glimpse again of that original joy: the ecstatic joy of creation came to expression again, though tempered, when the Creator said that his covenant wasn't just with the earth creature, not just with the sons and daughters of Adam and Eve. No, this was a covenant with all of creation. Almost echoing the giddy days of creation, the Holy One repeated seven times that this covenant, this wedding, this renewed homemaking, was with all living creatures. Indeed, this covenant was with the very earth! Renewed joy!

And then three times he said that he would never again destroy the earth by flood. Joy and relief!

And then . . . well, then the Creator set a bow in the sky: it was a symbol of his covenant, something to remind him — not to remind the covenant partners, but to remind him! — of his promise.

And the bow was unspeakably beautiful, but it was a bow.
And it was pulled tight as if loaded with an arrow ready to fly.
And it was aimed right at the heart of God, as if God were saying,
     "If I should break this covenant, then let the arrow fly!"
An ominous symbol. Among the heavenly host there was joy,
     but yet dis-ease.
     Joy at covenant, dis-ease about where all this would lead.
     Joy at the renewal of home, dis-ease about the fear of violent
          homebreaking.

And we had a sinking feeling that one day this arrow would fly,
     and pierce the very heart of God.
But that it wouldn't be because God broke covenant.

The Meaning of Home

Gee, but it's great to be back home,
Home is where I want to be.

Simon and Garfunkel[1]

Home is the place where, when you have to go there,
They have to take you in.

Robert Frost[2]

"What comes to mind when you think of home?" the teacher asked.[3] "Especially what do you miss?" The replies by many students, most of them far from home for the first time, were fast and furious.

"The first sense that comes to mind is smell," replied Lori. "Most powerful would be my mom's kitchen oven smells: vanilla, homemade bread, roast, or cookies. Next is the smell of my dad when he's leaving for work and the ever-present doublemint gum on his breath. I really miss them, even though I was very happy to leave."

"I miss making pasta with dad," replied Hannah. "And I miss having

---

1. Simon and Garfunkel, "Keep the Customer Satisfied," from *Bridge Over Troubled Waters* © 1970 Columbia Records.

2. Robert Frost, "Death of the Hired Man," from *North of Boston* (New York: Henry Holt and Co., 1915).

3. The conversation recorded here is in the first person singular because it comes from Steven Bouma-Prediger's teaching experience. The names of the students have been changed.

him tuck me in every night. He would always ask me about the next day and kiss my forehead. And I miss doing pottery with my mom. We would stay up till three in the morning doing pottery in her studio."

"I miss my family and friends," said Abraham, a student from Ethiopia who was now, for the first time in his life, a very long way from his ancestral home. "My home is the temple of my soul, a place of happiness and sadness. A friend is happy to be with me. He feels joy in being with me. I am still starving of these spiritual meals. I miss my family and friends very much."

Karla could no longer keep quiet, bursting out, "I miss so much! Most of all, it is hard here always putting on a show. I feel there is no single place here where I can just be me. It's exhausting! I miss home in the sense that I feel accepted there and can just be me. At home I don't need to play any game or smile or pretend I am happy. At home I could cry. Here there is nowhere to be alone, to cry."

"Frankly, I don't miss anything, not yet anyway," commented Jon, who had been waiting, somewhat nervously, to get into the discussion. "I couldn't wait to leave home, go to college, get out on my own at last. I felt stifled by my mom, and my dad wasn't around much. My folks divorced when I was nine. I'm glad to get away. I finally feel free."

"I have had three places that gave me the feeling of home — my grandma's house, my cottage, and my house," Mary volunteered, somewhat hesitantly, anxious about how her peers would receive what she was about to say. "My grandma died when I was nine years old and I have not been back to her house since. This is the place I most sorrowfully call my home. I miss the smell of her house, swinging in the old oak tree, and I miss the happy visits."

Cathy sat quietly over near the window. It was obvious from previous conversations and her journal entries that her home life was very painful. When she wasn't at college, she lived uneasily with her mother. She was estranged from her father, who lived in a different city but was near enough to be a nuisance. Her one brother was, in her terms, "a mess." She was bright and articulate but reluctant to speak up; but then, surprisingly, she spoke. "I miss nothing," she said in a near whisper. "I dread school breaks and summer vacation. I don't want to go home." Her voice trailed off into silence. Her courage in speaking out was a testament both to her and to the openness of this class. Such honesty is not easily achieved. And because not all student experiences of home are happy, her voice needed to be heard along with the others.

Sue was sitting in the back. I could tell she was listening intently, and I hoped she would add her voice to the mix. But I understood why she did not: for her to express her thoughts would simply be too painful, because she was too vulnerable. From what she had hinted in occasional confidences, her life bore the scars of abuse. Home was a place not only of great pain but also of deep anger. And profound sadness. I felt helpless to do anything. I hoped and prayed she was seeing someone in the counseling center or at least had a close friend with whom she could confide.

For some people, home is a place of very fond memories, a place they palpably miss, a place for which they often long. For others, home is a place of painful memories, a place they rarely if ever miss, a place from which they long to escape. For most of us, perhaps, home is a mixture of both joy and sadness, and we feel both a longing to return and a longing to leave. Home is an ambivalent place.

In the opening lines of their song "Keep the Customer Satisfied," Simon and Garfunkel give voice to a yearning for home. This yearning, as they tell it, is occasioned by being "on the road so long, my friend" that "if you came along I know you couldn't disagree." Road weary, our peripatetic traveling salesman — always striving to keep the latest customer satisfied — voices a common desire: to be at home. This is also expressed in one of the all-time American movie favorites, *The Wizard of Oz,* when Dorothy, having returned to her Kansas farmhouse and family, exclaims, to a musical crescendo: "There's no place like home, there's no place like home!" But the Robert Frost epigraph above reveals quite a different attitude and feeling. In his poem "Death of the Hired Man," home is not something for which one longs; rather, it is a place where one is taken in, but begrudgingly and only out of necessity. Duty, not affection or love, is the motive for giving shelter.

Home. Homelessness. Longing for home. Ours is a culture of displacement, exile, and homelessness. Socioeconomic homelessness is growing, with many people seeking adequate housing. Ecological homelessness is increasing, with its sense of alienation from a degraded and defiled earth. And a profound spiritual homelessness pervades postmodern culture, so that for an increasing number of people today, the experience of the world as home, as a place where we know the rules and responsibilities of the house, is lost. A nomadic homelessness dominates the contemporary horizon.

In this chapter we intend to explore the central question of what a home is. Given that we early twenty-first-century Westerners, in many ways and for many reasons, do not feel at home in the world, what exactly does it mean to have a home or be at home? We will first describe various categories of displacement, the different ways a person can be and can feel not at home. Then we will get at the notion of home by talking about boundaries: we might say that, at a minimum, home is a bounded space of identity and security. But social, ethnic, gender, and economic boundaries can often be oppressive and render us homeless. Thus the problem of boundaries will provide an entry into an in-depth phenomenology of home. Home is many things: a place of stability and familiarity, a site of dwelling, a storied place of memory-shaped meaning, a berth of rest and security, a locus of welcome, an abode of embodied inhabitation, a point of orientation, a web of affiliation and belonging. But as the student voices above illustrate, sometimes we know what home is by what it is not.

Categories of Displacement

The gray-haired woman shuffled through the door into the dining area, her thirty-something son in tow. They exchanged angry words, then quickly got some rice and beans and sat down. Road-weary and dog-tired from a long day on the Los Angeles streets, they slumped into their seats. And they gulped down the meager meal we were serving that chilly night. Alice Marie and James had no house and no home. They were, by most typical understandings of the word, homeless.

The people who had gathered at the soup kitchen were just a small sampling of many in the "City of Angels" who have no permanent place of residence. Some were sleeping out of doors — the roofless. Others were sleeping in the local shelter — the houseless. And still others were sleeping in squatters' camps — those in insecure housing. All three groups of people were homeless: they had no house or home, and that condition was almost always not of their own choosing. While having a house does not necessarily mean you have a home, is it possible to feel at home without some sort of secure dwelling?

Jimmy had a roof over his head, and it wasn't a homeless shelter, so he wasn't officially roofless or houseless. But his housing was not much more secure than those in a Los Angeles squatters' camp. He lived alone in the backwoods of western North Carolina in what he called "my shack." He had no running water or indoor plumbing, and his roof barely kept the rain out. The walls were beginning to slip and sag. He didn't want it to be that way, but there it was. Jimmy was among the inadequately housed, those who had a house but without basic facilities and in ill repair. Technically, perhaps, you could call it a house, but that would be a stretch. But did he have a home? Soon, Jimmy would be thankful to learn, he would be a candidate for a new dwelling, courtesy of the local chapter of Habitat for Humanity.

If the inadequately housed are an often overlooked group, so are the well-housed homeless. Sally had a mansion in north suburban Dallas, a house with seven bedrooms and five bathrooms, a three-car garage, and a four-lane pool. Her house was elegantly appointed and artfully decorated. But it became painfully clear during casual conversation at dinner that, while she had a beautiful house, Sally still lacked a home. She lamented that, since moving into the house three years earlier, she had never felt at home. "Something was missing," she said, admitting that she felt empty inside even though she "had it all." Though she had more than adequate shelter, Sally was homeless, too. While a house of some sort may be necessary to have a home, is it sufficient? What is it that the well-housed homeless lack?

Henny spoke with a thick Dutch accent that betrayed her place of birth. As a young woman, she had moved to Canada with her new husband after World War II had devastated their home country. Like many in the Netherlands, they left their homeland for good in search of a better life elsewhere — in their case, Ontario. From one home to a new home. Also, a new language, a new church, new customs, new friends. Henny was an immigrant, a person who voluntarily left her native country and took up permanent residence in another country. What do immigrants leave behind, and what is it they build in their new homeland? When does a new house in a new community in a new country feel like home?

Juan fled his homeland fearing for his life. A farmer in northern Guatemala who wished only that his fields could be more fertile and his life more fair, Juan had joined with some neighbors to protest repeated injustices concerning the village lands. Because of that protest, he had been branded a threat to the government in power — a subversive and a revolutionary. But Juan was no Communist or violent revolutionary. Like his compadre to the south, the martyred Salvadoran archbishop Oscar Romero, Juan wanted only that justice be done, that campesinos like him be treated fairly. He desired only a decent life for himself and his family.

The trucks came at night. Rumbling through the dusty streets of Juan's village, they came first for his neighbors Rodrigo and Felipe, and then for his friend Esteban. Not one of them was seen again. They were "disappeared." So, fearing he would be next, Juan fled north, all the way through Mexico, and at last to the United States. He ended up in Los Angeles, where a cousin was waiting for him. With the desperate hope that he would soon be able to return to his wife and children, Juan looked for work and prayed that the army trucks would go away from his town. Juan became a refugee: a person who flees to a foreign country to escape danger or persecution but always hopes to return home. Despite his fear of being caught and deported as an "illegal alien," he was grateful for a place of relative safety. But Juan remained restless, because his temporary dwelling place lacked everything he held most dear: family and friends, the land he knew, and familiar traditions he practiced. Could his home-away-from-home ever feel like home?

Tenzin Gyatso had no ordinary childhood. He was born into a Tibetan peasant family, but he was identified as the reincarnation of the thirteenth Dalai Lama at the age of two. He then began a rigorous educational program in which he eventually earned a doctorate in Buddhist philosophy and spirituality. At the tender age of fifteen, even before his education was complete, he became head of the Tibetan government. And when the Chinese army rolled into Tibet in 1959, the Dalai Lama was forced into exile. Since then he has lived in Dharmsala, India, as the head of Tibet's government-in-exile, and he has won the respect and favor of many throughout the world because of his work toward peace and justice for all peoples.

Like an immigrant, an exile moves from an old home to new home. But, unlike an immigrant, an exile does not freely choose to leave his or her homeland. An exile is banished or expelled from his or her native land and usually has little hope of returning. When you yearn to be somewhere else, and where you are is not of your own choosing, can it be home? Do exiles ever feel at home?

Estella dropped off her daughter and son, Maria and Ramon, at the school steps. The principal, fluent in Spanish, welcomed them warmly to Washington Elementary School in Holland, Michigan. She had missed them. Maria and Ramon had started school at Washington the previous year, only to move south to Texas in November. They had returned to Holland in May, but had not come to school. Now they were back at the start of a new school year, and they were excited to see old friends and play-mates. Estella and her husband, Eduardo, were migrant workers. They came to southwest Michigan each spring and moved to Texas every fall as they followed seasonal work in the agricultural fields.

Unlike an immigrant, refugee, or exile, a migrant moves regularly and seasonally during the year, usually in order to find work. The moves are often from one home to a new home and back to an old home — even if it is not always to the same house. What or where is home for the migrant? Can a person have two homes in two different places, as do some "snowbirds," who live in Florida during the winter months when their homes in Michigan or Quebec are snow-bound? Those retirees, however, have the luxury of choosing to live that way, whereas migrant workers face the vagaries of weather and work and have little choice about it. Where and what is home for the migrant?

Sam was gone again. He always seemed to be gone. Last year it was Patagonia for three weeks, and then a month in South Africa. This past summer it was three months in Australia and New Zealand. He was talking about going on an extended trip to China next. His friends wondered when he found time to work. His true friends sat through seemingly endless slide shows and picture albums. Sam's wanderlust made him a perfect example of the perpetual tourist. A tourist is someone who freely travels away from home for relatively short times for the purpose of business, education, or pleasure. Most tourists' travels are of short duration, and after a while they long for home. No matter how beguiling a destination may be — the gently rolling hills and conviviality of Prince Edward Island, Canada, or the friendliness and gentle beauty of Beaver Island, Michigan — it doesn't feel like home. People like Sam, by contrast, seem to be on the road more often than they are at home. Or is the road, in their case, home? If so, what is it that allows the inveterate tourist to feel at home on the road? Or is Sam just another example, less obvious perhaps, of homelessness?

Looking at the tourist brings up the ninth and last category of displacement: the postmodern nomad. Like Kenneth, whom we met in the first chapter, Paul is very successful and highly respected in his field. Yet, while he has an apartment in one city, you couldn't really say that Paul has a permanent residence. In fact, he chose the apartment because of its proximity to the local airport. Paul did not become successful by staying in one place; he's always on the move, and he seems to spend most of his time on airplanes or at airport hotels, moving from one meeting to another, one consulting job to the next. Paul is a postmodern nomad.

But Paul's nomadic lifestyle is in marked contrast to that of the traditional nomads such as the Masai, who have been nomadic for thousands of years. These proud people continue to live a nomadic life in the savannas of east Africa (what is now Kenya and Tanzania) with their many sheep and goats. To our Western way of thinking, they have no fixed residence; nevertheless, they have a clear sense of place within a geographically circumscribed area. The borders of their territory are well defined, and their movements are determined largely by the need for water and grazing land for their animals. Like the migrant, the traditional nomad moves from home to home. But it is all home, because, while they are peripatetic, traditional nomads are anything but homeless.

The postmodern nomad, by contrast, has no sense of place: he merely roams from one place to another. Or, more precisely, he wanders from no place to no place, since no particular place takes on sufficient significance to distinguish it from any other. No specific place is invested with enough story-soaked meaning to make it a place to which one would want or need to return. Hence, seeking personal freedom and professional success, Paul finds himself caught in an iron cage. Thinking he is well connected, Paul discovers that he has few significant relationships; feeling well oriented, he learns that he is actually adrift, a homeless postmodern nomad.

The homeless on the street, the inadequately housed, the well-housed homeless, the immigrant, the refugee, the exile, the migrant, the tourist, the postmodern nomad — these are different ways of being and feeling displaced, alternative forms of homelessness. Each in its own way illuminates what home is. Like the negative of a photograph, each provides some insight into what the positive might be. In one way or another, all of the people we have described thus far are displaced: they are excluded from some place and have no remaining connection to it. Such displacement, in its various forms, is at the heart of homelessness. On the other hand, to be "placed" is to have a sense of connection, loyalty, affection, and identity within a particular context — a location, a house, a community, a nation. Those contexts, or emplacements, are bounded: they are set off by boundaries as the special places they are — as home. The problem is that geographical, cultural, emotional, religious, familial, and physical boundaries are constitutive of homemaking, and yet they are deeply ambiguous.

The Problem of Boundaries

"Secret video exposes plight of homeless." The front-page headline of *The Toronto Star* on May 21, 2002, was accompanied by pictures of body-to-body conditions in one of Toronto's homeless shelters. While the United Nations stipulates that refugee camps should allow for at least four and a half to five square meters of space per person, in the Toronto shelter as many as four people could be found lying in a space that size. The problems in the shelter are complex, but they are fundamentally problems of boundaries.

While notions of "personal space" are culturally constructed and differ throughout the world, it seems to be a universal human requirement that some sense of personal space is necessary for all people. An invasion of that space, a transgression of those boundaries, invariably causes tensions, often violence, and sometimes the spread of disease (especially tuberculosis in homeless shelters). Indeed, one of the tragedies of homelessness is precisely the stripping of homeless people of all sense of boundaries so that "they have no stabilizing walls against which they can lean for the identity and security so critical for personal and family dignity."[4]

Boundaries, it would seem, are constitutive of life. For example, clear boundaries must be established to determine the difference between friendliness and sexual harassment. Churches and volunteer organizations working with children need to set up clear behavioral boundaries in relationships between adults and children. Professors must either have windows on their office doors, or those doors must be kept open when they are alone with a student. Conflict of interest rules must be developed and followed for the ethical conduct of affairs in business, politics, the church, and the academy. And any family knows that, in the rules of the household, boundaries — agreed upon or, if necessary, imposed — are indispensable if the home is to be a place of security and comfort for all.

But how do we talk about boundaries and borders in a post-9/11 world that is characterized by a xenophobic "war on terrorism" and the U.S. Homeland Security Act? When borders are guarded with a fortress-like vigi-

---

4. Caroline Westerhoff, *Good Fences: The Boundaries of Hospitality* (Boston: Cowley Press, 1999), p. 15. It is for this reason that those who work with street people are careful to recognize and respect what little boundaries they are able to erect around themselves — whether it be their grocery cart, doorway, park bench, or squat in the woods.

lance and bolstered by an ideological demonization of the "other," how can we speak of them as constitutive and necessary? When we view other peoples or cultures "outside" the bounds of our civilization as forces of "chaos" that would undermine the well-constructed and self-serving "order" established "inside" our geopolitical, economic, and cultural boundaries, how can we meaningfully speak of boundaries as good dimensions of human life?

While these problems have been heightened since the tragic events of September 11, 2001, they are not new to anyone paying attention to postmodern discourse. Boundaries require categories of "in" and "out," and thus boundaries necessarily marginalize. The "other" who is not in is relegated to being out, on the margins of the space constructed by such boundaries.[5] The ethical impulse of postmodernity has been to overcome this violent marginalization.[6] But since the "other" is constituted as other by the imposition of someone else's notion of boundaries, something has to be done about boundaries. The postmodern turn is to recognize the constructed character of all such boundaries and thus their inherent "deconstructability." Henry Statton puts it this way: "Deconstruction is not a defense of formlessness, but a regulated overflowing of established boundaries . . . so the point is *not* that we can get along without demarcating boundaries, but rather that there is no 'boundary fixing,' that cannot itself be questioned."[7] The questions that are raised will come from the perspective of the marginal, from those who are relegated to the outside. But there is another question that we must ask: If we still need some kinds of demarcated boundaries, how will they be drawn? What criteria will people use to draw up boundaries, even if these boundaries are never finally fixed? This, we suggest, is a deeply theological question.[8]

5. A quintessentially American metaphor for all of this is provided by baseball: it is the game about leaving home and trying to find one's way back to home. If one is ruled "out," there is no path back home. To be "safe," then, is to be "in" — still on the path home, if not already "safe at home."

6. Michael Purcell speaks of a "non-allergic relation with alterity" in "Homelessness as a Theological Motif: Emmanuel Levinas and the Significance of Home," *Scottish Journal of Religious Studies* 15, no. 2 (Autumn 1994): 89. Walter Truett Anderson speaks of postmodernism as "the age of overexposure to otherness" in *The Truth about the Truth: De-confusing and Reconstructing the Postmodern World* (New York: G. P. Putnam's Sons, 1995), p. 6.

7. Henry Statton, *Wittgenstein and Derrida* (Lincoln, NE: University of Nebraska Press, 1984), p. 34.

8. Mark C. Taylor expresses the deconstructive spirit well: "Settling inevitably unsettles. Since every place presupposes a certain displacement, there can be no settlement(s) without

In a postmodern context, then, we see frequent use of "boundary" or "border-crossing" discourse. The boundaries that have kept various academic disciplines in an apartheid-like arrangement of separation are being dismantled by interdisciplinary discourses such as semiotics. The borders that distinguished cultures are transgressed in the production of "hybrid" art forms, music, styles, and even identities.[9] These shifting borders undermine and redraw the common configurations of culture, power, and knowledge. Since sociocultural borders — together with ethnic, sexual, and behavioral boundaries — map our existence in monolithic, homogenizing, and exclusionary ways, Henry Giroux calls for a pedagogy and cultural criticism that crosses borders, arguing that we need "forms of transgression in which existing borders forged in domination can be challenged and redefined."[10] Indeed, Giroux argues that modernity — and its economic muscleman, capitalism — is a culture dedicated to the colonization of difference by creating "borders saturated in terror, inequality and forced exclusions" (p. 33). In these terms, postmodernism "constitutes a general attempt to transgress the borders sealed by modernism, to proclaim the arbitrariness of all boundaries, and to call attention to the sphere of culture as a shifting social and historical construction" (p. 55).[11]

However, this does not mean that Giroux's pedagogy of border crossings leaves us in a borderless wasteland with no identity or citizenship. In a world of "lived homophobia, racial oppression, and escalating economic inequality," an apolitical postmodern aestheticism of bricolage and pastiche will not do (p. 240). Rather, Giroux says that we need a pedagogy that

neglect." "Unsettling Issues," *Journal of the American Academy of Religion* 62, no. 4 (Winter 1994): 949. Our question is whether it might be possible to settle, indeed be placed, without neglect.

9. In his collection of essays, *Border Crossings: Christian Trespasses on Popular Culture and Public Affairs* (Grand Rapids: Brazos Press, 2000), Rodney Clapp employs such a metaphor to suggest the fruitful interchanges that happen when disciplinary, cultural, and religious borders are crossed.

10. Henry Giroux, *Border Crossings: Cultural Workers and the Politics of Education* (New York/London: Routledge, 1992), p. 28.

11. In *Truth Is Stranger Than It Used to Be: Biblical Faith in a Postmodern Age* (Downers Grove, IL: InterVarsity Press, 1995), Richard Middleton and Brian Walsh argue that postmodern criticism attends to both the constructed and the oppressive character of home. See also Brian J. Walsh, "Homemaking in Exile: Homelessness, Postmodernity and Theological Reflection," in Doug Blomberg and Ian Lambert, eds., *Reminding: Renewing the Mind in Learning* (Sydney: Centre for the Study of Australian Christianity, 1998).

enables students "to be border-crossers in order to understand Otherness on its own terms, and . . . to create borderlands in which diverse cultural resources allow for the fashioning of new identities within existing configurations of power" (p. 245). If all we have is border crossing and boundary blurring in a postmodern context of radical pluralism, then we have no place from which to make ethical judgments, no borders or boundaries the transgression of which constitutes oppression, no ability to distinguish the cry of the oppressed from the arrogant exclamations of the oppressors. We need to cross borders, says Giroux, and create new borderlands.[12] But Giroux fails to ask how these borders are determined. What criteria will be used to erect those borders? In short, boundaries are both constitutive of life — all of life, not just human life — and also deeply problematic. We can investigate their ambiguity more closely by returning to the themes of poverty and homelessness.

Mary Douglas describes "patterning" in a culture as the imposition of a symbolic order "whose keystone, boundaries, margins and internal lines are held in relation by rituals of separation," in which the defiling pollution on the outside of the boundary is kept from infecting the inside.[13] While this anthropological observation has its origins in ancient texts (e.g., Leviticus) and so-called primitive tribes, postmodern critical geographers discern a similar patterning going on in the modern city. Consider David Sibley's depiction of a "geography of exclusion":

> There is a history of imaginary geographies which cast minorities, "imperfect" people, and a list of others who are seen to pose a threat to the dominant group in society as polluting bodies or folk devils who are then located "elsewhere." This "elsewhere" might be nowhere, as when genocide or the moral transformation of a minority like prostitutes is advocated, or it might be some spatial periphery, like the edge of the world or the edge of the city.[14]

12. Giroux's postmodern critical pedagogy espouses a discourse that is "multiaccentual and dispersed and resists permanent closure" (p. 29), because it is rooted in no "master narratives" that are "monolithic" and "timeless" (p. 76). Such pedagogy is to be preferred, he insists, because such multiplicity creates "more democratic forms of public life" (p. 76). It seems to us, however, that his own affirmation of radical democracy is nothing less than a "master narrative" that would appear to carry "timeless authority."

13. Mary Douglas, *Purity and Danger* (London: Routledge and Kegan Paul, 1966), p. 41.

14. David Sibley, *Geographies of Exclusion: Society and Difference in the West* (London: Routledge, 1995), p. 49. Rosemary Haughton makes a similar point, though without the geo-

The boundaries between the rich and the poor are erected by the powerful in order to reduce the threat of their own defilement. Slums are *down*town, as opposed to the suburbs, which are *up*town. The topography of the poor is identified with filth, disease, excrement, and foul odors. James Duncan and David Ley make this point well: "Topography is also therefore a science of domination — confirming boundaries, securing norms and treating questionable social conventions as unquestioned social facts."[15] And all of this legitimates the rhetoric of "clean-up campaigns."[16] The unhomogenized other is identified with the forces of chaos that threaten from outside the well-ordered homes of cleanliness and purity of the inside. Boundaries, then, are violently exclusionary, especially for the most vulnerable, those who do not have the resources to erect their own boundaries and to overcome the boundaries of domination that oppress them.

We return to the Toronto homeless shelter, where the most basic boundaries of personal space cannot be respected. These people find

---

graphical specificity of Sibley. She says that homeless people are objects of fear and suspicion because "they don't fit in and their 'not belonging' is a threat to the sense of stability everyone wants. It could happen to us: perhaps if we can blame them and remove them we shall feel more secure" ("Hospitality: Home as the Integration of Privacy and Community," in Leroy Rouner, ed., *The Longing for Home* [Notre Dame, IN: University of Notre Dame Press, 1996], p. 213).

15. James Duncan and David Ley, "Introduction: Representing the Place of Culture," in James Duncan and David Ley, eds., *Place/Culture/Representation* (London and New York: Routledge, 1993), p. 1

16. Sibley (*Geographies of Exclusion*, p. 61) graphically makes his point by citing the character Travis Bickle from Martin Scorcese's film *Taxi Driver*. Speaking to a presidential hopeful in his cab, Bickle says:

> You should clean up this city here because this city here is like an open sewer, it's full of filth and scum and sometimes I can hardly take it. Whoever becomes the president should just really clean it up, you know what I mean. Sometimes I go out and I smell it. I get headaches, it's so bad, you know, they just like never go away, you know. It seems like the president should just clean up the whole mess here, should just flush it down the fucking toilet.

A further comment on Sibley: while Sibley's book powerfully unpacks the oppressive dynamics of a geography of exclusion, he has very little to say about geographies of inclusion. This is the question we have raised relative to both the deconstructive demarcation of new boundaries and Giroux's notion of new borderlands, and it returns in relation to Sibley. If geographies of exclusion are to be rejected, but boundaries are constitutive of human life (a point that Sibley grants), how do we make space, which is bounded, more hospitable? What are the characteristics of boundaries that do not violently exclude?

themselves in this situation for various reasons. The racist boundaries of our society (most of the men in the newspaper photo were aboriginal), combined with economic boundaries imposed by a neoconservative political regime (which abandoned progressive housing and social policy in favor of tax breaks), and the not-in-my-backyard geocultural boundaries (which have limited the ability of social service and volunteer agencies to provide shelters throughout the city) — all these things have conspired in a geography of exclusion to keep certain people out of sight and out of mind. Boundaries have put these people in this situation, and yet it is precisely the unconscionable transgression of boundaries of personal space that brought public attention to their plight. Therefore, when we recognize the profound ambiguity in our boundary construction, we need to reflect further on the necessity of boundaries.

The Necessity of Boundaries

"Strangers," says Walter Brueggemann, "are people without a place." They are "displaced persons" because the "social system . . . has . . . assigned their place to another and so denied them any safe place of their own."[17] In ancient Israel they were often people whose "boundary stones have been moved" (Deut. 19:14; Prov. 22:28-29; 23:10-11; Amos 5:7; 6:12; Isa. 5:7-10; 10:13). To be placeless is to live in the tenuous vulnerability of life without the bounded security of home and shelter.[18] Boundaries that demarcate in and out, mine and yours, ours and theirs, my body in distinction from other bodies, private and public, are necessary if life is to be secure. Strangers are people who have been stripped of such boundaries.

A boundary, says Caroline Westerhoff, is "that which defines and gives

---

17. Walter Brueggemann, "Welcoming the Stranger," in *Interpretation and Obedience: From Faithful Reading to Faithful Living* (Minneapolis: Fortress Press, 1991), p. 294.

18. This is why Ed Loring argues that housing, i.e., bounded and secure space for living in, is foundational to life. Reflecting on years of ministry among the homeless, Loring argues that housing is a basic necessity of life and thus precedes employment, sobriety, education, health, evangelization, and even the struggle for justice. See his provocative article entitled "Housing Comes First" in *The Other Side* 38, no. 3 (May/June 2002): 32-33. In the wilderness, shelter is second only to air in the priorities for survival. You can live three minutes without air, three hours without shelter (in difficult conditions), three days without water, and three weeks without food.

identity to all kinds of systems." Such boundaries can be concerned with "physical borders and property lines, as well as names and stories, traditions and values." Boundaries are constitutive of identity and, "unless we can draw a line — a boundary — and say that something lies outside its domain, then we can speak about nothing that lies inside with deep meaning."[19] Westerhoff continues: "Boundaries are lines that afford definition, identity and protection — for persons, families, institutions, nations. . . . A boundary gives us something to which we can point and ascribe a name. Without a boundary, we have nothing to which we can invite or welcome anyone else."[20] Without boundaries there can be no sense of "place" as home, as a site of hospitality, security, and intimacy with local knowledge. Without boundaries there is no locality and thus no sense of membership in a particular community, family, or neighborhood with an identity distinct from other communities, families, and neighborhoods. In short, identity itself is impossible without boundaries.[21]

Christine Pohl's discussion of hospitality makes the same claim. "Hospitality," says Pohl, "is fundamentally connected to place — to a space bounded by commitments, values, meanings."[22] Boundaries are necessary conditions for hospitality because they provide definition of the space being entered and give identity to both host and guest. Pohl goes on:

> Boundaries are an important part of making a place physically and psychologically safe. Many needy strangers (e.g., refugees, homeless people, abused women and children) come from living in chronic states of fear. A safe place gives them a chance to relax, heal, and reconstruct their

19. Westerhoff, *Good Fences*, p. xi.

20. Westerhoff, *Good Fences*, p. 7. Providing a phenomenological description of the inhabitation of a room, Edward Casey makes a similar point: "Indeed, to be in an intimately inhabited room is not merely to tolerate but to *require* boundaries" (*The Fate of Place: A Philosophical History* [Berkeley: University of California Press, 1997], p. 294).

21. Interestingly, the agenda of global consumerism is precisely to eradicate such borders — cultural, political, economic, and communal boundaries — in favor of a borderless homogeneity of global consumers who have no attachments to place and no distinct identities. That such an economic/cultural consumerist agenda bears striking similarity to the decentered pluralism of postmodern discourse has been noted in Nicholas Boyle, *Where Are We Now? Christian Humanism and the Global Market: From Hegel to Heaney* (Edinburgh: T&T Clark, 1998).

22. Christine Pohl, *Making Room: Recovering Hospitality as a Christian Tradition* (Grand Rapids: Eerdmans, 1999), p. 134.

lives. If hospitality involves providing a safe place, where a person is protected and respected, then certain behaviors are precluded and certain pragmatic structures follow. (p. 140)

In summary, boundaries provide "the kind of ordering necessary to life" (p. 139).

Homemaking, like worldbuilding, is a world-ordering enterprise.[23] To turn space into place is to establish normative boundaries that bring a certain kind of order to the life lived within those boundaries. As we shall argue in Chapter 5, ecology has to do with discerning and obeying the "house rules" of the planet. What is true of the *oikos* known as Planet Earth is true of any home, any *oikonomic* structure. To be home is to be at a site where certain kinds of rules are obeyed, certain kinds of order are constructed.

Of course, we are now back to where we started. Boundaries provide an ordering to experience and space, and that ordering makes certain people and certain behaviors out to be defiled, polluted, and threatening. Some are ruled out of order. So boundaries are constitutive of life; yet they are also invariably an ideological legitimation of our geographies of exclusion. Edward Said, who knows something about the reality of the exilic homelessness of his own Palestinian people, describes the ambiguity of boundaries and borders: "Borders and barriers, which enclose us within the safety of familiar territory, can also become prisons, and are often defended beyond reason or necessity."[24] Rosemary Haughton concurs: "The impregnable home where the only comers are clones of the hosts becomes not a home but a fortress and a prison combined."[25]

Boundaries used to erect fortresses of self-protection, then, can never be refuges of hospitality. The walls are simply too thick, the barriers too impenetrable. But boundaries that demarcate definite spaces and identities need not be exclusionary. Borders need not create prisons. Martin Heidegger evocatively suggests that a "boundary is not that at which something stops but . . . the boundary is that from which something *be-*

---

23. Peter Berger, *The Sacred Canopy: Elements of a Sociological Theory of Religion* (Garden City, NY: Doubleday/Anchor, 1967), pp. 19-24.

24. Edward Said, "Reflections on Exile," in R. Ferguson et al., eds., *Out There: Marginalization and Contemporary Cultures* (Cambridge and London: MIT Press, 1990), p. 365.

25. Haughton, "Hospitality," p. 215.

gins in its essential unfolding."[26] Boundaries can be horizons that provide a sense of orientation, yet are dynamic. Boundaries are not there so much to stop something from coming in (though that remains part of the safety-producing function of boundaries) as they are to provide a context for a certain kind of unfolding or opening up that happens within those boundaries.

This is an important point: boundaries need not be exclusionary, borders need not create prisons. Indeed, one can argue that, properly understood, boundaries provide both definition and openness, structure and flexibility. Westerhoff uses the analogy of the cell membrane to describe boundaries that are open and yet function to provide identity:

> Like a cell membrane, a boundary must be semi-permeable: admitting and containing what is necessary for sustaining and enriching life, discharging and excluding anything that does not belong within its borders. A membrane that allows for anything and everything to enter and leave is a membrane that is no longer functioning. The cell — the system — is now dead or dying. A healthy boundary is firm enough to hold, but not so tight that it binds, confines and cuts. It is flexible enough to allow movement and change within time and circumstance, but not so loose that it encourages sloppiness and aimless wandering. A boundary that is too rigid fosters stiff and brittle attitudes; it is always in danger of freezing and cracking. One that is too porous encourages attitudes of carelessness and disorder; it will rot and crumble.[27]

For some, this discussion of boundaries and borders is perhaps most powerfully engaged when focused on home. For example, Rosemary George argues:

> One distinguishing feature of places called home is that they are built on select inclusions. The inclusions are grounded in a learned (or taught) sense of kinship that is extended to those who are perceived as sharing the same blood, race, class, gender, or religion. Membership is maintained by bonds of love, fear, power, desire and control. Homes are manifest on geographical, psychological, and material levels. They are places

---

26. Martin Heidegger, "Building, Dwelling, Thinking," in David Farell Krell, ed., *Basic Writings* (San Francisco: HarperCollins, 1977), p. 356.

27. Westerhoff, *Good Fences*, p. 83.

that are recognized as such by those within and those without. They are places of violence and nurturing. A place that is flexible, that manifests itself in various forms and yet whose every reinvention seems to follow the basic pattern of inclusions/exclusions. Home is a place to escape to and a place to escape from. Its importance lies in the fact that it is not equally available for all. Home is the desired place that is fought for and established as the exclusive domain of a few. It is not a neutral place.[28]

But while George accents the potentially dangerous side of home, Emmanuel Levinas see things somewhat differently. He says: "The privileged role of the home does not consist in being the end of human activity but in being its condition, and in this sense its commencement."[29] In other words, human cultural engagement within the world has, as its ontological condition, the dwelling, security, and refuge that is the bounded space of home. But this dwelling that is home, Levinas continues, "answers to a hospitality, an expectancy, a human welcome" (p. 156). What unfolds within the home is a cosmic gentleness and intimacy characterized by welcome. And thus, Levinas argues, "[t]he possibility for the home to open to the Other is as essential to the essence of the home as closed doors and windows" (p. 173).

Home, as bounded space, must have windows and doors that can be closed, but they are not sealed doors and windows. They can and must be opened. An open door is a threshold both for those entering and those departing; it is the place between places, fraught with anxiety and danger, for people moving in both directions. But whether those departing leave with a spirit of embrace and service to the world, and whether those entering feel that they are coming into a safe place of welcome, depends on the kind of unfolding character of the bounded place that is identified as home. Our analysis of boundaries, then, invites — indeed, requires — phenomenological reflection on home.[30]

---

28. Rosemary George, *The Politics of Home: Postcolonial Relocations and Twentieth-Century Fiction* (Cambridge, UK: Cambridge University Press, 1996), p. 9.

29. Emmanuel Levinas, *Totality and Infinity: An Essay on Exteriority,* trans. Alphonso Lingis (Pittsburgh: Duquesne University Press, 1969), p. 152.

30. The phenomenological description that follows was first developed by Steven Bouma-Prediger in "Yearning for Home: The Christian Doctrine of Creation in a Postmodern Age," in Merold Westphal, ed., *Postmodern Philosophy and Christian Thought* (Bloomington: University of Indiana Press, 1999).

A Phenomenology of Home

What is a home? What does it mean to be at home? What is it that home-less people do not have that renders them homeless? And how would the jet-setting global consumer, the postmodern nomad, recognize home if she ever found one? Acknowledging the dangers inherent in any kind of phenomenological description of such a clearly constructed reality as "home," and not wishing to fall prey to either the Scylla of constructivism or the Charybdis of essentialism, we nonetheless need to reflect on the ba-sic phenomenological contours of what might count as "home."[31] At the risk of sounding overly schematized, we offer eight characteristics of home.[32]

First, home is a place of permanence. To be "at home" somewhere is more than simply having a place to stay. We sometimes stay in motels or hotels, perhaps even for relatively long periods of time; but we typically do not consider or call such places home, because motels and hotels signify transience and unfamiliarity, while home is a place of permanence and fa-miliarity. No matter how long we have been there, we are always guests in motels. Likewise, a community of squatters under a bridge may have some

31. By "phenomenology" we are not referring to the exact science of apodictic certainty found in the early Husserl. Rather, following the hermeneutical turn in phenomenology identified with Heidegger, Merleu-Ponty, and Ricoeur, we mean by phenomenology a mode of philosophical reflection whose "central point has to do with noticing what is too obvious to be seen, with finding the glasses we've been wearing," in the words of Merold Westphal (*God, Guilt, and Death* [Bloomington, IN: Indiana University Press, 1984], p. 13). This task of noticing the familiar, of seeing the overlooked, "is not motivated by the desire to be rigor-ously scientific, but rather by a passion for self-understanding that is itself neither detached nor disengaged" (Westphal, p. 22). This phenomenology, as Langdon Gilkey says, "seeks to in-terpret the latent *meanings,* i.e., unveil the implicit structures of man's being in the world. . . ." *Naming the Whirlwind: The Renewal of God-Language* (Indianapolis and New York: Bobbs-Merrill, 1969), p. 280. Such a method is certainly not a matter of offering decisive proofs of its conclusions, but rather a disciplined descriptive proposal for intuitive recognition.

32. It should be said that these are normative statements that do not describe most "homes" in an upwardly mobile, economically driven society of insatiable affluence — or a violent society of spouse abuse and child neglect. See Paul Wachtel, *The Poverty of Affluence: A Psychological Portrait of the American Way of Life* (Philadelphia: New Society, 1989); David Myers, *The Pursuit of Happiness* (New York: William Morrow, 1992); David Myers, *The American Paradox: Spiritual Hunger in an Age of Plenty* (New Haven: Yale University Press, 2000); and Alan Durning, *This Place on Earth: Home and the Practice of Permanence* (Seattle: Sasquatch Books, 1996).

semblance of shelter; but the insecurity of that environment and the lack of any lasting tenure in that space (not to mention its inhospitable character) makes homemaking, in any meaningful sense of the word, impossible. Thus, while shelter may be necessary for the experience of home, shelter is not sufficient.

Home, by contrast, signifies a certain degree of spatial permanence, an enduring presence or residence. In a speed-bound culture, every highly mobile person is a victim of at least some form of homelessness because there is no time to foster a sense of enduring emplacement.[33] Indeed, even traditionally nomadic peoples do not live in a world of sudden displacements; they, too, function within a context of a permanently sheltering structure of tribe and place. Remove an aboriginal child from his tribe, strip the people of their traplines, transport them to a different landscape, and you will render them homeless.

Second, a home is a dwelling place. A home is not just a place of permanence, for home is not the same as house. "The notion of dwelling," says Susan Saegert, "highlights the contrast between *house* and *home*."[34] The common expression "make a house a home" points to an important difference between house and home. A house is a domicile, while a home is a dwelling. A house is a building, whereas a home is an abode. A house is made of brick or wood or sod or thatch; a home is made of memories and stories and relationships. A house is space devoid of any deep meaning, while a home is a place filled with psychological resonance and social significance. A house is a space of residence, while a home is a place of (in)dwelling.

Therefore, while houses can be bought and sold on the open market, homes can be neither bought nor sold. A home is not a commodity and thus cannot be commodified. Kimberly Dovey says: "Home is a relationship that is created and evolved over time; it is not consumed like the prod-

---

33. In *Staying Put: Making a Home in a Restless World* (Boston: Beacon Press, 1993), Scott Russell Sanders resists the "vagabond wind" of his culture (p. xv), and says, "Only by knocking against the golden calf of mobility, which looms so large and shines so brightly, have I come to realize that it is hollow. Like all idols, it distracts us from true divinity" (p. 117).

34. Susan Saegert, "The Role of Housing in the Experience of Dwelling," in I. Altman and C. Werner, eds., *Home Environments* (New York: Plenum Books, 1985), p. 287. The classic essay on dwelling is Martin Heidegger, "Building, Dwelling, Thinking," in *Basic Writings*, p. 323.

ucts of economic process. The house is a tool for the achievement of the experience of home."[35] This is why indigenous Hawaiians have advocated for a richer approach to homelessness than shelters and public housing, something called 'ohana housing, which seems somewhat akin to the New Zealand Maori notion of the marai, composed of people "connected by ties of love and loyalty, duty and obligation." And 'ohana housing attempts to engender such communal relatedness by recalling "that 'home' is more than a roof over one's head and 'residing' more than a matter of having a place in which to eat and sleep."[36] So a dwelling is more than a building; home is more than house.

Third, home is a storied place. Homemaking transforms space into place. Certain practices turn spaces without stories into narratively formed places. They endow a place with meaning. Brueggemann argues: "Place is space which has historical meanings, where some things have happened which are now remembered and which provide continuity and identity across generations. Place is space in which important words have been spoken which have established identity, defined vocation, and envisioned destiny."[37] A house becomes a home when it is transformed by memory-shaped meaning into a place of identity, connectedness, order, and care.

We could say that careful and protective dwelling is itself always rooted in and directed by those historical meanings that made this space into the dwelling place of being-at-home. In other words, the boundaries of homemaking are narratively formed. John Berger says: "The mortar which holds the impoverished 'home' together — even for a child — is memory. . . . To the underprivileged, home is represented, not by a house, but by a set of practices. . . . Home is no longer a dwelling but the untold story of a life being lived."[38]

Some, perhaps many, of the meaning-making practices and stories have to do with rituals. According to David Saile, rituals transform "inert

35. Kimberly Dovey, "Home and Homelessness," in Altman and Werner, eds., Home Environments, p. 54.

36. Judith Modell, "(Not) In My Back Yard: Housing the Homeless in Hawaii," in Jan Rensel and Margaret Rodman, eds., Home in the Islands: Housing and Social Change in the Pacific (Honolulu: University of Hawaii Press, 1997), p. 201.

37. Walter Brueggemann, The Land: Place as Gift, Promise and Challenge in Biblical Faith (Philadelphia: Fortress, 1977), p. 5.

38. John Berger, And Our Faces, My Heart, Brief as Photos (New York: Vintage Books, 1991), p. 64.

physical and spatial fabric into living, participating, and richly experienced home places," and in so doing, "not only is the physical environment transformed but so too are the human participants and their relationships with the changed place."[39] Housebuilding and housewarming, spring cleaning and Thanksgiving dinner, Easter and Christmas, births and birthdays, weddings and funerals — all of these events, with their ritual practices, generate stories and thus provide the meanings that make a house a home. Without stories, without particular memories, there is neither home nor identity.[40] Once we have forgotten the stories, there is no home to return to, because there is no place, or even potential place, that could be shaped by those stories. Houses become homes when they embody the stories of the people who have made these spaces into places of significance, meaning, and memory.

Fourth, home is a safe resting place. In contrast to a war zone, a site of danger and fear, home is a refuge, an asylum of safety and security. Home is where one can be relaxed and at ease rather than tense and anxious. Saile says that home is "a secure and familiar base from which people explore their world, physically and psychologically, and to which they return for rest, regeneration, and a sense of self-identity."[41] Edith Wyschogrod says that the metaphor of home as bed or lodging "suggests that home is a milieu of safety, that at home one can drop one's wariness, allow oneself to fall asleep."[42] Or, as Bruce Cockburn sings, "Make me a bed of fond memories/Make me to lie down with a smile."[43] Home is a place constructed in such a way that we are safe to rest.

---

39. David Saile, "The Ritual Establishment of Home," in Altman and Werner, eds., *Home Environments*, p. 87.

40. Memory, however, is ambivalent, for some homes are precarious — or worse, painful. A home that is rooted in stories of conflict with others becomes a fortress of protection against those demonized others (we think of tribal/ethnic conflicts from Bosnia to Northern Ireland to Rwanda). The narrative foundation functions here to make home a deeply ambivalent reality. Conversely, homes are as precarious as the narratives on which they are founded. What happens to the identity of a home, or a homeland, when it becomes clear that the narratives that were taken to be stories of bravery, fidelity, and discovery are revealed to be narratives of cowardice, broken trust, and conquest?

41. Saile, "The Ritual Establishment of Home," p. 92.

42. Edith Wyschogrod, "Dwellers, Migrants, Nomads: Home in the Age of the Refugee," in Rouner, *The Longing for Home*, p. 189.

43. Bruce Cockburn, "Joy Will Find a Way," from the album, *Joy Will Find a Way* ©1975 Golden Mountain Music.

And beyond our present nomadic restlessness, home can be a place of "enough," of satisfaction, of peace. In stark contrast to the insatiable activity of our consuming culture, at home we can find Sabbath rest and thus cultivate contentment in place of envy, generosity rather than greed, moderation in contrast to overconsumption. And when a space becomes a dwelling place of homemaking, it is not viewed as an anxious achievement, but received as a gift. Gratitude not privilege should mark those who inhabit a home.

Heidegger is instructive when he notes that to *dwell* is "to be set at peace."[44] Like the biblical term shalom, to be at peace is to dwell in a particular place in a way that respects the integrity of others. Not held captive by what others think or driven by the need to polish our own self-image, we are not only free to be ourselves but also to let others be themselves. In so doing, we can know and truly be known. A home is a place of vulnerability and trust. In short, the dwelling that is home is a place of safety and rest.

Fifth, home is a place of hospitality. If homes are to resist the temptation to become self-enclosed fortresses — that is, if homes are to have windows and doors that are open — then they must be sites of hospitality. In a fortress the boundaries are high and thick and tightly secure; everyone is a stranger, and there is no room for others. In a hospitable home, by contrast, the boundaries are low and thin and loose; few are strangers there, and there is always room for the others. A fortress of hoarding possessiveness versus a home of openhanded hospitality. In this sense, home is a kind of hospice, a welcoming and caring abode for those — that is, all of us — who are terminally ill.

Such hospitality was at the heart of Dorothy Day's vision for the Catholic Worker Communities.[45] Day was dependent for her views on the philosopher Emmanuel Mounier, who argued that property was an extension of the body of a human being. In capitalist societies, however, "the tendency is for property (or place) to be used simply as the physical extension of one's sphere of control," so that "it becomes a protective shell, making oneself less vulnerable to the intrusion of the world." Mounier noticed that, "by using property (or space) in a protective, defensive manner, one becomes unavailable to the outside world. His property insulates and isolates him."[46] In contrast to such at-

44. Heidegger, "Building, Dwelling, Thinking," p. 327.

45. Dorothy Day, *The Long Loneliness* (San Francisco: HarperSanFrancisco, 1997).

46. Cited by Belden Lane, *Landscapes of the Sacred: Geography and Narrative in American Spirituality* (New York: Paulist, 1988), p. 206.

tempts at insulation and isolation, Rosemary Haughton emphasizes that "hospitality means a letting go of certainty and control — and paradoxically it's only this letting go that allows the richness of growth and change that makes real and not pretended continuity possible."[47] In other words, hospitality is what constitutes home as home yet keeps home open, keeps the boundaries suffused with welcome and protection, not exclusion.[48]

Sixth, home is a place of embodied inhabitation. This trait assumes that there is a distinction between a temporary occupant and a permanent inhabitant, between merely living in a place and becoming rooted in a particular place, by virtue of intimate knowledge and care. David Orr perceptively describes this important distinction between residing and dwelling, paying particular attention to matters of ecology:

> The resident is a temporary and rootless occupant who mostly needs to know where the banks and stores are in order to plug in. The inhabitant and the particular habitat cannot be separated without doing violence to both. . . . To reside is to live as a transient and as a stranger to one's place, and inevitably to some part of the self. The inhabitant and place mutually shape each other.[49]

Elsewhere, Orr expands on this distinction:

> A resident is a temporary occupant, putting down few roots and investing little, knowing little, and perhaps caring little for the immediate locale beyond its ability to gratify. . . . The inhabitant, by contrast, "dwells," as Illich puts it, in an intimate, organic, and mutually nurturing relationship with a place. Good inhabitance is an art requiring detailed knowledge of a place, the capacity for observation, and a sense of care and rootedness. (p. 130)[50]

Thus, while residents require only "cash and a map," inhabitants "bear the marks of their places," and when uprooted they get homesick (p. 130). In-

---

47. Haughton, "Hospitality," in Rouner, *The Longing for Home*, p. 214.

48. These themes are discussed in greater depth by Miroslav Volf, *Exclusion and Embrace: A Theological Exploration of Identity, Otherness, and Reconciliation* (Nashville: Abingdon, 1996).

49. David Orr, *Ecological Literacy* (Albany: SUNY Press, 1992), p. 102.

50. The reference to Ivan Illich is to his essay "Dwelling," *Co-evolution Quarterly* 41 (Spring 1984).

habitants know and treasure what is homemade, homegrown, and home-spun. For the inhabitant, there is a place of dwelling where one finds iden-tity, from which one derives meaning, and apart from which one feels a bit lost and lonely.

Inhabitation is a matter of being, as Edward Casey puts it, "not merely *at* our destination but fully *in* it."[51] We live not as strangers to our place, but fully in our place as knowledgeable and caring dwellers. Home, we have said, requires care and cultivation, but that care and cultivation is al-ways located in a particular place (p. 175).[52] So inhabitation requires atten-tion to one's habitat, and to one's nonhuman neighbors as well. Inhabita-tion requires intimacy with and love for our coinhabitants, for only then are we at home in that place.[53] Thus the place itself functions as another boundary for homemaking. We should note that inhabitation is a two-way street. We not only shape a place according to our own home-making ways, but we are shaped by the places we inhabit. Kimberly Dovey ob-serves: "We not only give a sense of identity to the place we call home, but we also draw our identity from the place."[54]

Seventh, home is a place of orientation. To elucidate this meaning of home, we might find it helpful to reflect on homesickness. What is it to be homesick? Think of children away from home, perhaps at a summer camp. Or recall your first week or two at college. Or the first months you lived in a foreign country. As is often the case with children, homesickness can even have physical symptoms — upset stomach, loss of appetite, insomnia. Com-mon to almost all such experiences is a kind of disorientation. When we are homesick, we feel emotionally out of sorts and out of kilter. We get lost,

51. Edward Casey, *The Fate of Place: A Philosophical History* (Berkeley: University of California Press, 1997), p. 121. For a brilliant set of reflections on how we can better under-stand and care for our place-world, see Casey's *Getting Back Into Place* (Bloomington, IN: Indiana University Press, 1993).

52. We have discussed the implications of inhabitance with respect to higher education in our article "Education for Homelessness or Homemaking? The Christian College in a Postmodern Culture," *Christian Scholar's Review* 32, no. 3 (Spring 2003).

53. See Wes Jackson, *Becoming Native to the Place* (Washington, DC: Counterpoint, 1994). This love of place includes more than the human, as Terry Tempest Williams elo-quently says: "The landscapes we know and return to become places of solace. We are drawn to them because of the stories they tell, because of the memories they hold, or simply be-cause of the sheer beauty that calls us back again and again." *Refuge: An Unnatural History of Family and Place* (New York: Vintage, 1991), p. 244.

54. Kimberly Dovey, "Home and Homelessness," in *Home Environments*, p. 41.

turned around, or mixed up more quickly and easily. Familiar things — places, customs, languages — are now unfamiliar. The habitual ease with which we once negotiated much of everyday life is gone: When does the mail come? Where do I get the car repaired? How do I make a long-distance call? Because home functions as a point of orientation around which our world is rendered meaningful, we no longer feel "at home." A geography of home consists of more than the lay of the land, and our unique topography involves more than merely our *topos* as a point on a map, important as that is.

In other words, home provides order and direction to our lives. It functions, as Eliade has put it, as an *axis mundi* for life.[55] Home is the axis of the world, the point of orientation, around which all else makes sense. Dovey likewise describes home via the ordering of environmental experience and behavior: "Being at home is a mode of being whereby we are oriented within a spatial, temporal and sociocultural order that we understand."[56] Home is the center of our spatial world, the ordering memory of the past, and the taken-for-grantedness of everyday practices and discourse.[57]

For Edward Relph, this idea of orientation is connected to the notion of "roots": "To have roots in a place is to have a secure point from which to look out on the world, a firm grasp of one's own position in the order of things, and a significant spiritual and psychological attachment to somewhere in particular."[58] Writing in the aftermath of World War II, the great French mystic Simone Weil describes the importance of roots:

> To be rooted is perhaps the most important and least recognized need of the human soul. It is one of the hardest to define. A human being has roots by virtue of his real, active, and natural participation in the life of a community which preserves in living shape certain particular treasures of the past and certain particular expectations for the future.[59]

For Weil, this sense of rootedness is brought about, in part, by place. Home is a rooted place from which we can orient ourselves, get our bear-

55. Mircea Eliade, *The Sacred and the Profane* (New York: Harcourt Brace Jovanovich, 1959).

56. Dovey, "Home and Homelessness," p. 35.

57. An illuminating example of a personal journey from acknowledged placelessness to a deepened sense of place can be found in Alan Thein Durning, *This Place on Earth*.

58. Edward Relph, *Place and Placelessness* (London: Pion, 1976), p. 38.

59. Simone Weil, *The Need for Roots* (London: Routledge, 1952), p. 41.

ings, and find direction. Home provides an anchor that prevents us from being set adrift amidst the flow. Like turtles instinctively returning to their place of birth or salmon seeking their spawning grounds, we "home in" on home.

Eighth and last, home is a place of affiliation and belonging. Think of the resonances of home team, hometown, and homeland. Home is where we find our place and gain our identity. Just ask any long-suffering Chicago Cubs fan or proud Torontonian or persecuted Palestinian. Not only a point of orientation, home is a locus of recognition and acceptance. Jürgen Moltmann puts it this way: "I am 'at home' where people know me, and where I find recognition without having to struggle for it."[60] When we are homesick, we long for the familiar and familial bonds of affection derived from membership in our clan or group. Even when those bonds of affection are strained or absent, we nonetheless find ourselves returning to that place where we know we will find refuge. Recall Robert Frost's famous line from "Death of the Hired Man": "Home is the place where, when you have to go there, they have to take you in." That is, home is where you are taken in, at the very minimum, even if neither you nor your family find the prospect pleasant. More positively, as Frederick Buechner puts it, home is "a place where you feel you belong, and which in some sense belongs to you."[61] As Nicholas Wolterstorff poignantly observes, reflecting on the untimely death of his twenty-five-year-old son: "When someone loved leaves home, home becomes mere house."[62]

Related to the experience of homesickness is that of homecoming. In times of war, when soldiers return from places of conflict, we often speak of their homecoming. Many American high schools and colleges have "homecoming" for their graduates, usually once a year. And we often refer to Christmas as a time of homecoming for family members who now live far away. In these instances, our language reveals that home has to do not primarily with space but with indwelt and intimate place. The home to which we, the soldiers or graduates or family, come when we participate in a homecoming is a webbed network of relationships and shared stories and memories that may or may not be fixed to a particular location. For

---

60. Jürgen Moltmann, *God in Creation* (San Francisco: Harper and Row, 1985), p. 46.

61. Frederick Buechner, *The Longing for Home* (San Francisco: HarperCollins, 1996), p. 7.

62. Nicholas Wolterstorff, *Lament for a Son* (Grand Rapids: Eerdmans, 1987), p. 51.

example, while a college homecoming almost always involves visiting the existing alma mater, a return home to visit parents at Christmas may not mean stepping inside the old house. Indeed, returning "home" when your parents' home is no longer the house you grew up in is often a strange and unsettling experience: this new house (or apartment) they have simply does not feel like home. And yet it is a homecoming. Despite the different location, it is still a place peculiarly shaped according to the life projects and unique identity of your family. After all, your picture still hangs on the wall or sits atop the piano.

Notice that in homemaking there is a process of appropriation in which the place and the relationships within that place are taken as one's own. And this appropriation goes both ways. The place somehow belongs to us, and yet we belong to the place. We belong to the web of interconnected relationships that make up the place, and yet they belong to us. And so again, there are boundaries to be erected and respected: to belong here is not to belong elsewhere. To be on the inside of this home necessarily entails that others are on the outside of this home, those who do not belong at all or in the same way.

In short, home is a place of belonging, of recognition and acceptance rather than disdain and rejection. At home we feel included, we belong, and we have friends. When we are not "at home," we feel like outcasts, are disinherited, and have few friends. In the fellowship of home there is a plenitude of healthy relationships, while outside the home — or in a dysfunctional home — we often experience a poverty of relationships.[63]

What insights has this phenomenology given us? First, home is a place of permanence. Whether connected to a stable location or not, home signifies what endures over against what is transient. At home we are host, not guest. Second, home is a dwelling place. Saturated with meaning, home is no mere domicile. We are at ease at home because we know the way around, we know the family customs, the quirks and the jokes — the "rules of the house." Third, home is a storied place. A home is a dwelling made familiar and particular by the stories that have shaped it. At home, the stories we remember recall our common past and infuse our hoped-for

---

63. This, again, is a normative description. We fully well realize the dangers of oppressive (sexist, racist, ethnocentric, nationalist, etc.) communities, and the great pain many suffer when homes are sites of rejection and abuse. For an interesting collection of essays on home written by women, see Mickey Pearlman, ed., *A Place Called Home: Twenty Writing Women Remember* (New York: St. Martin's Press, 1997).

future. Fourth, home is a safe resting place. Home is a berth where we are secure and at rest because of the mutual respect everyone has for the integrity of the inhabitants. Fifth, home is a place of hospitality. At home, we take family in; ideally, we also welcome the stranger because we are at ease, without fear. Sixth, home is what we inhabit. More than merely where we reside, ecologically understood, home is our habitat, and as such, it includes our nonhuman neighbors. Home roots us in the sights, smells, and sounds of a particular piece of earth. Seventh, home is a point of orientation. From home our world is made meaningful. Away from home we become homesick. Eighth, home is a place of affiliation and belonging. Home is, minimally, where they have to take us in, like it or not. Ideally, it is where we are loved and cherished even though we are known. Home is where we have a shot at being forgiven. Barbara Kingsolver just about covers it all when she exclaims:

> I've spent hundreds of pages, even whole novels, trying to explain what home means to me. Sometimes I think that is the only thing I ever write about. Home is place, geography, and psyche; it's a matter of survival and safety, a condition of attachment and self-definition. It's where you learn from your parents and repeat to your children all the stories of what it means to belong to the place and people of your ken.[64]

The Ambivalence of Home

As Frederick Buechner puts it, we are suspended between "the home we knew" and "the home we dream," and so we long for that place "where you feel that all is somehow ultimately well even if things aren't going all that well at any given moment."[65]

But what if things seldom went well at home? What if your home was always transient, never permanent? What if, to you, "home" is a place so identified with such broken memories of violence, neglect, and abuse that it can never be a site of dwelling, inhabitation, safety, hospitality, and belonging? What if the experience of home has left you deeply disoriented in the world? Is it possible that all we have conjured up in this chapter is what

---

64. Kingsolver, *Small Wonder* (New York: HarperCollins, 2002), pp. 197-198.
65. Buechner, *Longing for Home*, p. 7.

David Sibley calls a "happy phenomenology of home" that is too romantic and benign?[66] Bruce Cockburn puts it this way:

> O sweet fantasia of the safe home
> where nobody has to scrape for honey at the bottom of the comb
> where every actor understands the scene
> and nobody ever means to be mean
> catch it in a dream, catch it in a song
> seek it on the street you find the candy man's gone
> I hate to tell you but the candy man's gone.[67]

If we take a mere glance at the street or in the homeless shelters, indeed a brief glimpse into the heart of family violence and alienation in North America, we discover that home often degenerates into a precarious site of transience, meaninglessness, forgetfulness, fear, violence, disrespect, disorientation, and estrangement. Even if our phenomenology does disclose real and normative dimensions of homemaking, we are still left with a culture of homelessness, with few resources, it would seem, with which to begin a process of constructing lives that are hospitable to all and with a home for all. So where do we go from here? We go to the street. We need to dig deeper into the socioeconomic homelessness that has plagued Western society.

66. Sibley, *Geographies of Exclusion,* p. 94.
67. Bruce Cockburn, "Candy Man's Gone," from *Trouble with Normal* ©1983 Golden Mountain Music Corp.

Wine, Money, and the Homebreaking King

Deuteronomy 15:1-18 and 1 Kings 21

When it came to special occasions, you always wanted a wine from Naboth's vineyard. These were fine wines, exquisite vintages. Somehow all of the right conditions came together with a Naboth's vineyard wine: carefully and lovingly tended vines, perfect soil conditions, a wonderful microclimate, and vintner skills passed down from generation to generation in Naboth's family.

But there was something more about Naboth's wines. I don't quite know how to explain it, but is it possible to say that a wine has the taste of "covenant" to it? Is it possible to drink a wine and know who you are, know where you came from, know in the very drinking of it that you are a child of promise? Well, that's what it was like to drink Naboth's wines. Some wines make you forget. A glass of Naboth's vineyard wine, shared with friends in the fellowship of a good meal, made you remember.

You remembered that God had promised this land as a place of home-making to our mother and father, Sarah and Abraham. You remembered that you were once a slave in Egypt. You remembered how God had liberated you from that oppressive empire and led you on an exodus journey through the wilderness. You remembered that God sustained you in the wilderness with manna, quail, and water flowing from rocks. You remembered that the land of our homecoming was received as a gift from our extravagantly generous God.

Maybe that was it. You remembered that the land is a gift. And you could taste the goodness of that gift with every sip of Naboth's wine. Naboth knew that the land, his vineyard, his wine, was a gift. And he cared for and tended that land with the tenderness of caring for a precious gift. He knew that he had received the land as an inheritance — not just from his father, but from the very God of Israel. And so, in an act of praise and gratitude, Naboth made some of the finest wines in Israel.

You know how the conversation often gets a little muddy after a few glasses of wine? Well here's the amazing thing: drinking Naboth's wine tended to lead the conversation into deeper clarity. The clarity of Torah. I'm not saying that every conversation over a glass of this fine wine turned to a discussion of Torah, but frequently enough it did. Whether it was the wine itself or that the wine got us thinking about Naboth and the faithful witness of his family over the years — I don't know. But we had many wonderful conversations around a couple bottles of Naboth's wine. Remembering that we are a people of promise, that we were once slaves and that the land is a gift, we would also remember that the Torah calls us to be a people of generosity and justice. We would remember that security in the land depends on how we treat the orphan, the widow, and the stranger. We would remember that the portion of our crops and our goods that we gave to the priests for distribution to the poor was the sacred portion (Deut. 26:13). We would remember that the seventh year was a Sabbath year, a year of rest for the land and for the forgiveness of our debts. And we would remember that, if there was anyone in need in the community, we were not to be hardhearted or tightfisted toward neighbors, but to be openhanded to them.

Again, I'm sure it's not just the wine that made us remember and meditate on these things. You see, we had seen brother Naboth live this way. I remember that one Sabbath year Naboth set free a slave who had become terribly indebted to him a few years earlier. Naboth freed the man of his debts and his service, and he didn't send him away empty-handed either. He gave the man a number of animals from his barn — some goats, chickens, and even a cow — and a couple bags of seed from his threshing floor. And Naboth sent the man off with a case of his finest wine as well!

We were at Naboth's house for dinner that night, and I asked him about the wine. I could understand the animals and the seed: these were necessary if this man was to begin to build a livelihood for his family again. But wasn't that wine a little over the top? Naboth reminded me that Moses required all of this when he gave us the law of the Sabbath year.

Now you know what happens when a few Jews get talking Torah over a glass of wine.

"Yes, but *why* did Moses require that we should give liberally from our wine cellar to a released slave?" I asked.

"So he can rejoice, my friend, so he can rejoice," Naboth replied.

So he can rejoice! That pretty much sums up Naboth's life. A life of rejoicing in being a covenant child, in tending the earth. A life of joyful homemaking and joyful generosity in the Promised Land. A life of rejoicing. Until Naboth's next-door neighbor had designs on Naboth's land, that is. That's when joy turned to sorrow.

Loving your neighbor, caring for your neighbor, seeking justice for your neighbor, being openhanded to your neighbor — such neighborliness was at the heart of covenantal homemaking. Naboth's problem was that his neighbor was the king. You would think that King Ahab of Israel would know something about covenantal neighborliness (Ps. 72; Deut. 17:14-20). But he didn't. And as you will hear in the tale I tell, he didn't know anything about the land as gift and inheritance either.

My hunch is that he also couldn't tell a fine wine if it bit him . . . well, never mind.

Like many of us, the king liked his fresh vegetables. No problem with that. But he wanted his vegetables — and pretty much everything else — right away. He was not a man who liked to wait for things. When he wanted something, he wanted it now! Sounds like typical king behavior, doesn't it? Seems like the richer and more powerful they get, the more of a spoiled brat they become. So here we have a spoiled brat of a king who liked his vegetables really fresh, but the vegetable farms that supplied the royal table were about a half hour away. What was the impetuous, couldn't-wait king supposed to do? He looked out his window one day and thought to himself that the next-door vineyard would make a fine vegetable garden, a kind of greengrocer convenience store right next door.

So Ahab walked over and found Naboth pruning a grapevine.

"Good morning, Naboth," the king said.

"Good morning, your highness," replied Naboth.

"Listen here, my good man," began the king, "I've got a deal for you. Give me your vineyard, so that I may have a vegetable garden close to my house, and I will give you a better vineyard for it; or if you prefer, I'll give you its value in money."

Naboth could hardly believe his ears. He looked around his vineyard, this vineyard that had been tended by his family for generations, this vineyard that was a portion of the inheritance of his ancestors when they entered the Promised Land. Could the king have really just asked him to give it up? Naboth's answer was short and to the point: "The Lord forbid that I should give you my ancestral inheritance."

Give you something that isn't mine to give? Give you something that

I've received as a gift, as an inheritance to tend and keep? Give you covenantal land given to me as an inalienable trust? Give you my home for the sake of your culinary convenience? Give up this vineyard that takes years and years to cultivate so you can plow it all under and plant vegetables? The Lord forbids such a thing. And you know he meant it, because the Lord does forbid such things. The Lord forbids such self-centered, unneighborly expropriation. The Lord forbids reducing the land to a commodity to be sold off to the highest bidder!

Well, kings don't like to be told no, so Ahab went home in a sulking mood and went to bed. If he couldn't have vegetables from Naboth's land, well, then he wouldn't eat anything at all. But when Queen Jezebel came home, things started happening.

"What's the problem, honey?" she asked. "Why are you so depressed?"

Now the way I heard it, Ahab's answer was kind of interesting. You know what he said? "I'm depressed because I spoke to Naboth the Jezreelite and said to him, 'Give me your vineyard for money; or else, if you prefer, I'll give you another vineyard for it.' But he answered, 'I will not give you my vineyard.'"

Listen closely to what the king said — and also to what he didn't say. First, notice that the order of things has changed. When he actually spoke to Naboth earlier, he offered him first another vineyard and then, second, the possibility of money for his land. But, in recounting the story to his wife, he changes the order. Why? Might it be that the issue was always money for Ahab? Could it be that, for him, land is simply a piece of real estate, something to be bought by the highest bidder? Might it be that the king was really that far removed from a covenantal understanding of land and home?

When you notice what he *didn't* recount from his conversation with Naboth, it becomes clear that he is indeed far removed from covenantal life. Naboth said, "The Lord forbid that I should give you my ancestral inheritance." But Ahab tells Jezebel that he said, "I will not give you my vineyard." No reference to what God forbids or to the language of ancestral inheritance.[68] Like all of us, Ahab hears what he wants to hear.

68. Actually the slippage in the text has a previous step. The narrator says, after the interchange between Ahab and Naboth, "Ahab went home resentful and sullen because of what Naboth the Jezreelite had said to him; for he had said, 'I will not give you my ancestral inheritance'" (21:4). Notice that, while the narrator includes the language of inheritance, he drops the opening exclamation, "The Lord forbid!" This would seem to be an intentional

Jezebel, for her part, has heard enough. She had not grown up in Israel's covenant, and, for a worshiper of Baal like her, neither what God forbids nor the Jewish language of inheritance is relevant. All that matters is that the king gets what he wants. "Get up, Ahab, and start acting like a king. Go and eat. I'll take care of this business with Naboth, and I'll give you his vineyard." Just like that. "I'll give you Naboth's vineyard" — as if it were somehow hers to give. As if it were the divine right of kings and the presumption of the powerful to get what they want when they want it.

The story that follows is devastating. I was actually there when it happened. A royal decree showed up declaring that a fast would be observed in a couple of days. I was already suspicious of this fast, because the Torah requires only one fast day, the Day of Atonement, the day that begins a Sabbath year, the day of forgiveness of sins and of debts. But Queen Jezebel had declared a fast day for no apparent reason. When I arrived at the gathering on the appointed day, I noticed that Naboth was seated up front with the nobles and elders. Before we knew it, two men whom I recognized to be lackeys of the royal court jumped up and shouted at Naboth, "You have cursed God and the king." The elders and members of the royal court grabbed Naboth and dragged him outside the city gates.

By the time I had pushed my way through the crowd, it was too late. There lay my friend Naboth in a pool of blood, his body bruised and broken, with large rocks all around him. They had stoned him to death.

Shortly after that, the queen received a note: "Naboth has been stoned; he is dead." This was even more succinct than Naboth's original response to Ahab. When Jezebel heard that, she said to Ahab, her husband: "Go, take possession of the vineyard of Naboth the Jezreelite, which he refused to give you for money; for Naboth is not alive, but dead." When Ahab heard that Naboth was dead, he went next door and took possession of Naboth's vineyard.

Naboth has been stoned. He is dead. So go, take possession. It all hangs together. Jezebel had not even referred to the possibility of giving Naboth another vineyard. He wouldn't take money, and as far as she was concerned, that's all that mattered. He was offered money, and he refused. So he was stoned.

That's the way it always goes. Once someone forgets that the land is an inheritance, that it is a gift, and once someone reduces land to its monetary

---

slippage, as though the narrator is only heightening the sense of Ahab's covenantal ignorance born of amnesia.

value, then those with the most money, those with the most power, will have their way with the land. And if someone should get in their way, well, that combination of death and possession will always raise its ugly head. And people of the covenant, people of inheritance — people like my dear friend Naboth — will always lose. They will lose their land, lose their home, and lose their life.

But the homemaking God of covenant will not have it. The God who gives land as a gift, the God who gives land for tilling and keeping, the God who sets land and all of life in the context of covenantal neighborliness and openhanded justice will not tolerate tightfisted violence and dispossession. Therefore, as we saw the king making his way to take possession of our friend's vineyard, we also saw the prophet Elijah slip into the vineyard from the other gate. When they met, there were no preliminaries, no "good morning, your majesty" or "lovely day, your highness." Elijah went right to the point: "Thus says the Lord: Have you killed, and also taken possession?"

"Naboth is dead, go and take possession" is the normal course of affairs for a royal vision of land and power. But this is not the vision of the covenant-making God. Dispossession and homelessness is the normal course of affairs for a world in which land and home is a matter of real-estate investment. Not so for the God of Israel. Not so for the God of inheritance. Not so for the God of homemaking.

"So, listen up, Ahab," the prophet continued, "Thus says the Lord. . . ." "Thus says the Lord" who forbids such violence, such expropriation. "Thus says the Lord" of Naboth and his ancestors: "In the place where the dogs licked up the blood of Naboth, dogs will also lick up your blood."

The tension in the air was so thick you could have cut it with a knife. The king replies, "Have you found me, O my enemy?" Can you imagine that — a king of Israel acknowledging that a prophet of the Lord is his enemy!

And then, speaking in a voice that was somehow both his own and God's, the prophet replied: "I have found you. Because you have sold yourself to do what is evil in the sight of the Lord, I will bring disaster on you; I will consume you, and will cut off from Ahab every male, bond or free, in Israel; and I will make your house like the house of Jeroboam son of Nebat, and like the house of Baasha son of Ahijah, because you have provoked me to anger and have caused Israel to sin."

I will, I will, I will. . . . While you and your wife, for whom there is a similar judgment, have acted like it is your royal prerogative to act as you see fit, let me tell you who has the authority to act in this world. I do. And I will act to bring on you and your house a dispossession even more devastating than what you have done to Naboth. By your violence and breaking of the covenant, you have forfeited your right to an inheritance in Israel. By breaking the home of Naboth, you will be rendered homeless yourself. By taking possession through a violent act of dispossession, you will be dispossessed. You yourself, Ahab, will meet death outside of covenant with your God.

Those of us who were witnessing this confrontation between king and prophet almost cheered. Those of us who loved Naboth, who had been instructed in faithfulness through his witness, who had tasted the goodness of covenant in the very wine that came from this wonderful vineyard — we felt vindicated that this judgment would befall Ahab and his house. We were happy that the utter homelessness that death had brought to our friend Naboth would now be visited on the royal household.

But it didn't happen. At least not right away. Rather than have Elijah arrested for treason against the king, rather than having him stoned as Naboth was — because Elijah really *had* cursed the king — Ahab did the totally unexpected: he tore his clothes, put on sackcloth, and began to fast. The irony is pretty heavy, isn't it? First Ahab fasts in a sullen sulk, and then his wife declares a deceitful fast of entrapment against Naboth. But now he really does fast. No vegetables or meat for King Ahab, not from Naboth's land and not from anyone else's.

And the God who takes initiative, the God who is sovereign over life and death, changes his mind . . . at least for a time. He speaks again to Elijah and says, "Because Ahab has humbled himself before me, I will not bring the disaster in his days; but in his son's days I will bring the disaster on his house."[69] A stay of execution.

I don't know how Elijah felt about it, but I've got to confess that I was initially outraged. Naboth's blood still stained the soil outside the city gate. My friend's family was still left without a father and husband. I wanted vengeance. I wanted justice. I wanted Ahab and his family to be disinherited, to be homeless because of their violence and breaking of covenant.

All of that happened, but not soon enough for me. As I look back on those events, though, on this story of homemaking and homebreaking,

---

69. In 2 Kings 10:1-17, this prophecy is fulfilled in the destruction of Ahab's complete household.

this story of land as covenantal trust or commercial commodity, this tale of life and death, of the fine wine of faithfulness and the bitter draught of deceit, I find myself brought back again to the God of faithfulness, of life, of covenant. I find myself drawn back to this homemaking God. And I find again that I need to learn from my friend Naboth the virtue of trust. Trust in this God who calls forth trust. Trust in this God who gives us homes and our very lives in trust. Trust in the God of trust — because without trust there can be no home and no homecoming. There can't even be justice.

Socioeconomic Homelessness

sunshine
on downtown eastside sidewalks
glows fresh crimson
like rose petals fallen
from ransacked gardens of the broken-hearted

Bud Osborn[1]

Any discussion of homelessness must begin on the streets of our cities. It is there that we meet the displaced and discarded, the exiled and the expatriate, the refugee and the rejected. It is on the streets that we see the face of socioeconomic homelessness in all of its pain and anguish. And it is there that we must confront the ethical contradiction of unspeakable wealth and opulence side by side with debilitating poverty and hopelessness. If we are ever to meaningfully realize a dream of life "beyond homelessness," then homecoming must come to the streets of our cities. We begin with two vignettes from the streets of Toronto.[2]

---

1. Bud Osborn, "Down Here," *Hundred Block Rock* (Vancouver: Arsenal Press, 1999).

2. The narratives in this chapter are written in the first-person singular because they are the experiences of Brian Walsh. While these stories and the analysis are about Toronto, there is a certain universality to the realities of homelessness throughout North America, and indeed the "developed world." It is important, however, to both the method and the substance of this book's argument to locate our analysis in particular places. If we are attempting to confront the socioeconomic realities of displacement, the last thing we need is for the analysis to be placeless.

The Streetcar Sped Away

The streetcar sped away as I was running across the street, and I groaned: it meant a five- or ten-minute wait for the next one. Not a long time, really, but this was one of the coldest days of the winter. As I reached the other side of the street, I immediately heard the words, "Excuse me, but can you spare some change?" I turned and looked at the tall man who was wearing clothes that were certainly not up to the task of keeping a body warm on a day like this, and my hand immediately went for my pocket. Of course, I have some change, especially on a day like today. Out came a couple of dollars.

"Thanks, man, pray for the poor," my street neighbor said.

"That's right," I replied, "you have to pray for the poor."

"And the rich, too," he added, "you gotta pray for the rich."

"What's that?"

"You gotta pray for the rich. They really need our prayers, too."

"We need to pray for the rich?"

"Oh yeah, we gotta pray for the rich. See, they're all scared. They're all worried about their money, and afraid that someone is going to come and steal it. That's a terrible way to live. It's so lonely. That's why we gotta pray for the rich."

It became clear that this was an interesting young man.

As we continued to talk on that frigid street corner, I learned that Will was a Jamaican, that he was homeless, that he had to pick up his anti-psychotic drugs at one of the major shelters in the area, though he didn't stay there. When I asked him where he had stayed the previous night (when temperatures reached -25 degrees Celsius), he mentioned an empty building nearby. "There's no heat, but a lot of us would rather stay there than in the shelters." I could understand that. The Toronto shelters had been hit with an incredible bedbug infestation, and sleeping there meant that, while you were warm, you were also going to be eaten alive.

I noticed that Will's nose showed the signs of frostbite. And while I was warmly dressed though shivering in the cold, Will had on only a light jacket and seemed to have all the time in the world to stand there and talk to me.

"You know," Will continued, "that the rich are scared of the poor. And if the rich ever gave the poor enough to live on, if the rich in the West ever gave the poor of Africa enough to be well fed, well, then the poor would be strong enough to come here and take everything from the rich. That's why the rich don't want to help the poor."

"You mean, the rich have to keep the poor in their poverty and hunger so they'll be easier to control?"

"Yeah, man, that's it. It's just like Bob Marley said [and here Will began to sing], 'You got to emancipate yourselves from mental slavery, none but ourselves can free our minds . . .' Bob Marley, man, he knew what it was about."

"That's right," I replied, "'Exodus, movement of Jah people,'" I said, not wishing to try to sing a Marley tune for this Jamaican brother. "Marley called for a spiritual liberation that would set the captives free."

"I don't know," Will mused, "but maybe the system has it all wrong. Maybe this system of the rich and the poor, the folks who have it all and those who have nothing, maybe this whole system is wrong."

"So, what do we do?" I asked.

"What if we tried out Jesus' way?"

"Jesus?"

"Yeah, you know, instead of this system, try out the kingdom of God."

"That's kind of what Bob Marley was about," I remarked.

"I don't know, maybe we've already tried it Jesus' way, and it didn't work — I don't know, man."

At this point the streetcar was now in sight, and while I was entranced by this conversation with Will, I was painfully cold and was looking forward to getting warm. As the streetcar approached, Will asked me if I could also give him a transit ticket, which I immediately did. How could I justify getting on a streetcar and leaving Will in the cold when I had extra tickets in my pocket? But it was clear that he was saving the ticket for later, because there was more panhandling to be done on this corner.

In our last few seconds together Will said: "I don't know, maybe when you get home you'll have a smoke, make a cup of coffee, and sit down and write a doctoral about what we just talked about."

Did he say a "doctoral"? A "doctoral"! Some kind of academic treatise on the plight of the homeless, the fears of the rich, the failures of the system, and the possibilities of emancipation — maybe even through Jesus? How did Will know that I was writing a book on these themes? How did he know that I was hanging out in his part of town precisely to get closer to the street-level experience of homeless people like him?

"Maybe I will," I replied. "Maybe I'll write a 'doctoral' on these things. If I do, I'll make sure you get a footnote."

"Okay, man, that's cool," Will called out as I boarded the streetcar.

That night I woke up at around 3:00 in the morning. It was another night of such cold temperatures that the city had announced a cold-weather alert: more emergency beds were being made available for the homeless, more street patrols were sent out, and various government buildings were to be kept open so that homeless people could get out of the cold. And I couldn't get back to sleep. All I could think of was whether Will was okay. Where was he sleeping? Was he warm enough? Somehow, knowing that he was out there somewhere and I was safe in my warm bed in my own home made it impossible for me to go back to sleep. So I prayed, but this time it was not for the rich. This time I prayed for Will.

I had gleaned from our conversation that Will sometimes ate at the Toronto Christian Resource Centre drop-in, where I was being hosted while working on this book. The next morning I went to the office as early as I could, still anxious about Will's fate that previous night. With great relief I spotted him eating breakfast as I came in. Another night in the cold. Another day to survive. Another prayer answered. Will made it through the night. What would happen if God started answering our prayers for the rich as well?

Nobody's Child

A few years earlier I was volunteering in a drop-in center for street kids. The center would be open all afternoon, and kids could come and hang out, get some basic medical care, check out the food and clothing banks, have a cup of coffee and play pool or Ping-Pong. My specialty was that last activity, and it was interesting what happened at the Ping-Pong table. The rule was clear: you play until you lose. Everyone agreed to the rule. And if that meant that some hotshot kid could beat all comers, then so be it, that kid stayed on the table all afternoon. That was, until I started playing. For some reason they changed the rule for me: instead of being bumped off the table every time I lost (which was at least half of the games I played), the kids would simply get in line in order to play me.

The rest of the staff found this very curious. These were not kids who were generally known to want to change the rules if those rules were in their own interest. And they certainly weren't kids who were known to want to bend over backwards to accommodate adults in their lives. That was precisely why so many of them were on the street. They had rebelled against what they experienced as the restrictive rules of their families and schools, and they had opted for the world of the street, where adult authority had little impact. But here at the center they were changing the rules precisely to keep an adult in the game.

It was during a match with one of the toughest kids in the center that it became clear what was going on. Phil was the kind of guy who other kids either stayed clear of or deferred to. It was clear from the way he carried himself and the seriousness of his gaze that this kid had seen a lot, had had to fight to survive, and wasn't about to take any shit from anyone. But he did want to play Ping-Pong. And if he showed up, it wasn't uncommon for other kids to simply allow him to walk to the front of the line. That's where he found me, the gray-haired guy in his mid-forties whom everyone wanted to play. So Phil and I started to play. He was good, and he was intense. For some reason he brought out the best in me, and the game was hard fought and close. I don't remember who won that first game, but it was clear that Phil was going to have another go at me. So we played again, and again, and again. No other kid dared protest. In fact, there was a bit of a crowd now watching this contest.

Then it happened. In the midst of a rally of shots that went back and forth, shots and countershots, where we both were making what looked like impossible saves on fantastic shots, it happened. As the sweat poured off each of us, as the game's intensity grew deeper and deeper, it happened. In the middle of a hard-fought rally, a smile broke out on Phil's face. He smiled! I had never seen this young man smile before, but there it was. And when we finished that particular rally, we both fell over laughing. Uproarious laughter, tears mixing with the sweat on our faces.

That's when I understood why all those kids wanted to play Ping-Pong with me. It wasn't because I was the great challenge, and it certainly wasn't out of deference to an adult. They wanted to play Ping-Pong with me — and especially Phil wanted to have a whole series of games with me — because I was an adult about the age of their fathers. Most of these kids had never, or at least very seldom, had this kind of experience with their dads. I was the dad-guy at the drop-in center. But not the dad who was responsible for their discipline. Not the dad they ran away from because of abuse.

No, I was the rec-room, Ping-Pong-playing dad that these kids, mostly young men, had always wanted.

Whenever I would talk to the kids in any depth, it became clear that even though "home" had been a site of such pain, such rejection, and such hurt, there was nonetheless a deep longing to go home. They still even referred to that place they had fled as home. And if they couldn't go home there, they would long for experiencing home in some other place.

An elderly woman named Dorothy Mortimer was at the drop-in center every day, dressed like someone's rich grandma. And that's what all the kids called her — "Grandma." Dorothy was the best security that we had in the place. If anyone was getting out of line, cursing and swearing, or acting in violent or intimidating ways, all the other kids would come down hard and bring that behavior to an end. You didn't act that way around "Grandma." They loved Dorothy so much that they wanted to make sure she didn't have to witness that kind of violence or rudeness. What was amazing about Dorothy was the way she talked to the kids. From her mouth came nothing but the sweetest — and even the most sentimental — language. She would refer to these street-tough kids as "my little darlings" or "my sweet angels." And the kids loved it. All the exterior toughness notwithstanding, these kids wanted to be someone's little darling, someone's sweet angel. They wanted Dorothy to be their grandma, and they wanted me to be the Ping-Pong dad. They wanted to be somebody's child.

ToniAnne gave this longing a simple, evocative expression in a short poem. ToniAnne had been on the street for a number of years, and like many street-involved girls, she longed to have a baby. If you can't have the family that you have run away from, then it is natural to try to create that experience of family for yourself. And so she had a baby. Of course, the baby was taken by the Children's Aid Society because it is impossible to raise a baby on the street. It was also clear that what ToniAnne needed was not to be a mother but to be a kid. One day she gave me a poem she had written entitled "Nobody's Child":

> I'm nobody's sweetheart
> I'm nobody's Child.
> I'm like a flower growing wild
> No mommy's kisses
> No daddy's smiles

Nobody wants me
I'm nobody's child.

Nobody's child. Home is where you belong. Home should be a locus of affection, a site of orientation and a place of hospitality and rest where you are rooted in deep memories. Home should be where you have a sense of security and permanence. Home should be where a child is wanted, protected, and loved. Neither Phil nor ToniAnne had such a home. Experiencing their lives as "nobody's child," they fear they are "nobody." And when you have no place in the world, when you have nowhere to go to call home, and the memories of what once was home are too painful to ever be healing, you lose your identity: nobody's child runs the risk of being nobody, period.[3]

Homelessness: A Socioethical Crisis

Homelessness has many faces in our time. In the above stories of Will, Phil, and ToniAnne we have met three of those faces. In their stories we begin to see the diversity of homelessness and some of its causes. Youth culture, dysfunctional families, inadequate schooling, adolescent rebellion, drugs and alcohol abuse — all of these factor into the crisis of homelessness that street youths like Phil and ToniAnne face. Other forces render Will homeless: poverty in Jamaica, mental illness, racism, the problems of homeless shelters, and a lack of affordable housing result in an eloquent person like Will begging for coins on the corner.

There are, of course, many more faces to homelessness. John Berger observes that "never before our time have so many people been uprooted. Emigration, forced or chosen, across national frontiers or from village to metropolis, is the quintessential experience of our time."[4] The twentieth century, says Berger, was "the century of banishment" (p. 67).

3. An excellent book on street-involved youth in Canada is Marlene Webber, *Street Kids: The Tragedy of Canada's Runaways* (Toronto, Buffalo, and London: University of Toronto Press, 1991). An interesting study of one particular American locale is Susan M. Ruddick, *Young and Homeless in Hollywood: Mapping Social Identities* (New York and London: Routledge, 1996).

4. John Berger, *And Our Faces, My Heart, Brief as Photos* (New York: Vintage, 1991), p. 55.

Refugees and immigrants experienced an economic and political banishment from their homelands, only to be impoverished and disenfranchised in their adopted "land of promise." Generations of families who have lived in poverty in the inner city find themselves banished from ever realizing the aspirations of their suburban neighbors. Street kids are banished from the local mall where they can get warm and hang out because they are an eyesore to the patrons and are trespassing on private property that is open only to those who have the economic means to consume the merchandise. And the urban poor find themselves banished from their own neighborhoods when urban renewal projects gentrify the area, displacing the very people who had for generations called this place "home," as impoverished and run down as it was. To better understand this phenomenon of socioeconomic homelessness, allow us to tell a story. Unlike the stories at the beginning of this chapter, which were true, the following story is a fiction, but one that sharply illustrates the dynamics of homelessness.[5]

A Tale of Compassion and Analysis

It all began with a church picnic. Families and friends gathered by the banks of a beautiful river on a day that just couldn't have been better. They had shared food, sung some songs, the kids were playing with the frisbees and balls, and the adults were catching up on each other's lives. But every now and then some of us could hear disturbing voices off in the distance: they were voices of alarm, voices crying out for help. Curiously, not everyone heard these voices, just a few of us. When we finally went to investigate the source of these disturbing sounds, we saw that someone was in the river and was in distress. A couple of us quickly jumped into the water and brought a young Somali woman to shore. And while we were wrapping her in blankets and giving her some warm tea, we heard other voices. Two more people were coming down the river, and they were

---

5. The general outline of this tale is not original with us. We have heard various people describe the realities of homelessness using such a narrative device. This telling is a development and an expansion of a version of the story presented by Joe Mihevc, a Toronto city counselor. Joe presented something akin to the first half of this story at a conference of Christian street workers called "Voices" on January 26, 2004. Jim Wallis tells a similar tale in *God's Politics* (New York: HarperCollins, 2005), pp. 204, 234.

drowning as well. Again, we jumped to the rescue and pulled out a couple of teenagers. But as we were getting them to shore, we saw that a few others were in the water, and then there were more and more. All kinds of people — from different ethnic backgrounds, different neighborhoods, and different circumstances — had been caught in that river's current and were drowning.

Before long we had quite a crowd of wet, cold, and shivering humanity huddled on the beach. Some of the other people who had been picnicking there that day complained that we were ruining their view of the river and disturbing their children, so we moved a little ways away to a site that wasn't as nice but was still adequate for us to continue our day together with this group of new friends. But it became clear as the sun was setting that we were not going to be able to just go home that night. More people kept coming down the river. So, while some went home to get tents, sleeping bags, and food, others stayed and continued to pull people out of that river. After all, this was a church picnic, wasn't it? Surely, following Jesus meant we had to reach out to these people, because he might say to us on the last day: "I was cold and drowning and you rescued me and gave me a cup of hot tea" (see Matt. 25:31-46).

After a few days of regularly pulling dozens of people out of that river, we set up a little field hospital, along with a food bank, an employment registry, and a shelter for people to stay in overnight. Some other churches got involved by volunteering time and money to our charitable venture. We even started our own little church on the site. The local government was impressed with what we were doing, so they gave us some money and paid for a few nurses and social workers to visit our riverside encampment. The local media featured our camp in a couple of magazine and newspaper articles, radio interviews, and even a television documentary.

And this went on for quite a while. But some of us started to wonder why all these people were floating down the river. Some asked, "Shouldn't we go upstream to investigate why all these people are falling into the river? Is it enough just to keep on rescuing them as they float by?" Others insisted that we couldn't afford to let anyone do that because, if we did, we would be short-staffed and wouldn't be able to save all the poor folks floating by. Some were even more adamant in opposing an investigation of the source of the problem; they insisted that this wasn't what the church was called to do. "Jesus cared for the individuals who appeared on his path and didn't waste his time trying to deal with larger 'social' problems," they reasoned. Some of those people even believed that our concern for finding the causes for this crisis was actually a denial of our faith. Some of them expressed this concern by worrying about our spiritual — and perhaps physical — safety. Others, who were not so polite, told us that our seeking causes for the people in the river was a "sell-out" of the heart of the gospel.

But the question wouldn't go away. A small group of us were sure that there was something going on upstream that we had to investigate. It simply didn't make sense to keep pulling these people out of the water if we didn't try to see why they kept ending up in the river in the first place. And so, with the worries, warnings, and even taunts of our friends, fellow shelter workers, and church members echoing in our ears, we began hiking upstream to find out why so many people were floating down this river — most of them drowning because of the current, some even dead. There were four of us: Phyllis, Greg, Marci, and me.

As we hiked, the terrain got rougher and rougher. When we came to a high bridge over the river, we found another group of people camped under the bridge. They had also been floating down the river, but somehow they had managed to drag themselves and each other out of the water. They were huddled together in poorly constructed shacks of cardboard and whatever other materials they could find. We asked them why they were there. How did they get there? Why didn't they come a little further downstream, where we could care for them? At first they just groaned about the conditions upstream that had put them into the water in the first place. And we couldn't quite make out what they were saying, but phrases like "no damn jobs," "my old man beat me," "no health card," "can't keep on top of my meds," and "I just don't know" kept coming up.

"So why don't you leave the bridge and come to the shelter?" we asked.

"I'd rather fight the rats than the bedbugs," one guy replied.

"Because here we at least have a community, and I can sleep with my boyfriend," a young woman said.

"I feel safer here than what I've heard about the shelters," another woman said.

It was with a real sense of sadness and a growing sense of doom that we left those "bridge people," after giving them a few blankets and some food, and continued upstream. We were sad because our compassion was real: we were pulling people out of the river, giving them shelter and medical attention, and were really trying to establish compassionate relationships with them. But some of them weren't too impressed with our best intentions. We also had a sense of doom because we didn't know what we were going to encounter upstream.

First we came to a tributary where some people were floating down hanging on to old pieces of furniture, inner tubes, and a life jacket or two. As we started up the tributary, we noticed two things right off: first, the terrain was getting rougher and the banks of the stream were very high; second, the stream was filthy and terribly polluted. As we made our way further up the tributary, we saw factories at the top of the banks, and workers were tumbling out of these factories, down the banks, and into the streams. Not all of the workers, but a good number of them. We pulled one man out and asked him what was going on.

"The factory is closing because the company is moving production to Mexico — or is it Indonesia or China? Whatever. All of our jobs are gone. Guess that's globalization for you, eh?"

"Well, yeah," we replied, "but what about unemployment insurance? Can't you get some benefits to tide you over until you can get another job?"

"I don't know, man. They said I wasn't eligible. That's why I'm in the river." And then we remembered that the rules for receiving unemployment benefits had become much more restrictive and had left guys like this worker out in the cold.

"Is everyone falling in the river from your plant?" we asked.

"No, some folks went up that other tributary over there. They're thinking they can find some kind of benefits there."

After giving this unemployed worker another one of our blankets and directions to the shelter downstream, we started up the tributary he had pointed to. As we hiked up this stream, we saw some tall buildings and what looked like a thriving city off in the distance. But along the banks of this stream (which was just as filthy as the last one) were houses and low-rise apartment buildings, all in disrepair and all precariously close to the bank, which was now becoming a cliff. Every now and then someone would fall out of one of those buildings into the water below. We had lots of experience pulling people out of the water, so we quickly jumped in and hauled out a thirty-something Jamaican woman and her two children.

"What happened?" we asked, "Did you also lose your job to globalization?" She looked at us with bewilderment in her eyes.

"No, I didn't lose my job! They'd never lay me off; I'm a very good worker. I just can't make it anymore on what they pay me. I'm so far behind in my rent and bill payments that I just got thrown out of my place, with my two kids here."

"You have a job?" we asked.

"Sure, I got a job. I got two jobs. I flip burgers at McDonalds in the afternoon, and I clean those office buildings at night. My sister watches the kids after school. But working sixty hours a week at minimum wage, man, I still can't keep up. And the landlord raised my rent fifteen percent last year. So here I am shivering on the side of this river with you folks, out of my home, and I don't know how I'm going to get to work tomorrow."

It's true, we thought. The minimum wage in Ontario had been stuck at $6.85 for years, and only recently was it raised to $7.15.[6] Even at sixty hours a week, there was no way that this mom could make enough money to feed and clothe her kids, pay the rent, and keep on top of the bills.[7] And the provincial government had abolished rent controls with the horribly misnamed "Tenant Protection Act" in the late 1990s.[8] And since the mid-1990s, not only had there been no rent-geared-to-income housing developed in Toronto, but very few new rental units had been developed in the city. Moreover, the waiting lists for public housing now had more than 71,000 households on it.[9] There was no place for this woman to go. No wonder she ended up in the river.

We called some of our friends to come and pick up this woman and her kids and take them to our family shelter for the night. But we knew that our shelter was way downriver from where she had lived, and we were already worrying about how she was going to get back and forth from her jobs in time to care for the children.

6. After many years of being stuck at $6.85 an hour, the minimum wage in Ontario was increased to $7.15 in the winter of 2004, and to $8.00 on February 1, 2007.

7. In 2003 more than a half million people in Toronto lived in poverty. *The Toronto Report Card on Homelessness, 2003* (Toronto: Municipal Government, 2003), p. 3.

8. From 1997 to 2002, rents rose in Toronto by 31 percent (*Toronto Report Card*, p. 3). In 2006 the Liberal government of Ontario introduced the Residential Tenancies Act, which begins to redress some of the injustices of the previous Act.

9. "From 2000 to 2002 only 3% of new housing construction was for rental units (873 units) compared to 97% for the home-ownership market (28,492)" (*Toronto Report Card*, p. 3). It needs to be added that, of those 873 units, none were for rent-geared-to-income apartments. Moreover, in the four-year period from 1998 to 2001, only 437 rental units were built in Toronto; during that same period no government-assisted rental units were built.

Back upstream, as we continued our journey, more and more people were in the water, hanging onto something for dear life. We were still looking for the people who came up this tributary for social assistance, but before we found them, we encountered a horrendous sight. The cliffs along the side of the river were, by this time, incredibly steep, and high above us we saw a swinging rope bridge that spanned the valley. It was a shabby, primitive bridge — just a long thick rope with thinner ropes on either side to hang onto. And while on one side of the river there were more of the fast-food joints and other service outlets (we noticed some big-box retail stores as well) that the Jamaican mom had been working in, on the other side of the river stood a huge building that looked like a hospital of some kind. Out of this hospital, assisted by people in white coats, came a steady line of people who looked scared and walked unsteadily. The hospital staff were taking them to the makeshift bridge and, with an encouraging smile and a pat on the back, sending them on their way to the city on the other side. But all kinds of these people could not make it across the bridge, and down they fell into the river. As each one fell, we leaped into the water and furiously tried to pull as many as we could to shore.

"What's going on here?" we asked one man in his late forties.

He just stared at us and made no reply. The woman we had pulled out of the water along with him was talking, but we couldn't make any sense of what she was saying. Then it dawned on us: this was a psychiatric hospital, and these were patients who were being "deinstitutionalized." Sounds like a good idea if you hate institutions, but these poor folks had no one to help them navigate their way across that bridge to the "normal" side of the river. And even if they got there, they probably would end up as road kill in our fast-paced, competitive society. More and more of these patients floated by. We called to inform our shelter downstream, and we suggested that they approach the city for more funding for psychiatric nurses and social workers to join our forces.

We climbed up the bank a little ways and sat down to rest in a grove of trees amidst the kind of garbage that you come to expect in urban ravines. Staying too close to the river meant we couldn't think because of all the people floating by. We were exhausted, cold, hungry, depressed, and angry — and we had to talk. But we just sat there for a while. A couple of us sobbed quietly, not sure we could take any more, not sure we could continue our journey upstream.

"Something's got to happen here," Phyllis said softly. "This has got to stop. We can't just let psychiatric patients fall off bridges, single moms get thrown out of their cheap little apartments with nowhere to go, and hard-working laborers get laid off with no employment benefits."

"Yes," I replied, rather academically, "as a society we have to change the conditions that are creating this tragedy."

"And it isn't just here, you know," Greg said. "This is happening all over the country. There are people floating downriver in every major city of the country, and throughout rural areas as well. You would think that the governments we elected would create systems and structures to make sure that this kind of thing doesn't happen. Isn't that why we pay our taxes? Don't get me wrong. I'm not saying that church people like us shouldn't keep pulling people out of the river, but this is getting ridiculous. Our tax dollars need to address the problems of homelessness. At least, we need to start building more units of affordable housing, instead of throwing all that money into the shelters."

"But that would require both a plan and a will to enact it," Marci said. "And that's exactly what we don't have. There is no national housing policy in Canada."

"Get out!" I replied. "Every advanced industrial society has a housing policy of some kind. Heck, even the Bush administration in the States has a housing policy that addresses homelessness!"[10]

"What you say about the U.S. is true," said Marci, "but Canada is the one exception to your comment about advanced industrial societies. We are the only such country with no national housing policy. Don't you remember when the federal government got out of social housing in 1993, supposedly because we just couldn't afford to do housing? The deficit was too great. So they offloaded housing to the provinces, and the provincial governments quickly saw it as a political hot potato and, in turn, offloaded housing to the cities."

"So at least it's still somebody's responsibility," said Phyllis. "Why doesn't the city do something about it?"

"With what money?" asked Marci. "With what *money?* The cities have the responsibility for housing the homeless, but they have no ability to

---

10. We refer to the McKinney Act of 1987. For an evaluation of the state of homelessness in American ten years after this Act became legislation, which demonstrates the parallels between the Canadian and American experience, see "Homelessness in America: Unabated and Increasing — A Ten Year Perspective," online at www.nationalhomeless.org/10yearsec.html.

raise the money to do so because the only taxation they can use is the property tax, and that just barely keeps the infrastructure of the city operating."[11]

"You've known this stuff all along, haven't you Marci?" Greg said. "You knew it when we started hauling people out of the river way back at the beginning during the church picnic. But you never told us."

"Actually, Greg, I did tell you, but either we were all too busy saving people from the river or we just didn't want to talk about the politics involved. You remember the opposition we got when we said that we needed to go upriver to see what was going on. For some reason, people felt that our compassion was going to be somehow compromised or disrupted or misdirected if we started to investigate what was upstream. You thought so yourself, Greg. I remember you said that what really mattered was for us to show solidarity with those who were drowning, that we should get into the water with them, that we should be their friends. That's all well and good, but now we can see that, if we are to be their friends, we have to find a way to stop these people from falling into the water in the first place. That's why we're sitting here, in this filth, shaking from the cold and wet, numb with our hopelessness!"

The tears came down Marci's cheeks. We sat in silence. Phyllis grabbed a blanket and wrapped it around Marci.

"Do you know what's upstream from here?" I asked Marci softly.

"I think so," she replied.

"Is it worse than what we have seen so far?" I asked.

"Well, I don't know if it's worse, but it's bad, and it's ugly, and it's scary."

"Are you ready to go?" Greg asked Marci, without looking into her eyes.

"Yes, let's go," she replied.

And so we continued our journey — past the psychiatric hospital, past

11. In June 2006 a new City of Toronto Act was passed by the Ontario Legislature. This act gives the city greater autonomy in managing its affairs and some new, though limited, authority of taxation. This is clearly a good step, but whether the taxation freedom will be sufficient to deal with the housing crisis is yet to be proved. We are convinced that, without further involvement and reinvestment from the provincial and federal levels of government, this crisis will continue to intensify. It also must be noted that this new act only applies to Toronto. All other municipalities remain under the old rules of strong provincial oversight and taxation limited to property taxes.

the closed-down factories, past the apartments that were hemorrhaging people. We were still looking for the people who had gone in search of the elusive thing called "social benefits."

As we rounded a bend in the river, there they were: hundreds and thousands of them lined up at shelter doors, in line at food banks, sleeping on sidewalks that ran along the edge of the river bank, and some falling into the river. Once again we were pulling people out of the river. Some were still clutching the check stubs from their social assistance payments. Marci sat down and put her head into her hands; somehow we knew that she'd been here before. But it was Greg who asked one of the victims the question: "You have a check in your hand. The government has given you some financial assistance. Why are you in the water?"

The man looked at Greg in utter disbelief. "The government can go to hell with their insulting little check. To hell with 'em!" He walked away in disgust.

We all turned to Marci. "Help us understand," Greg begged.

Marci's tear-stained face looked up at us, and her tone was one of utter exhaustion.

"Don't you remember what happened when the Conservatives were elected in 1995? Don't you remember that, along with halting a number of housing co-ops that were at the construction stage, they also cut social assistance payments by twenty-one percent? The already meager amount these people were getting was cut by twenty-one percent, and that has never been changed, nor has there been any increase since then.[12] You don't have to be an economist to figure it out. If your income was cut by twenty-one percent in 1995 and frozen at that level for the next ten years, then you have forty percent less money now than you did before 1995. Add to that the increased number of people in need and an incredibly limited supply of affordable housing, and you end up with people like the man we just pulled out of the river. He has no options. All that's available to him is food banks, shelters, and maybe another dip in that filthy river!"

So we began our journey back downstream, pulling people out of the river along the way. And as we walked we began to strategize. Marci started talking about how we needed to start developing policy initiatives, such as increasing the social-assistance and unemployment benefits. Phyllis

---

12. In 2004 the newly elected Liberal government in Ontario committed themselves to increasing social benefits, but not necessarily back to their 1995 levels.

wanted to get a group of people to stand at the entrance to the rope bridge in order to receive the "deinstitutionalized" patients and take them safely to the other side of the river. She was going to lobby churches, synagogues, temples, social groups, and government organizations to provide the funding for some decent supportive housing for these people. I decided that, because there was a connection between these victims in the river and the processes of globalization, I was going to go to the next "free trade" meetings and join the protesters, as well as get involved with alternative forums developing more just-trade laws.

Greg had been quiet on the way back, but just as we passed the bridge where the squatters were living, he said, "I'm running for city council."

"You are?" we all asked.

"Yeah, and I was wondering, Marci, if you would be my campaign manager."

Marci looked at Greg, and though her face was still tearstained, she cracked a small smile and said, "You bet!"

Then a pileated woodpecker flew by.

Why Socioeconomic Homelessness? A Structural Analysis

Martin Luther King Jr. once said: "We've got to begin to ask questions about the whole society. We are called upon to help the discouraged beggars in life's market place. But one day we must come to see that an edifice which produces beggars needs restructuring."[13] In other words, we need to hike upstream to see why so many people are homeless and impoverished within the wealthiest societies this planet has ever seen.[14] Are some people drowning in this river of homelessness because they are lazy and irresponsible? Do some people find themselves in poverty because they have made bad behavioral decisions, such as becoming addicted to gambling, drugs, or alcohol? Undoubtedly this is sometimes the case. But our story about going upstream demonstrates that there are larger, more structural and systemic issues that need to be addressed if we are to understand home-

13. Cited by Mark R. Gornik in *To Live in Peace: Biblical Faith and the Inner City* (Grand Rapids: Eerdmans, 2002), p. 197.

14. Ron Sider points out that "in the United States, over 35,000,000 people live in poverty in the richest society in human history" (*Just Generosity: A New Vision for Overcoming Poverty in America* [Grand Rapids: Baker Books, 1999], p. 27).

lessness in our time and respond appropriately. Most homeless people in North America are not disabled by drugs, mental illness, or physical affliction. Homelessness is not fundamentally a consequence of the moral and spiritual deficiencies of poor people; rather, it is "simply the endpoint, the 'logical' outcome for part of the population — the extremely poor — under conditions of industrial and urban decay." Indeed, anyone who has lived among the homeless would acknowledge that they "are not deficient and defective; they are resilient and resourceful."[15]

Out of his experience in the Sandtown area of Baltimore, Mark Gornik insists that "the source of collective inner-city struggle is not due in any way to personal failings, the force of nature, a lack of collective activity by the community, the presence of neighborhood 'pathology,' a lifestyle of sin, or any deficiencies in character or moral behavior. A lack of personal responsibility did not build the inner city."[16] Urban decay, rampant poverty, and a society-wide crisis of homelessness may all be rooted in pathology, but it is not the pathology of the victims. If there is pathology to be diagnosed, it is a societal pathology that has diseased the very structure of the economy and the shaping of public policy for the common good. If there is a cultural cause to homelessness, it is not to be discerned in a blame-the-victim diagnosis of a "culture of poverty," but it can be discerned in a victimizing and excluding culture of economic growth at all costs.

The themes recited in our story of going upstream are common throughout the postindustrial world. Gerald Daly offers a succinct summary of the structural issues: "Recent increases in homelessness are attributable to global economic changes, a severe shortage of affordable shelter for low-income households, and cutbacks in social programs."[17] Put these three factors together, and it doesn't take a rocket scientist or a Nobel economist to understand and predict the present crisis.[18]

15. Doug A. Timmer, D. Stanley Eitzen, Kathryn D. Talley, *Paths to Homelessness: Extreme Poverty and the Urban Housing Crisis* (Boulder, CO: Westview Press, 1994), p. 6.

16. Gornik, *To Live in Peace*, p. 50.

17. Gerald Daly, *Homeless: Policies, Strategies and Lives on the Street* (London and New York: Routledge, 1996), p. 1.

18. In fact, reading the literature on homelessness published since the mid-1980s is both tedious and depressing. The arguments are all the same. We have known for almost twenty years now that loss of jobs in a postindustrial global economy, government abandonment of affordable and rent-geared-to-income housing, and cutbacks in social welfare rates would

Globalization

Let's begin with globalization. Daly offers us a succinct definition: "Globalization is characterized by the concentration of economic control in multinational firms and financial institutions, worldwide networks of production, exchange, communication and knowledge, transnational capital, and a freer flow of labor, goods, services and information" (p. 5). What could such economic liberalization possibly have to do with the rise of homelessness in our city streets and around the world? After all, the rhetoric of globalization is that increased global wealth can only serve to help the poorest of the poor as the resources "trickle down" from the wealthy to the poor. And doesn't a "rising tide lift all boats"? In other words, if there is more wealth around, doesn't that actually make us all better off? Don't we need this kind of economic growth if we are to be able to afford social programs and if we are to have an economy robust enough to build housing for the population?[19]

Sounds good, but the evidence makes it clear that, if there is a rising tide, only those with enough resources to already own boats rise with it. The rest drown. A beggar on the streets of San Francisco forever demolished the "trickle-down theory" for us. As we were approaching, he shouted out, "Whatever happened to the trickle-down theory?" We stopped dead in our tracks. "I'll tell you what happened," he went on. "They kept it!" They — that is, those with the power to control capital — invested that capital, created wealth, and kept it. There was no trickling down of resources. Canadian singer/songwriter Bruce Cockburn describes such an economic culture as "hooked on avarice" in the following lyrics:

Trickle down give me the business
Trickle down supposed to give us the goods

---

render millions homeless. The analysis has been there and has been empirically proved in subsequent years. But this is one instance when social scientists are not rejoicing in being proved right.

19. Brian Walsh and Sylvia Keesmaat have addressed globalization as an imperial force in *Colossians Remixed: Subverting the Empire* (Downers Grove, IL: InterVarsity, 2004), especially chs. 1, 2, 5, 9, 10, and 11. See also Bob Goudzwaard and Leo Andringa, *Globalization and Christian Hope,* trans. Mark Vander Vennen (Toronto: Public Justice Resource Centre, 2003); Bob Goudzwaard, *Globalization and the Kingdom of God* (Grand Rapids: Baker, 2001); and Iain Wallace, "Globalization: Discourse of Destiny or Denial?" *Christian Scholar's Review* 31, no. 4 (Summer 2002): 377-91.

Cups held out to catch a bit of the bounty
Trickle down everywhere trickle down blood.[20]

Let's be clear about what Cockburn is saying here. It isn't just a matter of claiming that the trickle-down theory doesn't work, that the cups held out to catch a bit of the bounty remain empty. More devastatingly, Cockburn insists that a system "hooked on avarice" is necessarily a system of oppression, and that what really trickles down is "the blood of the poor."

While economic globalization as a process of the "opening of all national economies to the one global economy" may look to be little more than a process of trade liberalization, it is, in fact, a socioeconomic force of exclusion.[21] Homelessness is a consequence of poverty, and poverty is the result of unemployment or inadequate employment. We all know the devastating economic phrase "a jobless recovery." The economy can grow, but that does not necessarily bear any long-term or widespread growth in employment. Nor does economic growth seem to be an indicator of a narrowing of the gap between the rich and the poor.[22] Indeed, the opposite would seem to be true.[23] The poor are consistently excluded from a "new economy" that requires precisely the kind of highly developed set of knowledge skills that is unavailable to the poor.[24] The growth in employment is only at the highest end, with a concomitant decline in industrial labor due to automation. Where there are any jobs in the global economy

20. Bruce Cockburn, "Trickle Down" from *You've Never Seen Everything* ©2004 Golden Mountain Music Corp.

21. Bob Goudzwaard, "Globalization, exclusion, enslavement," *Reformed World* 46, no. 3 (Sept. 1996). See http://www.warc.ch/pc/rw963/01.html (p. 1). While Goudzwaard's analysis focuses on the negative impact of globalization in the Two-Thirds World, there are similar implications for the poorest populations of the "developed" world.

22. Bob Goudzwaard and Harry de Lange document the rising gap between the rich and the poor in the United States and Canada in *Beyond Poverty and Affluence: Toward an Economy of Care,* trans. and ed. Mark Vander Vennen (Grand Rapids: Eerdmans, 1994); the Canadian edition had the subtitle *Towards a Canadian Economy of Care* (Toronto: University of Toronto Press, 1994). All further references to this book will be to the Canadian edition.

23. For a comprehensive critique and alternative to the ideology of economic growth, see Herman E. Daly and John B. Cobb, Jr., *For the Common Good: Redirecting the Economy Toward Community, the Environment, and a Sustainable Future* (Boston: Beacon Press, 1989).

24. See Saskia Sassen, *Globalization and Its Discontents: Essays on the New Mobility of People and Money* (New York: New Press, 1998).

for the poor in postindustrial countries, they are to be found in the service sector. Whether we are talking about "McJobs" in the fast-food industry, cleaning office towers, or providing domestic help to double-income upper-middle-class families, the results are all the same: low-paying jobs, no health benefits, no security of employment, and no possibility of real advancement.[25] These are the jobs the working poor get, and those workers are just one missed paycheck away from the street.[26]

But even in the face of such a postindustrial service economy, there still aren't that many jobs. For not only are many jobs lost to technological automation, even more are lost because of free-trade agreements that both allow and encourage the flight of capital and of manufacturing from developed nations to less-developed economies. Is this a sharing of the wealth? No, it is a deepening of the misery. Why do businesses move capital and processing to the Philippines or Indonesia or China? Because these jurisdictions will have fewer environmental regulations, less stringent labor laws, lower wage expectations, relaxed investment laws, greater government incentives, and lower taxes because of the absence of comprehensive health and social programs in those countries. The result is economic oppression both overseas and in the developed world. The poor of the Two-Thirds World get near-slave working conditions and environmental degradation, while the poor of the richest nations remain poor as the rates of unemployment and homelessness continue to rise.[27] Globalization

25. Of course, our Two-Thirds World neighbors have other options. Those living in "economic processing zones" can find low-paying jobs in sweatshops or perhaps in "cash crop agriculture," which leave the workers' children impoverished and hungry, but provide cheap clothing and food to the "developed" world. For one critique of this system, see Naomi Klein, *No Logo: Taking Aim at the Brand Bullies* (Toronto: Random House, 2000).

26. Timmer et al., *Paths to Homelessness*, pp. 25-26. The authors go on to make an additional point: "Even the relatively few remaining manufacturing jobs have often tended to move from the inner city to the suburbs and non-metropolitan peripheries. The inner-city poor are disadvantaged by these moves because they do not have access to adequate transportation to these jobs and continued discrimination and high housing costs prevent them from moving nearer to the new job sites. The result is that those with the greatest need for jobs are the farthest from them" (p. 27).

27. A North American example of these dynamics is the Maquiladora program in northern Mexico, where U.S. plants have been set up on the Mexican side of the border because they can pay workers much less and the environmental protection laws are weaker. The products are then shipped back across the border to the United States for sale. Timmer et al. observe: "The obvious consequences of such an arrangement are cheaper products for U.S. consumers, a loss of jobs in the United States, lower wages within the United States, and

proves to be a foundational, structural force in the perpetuation of poverty and homelessness in our time. We cannot meaningfully address the crisis of homelessness and poverty without addressing globalization and its destructive impact, especially its impact on local impoverished communities both at home and abroad.

Lack of Affordable Housing

The second structural reality that we must consider is the serious lack of affordable housing available to the working poor, the unemployed, and the homeless. While real estate markets, government programs, urban decline, racism, various kinds of legislation, and problems of provincial/federal or state/federal relationships present a rather complex picture of the dynamics of homelessness, there is one starkly devastating fact that cannot be denied. If there are more people who are homeless or at risk of being homeless than there are houses, apartments, and rooms to provide them shelter, there is a crisis. And if the discrepancy between available affordable housing and the number of people in need continues to grow, then the crisis only deepens. This is the North American situation: as the number of needy people increases, the stock of affordable housing decreases.

According to a comprehensive study conducted by the Urban Institute (a nonpartisan economic and social-policy research organization), based on data collected in 1996, there were at least 2.3 million people in the United States who experienced homelessness that year. Note that the report said *at least* that many people; they concede that the number could have been as high as 3.5 million. The lower estimate would indicate that, as of the 2000 census, one out of every hundred Americans experienced homelessness. As many as 800,000 were on the streets at any given time.[28]

---

greater profits for U.S. multinational corporations" (*Paths to Homelessness*, p. 86). We find it amazing that no one has thought of accusing these U.S. companies of economic treason!

Especially oppressed in Maquiladora plants are the women: they have experienced violence, rape, murder, and forced pregnancy tests. See "A Job or Your Rights: Continued Sex Discrimination in Mexico's Maquiladora Sector," *Human Rights Watch* 10, no. 1B (Dec. 1998).

28. Martha Burt et al., "A New Look at Homelessness in America" (Washington, DC: The Urban Institute, 2000); see www.urban.org. This report was further developed by Burt and her colleagues into a book, *Helping America's Homeless* (Washington, DC: The Urban Institute, 2001).

These were the 1996 numbers, and nothing has happened in the intervening years to reduce those numbers — or even to quell the tide of increasing homelessness in America. One thing we can be certain of: things are worse now.

In Canada it is much more difficult to access accurate information on the size of the homeless population. Indeed, searching the Statistics Canada web-page proves to be a fruitless venture. Jack Layton wonders whether there is a conspiracy at work here. He asks: "Why is there no estimate of the number of homeless people in Canada? Could documenting the problem imply an obligation to address it? Without concrete numbers, estimates or well-informed ranges, planning and policy-making stand little chance of succeeding."[29] So, rather than giving national statistics, let's look at the country's largest city, Toronto.

From 1988 to 2002 the number of people who used shelters in Toronto rose from 22,000 to 32,000, an increase of more than 40 percent. One out of every eighty Torontonians had experienced homelessness. The number of children in the shelter system rose from 2,700 in 1988 to about 4,800 in 2002, an increase of 77 percent.[30] Remember, these are only the numbers of people who actually use the shelter system; they do not account for people who are "sleeping rough" in alleyways, on park benches, or under bridges. Nor do these numbers include all those people who are "doubling up," living in overcrowded, substandard housing throughout the city.

The reason that so many people are homeless in Toronto is that there is not enough affordable housing. From 1999 to 2003, the waiting list for subsidized housing in Toronto grew from 37,000 to 71,000 households, an

29. Jack Layton, *Homelessness: The Making and Unmaking of a Crisis* (Toronto: Penguin, 2000), p. 36. We should add, however, that in its 1988 "State of Emergency Declaration — Homelessness: A National Disaster," the Toronto Disaster Relief Committee (TDRC) declared: "Conservative estimates concur that about 200,000 Canadians are homeless." (www.tdrc.net) This would mean that about 1 in every 100 Canadians would have experienced homelessness in 1998 — the same ratio as in the United States in 1996. By April 2003 the National Housing and Homelessness Network (of which TDRC is an important player) had increased the estimate of national homelessness to 250,000.

30. These statistics are gathered from the report of the Mayor's Homelessness Task Force, *Taking Responsibility for Homelessness: An Action Plan for Toronto* (Toronto, 1999), p. 140, and from the *Toronto Report Card on Homelessness 2003* (Toronto: Municipal Government, 2003), p. 3. Important comparative information is also available in *The Toronto Report Card on Homelessness 2001* (Toronto: Municipal Government, 2001).

increase of 90 percent in four years.[31] This raises two questions. Why is there such a shortage of subsidized housing? And why are so many people in need of such housing in Toronto? The answer to the first question has to do with "downloading." Throughout the 1990s, the responsibility for affordable housing for the poor was first downloaded from the federal to the provincial government, and then the provincial government in Ontario downloaded the responsibility to the municipalities. While it would seem to make some sense to have the most local level of government take responsibility for housing its most vulnerable citizens, such a responsibility cannot be fulfilled without the financial resources to meet the needs. When the feds and the provinces added to the cities' responsibility to provide housing, they added no funding or the means to raise such monies through new forms of taxation.

What was the result? In 1995 the newly elected Ontario government canceled all new social housing, including 17,000 units of co-op and non-profit housing; in addition, no new units of affordable housing were built in the city of Toronto between 1996 to 2000. To put it starkly, spending on affordable housing went from $1.1 billion in 1994 to zero at the end of 1998. At the same time, the construction of rental apartments dropped to only thirty new units in 2000. Why? Because at that time the condominium market was much more lucrative for developers than was the rental market. In fact, many already existing rental units were lost because the owners of those units were converting them into condominiums. Since 2000, the situation has improved only marginally. In 1999 the Mayor's Homelessness Action Task Force argued that Toronto would need 2,000 new low-rent units a year just to meet the new demands the city was experiencing at that time. Given the absence of such new development, it is no surprise that there is a shortage of affordable housing and that the waiting list continues to grow at an alarming rate.

Why do so many people need affordable housing? Apart from the decline of rental accommodations, the other major factor has been the rise in rent prices relative to household income. Housing can only be "affordable" if someone actually has enough monthly income to pay the rent. From 1997 to 2002, rent prices in Toronto rose by 31 percent, while the average in-

31. Note that we are talking about households here, not individuals: 71,000 households would likely mean somewhere around 200,000 people — about 1 in 12 Torontonians are on the waiting list.

come rose only 11 percent.[32] Essentially, the rents of thousands of Toron-tonians rose at rates that outpaced the increase in their income by three to one. It is not difficult to understand why there is an affordability crisis.

Now let's turn to the situation in the United States. In 2003, 14.3 mil-lion American households paid out more than half their income for hous-ing; add to that the 17.3 million households that spend between 30 percent and 49 percent on housing, and you end up with three in every ten Ameri-can households having affordability problems concerning housing.[33] Let's be clear about what this means to the working poor in both Canada and the United States: in the absence of meaningful tenants-rights legislation and in the face of rising rents and an alarming gap between housing costs and household incomes, and without meaningful job security in the ser-vice sector and other areas of low-wage employment, the working poor are just one illness or layoff away from homelessness. One child gets seriously ill, and a parent must stay home from work, consequently losing wages or perhaps the job itself. The family falls behind in rent payments and is evicted and looks for shelter.

Not only are there problems of job security, health insurance, and ten-ant protection; there is also the inadequacy of any national standards for a minimum wage. The minimum wage is so inadequate in America that "households with one full-time minimum-wage earner cannot afford to rent a modest one-bedroom apartment anywhere in the country."[34] In-deed, in 2003 the average rent for a two-bedroom apartment in the United States was $791 a month; a family would need $15.21 as an hourly wage in order to be paying 30 percent of its income for that level of housing.[35] Un-til recently the federal minimum wage was set at $5.15 an hour. Obviously, two full-time minimum-wage workers could not afford a two-bedroom

32. *The Toronto Report Card on Homelessness 2003*, p. 32. For those households on social welfare, whose rates were cut by 21 percent by the Conservative government in 1995, the amount of allowance they receive for "shelter allowance" was frozen at $590.00 a month from 1995 to 2003.

33. Joint Centre for Housing Studies, *The State of the Nation's Housing, 2003* (Boston: Harvard University Press, 2003), p. 25. See http://www.jchs.harvard.edu/publications/mar-kets/son2003.

34. *State of the Nation's Housing*, p. 27.

35. From a study published by the National Low Income Housing Coalition and posted on the *USA Today* website: http://www/usatoday.cpm/money/perfi/housing/2003-09-08-rent. There would be some variation across the country because states have the right to in-crease minimum wage for their jurisdiction.

apartment on their income. Add to that picture the need to pay for child-care in order to have two parents working, and it's not difficult to see why a low minimum wage, high rents, and a lack of tenant protection all conspire against the American family.

And the availability of affordable housing is as grave in the United States as it is in Canada. According to the Department of Housing and Urban Development, the number of affordable housing units in the country fell at an accelerating rate in the late 1990s.[36] But what came to such distasteful fruit in the late 1990s had its roots in the 1980s. When Ronald Reagan became president in 1981, "the federal government spent seven dollars on defense for every dollar on housing"; but "when he left office in 1989, the ratio was forty-six to one."[37] The priorities of the Reagan administration were clear. And while the McKinney Homeless Assistance Act became law in 1987 (with amendments in November 1988), no administration since that time has done more than allocate federal funds to homeless shelters. There have been no significant government initiatives to address the crisis of affordable housing.[38]

Economic changes that have come in the wake of globalization and an absence of affordable housing have precipitated the present crisis of homelessness. But there is a third factor that has made its contribution to the crisis: the dismantling of the "social safety net."

36. Joint Centre for Housing Studies, *The State of the Nation's Housing, 2001* (Boston: Harvard University Press, 2001), p. 25. See http://www.jchs.harvard.edu/publications/markets/son2001. From 1997 to 1999, 300,000 units of affordable housing stock were lost, an overall decrease of 13 percent.

37. Richard Applebaum, "The Affordability Gap," *Society* 26 (May-June 1989): 9; cited by Timmer et al., *Paths to Homelessness*, p. 23.

38. Two further comments are in order. First, in 1992, President George H. W. Bush "vetoed the urban aid tax bill, intended to stimulate the production of affordable housing" (Daly, *Homeless*, p. 176). Second, it is important to add that most new affordable housing in America is built by private and nonprofit developers availing themselves of the benefits of the Low Income Housing Tax Credit program launched in 1986. "Since its inception, the LIHTC program has helped construct more than 800,000 units of affordable housing nationwide" (*Sharing the Dream: A Place to Call Home* [General Board of Pension and Health Benefits of the United Methodist Church, 2002], p. 1). See http://www.gbophb.org/news/features/affhous/. We will return to the role of nongovernmental institutions in the development of affordable housing.

Diminished Social Safety Net

There have always been homeless wanderers in our society. But the crisis of homelessness that we have been talking about in this chapter is a crisis unparalleled since the Great Depression of the 1930s. Whether we experience times of recession or economic recovery, the situation does not change: more and more people are homeless or at risk of homelessness. We seem to be in a state of perpetual crisis. Why? Consider the following. During the time that we have seen an emerging homelessness crisis in Canada and the United States, and a growing gap both between rents and incomes and between the rich and the poor, our nations have been under the sway of a neoconservative sociopolitical and economic agenda that believes that government should get out of providing social services, including housing. This neoconservative agenda claims that an affluent and growing global economy will be better able to remedy the social and economic problems that we have been considering than government agencies ever could. Government has no business in housing, these neoconservatives believe, and the market, if left to its own devices, will more efficiently produce housing and employment that will raise people up out of poverty.

In our above discussion of globalization we have already indicated our deep skepticism of such unfettered faith in the marketplace. The abandonment of housing by national governments has given the private market ample opportunity in the last twenty years to develop housing for the poor. The results have been devastating. Rather than produce affordable housing, the free market converts apartments into condominiums, gentrifies inner-city neighborhoods by displacing lower-income communities, "redlines" poor people so that they cannot get credit to buy or repair their homes, allows poor neighborhoods to deteriorate so that they become candidates for "urban renewal," raises rents beyond the reach of the poor, and lobbies for lax landlord/tenant legislation so that they can evict at will. If anything, "market forces are the source of, not the solution to, the problem."[39]

Let's be clear about the implications of all of this. Neoconservatism not only makes an ultimate authority of a market that will render more and more people homeless; it also insists that the government should not erect a social safety net to assist those who are the casualties of the market. Mark Gornik argues that "the end of welfare and a decreased social safety

---

39. Timmer et al., *Paths to Homelessness*, p. 24.

net" are goals that the "new economy" has "demanded."[40] So-called "inefficiencies" such as housing subsidies, minimum-wage standards, public healthcare, rent-geared-to-income units, and social-welfare programs must be purged from the system if it is to reach the potentials of wealth that the "new economy" promises for all. Such government programs, it is argued, function as disincentives for the poor to work and to raise themselves out of poverty.

The unquestioned premise of this, of course, is that "when we allow the market to do its sovereign work, then every poor person has the opportunity to get out of poverty."[41] But everything we have seen about the crisis of homelessness would seem to disprove that premise. Increased economic growth bears no positive relationship to alleviating poverty or homelessness; indeed, the opposite is the case. Poverty and homelessness rise hand in hand with the global economy: there is no trickling down of wealth. And Adam Smith's famous "invisible hand" seems only competent to rip away what few social safety mechanisms we had to soften the impact of those who fall off the economic treadmill. An "economic boom" is accompanied by a boom in food-bank use, child poverty, and more folks sleeping in shelters or under bridges.[42]

Of course, the reason constantly put forward when the social safety net was being dismantled was that we could no longer "afford" the luxury of such programs. Government deficits were out of control: we needed to get our "fiscal house in order," and therefore programs had to be cut. The fact that social programs and not military spending were cut is, in itself, telling. But there is a more sinister side to this story: to get our so-called fiscal house in order, we have to evict the most vulnerable from any house whatsoever. One might almost come to believe that the poor and the public funds spent on programs to alleviate poverty and homelessness are the major cause of any disorder in the fiscal house known as the public treasury. Thus, if the fiscal house is to be robust and healthy again, these people must be sacrificed. But what kind of house would that be? What kind of house requires the sacrifice of the most vulnerable? And would it be worth living in?

40. Gornik, *To Live in Peace,* p. 48.

41. Goudzwaard and de Lange, *Beyond Poverty and Affluence,* p. 49.

42. Greg deGroot-Maggetti, "Martin's Windfall a Cold Wind for Homeless" (Toronto: Citizens for Public Justice, 2001); see http://www.cpj.ca/budget/01/windfall.html.

Homelessness: A Socioethical Crisis Revisited

There is a sense of inevitability that hangs over the realities of homelessness in our time, and it is a seemingly intractable problem. There is widespread awareness of the crisis, and yet the inner cities are populated by thousands of people begging on the streets. There have been studies upon studies, with a fully operational homelessness industry consisting of shelters, drop-ins, clinics, and activist groups, but with "all of this expenditure of energy," there is "virtually no social transformation and none on the horizon."[43] Homelessness is an intractable problem because there is a stubborn and willful obstinacy that refuses to honestly name the causes of the problem and is unwilling to countenance socioethical change.

In the light of our structural analysis above, we should not be surprised by the stark conclusions of Philip Alston, the chair of the United Nations Committee on Economic, Social and Cultural Rights. In 1998, Alston said: "Homelessness is the predictable result of private and public-sector policies that exclude the poor from participating in the economic revolution, while safety nets are slashed in the name of 'global competitiveness.'" Alston goes on to say that "the situation is perpetuated by a deep reluctance to tackle the roots of the problem." Note that Alston does not say that there is a societal "inability" to tackle the problems. Rather, he insists that there is a "deep re-luctance" to tackle the roots of the problem. And that reluctance, he says, is a moral reluctance, rooted in the lack of a collective conscience. "Such con-cepts as the existence of a social contract, of community, of concern for the long-term good or even of public morality are discarded as people ignore the growing, simultaneous presence of high levels of prosperity on the one hand and of homelessness on the other."[44]

This lack of collective conscience came home to housing activists and the homeless themselves in Toronto in 1999. The mayor, Mel Lastman, had commissioned a task force on homelessness that was chaired by Anne Golden. In what became known as the "Golden Report," the task force of-fered a comprehensive series of 105 recommendations to address homeless-ness in Canada's largest city. Twice the authors insist that their report "dem-

43. B. Giamo and J. Grunberg, *Beyond Homelessness: Frames of Reference* (Iowa City, IA: University of Iowa Press, 1992), p. 151; cited by Gerald Daly, *Homeless*, p. 9.

44. Philip Alston, "Hardship in the Midst of Plenty," *The Progress of Nations 1998 — In-dustrialized Countries: Commentary* (Geneva: UNICEF, 1998); see http://www.unicef.org/pon98/indust1.htm.

onstrates that the problems are solvable and that the solutions are available." They then add: "On that basis we have a *moral* obligation to take the actions needed."[45] Two months after the report was released, Anne Golden spoke about its reception: she was "flabbergasted," she said, that while the report was widely lauded for the accuracy of its findings, together with the rationality and even frugality of its recommendations, it was clear that the report's proposals were not going to be acted on and that there was no sense of "moral obligation" among the legislators and civil servants who could actually do something to alleviate the homelessness crisis. While the report demonstrated that the crisis could be addressed with rather modest contributions from the public purse, it had become devastatingly clear to Golden that there was no political or civic will to do so.

Civic will, indeed, is the issue. Gerald Daly is right when he argues that "homelessness can be seen as a manifestation of a loss of shared common ground or abandonment of the notion of the public realm in a civic society."[46] What else would we expect when a neoconservative socioeconomic agenda, married to the forces of globalization, endeavors to privatize every dimension of human life? The whole idea of a civil society rests on the conviction that some things are public: some things, such as the environment, common spaces, and responsibility for the most vulnerable are public trusts and thus public responsibilities.[47] Such a notion of public responsibility, indeed of a public "commons," is decidedly alien to the proponents of neoconservative globalization. In the first instance, the individualism of the neoconservative side of this ideology insists that, if individuals cannot raise themselves out of poverty, that's likely the result of character deficiencies in the individual and not the responsibility of anyone else. In the second place, the economic agenda of the globalization side of this ideology finds it difficult to recognize any "good" that is outside the dictates of the global market. If the market does not produce affordable housing, it is difficult for the proponents of globalization to see that it might be a good thing for government or other agencies to produce such housing, that it might even be good to tax the wealthy and their cor-

---

45. *Taking Responsibility for Homelessness,* pp. 18-19; see also p. xi [italics in original].

46. Daly, *Homeless,* p. 14.

47. P. Williams says that "the rhetoric of increased privatization . . . functions as the rationalizing agent of public unaccountability and, ultimately, irresponsibility" (*Alchemy of Race and Rights* [Cambridge: Harvard University Press, 1991], p. 47; cited in Daly, *Homeless,* p. 4).

porations in order to raise the revenue necessary for such a public good. Such a taxation, this ideology proclaims, would be an unnatural intervention in the free operation of a global economy. Moreover, it continues, corporations are fundamentally responsible to their shareholders, whose expectations are clear, not to an amorphous thing called the "public good."

The power of this ideology, the intractable nature of homelessness, and the absence of political or civic will to take steps to address the realities of homelessness all indicate that the crisis before us is not narrowly economic in nature but is a crisis of culture and an erosion of the values that might shape the public good. Bob Goudzwaard and Harry de Lange argue that we desperately need to "develop a new public ethos and regauge today's values." If there is to be a cultural shift, it must entail a renewed economic paradigm "that proceeds from the assumption that people need to advance the interest of others. They must be willing to think inclusively. They must choose to be led by considerations other than self-interest, a principle that belongs inextricably to the thought-patterns of the industrialized societies."[48] In other words, we must abandon the ideological worldview of globalization, with its penchant for privatizing what is public, for absolutizing the impersonal forces of the "market," and for forsaking civic responsibility.

Another way to get at this crisis of culture, values, ethos, and worldview is to borrow the notion of *habitus* from the sociologist Pierre Bourdieu. Bourdieu wishes to account for the relative coherence of human social life. Why do certain patterns of behavior — both personal and cultural — manifest themselves in particular societies? Why do these particular "habits" of life — patterns of public/private distinctions (which differ from culture to culture), gender relationships, economic transactions, or practices of habitation — form in a particular culture? And why are they viewed and experienced as "reasonable" and even "natural" or "common sense" in their context? Bourdieu suggests that shared social "habits" are rooted in a shared *habitus,* which he defines as "a system of lasting and transposable dispositions which, integrating past experiences, functions at every moment as a matrix of perceptions, appreciations and actions and makes possible the achievement of infinitely diversified tasks." A *habitus* is "a *way of being,* a

---

48. Goudzwaard and de Lange, *Beyond Poverty and Affluence,* pp. 77-78. Goudzwaard makes the case for a "cultural" analysis of the history of capitalism in his *Capitalism and Progress: A Diagnosis of Western Society,* trans. Josina Van Nuis Zylstra (Grand Rapids: Eerdmans, 1979; rereleased, London: Paternoster, 1997).

habitual state . . . and . . . a *disposition, tendency, propensity,* or *inclination*" to behave in particular ways.[49] In other words, habitual patterns of behavior and ways of looking at the world are rooted in societally shaped and shared dispositions, values, and orientations.

But the crisis of homelessness in our time demonstrates that the *habitus of globalization* is one that is not concerned with providing habitation for the most vulnerable members of society. That there are millions of inhabitants who have no place to inhabit is testimony to the exclusionary nature of this dominant *habitus,* which has a disposition to dispossess certain people by legitimating economic, social, and political habits that provide comfortable habitation for some and homelessness for others.[50]

Anne Golden wants to know why the language of "moral obligation" in responding to the crisis of homelessness has no weight. The answer, we suggest, is that the language of moral obligation has meaning only within the context of a particular *habitus*. And the ideology of neoconservative globalization has so permeated our societal *habitus* that gentrification, displacement, tax cuts for the already wealthy, and the slashing of the social welfare net are perceived to be the normal habits of any "sane" government. If there is a "moral obligation," it is to "fiscal responsibility" (read: retreat from social problems), "trade liberalization" (read: remove barriers to capital investing wherever it will achieve the greatest profit), "free markets" (read: reduce the ability for sovereign nations to establish their own social, economic, and environmental policies), and "urban renewal" (read: cleaning up the streets by ridding them of the unsightly homeless population).[51]

---

49. Pierre Bourdieu, *Outline of a Theory of Practice* (Cambridge, UK: Cambridge University Press, 1977), pp. 95, 214; cited in Pierre Bourdieu and Loic J. D. Wacquant, *An Invitation to Reflexive Sociology* (Chicago: University of Chicago Press, 1992), p. 18.

50. Another way to put this would be to say that, while all human life requires some sort of *habitus* (or worldview) in order to have coherence, it is the constant temptation of any *habitus* to degenerate into an exclusionary ideology. Thus the larger question will be, how do we form a *habitus* (a worldview) and its concomitant pattern of societal, ethical, economic, and political habits (or way of life) that are inclusive rather than exclusive? What kind of *habitus* is necessary if we are to have a cultural praxis that insists on appropriate habitation for all? Brian Walsh has reflected on these problems at greater length in "Transformation: Dynamic Worldview or Repressive Ideology," *Journal of Education and Christian Belief* 4, no. 2 (Autumn 2000).

51. In the wake of Sept. 11, 2001, and the "War on Terrorism," we might add: "freedom" (read: America is open for business) and "democracy" (read: global control of oil stocks to fuel the global economy).

The moral consternation of much "liberal" analysis of homelessness is rooted in memories of post-Depression industrial economies that did in fact find room for housing policies that sought at least some semblance of inclusion for all.[52] Indeed, we are arguing that it is the dismantling of precisely such policies that has precipitated the present crisis. Why did the worldview that brought us the New Deal, together with state intervention to alleviate poverty and homelessness by means of a social safety net, collapse?

There are many reasons why the welfare state was untenable, but we will focus on only one: it was rooted in a weak *habitus*, the *habitus* of a kind of "post-care society."[53] The first priority of society is to seek economic growth in the forms of ever-increasing processes of production and consumption and an increase in the Gross National Product. Up to this point, liberalism and neoconservatism are in agreement. But liberalism acknowledges that there will be casualties of economic growth. Not everyone will benefit equally from this growth: the "invisible hand" will not, on its own, raise the standard of living of all people. So there is a role for the state to care for the poor, to make sure that there is at least a modicum of income distribution so that the disadvantaged may also benefit from the economic growth of society as a whole. Neoconservatives have greater faith (against all the evidence, as far as we can see!) in the powers of the market. Nonetheless, this liberal vision of the welfare state is that of a "post-care" society, because "care" comes only *after* economic growth.

Here is its greatest weakness. The foundational assumption of a liberal welfare state is that economic growth and abundance is a never-ending dynamic of a capitalist society. As long as the economy is growing, we can afford to redistribute wealth in small ways; we can afford to give everyone a chance to fulfill the "American dream"; we can afford to intervene when the invisible hand of the market economy doesn't seem up to the job. But what happens when there is an economic downturn? What happens if matters such as the OPEC oil embargo, rising inflation, and the success of the Asian economy in the 1970s result in an economic recession in the early 1980s? What happens to our public responsibility to the poor when there is

52. For a historical analysis that compares two of the most progressive jurisdictions regarding housing policy, see Alexander Davidson, *A home of one's own: Housing policy in Sweden and New Zealand from the 1840s to the 1990s* (Stockholm: Almqvist & Wiksell International, 1994).

53. Goudzwaard and de Lange, *Beyond Poverty and Affluence,* p. 64.

not the same kind of economic abundance to be spread around? Responsibility evaporates, liberalism dies, and neoconservatism takes its place.[54]

The problem with the liberalism of the past was that it was *too shallow:* its ethic was too thin to sustain a sense of civic solidarity and responsibility to the poor when it was perceived that we couldn't afford such responsibility anymore. Rooted as it was in an individualistic understanding of society, when the going got tough, self-interest again raised its ugly head. If Michael Walzer is right when he says that home is "a dense moral culture," the problem with Western society — whether liberal or neoconservative — is that it has no density, no foundation for homemaking.[55]

If it was an economic downturn that made the whole culture lose its ethical nerve and thus gave rise to neoconservatism, why doesn't an economic upturn result in a return to the ethical principles that for a while seemed too expensive? This would seem to be at the heart of Anne Golden's consternation. It is no longer the early 1980s; we are no longer in recession. There have been budgetary surpluses, not deficits — at least in Canada. So why don't we reinstate the programs that were dismantled? The money is there, the analysis has been done, and we know that real people are in need of these programs. Don't we have a "moral obligation"? The answer is, apparently, no. The economic growth of the last ten to fifteen years has done little to change the cultural mood regarding responsibility to the poor. That older liberal ethic, rooted as it was in assumptions of economic growth, has proved to be too shallow to sustain any kind of a renewed civic *habitus* that could creatively and ethically respond to the crisis of homelessness. Once that liberalism died at the hands of the recession and the prophets of neoconservatism, it would not rise again. The culture of fear has given birth to an ethos of individualism, scarcity, survivalism, and withdrawal from social responsibility.

But perhaps the *habitus* of globalization has other reasons to leave people homeless and not recognize any moral responsibility to the most vulnerable. While we agree with Bob Goudzwaard's claim that globalization is exclusionary at its core, perhaps globalization is just the latest ideological justification for an exclusionary dynamic that has even deeper

54. Linda McQuaig, *The Culture of Impotence: Selling the Myth of Powerlessness in the Global Economy* (Toronto: Penguin, 1999).

55. Michael Walzer, *Interpretation and Social Criticism* (Cambridge, MA, and London: Harvard University Press, 1987), p. 16.

roots.[56] Perhaps this moral abandonment has its own quasi-moral reasons. David Sibley argues that "the human landscape can be read as a landscape of exclusion" in which "power is expressed in the monopolization of space and the relegation of weaker groups in society to less desirable environments."[57] But what could be the moral justification for such a class-based geography of exclusion? In the face of Golden's question about "moral obligation," how can a society justify excluding the poor not only from the best real estate ("uptown" as opposed to "downtown") but also from the most basic rights to housing and livelihood? Sibley's answer: defilement, disgust, and disease. The dominant worldview views the poor as dirty, defiled, contaminated, and thus a threat to the ordered and habitual world of the middle and upper-middle classes. Sibley says that, at best, "the fear of infection leads to the erection of boundaries to resist the spread of the diseased, polluted others," and at worst it leads to cleanup programs that will attempt to locate these polluted others "elsewhere" (p. 25). "This 'elsewhere' might be nowhere, as when genocide or the moral transformation of a minority like prostitutes is advocated, or it might be some spatial periphery, like the edge of the world or the edge of the city" (p. 49). Within such a geography of exclusion, the poor, like our garbage, must go away — to another place. But there is no "away," and this kind of displacement amounts to an imposed and impossible placelessness.[58]

We should not miss the self-understood morality of such an ideology. Insofar as morality is a matter of making life safe and orderly, anything that will be a threat to safety and a force of disorder must be either eradicated or at least kept at a distance. Within this kind of *habitus* of exclusion,

---

56. Bob Goudzwaard, "Globalization, exclusion, enslavement," pp. 1-5.

57. David Sibley, *Geographies of Exclusion: Society and Difference in the West* (London and New York: Routledge, 1995), p. ix. Similarly, James Duncan and David Ley describe topography as a "science of domination," "confirming boundaries, securing norms and treating questionable social convention as unquestioned social facts" ("Introduction: Representing the Place of Culture," in James Duncan and David Ley, eds., *Place/Culture/ Representation* (London and New York: Routledge, 1993), p. 1.

58. J. Douglas Porteous and Sandra E. Smith argue that, in a capitalist culture that reduces dwellings to commodities and discards loyalty to neighborhoods and localities in an upwardly mobile global economy, policies of "domicide" will be common and seen to be morally justifiable. Domicide, they say, is "the planned, deliberate destruction of home causing suffering to the dweller." "In domicide someone or some group is responsible for the suffering; we cannot blame nature, God, or even 'the system'" (*Domicide: The Global Destruction of Home* [Montreal and Kingston: McGill-Queen's University Press, 2001], pp. 19-20).

establishing boundaries that keep the homeless out of our neighborhoods (the "not-in-my-back-yard" dynamics that homeless shelters, halfway houses, and affordable housing must constantly confront) is not seen to be a moral failure, but a moral success! Protecting one's family and community from contamination is a virtuous act.[59] If a *habitus* serves to shape human habitation, then anything that threatens the order of that habitation must be excluded. The poor remain homeless.

In summary, we have a crisis of homelessness because the demise of the shallow ethic of welfare-state liberalism finds its deepest psychological legitimation in a fear of defilement, which itself morally justifies a geography of exclusion and displacement. A geography of exclusion within the context of a neoconservative ideology does not deny that there is a homelessness crisis; it doesn't even deny that this is a moral crisis. But the individualism and the privatizing ethos of this ideology locates that moral crisis with the homeless themselves. It is *their* moral weakness that has left them homeless. In effect, they are getting what they deserve.

Emancipate Yourselves from Mental Slavery

Do you remember the panhandler Will singing Bob Marley songs on a freezing street corner in Toronto? While Will does not avoid acknowledging that his own mental illness is a contributing factor in his homelessness, he also helped us to think about larger systemic problems and their roots in a culture that legitimates rampant and debilitating poverty alongside unspeakable affluence. But Will also recognized that something deeper was going on here. That's why he got to talking about Jesus and the need to be emancipated from mental slavery. There is something about the socio-

---

59. Indeed, the "panic" that is often palpable in a community when news that a halfway house or a shelter or affordable housing is being proposed in the neighborhood is explained by what Stanley Cohen describes as a "moral panic." Cohen describes a "moral panic" as a "condition, episode, person or group of persons [that] emerges to become defined as a threat to societal values and interests" (*Folk Devils and Moral Panics* [London: McKibben and Kee, 1972]; cited in Sibley, *Geographies of Exclusion*, p. 39). People who are poor, addicted, homeless, suffering from mental illness, or are in any other ways deemed "deviant" function as stimuli to moral panics: their presence is itself a moral threat. Therefore, excluding such people from our neighborhoods, or even from receiving the benefits of our tax dollars, is deemed morally justified.

economic realities all around us that enslaves our minds and captures our imaginations so that we think that this kind of poverty, unemployment, homelessness, suffering, and displacement is normal — even natural. And so we need to be emancipated, Will sang. We need to have our imaginations set free to see and experience the world differently. We need a richer, deeper, and thicker *habitus,* a worldview rooted in a narrative that engenders a culture of hospitality and justice. We need a renewed imagination and renewed cultural practices that can counter a geography of exclusion with an ethos of inclusion.

We need to emancipate both our minds and our spaces for our friend Will, and for ToniAnne and Phil, and for the millions of people in North America and throughout the world who are treated as little more than social trash. If the economic dynamics of globalization and neoconservatism are forces for homelessness, we need an economics for homemaking to see us through this crisis. If our personal and cultural imaginations have been captivated by a fearful, self-protective, and myopic ideology of economic growth and "invisible hands," we need to be set free by a radical narrative of hospitality and homecoming. And if we are to enact an economics for homemaking, we will need to more deeply understand the relationship between housing and homemaking.

Architecture, Covenant, and Exile

The Book of Amos

Have you ever had an argument that simply wouldn't go away? Have you ever been in an argument with someone — a deeply serious argument — and years later you are still thinking about it? Almost as if that argument haunts you?

Well, I can't get Amos out of my head. It must have been twenty years ago that he showed up in Israel, and for twenty years I've wanted to believe that he was wrong. I just can't seem to let it go.

My name is Amaziah, and I have spent my life serving as a priest in the royal sanctuary at Bethel, in Israel. Almost all of those years I have served under King Jeroboam II.

Things were good in Israel at the beginning of Jeroboam's reign. Very good. Important international alliances had been formed, and the trade routes were secure; the borders of the kingdom had been expanded, and the economy was strong. Not since Solomon had we tasted the sweet fruit of empire, the luxury of wealth. Palaces and festivals, fine wines and strong drink, rich foods and the thriving of arts and letters — all this and more was the glory of Jeroboam.

And then Amos, a herdsman from Judah, showed up. At first I was actually impressed that such an unlearned fellow should be so well versed in the rhetoric of Israel's wisdom literature and its prophetic tradition. And those first seven oracles that he proclaimed were powerful, just the kind of sermon that I would have liked to preach in Bethel.

I was taken by his preoccupation with architecture as well. As he preached his oracles of judgment on the nations — on Syria, Philistia, Phoenicia, Edom, Ammon, and Moab — he consistently proclaimed judgment on the "strongholds" of these nations. These strongholds, or palaces, of the nations would be devoured, each time by fire. These architectural wonders that had been erected as the habitations of the elite and powerful, Amos said, would be the object of the wrath of God. In that seventh — and what I thought was the concluding — oracle against his own kingdom of Judah, Amos proclaimed that fire would come and destroy the strongholds of Jerusalem. Here was a judgment on our arrogant neighbors, our fellow Jews, to the south. Here was a judgment on the royal palace of the Davidic line and on the very Temple of Solomon! It was enough to take your breath away.

I was getting to like this man. I was even thinking of inviting him to preach at Bethel and maybe come over for a drink. But then he added an unprecedented eighth oracle. In each of his oracles he had used the same formula: "For three transgressions, and for four." The math is easy: three plus four equals seven. For seven transgressions would come the judgment on these nations, and on their architectural wonders. Seven! The number of completion. Once you get to seven, no more needs to be added. So when Amos gave seven oracles, concluding with Judah, the sermon was finished, right? Wrong. He added an eighth oracle, and this one was for the three transgressions of Israel, and for four. He sucked us all in. And before we could actually catch our breath, he actually listed the seven sins. In the other oracles, the seven was a kind of literary device, and Amos never really went beyond one or two sins. But for Israel — for us — he listed seven. According to him, we:

1. sell the righteous for silver,
2. sell the poor for a pair of sandals,
3. trample the heads of the poor into the dust of the earth,
4. push the poor out of the way,
5. tolerate father and son having sexual relations with the same young woman,
6. keep garments all night that had been given as collateral on a loan, in order to provide ourselves comfort as we sleep beside the altar,
7. drink wine in the sanctuary that was bought with fines imposed on lawbreakers.

I was, of course, flabbergasted. Somehow Amos had found a way to describe life that was normal in Israel, indeed, normal life in the *sanctuaries* of Israel — including Bethel — as if it were sinful. Such pernicious nonsense!

Oddly enough, Amos did not refer to architecture in that unprecedented eighth oracle. He said nothing about fire coming down on the strongholds. He did not mention judgment coming down on the sanctuaries, houses, and palaces. I took a little comfort in that. But I shouldn't have. You see, Amos's architectural preoccupation came out in his very next sermon, when he addressed the question of Israel's strongholds. But against us he was even more biting and more explicit than he had been against Judah and the nations. In fact, he invited the leaders of two pagan nations, the inhabitants of two pagan strongholds that he had already pronounced judgment on, to come to Mount Samaria to witness the judgment on Israel.

And here are the four things Amos claimed to see and invited the nations to see in Israel:

1. what great tumult there is within us,
2. what oppression characterizes our life,
3. that we have no understanding of what is right, and therefore,
4. our strongholds are built on violence and extortion.

From Amos's perspective, the social, economic, political, and religious structures that make life secure in the kingdom of Israel — the very way we order life in Israel — are nothing more than a tumult, a profound *dis*order. What I call order, the prophet calls chaos; what our societal structures have legitimated, the prophet declares to be an illegitimate bastardization of Yahweh's vision for covenantal life.

How does he know that there is a tumult? How does he justify calling order disorder? Where does he get off calling normal social, economic, and political structures chaos? Well, Amos says that if there is oppression in the streets and in the courts, if there is no fair dealing in socioeconomic life, if there is poverty and wealth side by side, if the strongholds of the powerful are erected on violence, if our communities are constructed in such a way that some are housed in opulence and others left homeless — then there is a tumult in the land, even if the rich and powerful don't notice it. Whether or not you see order or chaos, normal social and economic life or tumult, depends on where you stand. Amos decided to stand with those who had no standing in our society. I was standing on the other side.

The way I saw it, things were more complicated than Amos was acknowledging. There are certain kinds of economic mechanisms that need to be put in place if a society is to prosper. If there is to be economic well-being for the poor, there must be an increase in income for the rich. If you want to stimulate the economy, you need to give tax relief to the rich and not to the poor. If there is to be social order, you need to erect a certain kind of class structure and find ways to police society. If you are to have a broad sense of civic pride, even among the poor, you need to have strongholds, palaces, wonderful architectural structures to convey the wealth and power of your society.

For some reason, though, Amos just didn't catch these nuances of social organization. He didn't seem to get it that things were more complicated than his analysis suggested. He simply called Israel's order disorder. And then he proclaimed, against any geopolitical evidence that anyone could see on the horizon, that an enemy would come and besiege Israel, strip away its arrogant defenses and plunder its strongholds. All that seemed secure and provided a sheltered life for those dwelling in these strongholds would be destroyed. While the rich loll around on their couches, the lion will be devouring Israel.

I can remember that sermon like it was yesterday. My head was spinning, and a mixture of anger and anxiety was racing through my body. But before I could compose my thoughts and respond to this preposterous scenario, the prophet called out, "Shema!" Listen! Hear if you still have the ears to hear! And then he got even more specific. You want to know which strongholds, which buildings, which architectural wonders I have in mind? "I will punish the altars of Bethel." The royal sanctuary! The sanctuary that functions as the chapel of the royal house, the very house of God that is the foundation of all households, the stronghold that legitimates all strongholds will fall to the ground!

And if this house falls, so also will all the houses of its parishioners. "I will tear down the winter house as well as the summer house; and the houses of ivory will perish, and the great houses shall come to an end."

Now Amos was getting personal. Now he was addressing the question of strongholds with a specificity he had not used on any of the other nations. Whose houses were going to fall? The houses of the rich. The houses of those who have enough economic wealth to have both a summer and a winter home. He took specific aim at the architecture of opulence, the houses of inlaid ivory exported from Africa, the great houses of ebony. Hey, I lived in one of those houses.

Over the next days and weeks Amos kept showing up with his gloom-

and-doom message. It seemed that a common theme that paralleled his architectural preoccupation was justice: "You trample the poor," he said. "You turn justice to wormwood and bring righteousness to the ground," he proclaimed. And where there was an absence of justice and righteousness, he claimed, there was a breaking of covenant, and thus the blessings of covenant would turn to curses. Indeed, the promises of covenant would be reversed.[60]

As I've mentioned, the man's rhetoric was powerful. But more disturbing, his message had deep resonances with the Torah. Granted, these were dimensions of Torah that had not seemed as relevant to us during the success of Jeroboam's reign; but when Amos spoke of justice and righteousness, it awakened memories in my heart that been buried for a long time. Memories of my earliest Torah instruction from my father and mother. Memories of a covenant that required a certain kind of fruit to be born in our lives. Memories of care and justice for the poor, memories that perhaps had been suppressed because they were too dangerous.

You can see how this man was getting to me. But either he went too far, or I wasn't prepared to follow the implications of Torah justice and righteousness as far as he said was necessary. Yet, while his predictions of the fall of Israel seemed to be totally unfounded, I knew that prophets see things that the rest of us don't see. What made it impossible for me to accept his prophecy, however, was his attack on the royal sanctuary at Bethel. I know — I know what you're thinking: I was only upset because what Amos was saying threatened my job security as a priest. Please give me a little more credit than that.

No, my issue wasn't job security. My issue was that Bethel was a sacred place. The very name Bethel means "the house of God." Can a prophet speak in the name of God only to attack God's house? Bethel was the very "gate of heaven" where our father Jacob had a dream of a ladder in which easy access was allowed between heaven and earth. Could Amos really mean to suggest that this gate was closed? That this sacred space was desacralized? That the house of God was no more?

The implications were too devastating to bear. If God had no house in Bethel, if God had somehow become homeless, then no house was secure. No wonder Amos had so much to say about architecture! No wonder he connected the destruction of the sanctuary at Bethel with the destruction

---

60. See how Amos 5:3 is a reversal of Lev. 26:8, and Amos 5:11 is a reversal of Deut. 6:10-11.

of the winter houses and the summer houses, the houses of ivory and the great houses.

I knew that I had a duty to my king. Amos wasn't merely uttering blasphemy against the house of God; he was spreading treasonous thoughts against the royal household as well. I had no choice but to send a letter to King Jeroboam, which said: "Amos has conspired against you in the very center of the house of Israel: the land is not able to bear all his words." I said that Amos had prophesied the death of the king and that Israel would be taken into exile.

But I wasn't going to simply tell on Amos and expect the royal court to deal with him. I confronted him myself and told him to go back home to his sheep and never again prophesy at Bethel, for this was the king's sanctuary and a temple of the kingdom. That's when things got personal. And, if the truth be told, it's undoubtedly why this confrontation haunts me to this day and is difficult to even mention. Amos replied that there was a prophetic word for me because I had told him to stop prophesying.

> Your wife shall become a prostitute in the city,
> and your sons and daughters shall fall by the sword,
> and your land shall be parceled out by line;
> you yourself shall die in an unclean land,
> and Israel shall surely go into exile away from its land.

Crazy ravings, right? Offensive insults from a guy who had gone right over the top and couldn't handle criticism, right? Just becoming personal with what he'd been raving about, right?

Wrong. You see, while not all of his prophecy has come true, the first part did: my wife went off the deep end five years ago and left home. I don't know where she is, but some of my priest friends in Gilgal have said that there are rumors about her living there, and we can only imagine how she is supporting herself.

I am devastated. My home is broken and I am deathly afraid for my children, my land, my people. Could the rest of Amos's words come true? Could the homelessness of exile be the fate of Israel? Could it be that, because we have not followed justice and righteousness, because we have oppressed the poor and legitimated a society of homelessness, that the strongholds will fall? All of them?

Perhaps most disturbing of all was my last encounter with Amos. In his last oracle he said that he actually saw the Lord standing beside the altar in Bethel, and that God said, "Strike down the pillars until the thresholds shake, and shatter them on the heads of all the people" (Amos 9:1; authors' translation). He went on to say that God will fix his eyes on us "for harm and not good." Covenant reversed.

Amos wasn't just undermining the foundations of the sanctuary at Bethel; he was undermining the very foundations and pillars of Jewish identity. He went on to invert the very notion of our uniqueness, our election as the people of promise, by saying:

Are you not like the Ethiopians to me,
O people of Israel? says the Lord.
Did I not bring Israel up from the land of Egypt,
and the Philistines from Caphtor and the Arameans from Kir?

He was saying here that God's saving Exodus of Israel was not unique: God had done the same for the Philistines and Arameans. Maybe we could find a way to rebuild our lives even if an exile happened, and even if the temple and the palace and all of the other great houses were to fall. Maybe we could withstand such a shaking of the foundations. But how could we ever be at home again as God's covenant people if the very foundations of covenant were removed?

And yet Amos didn't leave us without any hope. He said: "The eyes of the Lord God are upon the sinful kingdom, and I will destroy it from the face of the earth — except that I will not utterly destroy the house of Jacob, says the Lord." If the rest of Amos's prophecy haunts me and leaves me with a deep disquiet in my soul, then that word "except" gives me hope. The destruction will not be complete.

Not surprisingly, when Amos whispered the possibility of hope during his last oracle, he returned to themes of architecture again. But instead of talking about strongholds, sanctuaries, and houses of opulence, he spoke of the tottering booth of David being raised up. Instead of the destruction of the architectural strongholds of the elite and powerful, we now hear language of a humble hut, of a booth that provides protection in the wilderness, of repairs being made. It was almost as if he was saying that permanent structures like palaces and temples would only legitimate another self-secure regime of opulence — a regime of homelessness rather than covenantal homemaking. No, if there is to be restoration, it will be the restoration of a sojourning community, a community following their God on a path of covenantal homecoming. They will have a restored canopy, but a canopy is what it will be. No pillars and thresholds here, just a tent where people can meet with their God.

There was one more thing in that final oracle. Why does God repair the breaches in this tottering hut, raise up the ruins, and engage in a rebuilding project? So that this community that is called to live in covenant with the Creator God will be able to expand the invitation of covenant to the nations. Israel is to be restored *so that* all nations will hear God's call and respond. If there is to be homecoming after exile, Amos insisted, it must be a homecoming for all peoples, not just us.

Twenty years later, I'm still struggling to understand all of this. Jeroboam is still on the throne, but there have been rumblings of military aggression coming out of Assyria. Remembering Amos's words to me, I look at my motherless children with deep anxiety, an anxiety that makes it difficult for me to imagine the restoration Amos was hinting at. But right at the end of that last sermon there was one other thing I hold onto. Amos said:

> I will restore the fortunes of my people Israel,
> and they shall rebuild the ruined cities and inhabit them;
> they shall plant vineyards and drink their wine,
> and they shall make gardens and plant and eat their fruit.

I'm pretty sure that I won't live to see that day of restoration. If everything Amos said is true, then I'll die in exile. But maybe the vision of a homecoming of my people, in solidarity with all the nations, drinking the wines of renewed covenant and eating the sweet fruit of faithfulness, can sustain me through the days of devastation that are coming. Maybe. . . .

From Housing to Homemaking

A house doesn't make a home
Don't leave me here alone.

U2[1]

The Grassy Narrows First Nation live on a reservation located eighty kilometers up a logging road from Kenora, Ontario. This Anishinaabe (or Ojibwa) community has been the site of some of the most severe social disintegration and ecological despoliation to be witnessed anywhere in North America. The community came to international attention in 1970 and throughout the next decade and a half because its waters had been poisoned when the Reed Paper company, upstream in Dryden, dumped more than 20,000 pounds of mercury into the English-Wabagoon River system. The local fisheries were closed, jobs vanished, welfare dependency increased, and as many as 1,000 people showed symptoms of Minamata disease, which was brought on by mercury poisoning.[2] By the mid-1980s the Grassy Narrows community demonstrated a numbness of spirit and utter hopelessness that rivaled any Third World community.[3]

Yet the people of Grassy Narrows date their real troubles to an event

---

1. U2, "Sometimes you can't make it on your own," from *How to Dismantle an Atomic Bomb* ©2004 Universal Music.

2. As recently as 2002, 86 percent of the Grassy Narrows residents tested showed signs of mercury poisoning. See Will Braun, "Treaties, Trees and Sharing," *CPJ Report: The Grassy Narrows Blockade* [see also: www.cpj.ca/native/03/grassy2.html].

3. As described by Anastasia M. Shkilnyk, *A Poison Stronger than Love: The Destruction of an Ojibwa Community* (New Haven: Yale University Press, 1985), p. 4.

that came before the mercury poisoning. They have consistently identified the forced relocation in 1963 of the band from their traditional settlement to a new reservation with government housing as the most devastating attack on their Anishinaabe identity and way of life. This relocation, forced on the people by Canada's Department of Indian Affairs and Northern Development, was enacted in the name of development. Surely, it was thought, access to better roads, healthcare, an on-site school, electricity, wage-paying jobs, more efficient infrastructures, and a higher standard of housing would make life better for the Grassy Narrows people and solve the problems of Indian poverty. That was the rhetoric of the federal officials; but it was also the rhetoric of assimilation. Remove the people from their traditional hunting-and-gathering grounds, insert them into a wage economy, educate their children in the ways of the dominant culture, and they will have only one of two choices: assimilate or die. The Grassy Narrows people found those two to be the same thing: assimilation is only possible if something dies, and what needed to die in this instance was the cultural heritage, beliefs, language, and worldview of a colonized people. Aboriginal peoples worldwide describe assimilationist policies as cultural genocide.[4]

Cultural genocide, however, is most effective if it is combined with a program of *domicide*. Douglas Porteous and Sandra Smith define domicide as "the deliberate destruction of home by human agency in pursuit of specified goals, which causes suffering to the victims."[5] Yi-Fu Tuan observes: "To be forcibly evicted from one's home and neighborhood is to be stripped of a sheathing which in its familiarity protects the human being from the outside world."[6] Such domicide, such forced eviction with its concomitant suffering and vulnerability, was imposed on the Grassy Narrows people.

While federal officials may have thought that white man's education and wage economy would be the most powerful assimilationist tools at their disposal, it was in fact the very physical shape of the settlement and the worldview out of which this new-built environment was developed that proved to be a devastatingly effective architecture of domicide. Like

4. See the essays in Diane Engelstad and John Bird, eds., *Nation to Nation: Aboriginal Sovereignty and the Future of Canada* (Toronto: Anansi Press, 1992).

5. J. Douglas Porteous and Sandra E. Smith, *Domicide: The Global Destruction of Home* (Montreal and Kingston: McGill-Queen's University Press, 2001), p. 12.

6. Yi-Fu Tuan, *Topophilia: A Study of Environmental Perception, Attitudes, and Values* (New York: Columbia University Press, 1990), p. 99.

most aboriginal tribes in North America, the Anishinaabe of Grassy Narrows is a clan-based society. On the original reservation "clan territoriality . . . played an important role in reinforcing the identity of the group and its place in the order of things."[7] Anatasia Shkilnyk notes that "on the old reserve clan-based family groups were separated by unspoken, yet well understood distances, and definite territories were allocated to them by custom and usage for trapping, hunting and gathering" (Shkilnyk, p. 65). The new reservation undermined this clan-based social structure, not only by taking children off the traplines and encouraging their fathers to enter the wage economy, but also by the very shape and structure of the new-built environment. In the first instance, housing allocation was determined by the federal Indian agent, who showed no respect for clan identities. Second, the space that was maintained between both clans and individual families within clans was erased via a model of suburban density (this, ironically, in the middle of the wilderness) that flew in the face of aboriginal sensibilities. Third, while the older settlement was constructed as a series of circular clan compounds, all with equal access to the running waters of the Wabagoon River, from which they gained much of their livelihood, the new settlement was established in a series of city-like linear blocks on a stagnant lake. For the Anishinaabe, both a connection to living water and the organization of life in terms of the circular pattern of the medicine wheel and the drum — representing the four directions of north, south, east, and west — are integral to a sense of well-being, wholeness, and being at home.[8] All of that was undermined by the simple act of providing the people with government housing designed on the principles of suburban planning.

One 71-year-old elder put it this way:

We don't live like the white man, that's not our way. The white man lives close together, but we don't. We like to live far apart, in families. On the

---

7. Shkilnyk, *Poison Stronger than Love*, p. 66.

8. See A. Irving Hallowell, "Ojibwa Ontology, Behavior and World View," in S. Diamond, ed., *Culture in History* (New York: Columbia University Press, 1960), pp. 19-52; see also Thomas W. Overholt and J. Baird Callicott, *Clothed in Fur and Other Tales: An Introduction to an Ojibwa World View* (Washington, DC: University Press of America, 1982). On the importance of the circle in an aboriginal worldview (in this instance, Plains Cree), see David Young, Grant Ingram, and Lise Swartz, *Cry of the Eagle: Encounters with a Cree Healer* (Toronto: University of Toronto Press, 1989), pp. 18-39.

old reserve, you knew your place. Everybody respected your place. . . . It wasn't private property, but it was a sense of place, your place, your force around you. . . . As soon as they started to bunch us up, the problems started, the drinking, the violence. This has a lot to do with being all bunched up.[9]

Home is a matter of knowing our place and knowing that our place will be respected, a place where we experience both identity and security. When people are stripped of that sense of place, deprived of the kind of space they feel is necessary to establish such a sense of place, they are rendered homeless.[10]

However, this elder also referred to the experience of a "force" that encompasses a sense of place. This is another important feature of the Anishinaabe experience of place. The Anishinaabe have a view, widely held by aboriginal peoples, that no space is empty and no matter is dead. All space is inhabited by spirits, and all matter is animated by the energy of the universe, the presence of the Great Spirit. Some places, however, are more spiritually suitable for human habitation than are others. The Grassy Narrows community believed that the old reservation site was a sacred place, specially blessed by the presence of Gitchi-Manitou; but the new site was already owned by a bad spirit, Machu-Manitou, who was in fact the nemesis of Gitchi-Manitou. Part of the evidence that demonstrated the spiritual difference between the two sites was that, whereas the original settlement was surrounded by many "places of power," where individuals could go for meditation and for more intense experiences of the spirit world, the new town site had relatively few of those places (Shkilnyk, pp. 70-73).

9. Cited in Shkilnyk, *Poison Stronger than Love*, p. 173. George S. Esber, Jr., found a similar aversion to crowding and a need for significant social space among the Apache ("Designing Apache Homes with Apaches," in Robert M. Wuff and Shirley J. Fiske, eds., *Anthropological Praxis: Translating Knowledge into Action* [Boulder and London: Westview Press, 1987], pp. 187-96).

10. On the importance of respect in an aboriginal worldview, see Stan McKay, "Calling Creation Into Our Family," in Engelstad and Bird, *Nation to Nation*, pp. 31-33. McKay brings respect and the symbolic importance of the circle together when he says: "Many teachings among the aboriginal nations of North America use the symbol of the circle — the symbol for the inclusive caring community, where individuals are respected and interdependence is recognized. In the natural order of creation, human beings are part of the whole circle of life. Aboriginal spiritual teachers speak of the re-establishment of the balance between human beings and the whole creation as a mending of the hoop" (p. 34). The Grassy Narrows relocation broke that circle of life as it was encoded in the built environment.

As a strategy for assimilation, the relocation of the Grassy Narrows reservation was an overwhelming success: "In the span of only one generation after the relocation of Grassy Narrows, the people's moral values and beliefs, the customary social relationships, political organization, and modes of production — all were rendered impotent, useless, even superfluous under the imposed conditions of the new reserve" (Shkilnyk, p. 174).[11] As one community member put it, "Now we have nothing. Not the old, not the new. Our families are all broken up. We are caught in the middle . . . between two worlds, two ways of life" (p. 85). Two worlds, two ways of life, two worldviews.

This story of profound homelessness in a northern Ontario tribe painfully illustrates the relationship between worldviews, housing, and the experiences of home and homelessness. Worldviews shape human life: they mold the discourse and experience of both place and home. Perhaps, if we discern more profoundly how home is shaped by worldview, we can avoid the kind of domicide that was imposed on the Anishinaabe of Grassy Narrows, develop a more holistic understanding of the relationship between housing and homemaking, and engender more culturally sensitive and appropriate housing policies and practices in our communities.

The Shape of Worldviews

In his foundational essay on cultural geography, *House Form and Culture*, Amos Rapoport wages a battle against all determinisms when it comes to understanding human habitation. Whether that determinism is rooted in

---

11. At least this was the case in 1985. But the spirit of the Anishinaabe people has not been totally defeated. In the late 1990s, and continuing to today, the community has been fighting against further attacks on their traditional ways of life in the form of clear-cut logging. Blockades have been set up and court challenges have been launched against Abitibi Consolidated, the wood and pulp paper giant. And, most encouraging, young people are at the forefront of this direct action to protect their land. Foundational to such a renewal of this community, however, has been a reclaiming of Anishinaabe language, culture, and spirituality. See Andrew Chapeskie, Iain Davidson-Hunt, and Roger Forbister, "Passing on Ojibway Lifeways in a Contemporary Environment," an essay presented at the 7th Annual Conference of the International Association for the Study of Common Property, June 20-14, 1998. (see www.taigainstitute.org). This essay demonstrates the adaptability of the Anishinaabe, how they use CD ROM technology to teach the Anishinaabe language, culture, and worldview.

climate, building materials, available technology, or economics, Rapoport insists that housing should reflect larger sociocultural dynamics. He argues: "Given a certain climate, the availability of certain materials, and the constraints and capabilities of a given level of technology, what finally decides the form of a dwelling, and molds the spaces and their relationships, is the vision that people have of the ideal life."[12] This vision, or *genre de vie*, or worldview, comes to expression in the built environment broadly conceived, and particularly in the house (pp. 34, 47, 58, 73-78). How we shape human habitation is most deeply rooted in communally shared worldviews, says Rapoport, and worldview-shaped habitation, in turn, shapes our lives as inhabitants of these dwellings, this built environment.

Similarly, Timothy Gorringe suggests that "all housing embodies an anthropology and therefore a view of society."[13] Moreover, Gorringe argues, "houses express, and are intended to express, a moral order" (p. 82).[14] And insofar as moral orders are spiritual in character, Gorringe says, it is possible to argue that "profound, creative, grace filled spiritualities produce grace filled environments," whereas "banal, impoverished, alienated spiritualities produce alienating environments" (p. 24).

But what exactly is the relationship between worldviews, housing, and home? How is housing an expression of worldview, and how does housing shape worldview? What are some implications of the worldview-housing relationship for the development of housing policy?

Ultimate Questions and Inhabited Answers

Housing, of some kind, is foundational to the experience of home. While a community of squatters under a bridge may well have an important experience of home under that bridge, the insecurity of that environment, the lack of any secure tenure in that space, and the sheer inhospitable character of the space makes homemaking, in any sustainable sense of the word, very difficult. Housing is necessary for the experience of home. This is why

12. Amos Rapoport, *House Form and Culture* (Englewood Cliffs, NJ: Prentice-Hall, 1969), p. 47.

13. Timothy J. Gorringe, *A Theology of the Built Environment: Justice, Empowerment, Redemption* (Cambridge, UK: Cambridge University Press, 2002), p. 109.

14. See also Karsten Harries, *The Ethical Function of Architecture* (Cambridge, MA: MIT Press, 1998).

the United Nations identifies the need for adequate human housing as a fundamental human right.[15] Indeed, where people are shelterless, they are being denied that fundamental human right.

Yet housing does not necessarily make for home. Houses can be bought or rented on the market; homes can be neither bought nor sold. As Kimberly Dovey puts it, "Home is a relationship that is created and evolved over time; it is not consumed like the products of economic process. The house is a tool for the achievement of the experience of home."[16] Home, we have argued, is more than lodging and something profoundly more than an economic commodity. Recall Michael Walzer's description of home as "a dense moral culture within which [people] feel some sense of belonging."[17] That "dense moral culture," together with its concomitant sense of belonging, is precisely what a fully functioning worldview provides in human life. And only when one's housing can be experienced in the terms of one's worldview — indeed, only when one's housing is, in important respects, *shaped* by one's worldview — can housing become home.

The notion of worldview has emerged in cultural anthropology, sociology of knowledge, and religious studies as a way to understand how humans shape their world into a site of inhabited meaning, a home.[18] Berger, Berger, and Kellner put it this way: "Any particular life-world is constructed by the meanings of those who 'inhabit' it."[19] Peter Berger affirms that sharing a worldview provides a community with a "sacred canopy," a mythic cover of protection, under which the day-to-day business of making homes, shaping community, and sustaining life together can happen.[20]

A worldview, then, is a vision *of* life that provides its adherents with a foundational understanding of how the world works. That means, however, that a worldview necessarily also functions as a vision *for* life that

---

15. Article 25, *Universal Declaration of Human Rights,* United Nations, Dec. 10, 1948.

16. Kimberly Dovey, "Home and Homelessness," in I. Altman and C. Werner, eds., *Home Environments* (New York: Plenum Books, 1985), p. 54.

17. Michael Walzer, *Interpretation and Social Criticism* (Cambridge, MA: Harvard University Press, 1987), p. 16.

18. For a comprehensive discussion of the history of the idea of "worldview," see David K. Naugle, *Worldview: The History of a Concept* (Grand Rapids: Eerdmans, 2002).

19. Peter Berger, Brigitte Berger, Hansfield Kellner, *The Homeless Mind* (New York: Vintage, 1974), p. 12.

20. Peter Berger, *The Sacred Canopy* (Garden City, NY: Anchor Books, 1969), esp. chs. 1 and 2.

gives direction for normative and life-giving ways to live.[21] A worldview shapes those who live in its embrace so that they develop certain habits, certain ways of relating to each other and the world, and these habits are the stuff of habitation.[22] We could say that worldviews are plausibility structures that provide fundamental answers to ultimate questions — questions that seem to bear some anthropological universality.[23] All cultures, all peoples, all religions answer at least these four questions:

1. Where are we? What is the nature of the world? Is this a safe or an insecure place? Is land a gift of the Great Spirit, a commons managed by the community, or is it a commodity for sale on the open market? Is our life here a temporary way station in a larger cosmic process, or is this world and this life all we've got? Is the world a place of inherent tensions or primordial peace? Is this world experienced as home for human beings? How do we relate to nonhuman creatures?

2. Who are we? What does it mean to be human? How are gender, ethnic, and generational relationships negotiated? How do we relate to the "other"? What is the role of men and women, children and the elderly? How do we relate to our ancestors? What is meaningful labor, and who should do it? What makes for human flourishing and well-being? If humans are homemakers, what does fully human habitation look like?

3. What's wrong? How do we account for the brokenness of life, for evil, for antisocial behavior (as determined by the worldview)? Where do we meet what most severely threatens our sense of order, security, and well-being? What is it that most profoundly renders us homeless?

4. What's the remedy? How do we find a path through brokenness, chaos, and insecurity so that life can be secure and whole again? Where and how might we find homecoming?

21. See James H. Olthuis, "On Worldviews," *Christian Scholar's Review* 14, no. 2 (1985): 153-64; this essay was also published in Paul A. Marshall, Sander Griffioen, and Richard J. Mouw, eds., *Stained Glass: Worldviews and Social Science* (Lanham, MD: University Press of America, 1989), pp. 26-40.

22. Christian Smith makes a similar point: "Whether it is obvious on the surface appearances or not, social institutions are inevitably rooted in and expressions of the narratives, traditions and worldviews of moral orders" (*Moral, Believing Animals: Human Personhood and Culture* [Oxford: Oxford University Press, 2003], p. 22). Housing and the construction of home is this kind of social institution.

23. Brian J. Walsh and J. Richard Middleton, *The Transforming Vision: Shaping a Christian Worldview* (Downers Grove, IL: InterVarsity, 1984). On plausibility structures, see Berger, *Sacred Canopy*, pp. 45-51.

We can see how these questions are implicitly answered in the kind of worldview that we meet among the Anishinaabe and other aboriginal tribes in North America. If the land is our mother (where we are), a world of profound harmony in which animals, plants, stars, moon, sun, and wind are among "all my relations," and we find our fundamental identity (who we are) in being children of the land, kin to the animals, and members of a clan, then homemaking will require that we maintain this sensitive balance of relationships. The basic problem in the world (what's wrong) is that human beings overstep their bounds, act in arrogance rather than humility, and thereby destroy the balance of the wheel of life. Moreover, some human beings, by means of colonial violence and exploitative control, have stolen our land, separated us from our mother, and imprisoned us on reservations of their own making. We have been rendered homeless not just because of our own arrogance but also because of the arrogance and genocidal intentions of others. The only solution (what the remedy is) will be to return to the land, reconnect with the Great Spirit, strengthen the ties of family and clan, remember anew the old stories, and restore the ancient rituals.[24]

In this worldview the land is a homeland. When this worldview is lost, there are devastating consequences in the aboriginal community. Losing the land means quite literally that aboriginal peoples face profound homelessness. Indigenous knowledge disappears; native languages are lost; the structures of clan and tribe collapse. Alcoholism, substance abuse, violence, and suicide become rampant. Not only are many native people on the streets in the cities, even more are languishing on reservations: they are bored, have nothing to do and no place where they can live out their indigenous worldview. It is not surprising that native peoples are disproportionately represented in the prison system. Many say that there isn't that much of a difference between the reservation and prison: both are forms of incarceration.

Homecoming for this community cannot mean the provision of government housing on reservations and native public housing in the cities. Housing is indispensable, but it is not enough. Prefabricated three-bedroom dwellings can never begin to approximate the experience of

---

24. While these themes are common to most aboriginal worldviews in North America, our source for these particular images is from the Dene nation of the Mackenzie Valley. See Thomas Berger's royal commission report, *Northern Frontier/Northern Homeland: Report of the Mackenzie Valley Pipeline Inquiry* (Ottawa: Supply and Services Canada, 1977), pp. 94-95.

home on the trapline, in the longhouse, or in the traditional community. Indeed, there is something about these poorly constructed, prefabricated structures that actually militates against any sense of homecoming. Nor do 1960s-style public-housing apartments in urban centers meet aboriginal needs. These may be habitations, but they seem to provide no space for the telling of stories and the fostering of other habits that give aboriginal communities their identity.

Founding Stories and Storied Places

Houses become homes when they embody the stories of the people who have made these spaces into places of significance, meaning, and memory. Home is fundamentally a place of connection, of relationships that are life-giving and foundational. And that connectivity includes the past, for homes are shaped by memories of important transitions, events, and experiences. Once these stories are forgotten, there is no home to return to because there is no place, or even potential place, that could be shaped by those stories.

The New Zealand phrase "he's totally lost the plot" is instructive here: it means being "off his rocker," lacking sanity, losing one's sense of direction and identity. That is what happens when a people lose their memory, when they become story-less. This is tragic under any circumstances, but all the more tragic when the amnesia is a defense mechanism against either the ridicule of the present or the pain of the past. And just as good therapists help clients reconnect their life stories (because, without such reconnection, emotional health is not achievable), so also do people in times of cultural and historical crisis need to reassess — and reclaim — their founding stories. Christian Smith argues that humans "are animals who most fundamentally understand what reality is, who we are, and how we ought to live by locating ourselves within larger narratives that we hear and tell, and that constitute what is for us real and significant."[25] When such narratives collapse, we are lost in the dislocation, fragmentation, moral paralysis, and disorientation of homelessness.

25. Smith, *Moral, Believing Animals,* p. 64. Responding to the postmodern "incredulity" toward all metanarratives, Smith comments: "We have no more dispensed with grand narratives than with the need for lungs to breathe with. We cannot live without stories, big stories finally, to tell us what is real and significant, to know who we are, where we are, what we are doing, and why" (p. 67).

On one level we have the problem of how a built structure can be home for a family or community when that structure appears to be a generic dwelling with no sense of memory or story. How can aboriginal peoples in Canada ever "make home" in a dwelling that is little more than a prefabricated shelter or a homogeneous public housing complex? Can such spaces easily be transformed to hold the memories, myths, and founding stories of an aboriginal people? The answer would appear to be no. But this isn't just because the building is too neutral of meaning, too generic. Indeed, we contend that no built structure is generic.

Buildings communicate, in their very built form, the worldview of the architect or the society that has designed them. They are, in the language of architecture, "legible."[26] Karsten Harries argues that there is "a sense in which every building cannot but tell us something about its function and the kind of society that gave rise to it."[27] And all buildings tell the story of their builders. While prefabricated buildings seem to be generic and certainly have limited legibility, they nonetheless speak of the modernist worldview that was at the heart of their design. If homes are machines for living in, as Le Corbusier said, and we attempt to design "one single building for all nations and climates,"[28] it is not surprising that modernist architecture applied the criteria of mass production, standardization, and uniformity to housing.[29] But there is nothing generic about this housing. Rather, the eschewing of historical reference and the commitment to func-

26. Eric O. Jacobsen, *Sidewalks in the Kingdom: New Urbanism and the Christian Faith* (Grand Rapids: Brazos Press, 2003), p. 106.

27. Harries, *The Ethical Function of Architecture*, p. 130. This architectural legibility, however, needs to be placed in the context of a wider sense of what Albert Borgmann calls the "eloquence of reality" (*Crossing the Postmodern Divide* [Chicago: University of Chicago Press, 1992], pp. 118-19). If natural reality has no voice, no eloquence, then any notion of the legibility of the built environment will necessarily be thin and weak. Harries puts it this way: "But to hold that there is nothing that transcends human beings and speaks to them, that reality is itself mute and meaningless, means nihilism. If there is to be an alternative to nihilism, it must be possible to make some sense of and learn to listen to the language of things" (p. 133).

28. Le Corbusier, cited in David Ley, "Modernism, Postmodernism and the Struggle for Place," in John A. Agnew and James S. Duncan, eds., *The Power of Place: Bringing Together Geographical and Sociological Imaginations* (Boston: Unwin Hyman, 1989), p. 47. Gorringe describes this kind of standardized approach to domestic architecture as the "McDonaldization" of housing (*Theology of the Built Environment*, p. 110).

29. Gorringe says: "Mass housing represents an institutionalized, regimented, view of human nature," and "mass produced housing leads to mass produced lives" (*Theology of the Built Environment*, pp. 100, 102).

tion over adornment that we see in modernist architecture — especially in Bauhaus, Brutalism, and the International Style — loudly proclaims a particular industrialist, rationalist, and narrowly defined progressivist vision of history. Indeed, we could say that these buildings, in their very form, symbolize a particular worldview that is embedded in a particular cultural story or myth.[30]

The problem is that this particular story, this worldview, is deeply at odds with the vision of life that has animated North American aboriginal culture for many generations. The issue is not that the built environment where the aboriginal community had to live was too generic and devoid of meaning to sustain a robust aboriginal community and self-identity; the problem is that this built environment spoke a language both alien and alienating to that aboriginal identity. These buildings conveyed an industrial and modern worldview that could never be the site of home for a people deeply committed to a nonindustrial and traditional vision of life. In other words, modernist architecture, and especially public housing, took a homogeneous, "one-size-fits-all" approach to housing that assumed all people and their housing needs were essentially the same.[31] But this homogeneous standardization, rooted in the arrogant universalism of a modernist worldview, failed to understand deeply enough the diversity of communal housing needs, needs that are rooted in the diversity of communally shaped worldviews and grounding narratives.

Mythic Power and Symbolic Place

This leads to a third dimension of worldviews, namely, the way they are embodied and carried in symbols. It is ironic that a modernist architectural tradition that eschewed the ornamentation of facades nonetheless could not avoid the symbolization of its own built environment. Not only do tall bank towers of the International Style symbolize the phallic power of the corporations that are housed in them, but the modern house —

30. See Smith, *Moral, Believing Animals,* ch. 4; see also Alasdair MacIntyre, *After Virtue: A Study in Moral Theory* (Notre Dame, IN: University of Notre Dame Press, 1984), ch. 2.

31. Commenting on the infamous Pruett Igoe complex in St. Louis, Peter Hall says: "The cold brutality of the architecture made the blocks feel bleak and comfortless, and alienation, loneliness, and stress became common experiences" (*Cities of Tomorrow* [Oxford: Blackwell, 1988], p. 238; cited by Gorringe, *Theology of the Built Environment,* p. 99).

whether it be the detached house in the suburbs, the elegant terraced housing of the United Kingdom, or the gated communities of North America — bears distinctive symbolic meanings. For example, the Victorian home was a display of the virtues of polite society, the boundary between public and private space, the "castle or fortress offering protection against the cruel world outside."[32] In industrial society, "the house stands out primarily as a symbol of social status,"[33] where status is determined primarily in terms of tenure, location, and type of dwelling. That is, status is conferred according to whether the inhabitants are renters, homeowners, or under public subsidy; whether they live in the "right" part of town; and whether they live in a detached house, a condominium, a public housing apartment, or the like.

Home functions symbolically in two ways: by the symbols that adorn the home and by the home itself. A space is transformed into a place, we have suggested, when it tells a story. And stories are carried in human life by symbols. A cross in the hallway, family wedding pictures on the mantle, an altar to the ancestors, totems at the entrance way, a television in the center of the living room, the dream catcher with the little pouch of tobacco in the front hallway, the "head of the table," the "master bedroom." Home is a site of culturally meaningful and shared symbols that remind the inhabitants of the founding story; and those symbols go a long way toward adapting various forms of housing into homes. A mezuzah on the doorpost with the words of the *Shema* ("Hear, O Israel. . .") identifies a home as Jewish, regardless of the rest of the architecture.

But the home itself is also symbolic. Beyond the symbols with which we adorn our dwellings, it is important to note that diverse architectures — varied constructions of inside/outside, public/private, house size, building materials, and location — are symbolic of class, status, cultural identity, and, most foundationally, worldview. An oversized house in the suburbs on an acre and a half lot with a three-car garage may have the external and internal symbols of Judaism, Islam, Christianity, or any other worldview; but the very structure of the house may well be more revealing of the practiced worldview of its inhabitants than these more traditional symbols. Only by

32. Mike Hepworth, "Privacy, Security and Respectability: The Ideal Victorian Home," in Tony Chapman and Jenny Hockey, eds., *Ideal Homes? Social Change and Domestic Life* (London and New York: Routledge, 1999), p. 21.

33. Hepworth, "Privacy, Security and Respectability," p. 39.

understanding the symbolic character of home — how different kinds of built environments symbolize different home-constituting memories and ways of answering foundational worldview questions — will we be able to address a diversity of housing needs with sensitivity and integrity. As Douglas Porteous and Sandra Smith say, "Home is a second body, which is seen as a symbol of self and self-identity. Home shapes you and, in turn, is shaped in your image."[34]

Basic Practices and Built Environments

Winston Churchill said, "We shape our buildings and then our buildings shape us."[35] Rapoport also argues that there is a dialectical relationship between housing form and cultural behavior, because the built form is both a physical embodiment of patterns of human behavior, desires, motivations, and feelings, and serves to shape and engender a certain way of life. Buildings both "reflect the values of a community and also influence them."[36] James Howard Kunstler says that buildings "possess anthropomorphic qualities that reflect human qualities and aspirations which we, in turn, project onto them — a reinforcing feedback loop."[37] The built environment is one of the most enduring ways in which we put our worldviews into action.

David Orr acknowledges this and draws an important pedagogical conclusion. If buildings "behave" in certain ways, and demonstrate certain "legibility," then perhaps we "must begin to see our houses, buildings, farms, businesses, energy technologies, transportation, landscapes, and communities in much the same way that we regard classrooms. In fact, they instruct us in more fundamental ways because they structure what we see, how we move, what we eat, our sense of time and space, how we relate to each other, our sense of security, and how we experience the particular places in which we live."[38] Buildings have pedagogical power.

34. Porteous and Smith, *Domicide: The Global Destruction of Home,* p. 54.

35. Cited by Jacobsen, *Sidewalks in the Kingdom,* p. 111.

36. Rapoport, *House Form and Culture,* p. 16.

37. James Howard Kunstler, *Home from Nowhere: Remaking our Everyday World for the 21st Century* (New York: Simon and Schuster, 1996), p. 136.

38. David Orr, *The Nature of Design: Ecology, Culture and Human Intention* (New York and Oxford: Oxford University Press, 2002), p. 31.

Whether one lives in a traditional longhouse, a split-level rancher in a North American suburb, a public-housing apartment in Toronto, an old-order Mennonite community, or a clan compound in Nigeria, it will profoundly shape how one experiences the world. But each of these dwellings, each of these built environments, is itself an expression of the vision of life, the overarching narrative, the guiding symbols, and the cultural practices of those who had the power to construct these sites of habitation.

The model sketched here is essentially a four-part explication of how worldviews are structured and work in human life. Worldviews answer ultimate questions at the heart of human life in terms of a grounding and directing narrative or myth that is encoded in symbols and embodied in a way of life.[39] This model could be diagramed as follows:

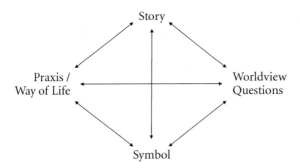

In this model, deeply formative, sacred, even mythic memory provides the template on which ultimate answers are given to ultimate questions. These answers to worldview questions are narratively based and encoded in symbols that give them powerful visual presence and abiding memory. The praxis, or way of life, of a community is embedded in the community's grounding story, confronted by its most powerful symbols, and is an expression of the way in which the community implicitly (and sometimes explicitly) answers ultimate worldview questions. But the model is actually more dynamic than this description would suggest: a reciprocal relation-

39. This model was developed by N. T. Wright in collaboration with Brian Walsh; it was first articulated in Wright's book *The New Testament and the People of God* (Minneapolis: Fortress Press, 1992).

ship exists between all the components of a worldview. A sense of failure or even a forgetting of a grounding narrative brings into question the power of various symbols and requires different kinds of answers to worldview questions.

So the Anishinaabe worldview crisis is evident in the new reservation when the children begin to forget (or are no longer taught) Ojibwa myths and the community ceases to observe rituals such as naming ceremonies and vision quests. Alternately, overexposure to various kinds of symbols and images alien to one's indigenous worldview might lead one to a different set of answers to worldview questions. How does an Anishinaabe youth answer the "who are we?" question when she meets negative images of "Indians" on television, or more perniciously, images of beauty and success that are expressive of the dominant culture?

To make this dynamism more evident, let us focus on the reciprocity between story and praxis. As we have already seen, it is not just the case that we shape the built environment in terms of our grounding stories. The built environment in which we live also shapes our stories.

Houses and Homes

From the 1920s to the 1960s, Robert Moses realized his vision for the modern city as the chief planner for New York City. Pursuing an aggressive agenda of "urban reform," Moses made New York City into a metropolis of modern architecture whose skyline became increasingly higher and its crisscrossing freeways increasingly ubiquitous. This was going to be a city for cars, and if that meant that freeways had to cut through cohesive neighborhoods, well, so much the worse for those communities. Some things need to be sacrificed in the name of that most powerful of all modern myths, the myth of progress. One cannot live in New York City without confronting the worldview, together with its urban symbols, of Robert Moses. Marshall Berman says that "his work still surrounds us, and his spirit continues to haunt our public and private lives." Mourning the loss of his own neighborhood, Berman says that he "felt a grief that, I can see now, is endemic to modern life. . . . All that is solid melts into air."[40] Not to

40. Marshall Berman, *All That Is Solid Melts Into Air* (New York: Simon and Schuster, 1982), pp. 294-95.

put too fine a point on the matter, Robert Moses's vision of the city rendered Berman and many other New Yorkers homeless.

What happened in New York has been repeated around the world to varying degrees. If houses are constructs rooted in worldview, what happens when the structures of the built environment change and people of a community find themselves in an alien built environment, one that is not only very different from what they are used to but, even more devastatingly, undermines their own worldview? What happens if they find themselves in housing that not only tells a story that is alien to their own but seems destructive of their most foundational narrative? They will feel groundless, out of touch, disoriented, and homeless. In short, they will suffer from a worldview crisis.

Consider the recent research on Samoan migrations from their island homes to city life in Hawaii. Like the Anishinaabe and other indigenous peoples around the world, Samoan life is deeply embedded in kinship relationships and responsibilities that go far beyond the immediate family and even blood ties. A traditional Samoan village has a concentric structure revolving around the *malae*, the sacred ground in the center; a secondary ring of houses *(fale)* with a large guest house near the center; a chief's house *(maota)* that would command a view of the wider village; and then other smaller huts and cook houses radiating out from that center. The wall-less construction of Samoan houses, together with the open public nature of the central *malae*, creates a culture of oversight and supervision. Indeed, the young unmarried men and women sleep in different places under the watchful eye of the whole community, but especially of the chief and his wife. There is here "a kind of collective strategy for controlling behavior by providing an audience for it, an audience whose approval mattered a great deal to the performers."[41]

Traditional Samoan life transpires in a public arena. What we North Americans call private life is strongly discouraged or is circumscribed both by the absence of walls and by powerful norms of social life that keep people in constant social interaction. In contrast to the walled houses of the Europeans *(palagi)*, the primary feeling in a traditional

41. Robert Franco and Simeamativa Mageo Aga, "From Houses without Walls to Vertical Villages: Samoan Housing Transformations," in Jan Rensel and Margaret Rodman, eds., *Home in the Islands: Housing and Social Change in the Pacific* (Honolulu: University of Hawaii Press, 1997), p. 179.

Samoan village is openness, movement between houses, and shared space.

What happens if the very symbolism of the wall-less house is taken away and a young Samoan is removed from her community? If she lives in a two-bedroom apartment in a sixteen-story public-housing complex in Hawaii, where does she look? Where will she receive instruction and support as a parent? Who will even see her if she is in difficulty? And with walls all around her, where will her gaze rest? Without open discourse among neighbors, where will she hear the stories that will make her life meaningful and give her a perspective from which to understand the world? Most likely her gaze will be directed at the television set. "The television targets individual attention away from the broader social interaction of the *malae* and disrupts normal patterns of family communication and socialization. Within the *palagi*-style living rooms, the television is the focal point of an implicitly identified viewing area. . . ."[42] As if the transfer from a village without walls to a boxed-in apartment wasn't enough to assault her identity and threaten her worldview, the television confronts her with an alien vision of life: alternative narratives shape her grounding story and memories differently, and commercials capture her children's imaginations with images that go far beyond the images they would have encountered at the *malae*.

What are the consequences of this change in built environment, this shift in way of life from the *malae* to the city? This woman is sheltered, but she has been made fundamentally homeless. And without that home-making context of shared worldview and community life, things begin to fall apart for the Samoan diaspora. Young mothers who always had role models around them for the discipline of their children are at a loss: they are alone and have no social supports. And young men, used to being together but under the watchful eye of the village, especially the chief, still need to be together, but now it is in the destructive form of Samoan youth gangs. It's not New York, but the result is the same: all that is solid melts into air.

It is true that humans are incredibly adaptable creatures and their traditions and worldviews demonstrate rich flexibility.[43] But sadly, there are

42. Franco and Aga, "From Houses without Walls," p. 181.

43. Indeed, there are interesting examples of precisely this kind of adaptability within the Samoan community in New Zealand; see Cluny Macpherson, "A Samoan Solution to the Limitations of Urban Housing in New Zealand," in Rensel and Rodman, *Home in the Islands*.

too many stories of cultural domicide for us to ignore the way this adaptability often meets its limit when a community's worldview is assaulted on so many levels. We are not arguing that there is something "timeless" about indigenous culture. All culture is historical and subject to change. But not all cultures and worldviews embrace change in the same way. Aboriginal culture is neither static nor as enamored with the speed of change as is a modernist worldview.[44] Combine different sensibilities around time and change with an alien built environment, and the resulting experience of homelessness is not surprising.

Housing for Homemaking

This chapter has examined stories of homelessness amidst indigenous peoples. In the case of both the Grassy Narrows resettlement and the Samoan diaspora in Hawaii, people were "housed" in such a way that made them homeless. That experience of "housed homelessness," we have argued, is intimately connected to issues of worldview. In both of these cases, the housing was provided by a public agency. While we may question the motives behind the forced relocations of the past, and also question the wisdom of one-size-fits-all approaches to housing, we should assume that the providers of housing for the most vulnerable in our midst want to develop alternatives to the alienating, stigmatizing, and ghettoizing failures of public housing. Public housing agencies are committed to providing "adequate" housing; but one of this chapter's important conclusions is that adequate housing must be housing for homemaking. We must take care not to have too narrow an understanding of "adequate housing," where we provide forms of housing that shelter certain populations while stripping them of home.

We have argued that, while generic housing appears to be without any reference to worldview, in fact it proclaims loud and clear that this is the housing of a modernist worldview, and it is imposed on people for whom this housing could be nothing but demoralizing, debilitating, and dispiriting. Such housing, modeled on standardized designs and built with indus-

---

44. For further reflection on the relationship of time, change, and worldviews, especially in a modernist and postmodernist cultural context, see Jeremy Rifkin, *Time Wars: The Primary Conflict in Human History* (New York: Touchstone Books, 1987).

trial efficiency, is culturally insensitive to various populations that are in need of public housing. And while we may question whether this kind of generic modernism can ever satisfy the human longing for home even for modernists, the evidence is overwhelming that such standardized housing certainly inhibits homemaking for those who do not share a modernist worldview.[45] This analysis of the relationship between worldviews and homemaking suggests that responsible housing policy needs to take seriously the divergent worldviews of the target population.

International organizations such as the United Nations recognize adequate housing as a right. But if we expand our definition of adequacy beyond basic shelter, then perhaps we need to think of the right to not just housing, but to home. And if it is indeed the case that the experience of home has something to do with the integrality of housing and worldview, then housing policy would need to begin to reflect the pluralistic cultural context in which we construct our built environment. In this light, worldview-sensitive housing is a matter of social justice committed to a principled pluralism that both protects worldview diversity and encourages people to live integral lives that holistically reflect their grounding narratives, moral orders, and symbols.[46]

Finally, worldview-sensitive housing is committed to hospitality. This means that such housing is developed in the context of broader concerns for the common good, civility, and neighborliness. This is housing that respects the homemaking sensitivities of our neighbors and strives for communities in which our neighbors' differences are known, welcomed, celebrated, and given real space in the shaping of our shared built environment. However, we will not see a housing for homemaking emerge in a totalitarian economy that breeds homelessness. What we need is an economics for homemaking.

45. One of the central claims of the "new urbanism" is that the housing quintessentially symbolized in the modern suburb does not provide a rich enough architectural or social context for homemaking. See James Howard Kunstler, *The Geography of Nowhere: The Rise and Decline of America's Man-Made Landscape* (New York: Simon and Schuster, 1993).

46. For helpful reflection on pluralism, see Sander Griffioen and Richard Mouw, *Pluralisms and Horizons: An Essay in Christian Public Philosophy* (Grand Rapids: Eerdmans, 1993).

Economics for Homemaking

As we have seen, ours is a culture of disconnection. And the disconnectedness spawned by individualism and privatization has eroded what was already the weak social fabric of a liberal culture and its welfare-state social policies. A culture of disconnection to one's neighbor is a culture with a weakened sense of the common good and a diminished sense of public responsibility. It is a culture, to use Bourdieu's terms, that has a *habitus* not strong enough to insist on sufficient habitation for all. Therefore, it's clear that we need more than a "technical fix" to address the crisis of homelessness in our time. The demise of the welfare state, together with the contradiction of rising economies paralleled by rising rates of homelessness and poverty, have laid bare a deeper crisis at the heart of our culture. The crisis of homelessness in our time is a spiritual crisis that is rooted in the spiritual captivity of our culture to an understanding of economic life that is, at its heart, idolatrous.[47] Any *habitus* for habitation, any renewed sense of public responsibility, any genuine homemaking will need to abandon that idolatrous understanding of economic life and embrace an economics for homemaking.

Wendell Berry sharpens the issues for us by distinguishing between two kinds of economy:

> There is the kind of economy that exists to protect the "right" of profit, as does our present public economy; this sort of economy will inevitably gravitate toward the protection of the "rights" of those who profit most. Our present public economy is really a political system that safeguards the private exploitation of the public wealth and health. The other kind of economy exists for the protection of gifts . . . and this is the economy of community, which now has nearly been destroyed by the public economy.[48]

The "rights of profit" or the "protection of gifts"? The "private exploitation of public wealth" or "the economy of community"? Which is more likely to

---

47. On the idolatry of "economism," see Brian Walsh, *Subversive Christianity: Imaging God in a Dangerous Time* (Seattle: Alta Vista College Press, 1994); see also Bob Goudzwaard, *Aid for the Overdeveloped West* (Toronto: Wedge Publishing, 1975), ch. 2.

48. Wendell Berry, *Sex, Economy, Freedom and Community* (New York: Pantheon, 1993), p. 138. See also Berry's essay "Two Economies," in his book *Home Economics* (New York: North Point Press, 1987), pp. 54-75.

safeguard the "rights of the homeless"? Which is more likely to have a social ethic that would protect the most vulnerable in the community?

The contrast between these two kinds of economies has profound parallels in the Bible. Walter Brueggemann contrasts a "royal/urban" economy with a "covenantal/prophetic" economy. The "royal/urban" perspective "affirmed that the 'haves' are entitled to have, whether the haves are the king, the nobles, the wealthy landowners, or the managers of legitimated bureaucracy." Since "possession gives legitimacy," those who have possession of resources like land, wealth, and housing will then "construct social values and social procedures as well as law so that the haves may have and legitimately seek more."[49] Sounds like the neoconservatism of our own day.

But, says Brueggemann, there is an alternative economic vision found in biblical faith. A covenantal/prophetic perspective "holds that the haves and the have-nots are bound in community to each other, that viable life depends upon the legitimate respect, care, and maintenance of the have-nots and upon the restraint of the haves so that the needs and rights of the disadvantaged take priority over the yearnings of the advantaged" (pp. 276-77). There is nothing naïve or romantic about this economic vision. Classical economic theory is correct: humans are self-interested, indeed, deeply selfish creatures. But rather than take that as a normative given for economic life, a biblical vision responds to such selfishness by prioritizing the needs of the poor and restraining the acquisitive appetites of the rich. Otherwise, the poor will always be oppressed, and the rich will continue to rule with an agenda of privatization and legal structures that protect their rights of profit. Against such privatization, a covenantal/prophetic vision of economic life "regards property as a resource for the common good, as a vehicle for the viability of a whole society, as the arena for the development of public responsibility and public compassion." And when responsibility and compassion become public, they take the shape of justice.

Justice rooted in compassion and public responsibility for the common good is what a biblical economic vision is all about.[50] Wendell Berry says: "By 'economy' I do not mean 'economics,' which is the study of money-making, but rather the ways of human house-keeping, the ways in which the

---

49. Walter Brueggemann, "Reflections on Biblical Understandings of Property," in *A Social Reading of the Old Testament* (Minneapolis: Fortress, 1994), pp. 276-77.

50. See Gerald Vandezande, *Justice, Not Just Us: Faith Perspectives and National Priorities* (Toronto: Public Justice Resource Centre, 1999).

human household is situated and maintained within the household of nature."[51] This is a view of economic life that is rooted in the most ancient meaning of the very word *economy*. The Greek word *oikonomia* has to do with the "rules" *(nomos)* of the "household" *(oikos)*. *Oikonomia* "means the management *(nomos)*, or care exercised by the economist, or steward *(oikonomos)*, for the household *(oikos)* and for that within it that is entrusted to him."[52] Will the household be managed in such a way that public resources are developed and shared to the benefit and livelihood of all members of the household?[53] Only such a household is considered to be a good economy; only such a household is obeying the rules of the household.

Within such a vision, getting one's "fiscal house in order" *means* protecting all the members of the household and making the household fruitful so that all can benefit. Indeed, Douglas Meeks wisely notes that "the conditions that exclude some from the household distort the life of all those who are already in the household."[54] If people experience good economic life under the norms of inclusion, welcome, and justice, then economic structures that exclude and oppress people erode the very foundations of all economic life. Whether we are talking about the thin and shallow moral foundation of liberalism or the myopic faith in the market of neoconservatism, the result will be the same: both poor and rich will live distorted, broken, and constricted economic lives. Furthermore, in important respects, we all will be rendered homeless.

Oikonomia provides us with a *habitus* for habitation, and "care" is at the heart of such a *habitus*. Goudzwaard and de Lange describe liberalism as a "post-care" society. An economics for homemaking, however, would

51. Berry, *Sex, Economy, Freedom, and Community*, p. 99.

52. Bob Goudzwaard and Harry de Lange, *Beyond Poverty and Affluence: Toward an Economy of Care* (Grand Rapids: Eerdmans, 1995), p. 56; see also Goudzwaard and Leo Andringa, *Globalization and Christian Hope* (Toronto: Public Justice Resource Centre, 2003), p. 13. Ross Kinsler and Gloria Kinsler comment that *oikos*, or *oikia*, "refers not just to the physical house but also the home, the family, the belongings, the household and all its inhabitants" (*The Biblical Jubilee and the Struggle for Life* [Maryknoll, NY: Orbis, 1999], p. 66).

53. Such a question is at the heart of Herman Daly and John Cobb's economic theories in *For the Common Good: Redirecting the Economy Toward Community, the Environment, and a Sustainable Future* (Boston: Beacon Press, 1989), esp. in ch. 7, where they contrast "chrematistics" (economy driven by self-interest, greed, and short-term gain) with "oikonomia" (an economics for community, sustainability, and justice).

54. M. Douglas Meeks, *God the Economist: The Doctrine of God and Political Economy* (Minneapolis: Fortress Press, 1989), p. 43.

be a "pre-care economy" that reverses the relationship between economic growth and care for the most vulnerable by prioritizing justice over narrowly defined notions of economic efficiency.

> In an economy of care, economic needs or ends include more than what the output of production can satisfy. They also include what human culture needs to survive: the level of care required for the environment to remain fertile; the amount of care needed to sustain communities, so that people's care for each other will acquire continuity and tradition; and adequate care for employment opportunities and the quality of work.[55]

A pre-care economy is rooted in an "economics of enough" that makes economic forces serve people, not the other way around.[56] This is a worldview that considers justice, compassion, community, good work, and ecological responsibility as points of departure for economic life, not as (necessary) afterthoughts. That is a pre-care, not a post-care, understanding of economic life.

If economic life is all about fruitful and inclusive households, then ensuring that everyone has the opportunity to participate in the household is foundational. The reason we need social policies that will guarantee to everyone an adequate income, secure housing, equal access to healthcare, clean air and potable water, basic education, and a genuine opportunity for meaningful employment is not because the economy is a tightrope and we need to have safety nets for those who fall; rather, it is because the economy is a household that demonstrates its health only in its care for all its members.

Clearly, housing is crucial to such care, and a household — that is, an economy — that cannot find ways to house its members is a household that transgresses its most basic norms. In a powerful article entitled "Housing Comes First," Ed Loring argues that housing is absolutely essential in human life.[57] Reflecting the context of his ministry on the streets of Atlanta, Loring argues that housing precedes employment because you can't hold down a decent job without secure housing. Housing also precedes sobriety, because the despair of homelessness will often need alcohol or drugs to numb the pain. Housing precedes education, because you can't do your homework sitting in a shelter or on a park bench. And housing

---

55. Goudzwaard and de Lange, *Beyond Poverty and Affluence,* p. 87.
56. Goudzwaard and de Lange, *Beyond Poverty and Affluence,* p. 64.
57. Ed Loring, "Housing Comes First," *The Other Side* (May/June 2002): 32-33.

precedes both physical and mental health, because homelessness is a breeding ground for disease, and it makes you go crazy.[58] Housing is an absolutely essential precondition for human health and well-being.

Rights, Public Policy, and the Church

If it is true that housing comes first, then an economy of care insists that housing is a human right. Just as a member of any family has a right to the protection of life and to sustenance and care within that family, so do all members of that broader household of a society's economy have the right to housing. Article 25 of the Universal Declaration of Human Rights, proclaimed by the United Nations on December 10, 1948, declares:

> Everyone has the right to a standard of living adequate for the health and well-being of himself and of his family, including food, clothing, housing and medical care and necessary social services, and the right to security in the event of unemployment, sickness, disability, widowhood, old age or other lack of livelihood circumstances beyond his control.[59]

Moreover, the United Nations Committee on Economic, Social and Cultural Rights said in 1999 that a state violates these rights to adequate housing when there is a "general decline in living and housing conditions, directly attributable to policy and legislative decisions by States parties, and in the absence of accompanying compensatory measures. . . ."[60] Canada, the United States, and other industrialized nations, precisely those nations that have the economic ability to secure such foundational hu-

---

58. Loring also argues that housing precedes evangelization because "no church ought to call someone to accept Jesus Christ until it is ready to bring that person into a house and assist in the arduous task of making that house into a home" (p. 33). He concludes that "housing precedes the justice struggle" (p. 33) because the homeless cannot be expected to harness the energy to advocate for justice when they are expending all of their energy with the daily business of survival at its most basic level.

59. Cited in *State of Emergency Declaration: An Urgent Call for Emergency Humanitarian Relief and Prevention Measures* (Toronto Disaster Relief Committee, 1998), p. 1. See http://www.tao.ca/~tcrc/Booklet.htm#Booklet_on_State_of_Emergency. This document also cites the "International Covenant of Economic, Social and Cultural Rights of 1966, which also identifies housing as such a right.

60. Cited in *State of Emergency Declaration*, p. 11.

man rights, are in clear violation of the United Nations Declaration of Human Rights.

An economy of care is concerned about housing rights not just because such a right ensures access to the essentials for living, but because the protection of such rights ensures that all members of the household have the room to exercise their responsibilities as members.[61] Without a secure home, one has little ability to participate in society. People who have "no fixed address" have no way to make a contribution to that household. As Jim Ward puts it, "Homelessness is more than a lack of shelter: it is powerlessness and lack of control over one's life."[62] While the neoconservatives' foundational absolutizing of market forces proclaims that all is done in the name of freedom — free markets, free consumers, free business enterprises — the result of such an economy, as we have seen, is enslavement. In sharp contrast, an economy of care recognizes that freedom is for responsibility and service, not self-interest and personal wealth. Such freedom is possible only where common resources are protected, social rights are ensured, and care is the foundation of the economic household.

Rights need to be protected, and while it is the responsibility of all people and all societal institutions to ensure that rights are protected, it is also true that government has an important and unique legal role to play in protecting such rights. That is why governments signed the United Nations Declaration of Human Rights, not individuals or religious institutions or charitable organizations. But when governments adopt policies rooted in blind faith in the market and the legitimation of a growing gap between rich and poor, those governments commit sins of both omission (failing to protect these rights) and commission (following policies that will trample on the rights of the poor). The homelessness crisis has its origins in flawed public policy, and so it will be resolved only if better public

61. Our understanding of social rights and responsibilities is indebted to the "Charter of Social Rights and Responsibilities" of the Ottawa-based Canadian Christian political advocacy organization Citizens for Public Justice. This charter is available on its website: http://www.cpj.ca.

62. Jim Ward, *Organizing for the Homeless* (Ottawa: Canada Council on Social Development, 1989), p. 5 (cited in Marlene Webber, *Street Kids: The Tragedy of Canada's Runaways* [Toronto: University of Toronto Press, 1991], p. 138). Václav Havel says that homes are "an inseparable element of our human identity. Deprived of all aspects of his home, man would be deprived of himself, of his humanity" (*Summer Meditations* [Toronto: Knopf, 1992], pp. 30-31; cited by Daly, *Homeless*, p. 149).

policy is enacted. If it is impossible for a person making the minimum wage to rent an apartment, we must increase the minimum wage to become a living wage. If the waiting lists for affordable housing are getting longer and longer, we must build more affordable housing. If the housing industry is uninterested or unable to develop affordable rental housing, nonprofit organizations and housing co-ops must do the job. If the poor who manage to get into public housing are stuck there, we must develop programs to enable the working poor to actually buy housing at affordable rates with mortgage assistance.

If the poor are burdened more than the affluent are when sickness hits the family, we must develop a universal healthcare program. If the working poor are stuck in low-paying service-industry jobs with no prospect of advancement, we must establish creative educational and job-training programs. If welfare recipients find it necessary to go to food banks in order to feed their children, we must increase welfare payments. If "urban renewal" is displacing the poor, we must design urban plans that will not use "mixed housing" as a euphemism for displacement. If buildings are falling down, public transit is inadequate, and roads are dangerous in the inner city, we must provide funding for infrastructure renewal and give some jobs to the jobless of the community.

If inner-city schools are underfunded, we must insist on educational justice. If poor neighborhoods are underserved when it comes to libraries, parks, and recreational programs for the children, we must build libraries, develop parks, and offer programs for the "disadvantaged" children. If municipalities are stymied in their attempts to address poverty and homelessness by the agitations of "not-in-my-back-yard" neighborhood groups who oppose any affordable housing in their areas, we must appeal to national and international charters of rights to rule such folks out of order.[63]

Our point here is not to provide a shopping list of things that we think government needs to do. Rather, we are simply saying that policy options are available that can respond to real suffering, genuine injustice, and repeated violation of the rights of the poor, rights that our governments have acknowledged. There is no lack of creative proposals for the problems that beset us.

---

63. In Toronto, HomeComing is a coalition of supportive housing providers who have developed a creative booklet, entitled *Yes, in My Back Yard* (Nov. 2003), which suggests strategies to deal with the debilitating and community-destroying forces of Nimbyism ("not-in-my-back-yard").

We often hear two responses to these kinds of proposals. First, people often tell us to get in touch with reality: there is nothing "realistic" about our proposals, they argue. To which we ask, "Whose reality?" We agree with how Goudzwaard and de Lange put it: "We consider it unrealistic and even illusory to think that the economy can simply continue to develop along its current, antiquated patterns, while we remain oblivious to the consequences for people and the environment."[64] Reality looks quite different depending on whether you are a parent trying to decide whether to pay the rent or feed the kids, or a venture capitalist considering your portfolio over a glass of single-malt scotch. An economy of care, an ethos of public good, chooses to view reality from the perspective of the most vulnerable.

Second, people often reply that we are giving the "state" too much power and responsibility. Government is not — or should not be — in the business of healthcare or housing or social welfare, they argue. On one level, we agree. Government should not be "in business" at all! Instead, government has the responsibility to protect the common good. And just as all governments recognize that such protection entails ensuring the security of the population by police and military forces, so also, we argue, must governments ensure that the common good is protected via public policies that safeguard the rights of the poor. The policies we listed above amount to using public resources (tax dollars, public land, public healthcare, public spaces, and so on) for the public good. Or to put it in terms of an economy of care, these are policies that attempt to make sure that the household is a place of inclusion and not exclusion, for the benefit and fruitfulness of the whole.[65]

Of course, some will still say, "Been there, done that. This is just the tired old liberal rhetoric of the welfare state all over again." If we have learned anything from the demise of the welfare state, they will argue, it is that government is not a very good provider of most public services — and certainly not housing! Doesn't the disaster of the "projects" teach us that the government should stay out of housing? Well, no and yes. No, it doesn't follow that, because government has not done its job in housing very well, it should get out of housing. In fact, if we were going to follow

64. Goudzwaard and de Lange, *Beyond Poverty and Affluence*, p. 122.
65. Goudzwaard and de Lange offer a "Twelve Step Program for Economic Recovery" that offers suggestive proposals for the shape that such an economy of care might take (*Beyond Poverty and Affluence*, ch. 8).

that logic, we could advance arguments that government should get out of national security as well. What would we call the Vietnam War and the war in Iraq if not evidence of the U.S. government's incompetence in running an effective military? No one is making these kinds of arguments about the military budget.

But yes, there is something to the argument that says that large centralized bureaucracies on either national or local levels tend to fail rather miserably in providing the kinds of services that would be entailed in the policies listed above. And housing is indeed a glaring example of the ineptitude of such government bureaucracies.[66] But it also seems clear that the for-profit housing market will not develop enough affordable housing. This is why we suggested above that public resources need to be made available to nonprofit and co-op housing corporations, equipping them to do the job locally that government bureaucracy has proven less competent to do.[67]

Is there room, then, for increased emphasis on "faith-based initiatives" in addressing the homelessness crisis? Again, our answer is yes and no. Yes, faith communities must be involved in addressing this crisis. Whether they do it by investing in affordable housing through a pension fund,[68] supporting Habitat for Humanity,[69] or actually being involved in the production of affordable housing, faith communities have a role to play. And there is much to be said about partnering the resources of faith communities with public funds to bring about a public good. But faith communities need to be careful about any administration's emphasis on "faith-based

66. Kimberly Dovey argues that "the more that the production, control, and maintenance of home environments is dependent upon bureaucratic organization, then the more this organization both erodes and paralyzes the emergence of the experience of home." And where that experience is eroded, social breakdown and disrespect of the built environment is close behind ("Home and Homelessness," in I. Altman and C. Werner, eds., *Home Environments* [New York: Plenum Books, 1985], p. 55).

67. See James C. Scott, *Seeing Like a State: How Certain Schemes to Improve the Human Condition Have Failed* (New Haven: Yale University Press, 1998).

68. The General Board of Pension and Health Benefits of the United Methodist Church in the United States has an investment portfolio in affordable housing that has reached $1 billion. See *Sharing the Dream: A Place to Call Home.* Accessible online at http://www.gbophb.org/news/features/affhous/.

69. See Millard Fuller, *A Simple, Decent Place to Live: The Building Realization of Habitat for Humanity* (Dallas: Word, 1995). For an exciting story of Habitat for Humanity's housing transformation of the Sandtown community of Baltimore, see Mark Gornik's *To Live in Peace,* esp. ch. 5

initiatives" as a cover for a retreat from public responsibility. It is precisely this kind of retreat that has characterized the neoconservative movement in North America in recent years, and it has been a significant contributing factor to homelessness. In the face of an agenda of privatization that will prioritize profit over people, capital growth over community, and charity over compassionate justice, we need to insist that these matters "concerning our common polis require the involvement of political institutions."[70]

Wendell Berry offers us a sober warning. Recognizing that "the global economy does not exist to help the communities and localities of the globe," but rather "exists to siphon the wealth of those communities and places into a few bank accounts," Berry says that "those who wish to help communities to survive had better understand that a merely political freedom means little within a totalitarian economy."[71] And that is the heart of the issue. An economic worldview that is rooted in the rights of profit (which amounts to the rights of the most powerful and affluent) is a totalitarian economy in which the lives of all are determined by the aspirations and economic control of a few. The individualism of this worldview will necessarily result in homelessness not just because it can sustain no ethos of public responsibility and neighborly care, but also because such individualism destroys community when it is institutionalized in systems of economic control. Concluding that "the triumph of the industrial economy is the fall of community," Berry adds:

> But the fall of community reveals how precious and how necessary community is. For when community falls, so must all the things that only community life can engender and protect: the care of the old, the

70. Gornick, *To Live in Peace*, p. 228. Gornik offers a fair and incisive critique of the Bush agenda on pp. 227-29.

71. Berry, *Sex, Economy, Freedom and Community*, p. 129. In another place, Berry says: "That this economic system persists and grows larger and stronger in spite of its evident failure has nothing to do with rationality or, for that matter, with evidence. It persists because, embodied now in multinational corporations, it has discovered a terrifying truth: If you can control a people's economy, you don't need to worry about its politics; its politics have become irrelevant. If you control people's choices as to whether or not they will work, and where they will work, and what they will do, and how well they will do it, and what they will eat and wear, and the genetic makeup of their crops and animals, and what they will do for amusement, then why should you worry about freedom of speech? In a totalitarian economy, any 'political liberties' that the people might retain would simply cease to matter" (*Another Turn of the Crank* [Washington, DC: Counterpoint, 1995], p. 34).

care and education of children, family life, neighborly work, the handing down of memory, the care of the earth, respect for nature and the lives of wild creatures. (p. 133)

Such a failure of community, in the broad sense in which Berry describes it, is a necessary consequence of an economy that places economic growth, efficiency, and "freedom" over the care, respect, and compassion that is foundational to any healthy economic household.[72]

More than Bricks and Mortar

An economy of care is an economy for homemaking because it has a broad understanding of who is in the economic household and what a just stewardship of such a household entails. Thus it seeks to protect the right to adequate housing for all and seeks to foster housing that makes for home. This is an economy for homemaking. In contrast, the individualism of a free-market economy is destructive of community in two ways: it engages in economic development that prioritizes the bottom line of profits over the needs of any particular community, and this worldview's individualistic ethos knows nothing of the character and importance of community in human life.[73] This is an economy of homelessness.

In a previous chapter we argued that a sense of community is necessary if one is to experience any place as home. If people never meet on the sidewalk or on the bus because all transportation is by car, then the neighborhood will lack a sense of home. And if the buildings are ugly and imposing, if there is no connection between the buildings and the street, if there is no sense of historical continuity to the architecture, the neighborhood will lack a sense of home. If there is no protection of the local ecology, no local coffee shops or grocery stores (i.e., not part of a chain) or farmer's market, the neighborhood will lack a sense of home. Therefore,

---

72. "The ideal of 'limitless economic growth' is based on the obsessive and fearful conviction that more is always needed. The growth is maintained by the consumers' panic-stricken suspicion, since they always want more, that they will never have enough" (Berry, *The Gift of Good Land* [New York: North Point Press, 1981], p. 169).

73. The classic study of individualism in America is Robert Bellah et al., *Habits of the Heart: Individualism and Commitment in American Life* (Berkeley: University of California Press, 1985).

simply providing shelter does not constitute an economy for home-making. While it is absolutely crucial, housing that only provides security from the elements but fails to engender social, emotional, and psychological security can only result in a deeply diminished experience of home. Beyond refuge, home provides security, status, pride, self-respect, roots, privacy, and respite.[74] Housing does indeed "come first": there is no possibility of homemaking apart from secure housing. But an economy of homemaking is not satisfied with the mere provision of shelter.

So home is more than bricks and mortar. As Mark Gornik reminds us, "seeking the peace of the inner city . . . enjoins activity that enhances the social, physical, aesthetic, and economic world in which we dwell."[75] A single mother living on the fourteenth floor of a public housing apartment with three kids, little income, no friends or extended family, and tensions with the neighbors because the baby has colic, will have a hard time feeling that this is her home. If that high-rise is in an urban wasteland with no green space or parks, and is characterized by the ugliness that was the architectural style for so much of the last half-century, that physical and aesthetic impoverishment simply adds to her sense of being homeless. More than bricks and mortar, home includes community gardens and little-league baseball, neighborhood celebrations and art exhibits, dancing in the park and religious communities, learning centers and social clubs. Home is a place where families are raised, the elderly are respected, and the vulnerable are cared for. Home is where you have some sense of control over your communal identity and destiny. An economy of care seeks to engender and protect these various ways of homemaking.

While socioeconomic homelessness is a devastatingly painful dimension of the pervasive cultural crisis we are addressing, it is not the only form of homelessness. We must now expand the scope of our analysis and move from a discussion of socioeconomic homelessness to an examination of ecological homelessness. A homemaking economy of care is only possible within the broader context of an ecology of care. For, as Thoreau asks rhetorically, "What is the use of a house if you haven't got a tolerable planet to put it on?"[76]

74. Daly, *Homeless*, p. 149.

75. Gornik, *To Live in Peace*, p. 120.

76. Henry David Thoreau, *The Writings of Henry David Thoreau*, vol. VI, *Familiar Letters*, ed. F. B. Sanborn, enl. ed. (Boston and New York: Houghton Mifflin, 1906), p. 360. Thanks to Angela Emerson and Bill Pannapacker for tracking this down.

Homemaking in the Ruins

Isaiah 58

When it came right down to it, the center did not hold. What was the Temple if not the very center of the world? The very house of God? If that doesn't hold, nothing will. Not the monarchy, not the social order, not the legal structures, not the economy. If the house of God cannot be sustained, no house can be sustained. If God is homeless, we all are homeless. This was the crisis of exile. If the center does not hold, people are left with a profound identity crisis. What does it mean to be an Israelite, a child of Abraham, a covenant community, if there is no Temple, no monarchy, and no freedom to live out covenantal life on covenantal land?

The exiles of Judah were not rendered homeless simply by their forced removal to Babylon; they also remained deeply homeless when they returned to Jerusalem. With the major institutions gone and the city left in ruins, where was the homecoming? Where was the home to come back to? But the exiles had a lot of time to think while they were in Babylon. And from the vantage point of exile, they recalled the words of the prophets, words they had dismissed, words they had judged to be too harsh and too seditious to bear.

> Didn't the prophets say that our sin would bring this disaster upon us? And weren't they right? So, if the prophets were right about our sin, then how do we go about rebuilding our lives after our sentence has been served? We suffered from covenantal amnesia. We forgot the covenant, forgot the God who set us free from Egypt, and we disobeyed Torah in our idolatry. So if we are to rebuild our lives in fidelity, we must be a people of remembering. But what do we remember, and how do we remember it? Well, we need to remember our sin, and a time-honored way to do that would be through fasting.

And so the returned exiles engaged in fasts of remembrance. Specifically, they instituted fasts in mournful memory of the destruction of the Temple and the loss of the monarchy. The intent of all this fasting — this piety — was clear. They wanted to be a people of righteousness. They wanted to delight in the ways of God, to experience anew the presence of the Holy One in their midst, to renew covenant in faithfulness. They fasted because they wanted to rebuild their lives in the land of covenant. They wanted to come back to Jerusalem and rebuild home in the midst of its ruins.

But the prophet wasn't impressed — on two counts. First, he told them that fasting was a quick fix, a cheap grace, because it was a spiritual discipline empty of a comprehensive covenantal renewal. That is, fasting coupled with communal violence (quarreling, strife, and striking each other) and economic oppression (the exploitation of workers) was no piety at all. It may have looked like a path of renewed piety, but it was little more than a self-indulgent spirituality that changed little in the actual day-to-day lives of the people. The injustice, violence, and oppression that characterized Jerusalem before the exile still characterized communal life. Cultural practices that previously resulted in the homelessness of exile were not likely to provide a good foundation for homemaking in the ruins.

So, instead of this kind of empty piety, the prophet offered another option:

> Is this not the fast that I choose:
> to loose the bonds of injustice,
> to undo the thongs of the yoke,
> to let the oppressed go free,
> and to break every yoke?
> Is it not to share your bread with the hungry,
> and bring the homeless poor into your house;
> when you see the naked, to cover them,
> and not to hide yourself from your own kin?

Replace your introspective fasting, mourning, and paralyzing malaise with action, he is saying. This is the kind of fast, the kind of spiritual discipline, that is required of us. And Isaiah's language here goes beyond acts of benevolence, beyond acts of dutiful compassion and charity, to deal with structural realities as well. Sharing your bread with the hungry while not addressing the yoke that oppresses them actually makes you complicit in their oppression. So Isaiah carefully moves his rhetoric from loosening and untying the cords of injustice to setting free those who have been constricted by these cords, and then to taking the yokes — the very structures of oppression — and smashing them so that they can never be implements of oppression again. If we are to engage in a home-making that is worthy of the covenant, says Isaiah, our home must be a home of justice.

But Isaiah is up to something else in this oracle, something that is perhaps even more radical than this call to do justice. The issue for the returned exiles is how to rebuild home in the midst of the ruins of their former lives. They wisely acknowledge that life before the face of God requires that the covenant people be a community of memory. If it was forgetfulness that got them into this mess, then surely it will be a remembering that will put them back together again and provide the foundation for the making of home here.

So far, so good. But the question is, which memories? Which stories should the people remember? Isaiah clearly stands against a mournful fasting that would ensure that the Temple and the monarchy are not forgotten. Why? Because he doesn't think that these are very liberating memories. Indeed, to hark back to the good old days when God was safely domiciled in the Temple and the king lived safe and secure next door on his opulent throne would be to reintroduce an oppressive royal ideology of homelessness. As far as this prophet is concerned, you can forget the Temple and the monarchy.

Here is the prophet's second and even more profound point of contention with the community. Why live inside the future of a shattered past when there is a better past to remember, a set of memories that can more radically provide vision for a homecoming future?

Listen closely to Isaiah 58 and you will hear memories that are an alternative to the Temple and the monarchy. From the very first lines the prophet uses language that echoes the blowing of the trumpet on the Day of Atonement and the advent of the Jubilee year, language that recalls the only day of fasting actually commanded in the Torah.[77] Here is a fast of justice that is rooted in the deep Torah memories of Jubilee, one that is worth keeping because it requires setting the oppressed free. Here is a memory of homemaking because it requires the community to practice an economics of generosity and justice that insists we can shape a society of

---

77. On the Day of Atonement and the blowing of the trumpet, see Lev. 23:23-32; on the year of Jubilee, see Lev. 25:8-12.

homecoming only when the most vulnerable are provided the means and resources for homemaking.

When that is the kind of fast you keep and the kind of life you live, "then your light shall break like the dawn and your healing shall spring up quickly," because then "your vindicator shall go before you, the glory of the Lord will be your rear guard."

At this point the prophet moves from Torah memories of Jubilee back to Exodus images. When was the glory of the Lord your rear guard, but in the Exodus? And this image of returned glory could not be more different from the hope of a returning of the glory of the Lord to bless and re-consecrate the Temple. Here is a more dynamic memory of sojourning with God in the wilderness. Here is a memory of homemaking with God in a context that was distinctly inhospitable to habitation; but because the glory was their rear guard, life could be secure with the covenanting God. If home is rooted in remembering, then the memory of Exodus, when the homemaking God set free the captives from imperial homelessness and miraculously made a home with them in the uninhabitable space of the wilderness, is a memory that is foundational to covenantal homecoming.

Then the prophet evokes a third memory: if you follow a life of justice, if you offer your food to the hungry, then the Lord will satisfy your needs in parched places (an Exodus image again), "and you shall be like a watered garden, like a spring of water, whose waters shall never fail." A watered garden? What might that refer to? Certainly sounds like the Garden of Eden, doesn't it? What is your most primordial memory of being at home with God in the world? When was home like a well-watered garden, a source of fresh sustenance every day, all day? At the dawn of creation. At the beginning of our story of homemaking with a garden-planting God.

Jubilee, Exodus, and Creation — these are the covenantal memories of homemaking, says Isaiah. If you root your communal life in these stories,

> Your ancient ruins shall be rebuilt;
> you shall raise up the foundations of many generations;
> you shall be called the repairer of the breach,
> the restorer of streets to live in.

Rebuild your life on these stories, says Isaiah, and the streets will be secure enough for dwelling. Only on the basis of these memories will we construct a city of homes, a city for people to feel at home in, a city where no one is hungry because we are nourished by the practice of justice, and where no one is thirsty because our thirst for righteousness has been met.

Given this kind of covenantal memory, this kind of interpretation of Israel's story, it is not surprising that the prophet ends with the Sabbath:

> If you refrain from trampling the sabbath,
> from pursuing your own interests on my holy day;
> if you call the sabbath a delight
> . . . then you shall take delight in the Lord,
> and I will make you ride upon the heights of the earth. . . .

In radical contrast to all homemaking rooted in autonomous self-construction and anxious labor, Sabbath proclaims that the world is a creational gift that nurtures an attitude of basic trust. Trust in such a gift, and deep trust in the Giver, frames all of our homemaking activities, for Sabbath insists that the world ultimately depends not on our striving but on God's generous, world-sustaining love. Moreover, Sabbath is a radically egalitarian ordering of time and culture that is the alternative to an unbridled acquisitiveness that exploits our neighbors. The Creator's generosity celebrated in Sabbath calls us to construct homes of generosity, dwellings of love.

The returned exiles had a lot of work to do. There was a whole world to reconstruct. In the midst of this anxious busyness, the prophet says, "Remember Sabbath." Remember that this land, this creation, this city, this heritage is most deeply to be received as a gift in the attitude of grateful trust. Only by receiving this world as a gift will we be able to make this world into a home that is worth having, a home of generosity and hospitality, a home of justice and love.

Jubilee, Exodus, Creation, Sabbath — embedded in these we find a narrative that is worth living in. Here is a story that engenders a way of living that can make a home amid the ruins. People who live out of these memories are called repairers of the breach, restorers of streets to live in.

Ecological Homelessness

Crowded isles face growing piles of trash.
Oceans in deep trouble: U.S. must help.
Small rise in global temperature creates big problems.

The class discussion was animated. The students, all of them second-semester college seniors, were alternately hopeful and despairing. The topic of the day: home — that is, the world we live in and the world that they, on the cusp of graduation, would soon enter in a new and different way.

"I grew up in Michigan," said Janet, "but my parents both grew up in Ohio, and so for a long time I felt like my second home was the house where my mother was raised. But last summer I lived and worked in the Boundary Waters, so I still feel the tug of the Gunflint Trail in the northern tip of Minnesota. And because I had a wonderful semester abroad in Aberdeen, and because of the people, culture, and natural beauty I found there, I have an irreversible emotional attachment to Scotland. It feels like home when I close my eyes and walk through the cobbled streets down to the rowing team's boathouse, or to the train station where so many adventures began. The attachment I feel to so many places does not decrease my liking for one place or another, but it does increase the feeling of a type of homelessness."

"What do you mean?" asked Ari.

"I say 'homeless' not in the sense of living on the streets below the poverty level, but in the emotional sense of a lack of geographic affinity. I still feel that my roots are in my parents' home, where I grew up, but I have lived in other places, and now I face a new challenge of moving several states away for grad school. I have to ask myself the question, What is a home?"

"I can relate to that," said Ari in response. "But my sense of homelessness comes from the mess we're in. I mean, look around. We are a broken people living in a broken world. And this brokenness is undeniable, even though we often fail to recognize all that brokenness until we are nearly buried by it. Creation seems so big and sturdy, but it really is made up of these incredibly intricate parts that are so very fragile and susceptible to harm. We have forgotten how to be gentle. We have lost our sense of awe and respect, and we have neglected to consider the future we are in the midst of creating. We have plundered and raped our Mother Earth, all the while expecting her to forgive and forget. But that's impossible. She is not immune to the wounds we cause. Nor is she easily cured by the remedies we concoct when those wounds become too large to ignore."

"But most environmental problems don't really affect us," said Kevin. "Sure, the earth is somewhat 'wounded,' as you put it, but the earth is resilient. Besides, every day we get better technologies to fix most of our problems."

"But you fail to realize," continued Ari, "that our health is inextricably linked to the health of our planet. We poison our bodies while we're poisoning the earth, and if we are not extremely careful, if we don't begin to make alterations in the way we live, we will certainly perish."

"Don't be melodramatic," interjected Jon. "We won't perish. Sure, we have some problems, but they're not that bad. People have made such half-baked claims before about the end of the world, and look where we are now. Lots of advances in medicine, faster computers, smaller cell phones. I call it progress."

"I have to disagree, Jon," responded Paul. "Evidence of our brokenness surrounds us. Just pick up a paper or watch the news. All you have to do is look around for a few seconds and you will see it. Violence, weapons of mass destruction, land disputes, extinction, greed, civil war, famine, theft, rape, murder — on and on it goes. Do you feel the heartache?"

Silence. Many minds thinking, no lips moving.

"We live in a world where money is power and peace is weakness," continued Paul after a pregnant pause. "We are completely and utterly broken. Here in America, children are raising themselves as they sit in front of the modern fireplace, the TV, which is fueled by the logs of CBS, MTV, and

HBO. Parenthood has been replaced by pop icons, teen role models. Video games and prime-time television have overtaken family dinners, and money-hungry investors have usurped the religious leaders of our day. We have lost our sense of home."

Many nodding heads seemed to indicate significant agreement with this claim. "Listen to this from the jacket of a CD by Moby," said Paul.

> By 'Everything is Wrong' I mean EVERYTHING. I look around me. I'm typing on a plastic and metal and glass computer perched on a desk made from cut down trees and toxic paint. I sit in a building made of wood and bricks that were taken from the Earth on a street made of poisonous asphalt that was laid over an ecosystem that had thrived for hundreds of thousands of years. I'm clothed in cotton that was saturated with pesticides while it grew and treated and dyed with toxic chemicals while it was being processed. All of my possessions were made hundreds or thousands of miles away and shipped in styrofoam and plastic wrap via gas burning engines and destructive road and air ways to me. My food, although organically grown and completely vegan, is shipped from where it was grown to my local store and is often packaged in paper, plastic, metal, and toxic inks. I know tons of people who eat meat, smoke cigarettes, drive cars, use drugs, etc. even though they know that these things will ultimately hurt the quality (and length) of their lives. I live in an apartment building where no one is on a first name basis. I know more about idiot actors in Hollywood that I've never met than I do about the woman who lives next door to me (and is probably more interesting). While walking to work I inhale toxic exhaust from cars sitting in traffic. To make sure that eating three cans of oven cleaner will make you sick, or to make sure that pouring nail polish remover into your eyes will hurt you, we torture mice, rabbits, dogs, cats, etc. We use toxic chlorine bleach to keep our underpants white. We cut down the rainforests to drill for oil so we can drive to the video store. Do you see what I mean? Everything really is wrong.[1]

With that onslaught of words from a bonafide member of the pop-culture crowd, the discussion came to a close.[2] The silence was palpable. Moby's

---

1. Moby, from *Everything Is Wrong* ©1995 Mute Records.

2. While the names have been changed, this discussion is based on actual student papers and conversations (used with permission). Reflecting the ambiguity and ambivalence

words rang all too true, sailing like a dart to the heart. "Everything is wrong." And if so, what then?

Clearly, for these young men and women there was a feeling that the world is not the way it's supposed to be. And our sense is that many people today, not just the twenty-somethings, feel in their bones that something is wrong. The world is amiss. The earth is amuck. We are feeling homeless on our home planet. Though we perhaps rarely acknowledge it, we feel as though our home is no longer fit for human habitation. Is this perception based in reality? What really is the plight of Planet Earth?

Not all is well in the world, ecologically speaking. Each morning's newspaper greets us with more unsettling news. The headlines cited at the beginning of this chapter are just the proverbial tip of the (melting) iceberg.[3] A solid-waste crisis threatens to overwhelm tiny islands in the Pacific, such as the Tarawa Atoll, where 3,400 U.S. Marines died or were wounded in four days during November 1943. Broken bottles and plastic bags now pile up on a beach once heaped with human bodies. Rubbish has nowhere to go on this alluring "tropical paradise." And on our water planet, pollution, overfishing, and housing developments threaten the health of the oceans. Despite their vast and seemingly endless bounty, the oceans are not limitless, nor are they capable of continual self-cleansing, at least not at a rate that will stay ahead of the rate at which we are polluting them. So we need "a major overhaul" of federal policy, concludes a 413-page report of the U.S. Commission on Ocean Policy.[4]

The third headline refers to global climate change. The evidence is clear: the earth is warming, we humans are causing it, and the consequences are momentous for more than a few of us. For example, if you are one of the 5,000 people who live on Funafuti, in the Pacific island country of Tuvalu, you have to be very concerned: the land beneath your feet is literally disappearing. The rising ocean is engulfing your home-

---

of this issue, one paper is entitled "Sad State of Homelessness" but is subtitled "Why Homelessness Is Not Necessarily Hopelessness."

3. These first two headlines are from the *Chicago Tribune,* April 21, 2004, and May 20, 2004. The third headline is from the *Holland Sentinel,* May 23, 2004. These three are but a small and random sample. There are articles on some ecological issue virtually every day in the newspapers.

4. See http://www.oceancommission.gov/documents/prelimreport/welcome.html. Another comprehensive picture of the state of the world's oceans can be found in *The New Internationalist* 339 (Jan.-Feb. 2007).

land, toppling trees and forming inland lakes from fingers of salt water. Where will you go when your homeland is underwater? Who will take you in? Pacific islanders are not the only ones worried about their future; rising oceans threaten people from Alaska to Shanghai. As the local paper puts it, a seemingly small rise in global temperature is causing very big problems.

Thoreau's question, cited at the end of the preceding chapter, is absolutely crucial: What is the use of a house if you haven't got a tolerable planet to put it on? Providing homes for the homeless has no point if our home planet is in peril. Addressing the pervasive and pressing issue of *socioeconomic* homelessness, important as that is, makes little sense if we do not address the equally pervasive and pressing issue of *ecological* homelessness. Moreover, ecological destruction has a disproportionate impact on the poorest of the world's population, and it compounds their experience of homelessness.

As should now be clear, there is, unfortunately, more than one kind of homelessness. And while "street-people homelessness" is perhaps the most obvious and well-studied kind of homelessness, ecological homelessness is also widespread, even if less well examined. But what exactly is this phenomenon that we call "ecological homelessness"? What does ecological degradation have to do with "home"? And what are its causes? How are we to understand this form of homelessness?

The Plight of Planet Earth

This is not the place to present in any comprehensive way the multitude of data on the state of the earth; other sources are more than adequate for that task.[5] But we must get some accurate and informed sense of the vital signs of the planet, a sense of the scope and contours of our ecological homelessness. A number of perceptive and well-traveled observers have

---

5. For example, see Steven Bouma-Prediger, *For the Beauty of the Earth* (Grand Rapids: Baker Academic, 2001), ch. 2. For more extensive data, see Bernard Nevel and Richard Wright, *Environmental Science: Toward a Sustainable Future,* 8th ed. (Upper Saddle River, NJ: Prentice Hall, 2002); see also the *Annual Review* and other publications from the World Resources Institute, or the latest *Vital Signs* or *State of the World* from the Worldwatch Institute.

commented recently on our common environmental future, and their works give us a promising place to start.

In his eye-opening and riveting book, journalist Robert Kaplan provides a firsthand survey of the world scene in order to "find a paradigm for understanding the world in the early decades of the twenty-first century."[6] While he affirms in *The Ends of the Earth* that his travels "showed me how culture, politics, geography, history, and economics were inextricable," he admits that he found no "grand theory" or overarching paradigm (p. 9). However, Kaplan did find — from West Africa to East Asia, from Anatolia to Cambodia — gut-wrenching poverty, unceasing warfare, inescapable crime, futility and famine, despotism and disease.

Kaplan also found massive evidence of ecological degradation virtually everywhere. Once lush African rainforests had turned to asphalt-like laterite. Once fertile Nile River valley soil had washed to the sea or was now too salty for crops to survive. A once healthy Azerbaijani city is now a lunar landscape of tar and oil, with soil and water and air so lethal that people speak of ecocide. The once breathable air of Tehran is now among the worst in the world. The once potable water of Uzbekistan is now too poisonous to drink, and the once available water of the Aral Sea is gone like a phantom in the night. Kaplan's description of China, given both its geographical and demographic size, is especially portentous:

> Among populous developing countries, only Egypt and Bangladesh have less arable land per person than China. . . . This situation is about to become dramatically worse as the population grows, soil erodes, and urban settlements and transportation networks expand onto agricultural land. . . . Artificial fertilizers have already pushed crop yields to their attainable limit. Moreover, large-scale illegal logging to provide timber for everything from fuel to housing to mine-shaft supports is destroying Chinese woodlands by 10 percent every decade. Grasslands for cattle herds are being lost to desertification by as much as 3.7% a year. . . . An increasing percentage of irrigation water is being polluted by industrial wastes. Because irrigation is depleting the underground water table, forty Chinese cities have been beset by drinking-water shortages. (p. 299)

6. Robert Kaplan, *The Ends of the Earth* (New York: Vintage, 1997), p. 8; see also his much-cited article "The Coming Anarchy," *Atlantic Monthly,* February 1994.

In summary, our home planet is not well. Despite the lack of any grand theory of the world, any overarching explanation of its present anarchy or future promise, Kaplan concludes:

> I am sure of one thing: that even as some nations, including the United States, may be retreating into a fortresslike nationalism, this is only a temporary stage before the world tide of population and poverty forces us all to realize that we inhabit one increasingly small and crowded earth. The benighted part of the planet near the Liberian border where I, an American citizen, had found myself on that lonely night would, ultimately — on some not so distant morrow — become part of my planetary *home*. (p. 9)[7]

But how can we be homemaking inhabitants of this planetary home when ecological degradation renders it increasingly hostile to human habitation?

Mark Hertsgaard tells much the same tale. His ten-year odyssey around the world, and through nineteen countries, sadly revealed significant despoliation of the earth. For example, in the southern Sudan he found grinding poverty that was fueled by civil war, unrelenting famine, and a perpetual lack of clean water or decent healthcare. Hertsgaard rightly recognizes that "it seems to me a grave intellectual error to assume that the fate of the world's poor can be kept separate from the human species' larger ecological prospects."[8] Quoting the director for the regional office for Africa of the United Nations Environmental Program, he emphasizes that "it is impossible to deal with the environmental problems of Africa — soil erosion, deforestation, desertification, and, of course, [lack of clean] water — without confronting issues of poverty and development" (p. 47). Any attempt to address environmental problems must also address issues of social justice. Pollution and poverty, water rights and racism, human-induced climate change and hunger — all are wedded to-

---

7. Near the end of the book (p. 436), Kaplan observes: "Many of the problems I saw around the world — poverty, the collapse of cities, porous borders, cultural and racial strife, growing economic disparities, weakening nation-states — are problems for Americans to think about. I thought of America everywhere I looked. We cannot escape from a more populous, interconnected world of crumbling borders."

8. Mark Hertsgaard, *Earth Odyssey: Around the World in Search of Our Environmental Future* (New York: Broadway Books, 1998), p. 47.

gether. And they all conspire together to fill the refugee camps and create conditions ripe for genocide. To use what has become a common technical term, we must be concerned with "environmental justice," because a disregard for the health of the planet always goes hand in hand with oppression and violence against the most vulnerable.[9]

In Bangkok, Hertsgaard discovered air pollution so extreme it "seemed to have a tactile quality," as if you could "scoop up a handful of the stuff and splatter it against the wall like a dirty snowball." Water pollution was so bad that "the Chao Phraya River was virtually dead south of Bangkok" (pp. 85-87). In Leningrad he found that "its water was absolutely unsafe to drink thanks to a witch's brew of human and industrial waste that poured constantly into the Neva River" (p. 119). In Mayak, fifty miles north of Chelyabinsk, Russia, Hertsgaard learned of "the most polluted spot on earth," Lake Karachay, which "had accumulated an awesome 120 million curies worth of radioactivity and absorbed nearly one hundred times more strontium 90 and cesium 137 than was released at Chernobyl" (p. 136). It comes as no surprise that Chelyabinsk is the cancer capital of Russia.

In Beijing, Hertsgaard experienced firsthand China's "filthy skies and battered lungs" and confronted the worsening effects of acid rain, not only for China, but also for Japan, South Korea, and the rest of the world (pp. 168-69).[10] And the air is even worse in the Yangtze River city of Chongqing: its rates of lung disease are higher than any other Chinese city, and the water not much better because virtually all of the household sewage is dumped straight into the river. In Sao Sebastiao, Brazil, in the heart of Amazonia, Hertsgaard found bare and abandoned fields, hard-packed dirt, and soil that was spent after just a few years of cultivation — all where a

---

9. For more on environmental racism, as one form of environmental justice, see Steven Bouma-Prediger, "Poor and Oppressed Unite: Overcoming Environmental Racism," in Miguel de la Torre, ed., *Handbook of U.S. Liberation Theologies* (St. Louis: Chalice Press, 2004).

10. So important is China that Hertsgaard devotes an entire chapter to its environmental problems. Indeed, Hertsgaard remarks (p. 223) that "China thus brings together two of the most disturbing trends in global environmental affairs: the large, growing population typical of poverty and the high-impact consumption patterns promoted by Western capitalism. This combustible union makes China a sort of environmental superpower in reverse. Like the United States, the other environmental superpower, China wields what amounts to veto power over the rest of the world's environmental progress."

teeming rainforest once stood (p. 204).[11] His list goes on — place after place despoiled and degraded. Home defiled.

Like Kaplan, Hertsgaard found more than ample evidence that the earth is in peril. This led him to ask: "Can the human species bring its behavior into balance with the systems of nature that make our lives on earth possible?" (p. 289). His initial answer is pessimistic: "[H]umans seem addicted to forever wanting more of everything, yet there are billions who still lack the basic necessities"; furthermore, "political leaders talk about changing course, but they rarely do so" (p. 289). On further reflection, however, Hertsgaard comes to a different realization:

> But if humanity's environmental progress has been inadequate in the 1990s, it is not because people don't care. During my travels I encountered a high degree of concern about the state of the environment among average people the world over; it was one of the most consistent and encouraging findings of my entire journey. In hundreds of conversations with individuals from all walks of life, I found that the vast majority of people had not only heard about the gathering ecological crisis, they cared and were happy to talk about it. (p. 290)

But while concern for the earth "has become a worldwide phenomenon," according to a George Gallup poll,[12] ignorance and apathy and denial still loom large. As Hertsgaard puts it:

> Many people tell themselves that dangers like global warming and ozone depletion are so far off in the future that they don't really exist. On some level, these people may know better than that, but the possibility that we humans are dooming ourselves is simply too terrible a thought to absorb. It is much easier to pretend the danger doesn't exist, or adopt a childlike faith that everything will turn out all right in the end — surely the experts will think of something! — and burrow back into the routine of paying the bills, getting the kids off to school, and waiting for the weekend. (pp. 295-96)

---

11. Rejecting the common claim that population growth is to blame for ecological devastation in Brazil, Hertsgaard argues that "deforestation in Brazil is fueled far more by economic inequality and political favoritism than by demographic pressure" (p. 209).

12. Riley Dunlap, George Gallup, Jr., and Alex Gallup, *Health of the Planet* (Princeton, NJ: George Gallup International Institute, 1993).

Care and denial. Happy to talk about it and yet pretending it doesn't exist. On some level people know better, but it's too terrible a thought to absorb. Captured here is the radical ambivalence of people confronting their own ecological homelessness.

To rephrase Hertsgaard's question: Can human beings engage in homemaking on our home planet in ways that are sustainable? Or must our own housekeeping always be at the expense of keeping, caring for, and nurturing the ecological home that is the very foundation of any and all human homemaking? Must humans always construct a built environment that deconstructs the home planet?

These two perambulatory journalists provide much insight concerning the vital signs of the earth. But what do trained environmental scientists say? With authority, wit, and style, conservation biologist Stuart Pimm focuses on land, fresh water, oceans, and biodiversity in his survey, and in each of those cases the results are truly sobering. For example, within a few decades tropical forests have shrunk by about seven million square kilometers, to about half of their original size.[13] The consequences of this are enormous: more massive fires, degraded land, eroded soil, silted streams, and erratic weather. Furthermore, our fresh water is imperiled. Rivers are increasingly dammed, diverted, or have run dry. Aquifers are being drawn down faster than they can be replenished. And wetlands are disappearing. Pimm asserts that because "water is in desperately short supply in some parts of the world," wars over water will increase in the near future (p. 114).

With respect to the oceans, Pimm observes that "overwhelming evidence shows that we are destroying the oceans' ability to supply even what we take now" (p. 6). Many fisheries have collapsed, leaving ghost towns in their wake. A "dead zone" extends one hundred miles out into the Gulf of Mexico. And much of the ocean is already a biological desert. Finally, with regard to biodiversity, Pimm calculates that while the average natural extinction rate is no more than one in a million species per year, "in recorded history we have been liquidating animals and plants 100 times faster than the natural rate" and "the rate is now accelerating to between 1000 and 10,000 times the natural rate" (p. 7). And these pressing problems do not include global warming, a subject that Pimm acknowledges as absolutely

13. Stuart Pimm, *The World According to Pimm: A Scientist Audits the Earth* (New York: McGraw-Hill, 2001), p. 58.

167

central to the future of the planet and the effects of which may be much more than we expect or can presently know.

At the end of his environmental audit of the earth, Pimm offers this conclusion and poses these questions:

> Earth at the turn of this millennium is suffering from huge and unmistakable human impacts. Some — the loss of species, certainly, and the loss of tropical forests, most surely — are about to become irreversible. What does this mean for our future as human beings? What will Earth be like as our numbers double? (p. 233)

Despite this ominous conclusion, Pimm contends: "Our world is not doomed, it is not fatally wounded, but neither is it healthy. It needs attention, for without stewardship, its wounds will fester" (p. 8).[14]

Biologist Calvin DeWitt's analysis is consistent with those above and also quite disturbing. DeWitt writes that we humans "find ourselves to have significantly restructured the biosphere both biogeographically and trophically."[15] Indeed, he says in no uncertain terms: "We have exceeded our capacity to be responsible stewards, and in our over-reach, we have brought destruction and degradation as never before, on a grand scale" (p. 348). Because the earth is now "under human domination," and humans are "a principal geological force," DeWitt persuasively argues that we must be "stewards of the biosphere," and we "will have to discipline ourselves in another direction if we are to restore the freedom we have lost through the domination we have imposed" (pp. 347-48).[16] In his view, the four major issues we currently face are: disruption of planetary energy exchange, degradation of land and soils, destruction of forests and habitats, and loss of biodiversity.

We could cite more scientists, but these will suffice. As with the peripatetic journalists, so too with the environmental scientists, the conclusion is distressingly the same: the earth is not well — its vital signs are not good.

14. Earlier on (p. xiii), in reference to his own wife and children, Pimm states "Our children are always the main reason we mustn't make a mess of it."

15. Calvin DeWitt, "Biogeographic and Trophic Restructuring of the Biosphere: The State of the Earth under Human Domination, *Christian Scholar's Review* 32, no. 4 (Summer 2003): 347.

16. Likewise, Peter Vitousek and his colleagues honestly declare: "Humanity's dominance of Earth means that we cannot escape responsibility for managing the planet" (see Vitousek et al., "Human Domination of Earth's Ecosystems," *Science* 277 [1997]: 494).

We have good reason to feel homeless on our home planet. We are destroying the very matrix of life, bringing the notion of "domicide" to new and unthinkable heights.[17] Not only do we allow and sanction the destruction of the homes of economically marginalized people, we engage in dangerous and unsustainable practices that threaten any viable homemaking on Planet Earth.

Why Ecological Homelessness? A Sociocultural Analysis

Ecological degradation is sadly, seriously real. But some of us seem deaf or ignorant, in denial or indifferent. According to Thomas Berry, we are deaf and dumb. "Our scientific inquiries into the natural world," he argues, "have produced a certain atrophy in our human responses," so that "we cannot speak" to the forms of existence around us. "Emotionally we cannot get out of our confinement," he continues, "nor can we let the outer world flow into our own beings." Therefore, "we cannot hear the voices speak or speak in response."[18] We are unable to perceive either the wonder of the world around us or its tragic despoilment and ongoing destruction.

For others, the problem is ignorance. If only people knew the scope and severity of the problems, some insist, they would take action. There is solid evidence for widespread ecological illiteracy. For example, the National Environmental Report Card concludes: "As the results of the most recent surveys make clear, Americans lack the basic knowledge and are unprepared to respond to the major environmental challenges we face in the 21st century."[19] Or as educators Joe Sheldon and Dave Foster succinctly say, "The lack of [environmental] knowledge is a serious problem."[20] Whether or not overcoming ignorance is enough for all to be well, it is true that there is altogether too much we do not know.

17. J. Douglas Porteous and Sandra E. Smith, *Domicide: The Global Destruction of Home* (Montreal and Kingston: McGill-Queen's University Press, 2001).

18. Thomas Berry, *The Dream of the Earth* (San Francisco: Sierra Club, 1988), pp. 16-17.

19. See www.neetf.org/roper/roper.shtm, the website of the National Environmental Education and Training Foundation.

20. This is, in fact, the title of one of the sections of their article entitled "What Knowledge Is Required for Responsible Stewardship of Creation?" *Christian Scholar's Review* 32, no. 4 (Summer 2003). For a trenchant critique of ecological illiteracy and a compelling alternative, see David Orr, *Ecological Literacy* (Albany: SUNY, 1992), esp. part 2.

For Mark Lynas, denial is the root problem. We know enough, but we simply do not want to face the mess we have made. "We live in a society consumed by denial," says Lynas, where "politicians make the occasional speech about the gravity of the climate change crisis and then go right back to business. . . . [We] claim to be worried about global warming . . . but we still do remarkably little to change our own habits and lifestyles." Or, if we don't deny the problem, we deny that we have any responsibility:"It's someone else's problem and we vaguely hope that someone else will sort it out."[21] Denial in its many deceptive disguises clearly is very much with us.

Finally, many people seem apathetic: they simply don't care. In response to an editorial published in the local newspaper about the very real effects of global warming in Michigan, one person responded: "Yawwn, will someone turn on the Cubs game and hand me a cold beer, please?" Whether adopting a hedonistic ethic of "eat, drink, and be merry for tomorrow we die," or overcome by the ennui and cynicism of the times, many people lack the concern sufficient to move them to responsible action.

I hear nothing. I know nothing. It's not that bad and not my problem. I don't care. Deafness, ignorance, denial, indifference — a litany of human responses that evoke little or no sense of homelessness.

But others of us feel our home is no longer fit for human habitation. Like Aldo Leopold, we are aware that we live in a world of wounds.[22] While hard of hearing, we are not deaf to the groanings of the earth. And we know too much to claim ignorance. And on our better days we reject denial, for the evidence is too hard to evade. And we know and care too much to be indifferent. These four ways are not open to us.

This raises a number of important questions. What sociocultural conditions have contributed to this degradation and our deafness? What keeps us ignorant? What allows for our patterns of denial and what fuels our self-deception and deceit? And, finally, what cultural pressures allow for apathy regarding this wounded world of wonders? To use Pierre Bourdieu's language again, what is the *habitus* that legitimates habitat-destroying habits? This section is a modest attempt to address these questions. Our hope is that this discussion will provide some insight into

21. Lynas, *High Tide* (New York: Picador, 2004), p. 296.

22. Aldo Leopold, *Sand County Almanac* (New York: Ballantine, 1966), p. 197. Interestingly, James Speth gave the first chapter of his book *Red Sky at Morning* the title "A World of Wounds."

why we are facing ecological homelessness and feeling homeless on our home planet.

James Speth provides a convenient place to begin. In a chapter of his book *Red Sky at Morning* entitled "Ten Drivers of Environmental Deterioration," he clearly explains some of the underlying causes of global environmental degradation. His list of ten includes: population, affluence, technology, poverty, market failure, political failure, the scale and rate of economic growth, and, at a deeper level, the nature of our economic system, our cultural values, and globalization.[23] This list provides a handy framework, especially since he perceptively points to larger cultural, ethical, and religious factors that too often are not acknowledged or fully appreciated.

As Speth notes, human population pressures exacerbate virtually every environmental problem. Christopher Flavin seconds that assessment when he says that population growth is "a driving force behind many environmental and social problems."[24] For example, "as populations expand they place additional pressures on the resource base because other resources and options are not available to them," such as water and wood for fuel (Speth, p. 122). Population is so important an issue, says Lester Brown, that in our "demographically divided world," countries will either "break out or break down."[25] That is, in a world divided between countries whose populations are either stabilized and declining (e.g., Holland, Japan, and Italy) or quickly expanding (e.g., Pakistan and Ethiopia), countries with high birth rates and falling death rates will, in a matter of a few decades, either break out of the middle stage of the so-called demographic transition to a stage in which birth rates fall to a lower level and balance death rates, or they will break down because rapid birth rates and increasing population pressures will overwhelm the natural systems on which those countries depend, leading to higher human mortality rates and economic decline. Population is thus one driver of ecological deterioration. Just as overcrowding in a house, homeless shelter, or refugee camp puts pressure

23. James Speth, *Red Sky at Morning: America and the Crisis of the Global Environment* (New Haven: Yale University Press, 2004), p. 120.

24. Christopher Flavin, "The Legacy of Rio," *State of the World 1997* (New York: W. W. Norton, 1997), p. 16. Flavin lists population as one of the three major problems, along with global warming and loss of biodiversity, standing in the way of achieving a sustainable world.

25. Brown, *Eco-Economy* (New York: W. W. Norton, 2001), p. 213. For a thoughtful and informed Christian perspective, see Susan Power Bratton, *Six Billion and More: Human Population Regulation and Christian Ethics* (Louisville: Westminster/John Knox, 1992).

on the physical and social carrying capacity of a dwelling that many are required to share, so do excessive population rates threaten us with ecosystem collapse and its resultant homelessness.

Population, however, is not the only ingredient in determining environmental impact; affluence, or the level of consumption per person, is
also very important. For example, while world population increased four-
fold in the twentieth century, the level of consumption increased fivefold
and per capita fossil fuel consumption increased sevenfold (Speth, p. 124).
In other words, because of very high rates of consumption per person in
the wealthy countries of the world, those populations have a much greater
negative effect on the world's natural systems. Christopher Flavin notes:
"The annual increase of the U.S. population of 2.6 million people puts
more pressure on the world's resources than do the 17 million people
added in India each year."[26] If everyone lived as excessively as we in North
America presently do, we would need three planets to survive. Three planets. But we have only one, and "good planets are hard to find."[27]

Whereas "consumption" was a disease one died from in the nineteenth
century, it became a way of life in the twentieth century. Writing shortly after
World War II, the economist Victor Lebow proclaimed: "Our enormously
productive economy . . . demands that we make consumption our way of life,
that we convert the buying and selling of goods into rituals. We need things
consumed, burned up, worn out, replaced and discarded at an ever increasing
rate."[28] We have made consumption a god, and in doing so we have impoverished our planet and our own souls. As David Myers concludes in his survey
of contemporary American life: "Never before has a culture experienced such
physical comfort combined with such psychological misery. . . . We have bigger houses and broken homes, higher income and lower morale, more mental
health professionals and less well-being. We excel at making a living but often
fail at making a life."[29] Affluence is thus a second cause. Let us, then, call consumption what it really is: a disease that is killing us and the earth. Only a

26. Flavin, "The Legacy of Rio," pp. 18-19.

27. Mathis Wackernagel and William Rees, *Our Ecological Footprint* (Gabriola Island,
BC: New Society, 1996), p. 15.

28. Quoted in Speth, *Red Sky at Morning*, p. 127.

29. David Myers, *The American Paradox: Spiritual Hunger in an Age of Plenty* (New Haven: Yale University Press, 2000), p. 138; see also John DeGraaf, David Wann, and Thomas
Naylor, *Affluenza: The All-Consuming Epidemic* (San Francisco: Berrett-Koehler, 2001); see
also the videos "Affluenza" and "Escape from Affluenza."

group of humans so totally devoid of any sense of the earth as home could so carelessly sacrifice the earth on the altar of their own consuming greed.

A third driver of environmental deterioration is technology. Many new technologies have brought with them huge — and often unforeseen — environmental costs. Nuclear energy is Speth's classic example of how "technology is so often in the saddle, riding us," with devastating environmental consequences (p. 128).[30] Technology is environmentally ambiguous, a fact not often enough appreciated in a culture that is fascinated by technological control and imbued with technological optimism. Wendell Berry puts it with characteristic candor:

> I would argue that it is not human fecundity that is overcrowding the world so much as technological multipliers of the power of individual humans. The worst disease in the world right now is probably the ideology of technological heroism, according to which more and more people willingly cause large-scale effects that they do not foresee and that they cannot control.[31]

Furthermore, our ideology of technological heroism means not just being in love with the newest techno-toy; it includes an underlying attitude or way of thinking. Speth perceptively unmasks this when he speaks of "the very habits of thought that have traditionally made it easy for a new technology to escape rigorous public scrutiny and penetrate easily into the economy," that is, overly credulous reliance on experts, faith in the virtue of technology per se, and belief in the inevitability of progress (p. 129). In other words, we assume that experts know it all, that technology is always beneficial, and that newer is always better.

Albert Borgmann digs even deeper to show how we are blinkered to our own technologically oriented worldview and way of life. Our "technologically advanced style of life," he observes, is "essentially blind to itself" and "ignorant of its essential character."[32] We are inundated with informa-

---

30. Of course, certain technologies hold great promise to help alleviate ecological woe, e.g., hybrid-engine motor vehicles, solar and wind power generation, recycling and upcycling facilities.

31. Wendell Berry, *Home Economics* (New York: North Point, 1987), pp. 149-50.

32. Albert Borgmann, *Power Failure: Christianity and the Culture of Technology* (Grand Rapids: Brazos, 2003), p. 11. See also Neil Postman's classic book *Technopoly: The Surrender of Culture to Technology* (New York: Vintage, 1993).

tion, yet unaware of the ways in which we constantly replace natural things with technologically reconstituted items (e.g., CoolWhip for whipped cream), often with deleterious environmental effects. We cannot construct a home without using technology. But if the development of technology is driven by technicism and not by love and responsible stewardship, homelessness will always result.

Poverty is a fourth factor, and it is a factor that appears on everyone's short list of contributors to ecological degradation. A stunning fact is that half the people in the world live on less than two dollars (U.S.) a day.[33] A line of the hungry, standing shoulder-to-shoulder, would extend around the world at the equator almost thirteen times.[34] Furthermore, over one billion people live on fragile lands.[35] Speth observes:

> Many of the things they [the poor] are forced to do merely to survive degrade the environment: the search for fuelwood de-vegetates the land, making it more susceptible to erosion and fertility loss; the effort to produce more food depletes the soil nutrients and leads to overgrazing and clearing of forests and woody areas; and reducing fallow periods compounds these problems. (p. 132)

Global poverty remains one of the great challenges of our age. And as we have learned, we cannot address ecological integrity without being concerned simultaneously with sustainable economic development. We cannot address pollution without also tackling poverty, nor poverty without also pollution. Environmental problems and social problems are intertwined. As we have said in our discussion of socioeconomic homelessness, a geography of exclusion that disregards the rights of the poor to adequate housing is itself rooted in an ecology of exclusion.

A fifth driver of environmental decline is the failure of the current market economy to reflect the true cost of scarce natural resources, thus leading to the excessive use of those resources. Market price, in other words, is inaccurate. For example, the full cost of air pollution is not borne

---

33. *Global Poverty Report*, from the G8 Okinawa Summit July 2000; see www.worldbank .org/html/extdr/extme/G8_poverty2000.pdf.

34. Assuming two feet per person, a circumference of 24,906 miles, and about 852 million people who are undernourished (a figure obtained from the "The State of Food Insecurity in the World 2004" annual report of the U.N. Food and Agriculture Organization).

35. *World Development Report, 2003* (Washington, DC: World Bank, 2003), p. 59.

by the polluter who spreads it over the surrounding area; rather, pollution is "external" to the polluter. To use the language of neoclassical economics, resource depletion and pollution are "externalities." For example, metals "only appear cheap, because the stripped rainforest and mountain of toxic tailings spilling into rivers, the impoverished villages and eroded indigenous cultures — all the consequences they leave in their wake — are not factored into the cost of production."[36] Thus prices for many goods are an illusion because they do not reflect the actual cost.

One particularly telling example is the Gross Domestic Product. The GDP measures only economic activity, not true economic value (or disvalue): thus "a country could cut all its forests, drain all its aquifers, and pollute all its waterways, and the GDP would only go up, up, up" (Speth, p. 134).[37] Indeed, as some have noted, when crime, divorce, and disease go up, the GDP goes up as well. The GDP seems blind to both natural and social capital. By contrast, "in spite of what such signals as the GDP or the Dow Jones Industrial Average indicate . . . it is ultimately the capacity of the photosynthetic world and its nutrient flows that determine the quality and the quantity of life on earth."[38] All human economies are based on the economy of nature. Hawken, Lovins, and Lovins capture the heart of the matter:

> Capitalism, as practiced, is a financially profitable, nonsustainable aberration in human development. What might be called "industrial capitalism" does not fully conform to its own accounting principles. It liquidates its capital and calls it income. It neglects to assign any value to the largest stocks of capital it employs — the natural resources and living systems, as well as the social and cultural systems that are the basis of human capital. (p. 5)

36. Paul Hawken, Amory Lovins, and L. Hunter Lovins, *Natural Capitalism* (Boston: Little, Brown and Co., 1999), p. 3; see ch. 8 for an extended analysis of how our current economic system fails to properly value natural capital and of what must be done to correct it.

37. Given this problem, a more accurate measure of our collective well-being must be used. Several exist, with Daly and Cobb's Index of Sustainable Economic Welfare perhaps the most well known. See Herman Daly and John Cobb, *For the Common Good* (Boston: Beacon, 1989), pp. 401ff. In the Old Testament, it should be noted, a good society was defined not by the amount of economic activity but by how it treated the orphan, the widow, and the alien — those most vulnerable.

38. Hawken, Lovins, and Lovins, *Natural Capitalism*, p. 149.

In short, the market fails because it acts as if the economy of nature does not exist. Furthermore, this failure cannot be remedied simply by capturing externalities. While it is an instructive and helpful exercise, monetizing the goods and services of the natural world will not get us far enough.[39] We cannot correct the problem of externalities "simply by assigning monetary value to natural capital," since "many of the services we receive from living systems have no known substitutes at any price," and valuing natural capital "is a difficult and imprecise exercise at best."[40] Something more than tinkering is needed.

We need to emphasize this crucial insight. Our economic system is broken and needs serious repair. We have an economy "that cannot sustain economic progress, an economy that cannot take us where we want to go"; therefore, we need "a shift in our worldview, in how we think about the relationship between the earth and the economy."[41] More precisely, we need "recognition that the economy is part of the earth's ecosystem and can sustain progress only if it is restructured so that it is compatible with it."[42] In sum, we need an economy that respects the principles of ecology and uses them to shape economic policy. We need "a capitalism as if living systems mattered."[43] We need an emplaced economics, an economics that knows its place, rather than a displaced economics, an economics of no place.

Another cause of environmental deterioration is political failure. Narrowly construed, this means the failure of various public policies and government units to "make the market work for the environment rather than against it" (Speth, p. 134). For example, water could be used more efficiently if it was sold at its full cost rather than subsidized with an artificially low price. Air polluters could be required to pay the true costs for their pollution. Developers could be required to pay for the

---

39. See, e.g., the work of Robert Costanza et al., "The Value of the World's Ecosystem Services and Natural Capital," *Nature* (15 May 1997). See also Gretchen Daily, ed., *Nature's Services* (Washington, DC: Island Press, 1997), and Gretchen Daily and Katherine Ellison, *The New Economy of Nature: The Quest to Make Conservation Profitable* (Washington, DC: Island Press, 2002).

40. Hawken, Lovins, and Lovins, *Natural Capitalism*, p. 5.

41. Brown, *Eco-Economy*, pp. 3, 6.

42. Brown, *Eco-Economy*, p. 21.

43. Hawken, Lovins, and Lovins, *Natural Capitalism*, p. 9. They spell out this "natural capitalism" in considerable detail under four main principles: radical resource productivity, biomimicry, service and flow economy, natural capital investment.

lost natural goods and services of destroying wetlands. Powerful business and political interests conspire to thwart efforts to make the market tell the ecological truth, and we lack the political will or clout to curb those interests.

But beyond these efforts to internalize economic "externalities," important as they are, there are other examples of political failure. In explaining why most attempts at global environmental governance have failed, Speth highlights "three political fault lines" (Speth, pp. 107ff.). The first is "the environment versus the economy." Not long ago, North American newspaper headlines regularly cried "owls versus jobs," since politicians and interest groups were pitting the protection of the northern spotted owl against loggers and their livelihood in the Pacific Northwest. Though the rhetoric that protecting and helping the environment necessarily hurts the economy has been increasingly challenged and shown to be a false dichotomy,[44] this belief persists among many politicians, who lack the political imagination to envision or the political will to enact policies that make it a "win-win" situation for both the human and natural economies. This is a telling example of political failure.

The second fault line is "North versus South." The environmental agenda has been perceived to be an agenda of the world's rich Northern Hemisphere, a luxury of those countries that are already "developed." Moreover, many in the Southern Hemisphere are suspicious of international environmental treaties or agreements, and justifiably so, for the North has often acted in ways that do not engender trust. For example, after the Rio Earth Summit, the so-called developing countries were promised development assistance; however, support from the "developed" world actually declined. The credibility of the North often hangs on a slender thread, and talk is cheap. When we in the North do not put our money where our mouth is, our conversation partners from the South are not inclined to consider us serious or reliable. And thus a shift to the left in Latin American politics over the last few years is not surprising. The central issue is equity. Environmental frameworks must be equitable, where equity does

---

44. See, for example, Lester Brown, *Eco-Economy;* Hawken et al., *Natural Capitalism;* and William McDonough and Michael Braungart, *Cradle to Cradle* (New York: North Point, 2002). This last book is especially enlightening. From the first chapter, "The Book is Not a Tree," to the last, "Putting Eco-Effectiveness into Practice," the authors, a leading environmental architect and a leading environmental chemist, show again and again how taking care of the earth seriously actually helps the financial bottom line.

not mean that all are treated equally but that all are treated fairly. To be fair, equals must be treated equally, and unequals must be treated differentially. To treat all the same would be unfair. Governments in the North all too often lack the insight or courage to deal with the South "in a way that recognizes their aspirations and special challenges."[45]

A third fault line is "the United States versus the world." After thirty years of personal involvement in international environmental efforts, Speth sadly declares: "If there is one country that bears most responsibility for the lack of progress on international environmental issues, it is the United States." Indeed, Speth delivers a stinging — and in our view, well deserved — indictment of what he calls "persistent American exceptionalism, at times tinged with arrogance" (pp. 109-10). For example, as of June 2006, one hundred thirty-two countries have ratified the Biosafety Protocol of the United Nations Convention of Biological Diversity, but the United States has not. Nor has the United States signed the Kyoto Protocol to the U.N. Framework Convention on Climate Change. With evidence like that, it is difficult to dodge the charge of arrogant exceptionalism. This is yet another example of a major political failure. In a wide variety of ways, then, we have failed to construct a civic polity that preserves and protects the earth and its inhabitants; rather, we have a geopolitical system that engenders ecological homelessness.

A seventh driver of environmental degradation is globalization. We have dealt with this in previous chapters as one of the key reasons that socioeconomic homelessness is on the rise, so a brief explication of how it contributes to the earth's deterioration will suffice here. Recall that, in Daly's short definition, globalization "is characterized by the concentration of economic control in multinational firms and financial institutions, worldwide networks of production, exchange, communication and knowledge, transnational capital, and a freer flow of labor, goods, services, and information."[46] Examples abound: shoes from Singapore and T-shirts from Thailand; orange juice from Belize and McDonald's in Bejing; zebra mussels from Asia multiplying in Michigan lakes, and garlic mustard from Europe invading Michigan woodlands; the World Trade Organization and

---

45. The words of Indian environmentalist Anil Agarwal, quoted in Speth, *Red Sky at Morning*, p. 108.

46. Gerald Daly, *Homeless* (London: Routledge, 1996), p. 5.

the European Common Market; computers and the internet and global capital seemingly everywhere.[47]

Also recall that globalization, in our view, is a socioeconomic force of exclusion. While many have championed economic globalization as a means of alleviating poverty, the reality is quite different. The brutal reality is that the poor get poorer and become more numerous. Jobs disappear or go beyond the border. Benefits shrink or are gone like the wind. More people are on the street, or they are one paycheck away from that reality. The result of all this is economic oppression.[48]

While there are some reasons to believe that globalization helps us care for the earth — for example, by the spread of beneficial environmental technologies or easier access to needed information — there are many more reasons to believe that it does not. Rooted in a growth-at-all-costs imperative, economic globalization results in an expansion of environmentally destructive growth; a decrease in the ability of national governments to cope with environmental challenges; an increase in corporate power; the stimulation of the transportation and energy sectors, with largely negative environmental effects; the commodifying of resources such as water and the decline of local controls on resource use; and the rapid spread of invasive species, which result in biological homogenization (Speth, p. 145). Whatever the positive effects of globalization may be, they are outweighed by the manifest negative consequences. As Nobel laureate economist Joseph Stiglitz bluntly puts it: "Globalization today . . . is not working for much of the environment," nor is it working "for many of the world's poor," nor, in fact, "for the stability of the global economy."[49] In short, globalization is yet another hard driver of environmental degradation.

An eighth reason for ecological decline is the destruction of place. We in

47. For an illuminating analysis of where our everyday objects come from, see John Ryan and Alan Durning, *Stuff: The Secret Lives of Everyday Things* (Seattle: Northwest Environment Watch, 1997).

48. See, e.g., Bob Goudzwaard, "Globalization, Exclusion, Enslavement," *Reformed World* 46, no. 3 (Sept. 1996): http://www.warc.ch/pc/rw963/01.html; see also Goudzwaard and Harry de Lange, *Beyond Poverty and Affluence: Toward an Economy of Care,* trans. and ed. Mark VanderVennen (Grand Rapids: Eerdmans, 1994).

49. Quoted in Speth, *Red Sky at Morning,* p. 145. For a small sampling of criticisms, see Joseph Stiglitz, *Globalization and Its Discontents* (New York: W. W. Norton, 2002). For a searing indictment of the current international economic order, see David Korton, *When Corporations Rule the World,* 2nd ed. (Bloomfield, CT: Kumarian, 2001).

North America have increasingly become a "country of exiles," to quote the title of an important book by William Leach. While we feel "a need for continuity and stability, and for confident attachment to a place to be from," there is a "weakening of place as a centering presence in the lives of ordinary people," a wearing away of connectedness to place.[50] In other words, even while we long for home we are becoming exiles. Our discussion of globalization helps us see why. Globalization can never honor any place as home, because all places must be expendable. When economic profit is the paramount goal, we can expect the sacrifice of place. And without knowledge of and love for particular places, ecological homelessness is inevitable. In Leach's succinct summary: "In America today, 'nobody is at home'"(Leach, p. 14).[51]

Leach expertly chronicles this destruction of place and some of the resulting environmental effects. He explores highways on land, sea, and air, and the post-1980 conditions that have created them: corporate mergers, government deregulation, intermodal transport (the creation of standardized containers to carry freight by truck, rail, or ship). He delves into the life of the peripatetic business executive and the "expatriate style" that often goes with it, including the creation of a "landscape of the temporary." He examines tourism and gambling, and shows in each case how they are an affront to place. He takes on the modern university and higher education in general, criticizing the migratory faculty and the curricula that are detached from specific places. Leach concludes that there is in America "an unprecedented alliance against place" (p. 173). We can only agree. If caring for place presupposes knowledge of place, and knowledge of place is possible only over an extended period of time, then the nomadic, upwardly mobile lifestyle of many Americans is a recipe for environmental disaster.

Further evidence of our collective destruction of place can be found in the built American landscape, where we have in many ways constructed a country filled with ugly and inhospitable places. As James Howard Kunstler convincingly argues in his witty and rollicking tome *The Geography of Nowhere*, we have built "a landscape of scary places, the geography

50. William Leach, *Country of Exiles: The Destruction of Place in American Life* (New York: Pantheon, 1999), pp. 6-7.

51. While Leach's *Country of Exiles* is a perceptive diagnosis of a major problem, his award-winning *Land Of Desire: Merchants, Power, and the Rise of a New American Culture* (New York: Vintage, 1993) is an illuminating history of how, since roughly 1890, we in America have become preoccupied with comfort, acquisition, and consumption — in short, how we have confused the goods life for the good life.

of nowhere, that has simply ceased to be a credible human habitat."[52] He continues in no uncertain terms:

> Eighty percent of everything ever built in America has been built in the last fifty years, and most of it is depressing, brutal, ugly, unhealthy, and spiritually degrading — the jive-plastic commuter tract home wastelands, the Potemkin village shopping plazas with their vast parking lagoons, the Legoblock hotel complexes, the "gourmet mansardic" junkfood joints, the Orwellian "office parks" featuring buildings sheathed in the same reflective glass as the sunglasses worn by chain-gang guards, the particle-board garden apartments rising up in every meadow and cornfield, the freeway loops around every big and little city with their clusters of discount merchandise marts, the whole destructive, wasteful, toxic, agoraphobia-inducing spectacle that politicians proudly call "growth" (p. 10).

Outrageous claims, perhaps, but Kunstler demonstrates their truth with penetrating accuracy in his insightful analysis of architecture, the automobile, shopping malls, zoning regulations, housing patterns, building codes, and cities both alluring and depressing. The upshot is that we have made it very difficult to know our place, like any place, or feel at home, for it is hard to find a home or feel at home in a geography of nowhere. In such a culture, environmental degradation is inevitable. Kunstler concludes: "We will have to replace a destructive economy of mindless expansion with one that consciously respects earthly limits and human scale" (p. 275).[53]

A ninth factor in environmental deterioration is what we call the impulse for the "new-'n'-now." Leach labels this first aspect "the cult of the new," and Speth calls the second "contempocentrism."[54] Today we believe that new is better than old, and we assume progress is inevitable. As Leach describes it, we feel "the need to overturn the past and begin again, and to disregard all kinds of attachments in the interest of getting the 'new and improved,' whether goods, jobs, entertainment, or places" (p. 13). And we

---

52. James Howard Kunstler, *The Geography of Nowhere: The Rise and Decline of America's Man-Made Landscape* (New York: Simon and Schuster, 1993), p. 15.

53. Kunstler's more extensive prescription for what ails us can be found in his sequel *Home from Nowhere: Remaking Our Everyday World for the 21st Century* (New York: Simon and Schuster, 1996).

54. Leach, *Country of Exiles*, p. 13; Speth, *Red Sky at Morning*, p. 138.

live in a land of immediate gratification. We want it — whether "it" is a burger or a car, sex or a computer response — right now! We seem incurably impatient. The devaluation of the past and a culture-wide sense of collective dissatisfaction and insatiable desire are integral to consumer capitalism. It is no surprise that we have environmental degradation and ecological homelessness in a culture where there is a seemingly endless longing to consume what is new and where "we gotta have it now."

Related to this is the common belief that bigger is always better and growth is always good, what Speth calls our "growth-at-all-costs imperative" — where the growth is, of course, economic growth. We feel compelled to grow, as if our very survival depends on it. In the history of North America, geographic growth was seen as Manifest Destiny (no matter that native peoples stood in the way); so now economic growth is taken as necessary and inevitable. As historian J. R. McNeill has persuasively argued, "The overarching priority of economic growth was easily the most important idea of the twentieth century."[55] This "growth fetish" seems to infuse and animate much of contemporary culture. Economists wait with bated breath for the latest report from the U.S. Federal Reserve. Businesses determine success or failure based not on quarterly earnings or profits but on rates of growth. Cities, schools, and charities decide whether the year has been good based on how much growth they have had. What we fail to realize as we grasp for this fetish is that some kinds of growth are good and some are not, that some rates of growth are healthy and some are not, indeed, that growth itself is sometimes right and sometimes not. Growth is not intrinsically good. As Ed Abbey once reminded us, "Growth for the sake of growth *is* the ideology of the cancer cell."[56] In summary, our new-'n'-now and growth-is-good ideology is yet another driver of ecological decline.

The tenth (and last) reason for ecological homelessness is anthropocentrism. The belief that we humans are at the center of the universe contributes both to the degradation of our home planet and to our own sense of homelessness on earth. Many now recognize that the so-called developed world's worldview is overly human centered. Norman Wirzba puts it this way:

55. J. R. McNeill, *Something New Under the Sun: An Environmental History of the Twentieth Century World* (New York: W. W. Norton, 2000), p. 336.

56. Edward Abbey, *The Journey Home* (New York: Plume, 1991), p. 183. For confirmation of this in detailed medical terms, see Sherwin Nuland, *How We Die* (New York: Vintage, 1993), especially ch. 10 on cancer.

The eclipse of divine transcendence, once understood to be the source and goal of the world, created a hole that would be filled by human beings who now positioned themselves as the center or source of meaning and value. No longer microcosms of the creation, people are the autonomous beings who, in an expression of rational freedom, chart and direct the fate of themselves and the world. Again, the history of this development toward autonomy is complex. But what emerges is a self cut off from the world of which it is a part and a world shorn of all remnants of final causality. Nature, a self-regulating mechanism, stands as the arena on which reason and technique can be exercised.[57]

Having banished or pacified God, we have enthroned ourselves at the center of things. Following Protagoras, we believe that we humans are the measure of all things. With ourselves at the center and the world a machine, nature gets reduced to the status of an object — merely a resource to be used and, if necessary, abused. It is not difficult to see how such a perspective on the world and one's place in it sanctions the despoliation of the earth. Viewing ourselves as autonomous creatures, fundamentally unrelated to either God or the rest of creation, we have shaped a culture, an economy, and a built environment subject to no principles beyond our own self-aggrandizing aspirations and with no sense of kinship with other creatures or their habitats.

It is not surprising, then, that the eclipse of agrarian life, the predominance of technology, the abstract character of modern life, and the perceived irrelevance of God have also contributed to our inability to understand ourselves as God-wrought creatures and the world as divinely crafted and lovingly sustained creation. Without such understandings, the earth is dead matter, mere resource, the object of our sophisticated manipulation and supposed mastery. And the degradation of the earth grows apace. What we need to understand, Bill McKibben insists, is that "[h]uman beings — any one of us, and our species as a whole — are not all-important, not at the center of the world. That is one essential piece of information, the one great secret, offered by any encounter with the woods or the mountains or the ocean or any wilderness or chunk of nature or patch of night sky."[58] Nevertheless, the belief persists that we humans stand at the center of things. While it may well be that some sense of "cen-

---

57. Norman Wirzba, *The Paradise of God: Renewing Religion in an Ecological Age* (Oxford: Oxford University Press, 2003), p. 68.

58. Bill McKibben, *The Age of Missing Information* (New York: Plume, 1992), p. 228.

teredness" is constitutive of any profound experience of "home," it is also devastatingly evident that human autonomy is a very poor candidate for that center. Anthropocentrism is a recipe for ecological homelessness.

The Home Planet: The Earth as *Oikos*

We have been arguing that ecological degradation brings about a kind of ecological homelessness. We feel homeless on our home planet. But in what sense is this our home planet? And how do we experience this homelessness? What exactly is ecological homelessness? We must now turn to these questions, if briefly, to understand more completely this particular dimension of homelessness.

Our claim is that planet earth is the home planet. But what does that mean? It means that this planet is where we reside, indeed, the only place we know of in the universe where we can live.[59] After all, we are human, derived from the *humus,* dirt rich in organic matter, the stuff of life. The etymology of our generic name "human" should remind us that we are native to this planet. Viewing the earth from space, rising from behind the moon, astronaut Edgar Mitchell, in his now famous words, observed:

> Suddenly from behind the rim of the moon, in long slow-motion moments of immense majesty, there emerges a sparkling blue and white jewel, a light, delicate, sky-blue sphere laced with slowly swirling veils of white, rising gradually like a small pearl in a thick sea of black mystery. It takes more than a moment to fully realize this is Earth . . . home.[60]

The Earth Story has been told many times and in many places, and need not be repeated here. But the upshot is "the whole storied natural history is little short of a series of 'miracles,' wondrous, fortuitous events, unfolding of potential."[61] One is struck by questions of ontological and exis-

---

59. As Holmes Rolston III reminds us, given our propensity "to think of ourselves primarily as consumers, and secondarily as citizens, and only rarely as residents," we "must increasingly realize that we are earthlings — of the Earth — and that this is our home planet" (Rolston, *Conserving Natural Value* [New York: Columbia University Press, 1994], pp. 10-11).

60. Quoted from Kevin Kelly, ed., *The Home Planet* (Reading, MA: Addison-Wesley, 1988), pp. 42-45.

61. Rolston, *Conserving Natural Value,* p. 208; for one short version, see pp. 207-8.

tential contingency: why anything at all, and why this world rather than some other? In Annie Dillard's luminous prose:

> Certainly nature seems to exult in abounding radicality, extremism, anarchy. If we were to judge nature by its common sense or likelihood, we wouldn't believe the world existed. In nature, improbabilities are the one stock in trade. The whole creation is one lunatic fringe. If creation had been left up to me, I'm sure I wouldn't have had the imagination or courage to do more than shape a single, reasonably sized atom, smooth as a snowball, and let it go at that. No claims of any and all revelations could be so far-fetched as a single giraffe.[62]

The earth is a precious place, a "small pearl in a thick sea of black mystery," and the pearl itself is a miraculous mystery in more ways than we can count or could ever know. This one lunatic fringe of a world is where we humans dwell and where we belong — our home.[63]

This understanding of earth as our home planet is enriched when we attend to earth as *oikos*. The Greek word *oikos* (eco-) means house or household, thus "ecology" is the *logos* of the *oikos*, that is, the study of the household, and "economics" is the *nomos* of the *oikos*, the law or the rules of the household. So these two disciplines are linked etymologically: each studies the household that is the earth. More exactly, ecology is the study of individuals and populations, communities and habitats, life systems and dynamics of the household, and of what is required for living well.

---

62. Annie Dillard, *Pilgrim at Tinker Creek* (New York: Perennial Classics, 1998), p. 146. Elsewhere (p. 128) she says: "The creator . . . churns out the intricate texture of least works that is the world with a spendthrift genius and an extravagance of care. This is the point."

63. Some will perhaps object that "this world is not my home, I'm just a-passin' through," to quote the famous song. Here it is sufficient to emphasize that the biblical view is that the earth is and always will be our home. From Genesis to Revelation, the Bible affirms that we humans are bodily creatures — 'adām from the 'adāmāh, humans from the *humus* — made from the stuff of the earth and animated by God's Spirit. And Scripture insists that God's intention is to redeem and restore and transfigure the world, not to trash it all and start over after rapturing human souls off a burning planet. The biblical vision of God's good future is of a renewed heaven and renewed earth — of heaven on earth, a kingdom of peace and justice, a reign of shalom. God is not the great Destroyer but the grand Home-maker and Recycler. We are earthlings: the earth is our home, and the earth will be God's home. For more on this reading of Scripture, see Bouma-Prediger, *For the Beauty of the Earth*, ch. 4. The best books debunking the "Left Behind" eschatology are Barbara Rossing, *The Rapture Exposed* (Boulder, CO: Westview, 2004), and Craig Hill, *In God's Time* (Grand Rapids: Eerdmans, 2002).

Economics is the study of how to respectfully care for and manage the earth so that the various requirements of the household are met and sustained, so that the household is hospitable for all its inhabitants. Ecology is the knowledge necessary for good home economics.[64]

Therefore, our home planet is our common household: all of us, human and nonhuman alike, share the same house. As Larry Rasmussen says, "Habitat is the core meaning of all *eco* words: economy, ecology, ecumenicity itself," and therefore we should speak of "Habitat Earth."[65] If we take these terms seriously, they mean that the earth is one vast but single household of life.

If that's true, what happens when global warming or some other kind of environmental decline breaks through our deafness and ignorance, our denial and indifference? We feel homeless. We feel as though we are being deprived of our rightful habitat and alienated from our only home. Rasmussen says: "The forms of homelessness are at least two — deprivation and alienation," each evident today in "the destruction of home as habitat and the economic, cultural, and spiritual uprooting of people from their homes" (p. 95). In short, we feel a lack of something that is rightfully ours, and we feel estranged from that with which we long to have a healthy relationship, feelings that are prompted by the physical degradation of our earthly habitat and our displacement from our particular place. We *feel* homeless because we *are becoming* homeless.

Our understanding of ecological homelessness can be deepened if we turn from earth as home to earth as holy. Consider these words by Václav Havel, the poet, playwright, political revolutionary, and former president of the Czech Republic:

> As a boy I lived for some time in the country and I clearly remember an experience from those days: I used to walk to school in a nearby village

---

64. Economics as a discipline has confined itself to explaining market transactions between humans as if nature did not exist. Similarly, ecology has confined itself to studying natural systems as if humans did not exist. Neither discipline can accurately understand its own subject, or predict its behavior, in these isolated frameworks. For more on this, especially on how we can understand what economics and ecology share (concepts, models, problems), see "Globalization, Ethics, and the Earth," a position paper by the Earth and Ethics Working Group of the Commission on Theology of the Reformed Church in America, available at www.rca.org.

65. Larry Rasmussen, *Earth Community, Earth Ethics* (Maryknoll: Orbis, 1996), p. 91.

along a cart track through the fields and, on the way, see on the horizon a huge smokestack of some hurriedly built factory, in all likelihood in the service of the war. It spewed dense brown smoke and scattered it across the sky. Each time I saw it, I had an intense sense of something profoundly wrong, of humans soiling the heavens. I have no idea whether there was something like a science of ecology in those days; if there was, I certainly knew nothing of it. Still that "soiling the heavens" offended me spontaneously. It seemed to me that, in it, humans are guilty of something, that they destroy something important, arbitrarily disrupting the natural order of things, and that such things cannot go unpunished.[66]

Though he was innocent, as a boy, of any scientific understanding of how the world works, any knowledge of ecology, Havel had an intuitive sense that air pollution was literally soiling what should be clean, staining what should be pure, and thus it was an offense to the natural order, a violation of the way things are supposed to be. And with this sense came an accompanying awareness of moral culpability, because we humans are responsible for this offense.

Havel's notions of purity and impurity, cleanliness and defilement, presuppose the earth is holy. His feelings that humans were offending the earth make sense only if the earth and its creatures and systems are in some sense sacred. Likewise, Holmes Rolston says that, "if there is any holy ground, this is it" — this "enthralling earth," and therefore he sadly laments our continual abuse and neglect as a kind of defamation.[67] Barbara Kingsolver expresses a similar sentiment and sadness. In talking about our "blunt utilitarian culture," one of her characters spits out: "But where do you go when you've pissed in every corner of your playground?"[68] Or perhaps the twelve-year-old daughter of a friend expressed it most poignantly when, after reading that the population of tigers in the world has decreased

---

66. Václav Havel, *Living in Truth* (London: Faber and Faber, 1986), p. 136.

67. Rolston, *Conserving Natural Value*, p. 236.

68. Barbara Kingsolver, *Animal Dreams* (New York: HarperCollins, 1990), p. 240. A paragraph later, the narrator muses: "To people who think of themselves as God's houseguests, American enterprise must seem arrogant beyond belief. Or stupid. A nation of amnesiacs, proceeding as if there were no other day but today." If you believe we are "permanent houseguests," as the Bible affirms we are, "sleeping on God's couch," as Kingsolver puts it, then you can only agree with this assessment and share the anger and sadness it contains.

dramatically, she burst into tears and exclaimed that this should not be. Something is profoundly wrong with a world without tigers. Something sacred has been diminished.

No one is more eloquent than Wendell Berry in seeing the earth as holy: "The Bible leaves no doubt at all about the sanctity of the act of world-making, or of the world that was made, or of the creaturely or bodily life in this world. We are holy creatures living among other holy creatures in a world that is holy."[69] The world is holy. All that lives is holy. And thus, understandably, Berry concludes that "our destruction of nature is not just bad stewardship, or stupid economics, or a betrayal of family responsibility; it is the most horrid blasphemy. It is flinging God's gifts into His face, as if they were of no worth beyond that assigned to them by our destruction of them" (p. 98). Ecological degradation by our hands is not only an economic or ethical matter; it is a religious matter — more strictly speaking, a theological matter. It is blasphemy, an egregious affront to the living God, the holy homemaker who creates and sustains a holy heaven and a holy earth. Ecological homelessness, in this case, is defilement of what is sacred and contempt for the Maker of heaven and earth.

In speaking of our contemporary patterns of uprootedness, Kingsolver says that the urban "exodus from the land makes me unspeakably sad. I think of the children who will never know, intuitively, that a flower is a plant's way of making love, or what *silence* sounds like, or that trees breathe out what we breathe in. . . . I wonder how they will imagine the infinite when they have never seen how the stars fill a dark night sky. I wonder how I can explain why a wood-thrush song makes my chest hurt to a populace for whom wood is a construction material and thrush is a tongue disease."[70] A longing sadness for what we are losing and is already lost. An aching wonderment about how we will come to desire a future in which all God's creatures are at home. How will we reimagine our lives as homemakers and our world as home?

Ecological homelessness is widespread. In a world in which a popular musician sings "everything is wrong," even those with roofs over their heads feel homeless. We wonder what's the use of a house if you haven't got a decent planet to put it on. This leaves us with two questions: Where will

---

69. Wendell Berry, *Sex, Economy, Freedom and Community* (New York: Pantheon, 1993), pp. 98-99.

70. Barbara Kingsolver, *Small Wonder* (New York: HarperCollins, 2002), pp. 38-39.

we find hope for a restoration of our creational home, our God-given habitat for our homemaking habitation? And what are the habits of homemaking that will engender a restoration of this creational habitat? The question of hope occupies us throughout this book, and we will return to it in the concluding two chapters. The question of habits, however, is the question of virtue. If our present cultural *habitus* has been one of domicide and homelessness, then what would be the shape of a homemaking *habitus*, of homemaking virtues? If we have developed an economy that is essentially at war with the rest of creation, rendering us ecologically homeless, then what might a more peaceable life, a life of shalom, look like?

Much Depends on Dinner

Matthew 14:1–15:39

Much depends on dinner. Food is deeply symbolic in human life. What, when, where, and with whom you eat says a lot about who you are, what is important to you, and what counts as "home" in your life. Indeed, it is not surprising that when we have asked groups of people to "free associate" with the word "home," the word "food" invariably is one of the first to appear. Home is where you eat, for better or worse.

Much depends on dinner. Much has always depended on dinner. In the first century, dinner was a matter of life and death. Dinner was a matter of whether Israel's exile in her own land would ever come to an end. That is why first-century Jews were so concerned with matters of ritual purity with respect to eating. How you ate, and especially with whom you ate, could impact the very salvation of Israel.

You are what you eat, it has been said. Who you are, your status in society, your self-understanding, your place in the world, is reflected in what you eat and who you eat with. We know from the stories of Israel that Jewish identity as the chosen people of God — the heirs of Abraham, the people shaped by the Torah given through Moses — was an identity deeply connected to food. That's why Daniel and his friends refused to eat the royal food of the Babylonian court (Dan. 1:8-17). The issue wasn't a matter of culinary preference but of ritual defilement. This food, deemed unclean by the stipulations of Torah, would defile any covenant child who would consume it. Eat the empire's food, and you will find yourself increasingly feeling at home in the empire, and you will forget that you are in exile. In such forgetfulness, we have seen, there is only homelessness.

The problem Daniel and his friends faced remained an issue of deep symbolic importance during the time of Jesus. In the face of the assimilationist designs of the Roman empire, and living in a state of imperially imposed exile in their own land, first-century Jews knew that they had to do everything they could to maintain their unique identity as a covenant people. Subject to Roman rule and the encroachment of the symbols of Roman culture and stripped of most of the freedoms to live out covenantal life in the land as an inheritance, the people and their leaders hung on to any and all identity markers to maintain their Jewish distinctiveness. The Temple in Jerusalem was undoubtedly the most important physical symbol of Jewish identity, and Sabbath observance was the most important temporal symbol of covenantal faithfulness. But it was at the family dinner that resistance to pagan defilement and maintenance of Jewish distinctiveness was reinforced on a daily basis.

Eating kosher food, with the proper level of ritual cleanliness and with people whose lives would not defile the meal, was not only a matter of reinforcing Jewish uniqueness, it was also a way of hastening the coming redemption of Israel. If Israel's sin had caused her unbearably long exile, then Israel's holiness — manifest not least in her table fellowship — would hasten the return of God to Israel and the end of her exile. Holy table fellowship at home was key to bringing about the return from exile and the all-encompassing homecoming that all Jews longed for.

But when Jesus proclaimed, "The time is fulfilled, and the kingdom of God has come near," and that people should "repent and believe in the good news," he had something radically different in mind (Mark 1:15). If the kingdom is at hand, then he is proclaiming that redemptive homecoming is at hand. The longed-for return from exile is being accomplished in their midst; but this is a return that dramatically changes the rules of table fellowship because it dramatically extends the boundaries of home. No wonder Jesus was a constant source of controversy. He seemed to break all the rules of homemaking that were rooted in a covenantal understanding of identity, purity, and defilement. Not only did he allow his disciples to break the central temporal identity marker of Israel by plucking grain on the Sabbath (Mark 2:23-28); and not only did he allow his disciples to eat with unclean hands, thereby defiling the meal and all who share it (Mark 7:1-23); he also chose to eat with unclean lepers like Simon and traitorous tax collectors like Zacchaeus (Mark 14:3-9; Luke 19:1-10).

And Zacchaeus wasn't the only tax collector with whom Jesus ate. He also shared table fellowship at a great banquet hosted by Levi, who became one of Jesus' followers (Luke 5:27-32). The place was crowded with precisely the kind of people that the Pharisees and scribes imagined would inhibit and postpone the coming redemption of Israel. No wonder one of the things they charged him with was that he "[ate] with tax collectors and sinners" (Luke 5:30; 15:1). Moreover, when he did go to a proper dinner that was served with the appropriate purity in the home of a man of unquestionable piety, Jesus allowed a sinful woman to defile the meal. In an outpouring of grief, this woman wept over Jesus, washed his feet with her tears, and then repeatedly kissed his feet! Through the touch — indeed, the sensual touch — of that woman, Jesus was defiled, his host was mortified, and the redemption of Israel was delayed, or so the traditionalists thought. But not in the kingdom Jesus brings. This is a kingdom shaped by the breathtaking inclusiveness of forgiveness (Luke 7:36-50).

And it wasn't only that Jesus ate with sinners and defiled holy meals; it was that he was *always* eating and drinking. It seemed that wherever he went there was a party, and if the wine ran out, he was known to produce some more of the highest quality (John 2:1-11). So Jesus' enemies added the claim that he was "a glutton and a drunkard" to the charge that he ate with the wrong kind of people (Luke 7:34). But this complaint did not arise out of an asceticism that frowned on good food and fine wine. No, the problem was that such feasting was generally deemed inappropriate while Israel was in exile. In fact, the complaint about Jesus' relationship to wine and food is rooted in a larger issue: Jesus didn't appear to fast. Apart from his solitary fast in the wilderness for those forty days (Luke 4:1-13; Matt. 4:1-11; Mark 1:12-13), Jesus did not seem to keep the four annual fasts in mournful memory of the destruction of Jerusalem by the Babylonians (Zech. 8:19). Maybe he had read Isaiah 58 and thus wasn't too impressed with this kind of fasting, with its nostalgic memory of the Temple and everything it stood for.

So the religious leaders asked: "Why do John's disciples and the disciples of the Pharisees fast, but your disciples do not fast?" (Mark 2:18). And Jesus' cryptic answer: "The wedding guests cannot fast while the bridegroom is with them, can they? As long as they have the bridegroom with them, they cannot fast" (Mark 2:19). Fast to mourn your exile. Fast as the covenantal partner of God because your bridegroom has departed. But if the bridegroom is here, it is feast time, not fast time. If your bridegroom is here, exile is over. That's the audacious message of Jesus to Israel of the first century: exile is over and homecoming is now a reality in the presence of the returned groom. He engages in the feasting that is deemed appropriate only when the promises are fulfilled, because he believes that the kingdom he brings *is* the fulfillment of those promises. It is feast time because homecoming is offered in Jesus.

Much depends on dinner. Much depends on your dinner guests, where you eat, and what you eat. Jesus eats with tax collectors and sinners, and in doing so he proclaims that the kingdom of God is at hand and exile is over. But if exile is over, there must be a homecoming. And in the memories of Israel, such a homecoming would invariably take an exodus shape. Exodus is the story of God liberating his homeless people from the oppression of Egypt in order to bring them to a new home, a promised home.

Much depends on dinner. Matthew tells the story of an opulent feast of death in the palace of Herod. An over-the-top birthday party for the king, perhaps too much rich food, too much wine, and a bit of an erotic dance by the king's daughter. Before you know it, things get out of hand, rash promises have been made, and John the Baptist's decapitated head is on a platter along with the dessert offerings.

In contrast to this opulent feast of death, Matthew then tells a story of a radically different kind of meal. The contrast to Herod's decadent birthday bash is a messianic party in the wilderness — perhaps also a birthday party, but of a different kind. Jesus is in the wilderness, and the people are hungry. What will we eat? Where will we eat it? And how will food be provided? Jesus tells the crowds to get ready for a picnic in the wilderness, and then five loaves and two fish miraculously feed five thousand people, and there are twelve baskets of food left over. Food in the wilderness? Twelve baskets left over? Could this be a sign of a new Exodus? Could Jesus be a new Moses leading his people home? Manna in the wilderness? Could those twelve baskets (together with the twelve disciples) suggest a restoration of the twelve tribes of Israel? (See Mark 6:30-44; Luke 9:10-17; John 6:1-13.) Is this a party to celebrate the rebirth of Israel?

Much depends on dinner. Who gets invited to dinner and who is excluded? If this story of a new exodus is good news for Israel, for whom might it be bad news? If the first Exodus and subsequent conquest of the land of Canaan was good news for Israel, was it good news for the Canaanites and the other inhabitants of the land? Will this new Exodus in Jesus, this new homecoming, simply repeat the exclusions of the past? Will homecoming for Israel mean domicide for others? And if so, then how does that fit with the inclusive table fellowship that we have seen to be so scandalous about Jesus' practice?

Consider this: immediately after playing the new Moses in the wilderness with the feeding of the five thousand, Jesus enters a boat to cross a body of water. And the other side of that water is a territory that is decidedly gentile, not Jewish. While he is in that area, a woman whom Matthew calls a "Canaanite" comes to him and pleads for mercy for her daughter, who is tormented by a demon (Matt. 15:21-28).[71] It is very instructive that Matthew calls this woman a "Canaanite," because that term would have been anachronistic at the time. There were no Canaanites in the first century; no one had been called a Canaanite for hundreds of years. But here we have a woman identified as a Canaanite pleading for mercy. Remember that the first Moses had told the Israelites that, when they entered the land of promise, they would encounter seven nations — the Canaanites included — and they were to utterly destroy them and show them "no mercy" (Deut. 7:1-6).

Now we have Jesus crossing a body of water after feeding the new Israel in the wilderness. In terms of the narrative he is re-enacting, Jesus has crossed the Jordan and is now confronted with a "Canaanite" who is pleading for mercy. What should he do? According to the narrative of the first Moses, he should kill her. At first, Jesus does not answer. But she persists to the degree that the disciples ask him to send her away. He finally replies that he was sent only to the lost sheep of the house of Israel, and she is not part of that household. But the woman confronts Jesus more directly. Kneeling before him, she says, "Lord, help me." He replies, "It is not fair to take the children's food and throw it to the dogs." Much depends on dinner, and you weren't invited. "Yes, Lord," she answers, "but even the dogs eat the crumbs that fall from their master's table." Yes, I know much depends on dinner, but don't I at least get the crumbs? Even if I am supposed to be treated like a dog, isn't a dog part of the family household? This woman insists on sharing in the dinner of healing and restoration that Jesus has been serving. Recognizing the audacity of her faith, Jesus grants her request and heals her daughter. He shows mercy to a Canaanite and thus indicates that something about this new Exodus, this homecoming in Jesus, will reverse the exclusions of the first Exodus.

But there is more. A few verses later in this Matthew passage, Jesus is still in the same gentile territory, and there is yet another hungry crowd in

---

71. The exegesis that follows is dependent on the work of Grant LeMarquand, "The Canaanite Conquest of Jesus (Mt. 15:21-28)," in Essays in Honour of Frederik Wisse, *ARC, The Journal of the Faculty of Religious Studies* (McGill University, 2005): 237-47.

the wilderness. Once again Jesus takes the initiative and feeds four thousand people in the wilderness from meager resources. And how many baskets are left over? Seven full baskets. Why seven? Why were twelve baskets left over from the feeding of the five thousand? To symbolize the restoration of the twelve tribes of Israel. So why are seven left over this time? How many nations did Moses say were to be destroyed and shown no mercy in Canaan? Seven. The one Canaanite woman who receives mercy from Jesus symbolizes that the seven Canaanite nations will also receive mercy. The seven baskets indicate the reversal of the injunction to domicide in Deuteronomy, which was realized in the book of Joshua. The shalom of Jesus (Heb. *Yeshua*) is the reversal of the violence of Joshua.

Much depends on dinner. This dinner — with four thousand guests and seven full baskets left over — is the dinner of a new and inclusive kingdom. Homecoming is for all. But this can only spell trouble for Jesus.

Shalom and the Character
of Earthkeeping

All over this magnificent world God calls us to extend His
Kingdom of shalom — peace and wholeness — of justice, of
goodness, of compassion, of caring, of sharing, of laughter,
of joy, and of reconciliation. God is transfiguring the world
right this very moment through us because God believes in
us and because God loves us.

Desmond Tutu[1]

You hear the music in the background. Ten or so voices and an old organ.
The sacred hymn "Blessed Assurance" wafts through the little pink church
in Waxahachie, Texas, like a dove searching for a place to land. "Blessed assurance, Jesus is mine! O, what a foretaste of glory divine!" As the choir
sings on, you see Margaret and her husband, Wayne, in the first pew. Their
relationship has seemingly been soured forever by Wayne's adulterous
ways — with his best friend's wife, no less — and Margaret has met his en-
treaties for reconciliation with the stolidity of a stone wall. As the minister
reads the New Testament text for the day, the famous love chapter of 1 Co-
rinthians 13, Margaret slowly moves her hand over and gently grasps her
husband's. Their eyes meet, and without a word she grants forgiveness and
their reconciliation is made real.

Two rows behind them, in their Sunday best, sit Edna and her two
children, twelve-year-old son Frank and eight-year-old daughter Possum. A few months earlier, Edna's husband, the town's sheriff, was acci-

1. Desmond Tutu, *God Has a Dream* (New York: Doubleday, 2004), p. 128.

dentally shot and killed by a black teenager named Wiley, who was drunk at the time. Wiley was promptly hanged and dragged behind a truck by members of the local Klan, unhooded in the middle of a bright Sunday afternoon. Widowed in an early 1930s hardscrabble Texas town, with two young children to raise and no marketable skills, without even the knowledge of how to write a check, Edna has won — just the day before this church service — the coveted monetary prize for being the first to bring in the cotton crop. With the unlikely help of two one-time strangers — Moze, a vagabond black man who is savvy about planting and harvesting cotton, and Mr. Will, a blind W.W. I veteran renting a room in her house — and by her own backbreaking and hand-scabbing labor of many days and nights, Edna has managed to eke out enough money to pay her mortgage and keep her family together. Against all reasonable odds, Edna and her ragtag band of castoffs have defied the powers that be. They have also come to care for each other. When a tornado strikes, Mr. Will rescues Possum from an upstairs bedroom, and Edna leads Mr. Will to a storm shelter. At a town party, Frank asks to dance with his widowed mother.

This Sunday is Communion Sunday for Edna and her children in the wooden pew at the little pink church in Waxahachie. As the minister speaks the words of institution ("This is my body . . . this is my blood"), the choir begins to sing the familiar evangelical hymn "I Come to the Garden Alone." The chorus ("And He walks with me, and He talks with me, and He tells me I am his own") provides the backdrop as a silver tray containing plastic cups of grape juice is passed from person to person down the pews. Upon drinking the symbolic blood of Jesus, each person says to his or her neighbor, "The peace of God." In the company of those partaking of communion and passing the peace, you notice an elderly woman. This woman had been homeless, living in her car, when she was killed by the tornado that raged through town. But now she is among those celebrating the Lord's Supper. Behind the nameless woman, seated on the aisle near the back, you see Moze, an unexpected presence in this segregated white church. Furthermore, the Klan had run him out of town after viciously beating him. He had become yet another victim of racist violence, apparently destined for a vagabond life. But here he is, quietly taking communion in the little pink church.

Moze takes a cup of juice, drinks it, and serves Mr. Will, who is seated next to him. Mr. Will takes a cup, drinks, and serves Possum next to him, who takes a cup, drinks, and passes the tray to her big brother, Frank. As he drinks from the cup, Frank says to himself, "The peace of God." It is now his mother's turn. Edna drinks and she also repeats the words "The peace of God." When finished, Edna turns to her right and passes the cups of juice to her formerly dead husband, Royce, who, in turn, passes it to Wiley, his killer. Looking Wiley directly in the eye, Royce says, "The peace of God." With a subtle look that says all is finally well, Wiley drinks and wishes Royce "the peace of God." In the background you hear the words of the hymn, blanketing this scene of serene bliss: "The joy we share as we tarry there, none other has ever known." Ears and eyes reveal a time and place in which the peace of God is completely realized and joy is shared by all — life as we know in our gut it should be. Peace and harmony and joy: God's future of shalom.

This description is of the closing scene from the award-winning movie *Places in the Heart.* Its final surrealistic images are of life as it should be. Everyone, even the dead, is present in the little church, giving and receiving from each other the holy sacrament and offering the peace of God. Young widows and fatherless children, blind war vets and money-grubbing bankers, adulterers and killers, homeless women and Klansmen, black folks and white folks. This seemingly mundane ritual has been transfigured by director Robert Benton to portray heaven: life as God intends it to be, when all is set right. In his illuminating study of this film, Roy Anker comments: "This is, after all, what human life is for, this culmination of fellowship, reconciliation, and delight in the fullness of God's blessing."[2] It is a stunning cinematic vision of human reconciliation and of God's reuniting love, a vision of shalom. Anker continues:

> Within the all-encompassing love of God, the badly fractured world, a storm fraught with enmity and death, again becomes a garden, as the hymn suggests was God's intention for creation and history in the first place. While humans cannot fathom the mystery of love that is God, the iconic last image of dead men in forgiveness and reconciliation wordlessly defines what God is. The two men together in new life, imparting peace to one another, radiantly evoke the character of God's inmost self. . . . This is the destination toward which all the story's outcasts, and all people — even the Klansmen — journey. It is the place beyond words

---

2. Roy Anker, *Catching Light* (Grand Rapids: Eerdmans, 2005), p. 159.

that the heart knows, the place where all are reunited by the love of God, and all is made whole. (pp. 159-60)

Indeed, it is not just the final scene that discloses this vision of God's good future. The film as a whole is shot through with an aching for shalom. Benton's central point is that, in a world fraught with brokenness and violence, people yearn for healing and peace. In Anker's words:

The central datum of *Places in the Heart,* shown repeatedly in the film, is that people are beset, inside and out, by an enmity that wrecks people, families, societies, cultures, and nature itself — the physical and metaphysical landscape in which humanity has its being. People's deepest hope, then, is that somehow the human penchant for destruction might disappear so that the world might mend and heal. In quiet and profound ways, Benton dramatizes the desire of all people for a realm of trust, harmony, and intimacy where, at the very least, violence and discord are no more. (p. 145)

The preceding chapter described a world of ecological homelessness, a world groaning in travail, a world of ecological degradation, a world in which many are hunting for home and looking for hope. In this chapter we will attempt to describe ecological homecoming and homemaking. We will endeavor to put flesh on the biblical vision of shalom and wings on the Christian understanding of hope. We start with the biblical vision. What exactly is this vision of life as God intended it to be, life as it someday will be? We then explore what we call the virtues of shalom. What are the habits and inclinations of those who have imbibed the biblical story of shalom and seek to live it out in their lives? Moreover, what are the practices of earthkeepers? What actions spring from the virtues of peaceableness and justice, compassion and wisdom? And given the push and pull of our times, how do we counter the sociocultural pressures that render us homeless?

The Biblical Vision of Shalom

A vision of shalom *(šālôm)* is present throughout the Old Testament, but perhaps never more so than in the Hebrew prophets. Most evocative among them is Ezekiel, who speaks of "a covenant of peace" in which humans will no longer be threatened by wild animals "so that they may live in the wilds and the woods securely." Because "showers of blessings" will fall, "the trees of the field shall yield their fruit, and the earth shall yield its increase," and God will "provide for them a splendid vegetation so that they shall no more be consumed with hunger in the land." Here shalom encompasses a rich agricultural fruitfulness. But there is more. "They shall know that I am the Lord, when I break the bars of their yoke, and save them from the hand of those who enslaved them"; therefore, "they shall no more be plunder for the nations" but "shall live in safety, and no one shall make them afraid" (Ezek. 34:25-31). Safety and security, fertility and fruitfulness, liberation and freedom, dignity and respect — all signs of the future shalom of God. A place of permanence and dwelling, of belonging and of safe rest. In other words, Ezekiel's covenant of peace describes a future homemaking and homecoming.

Isaiah also envisions a kingdom of shalom. In wildly suggestive language, he says:

> The wolf shall live with the lamb,
> the leopard shall lie down with the kid,
> the calf and the lion and the fatling together,
> and a little child shall lead them.
> The cow and the bear shall graze,
> their young shall lie down together;
> and the lion shall eat straw like the ox.
>
> (Isa. 11:6-7)

Under what conditions could anyone imagine such a world of ecological harmony? When could it ever be said that "they will not hurt or harm on all my holy mountain" (Isa. 65:25)? Only when the spirit of the Lord rests on the coming king: "the spirit of wisdom and understanding, the spirit of counsel and might, the spirit of knowledge and the fear of the Lord" (Isa. 11:2). Only when one comes to rule with righteousness *(sedāqāh)* and justice *(mišpāṭ)*. Only under such a Spirit-filled rule will a peaceable kingdom come to be — in a time when violence and destruction are no more. Peaceful habitation, genuine homecoming, is possible only if justice and righteousness first dwell in the land.

This is not the way it is now; nor was it Israel's reality after the exile. Shalom, justice, and righteousness were still supplanted by enmity, oppression, and exploitation. But the ancient prophetic voice of Isaiah won't have it. The prophet has two words for a world of weeping and distress, two radical words that imagine a different way of life: "No more."

No more weeping.
No more cries of distress.
No more premature deaths.
No more expropriation of land.
No more injustice.
No more cash crops.
No more children for calamity.
No more laboring in vain.

Why not? Because God is making a new heaven and a new earth. Creation will again be a site of joy and delight. Jerusalem will once again be a city of shalom. Indeed, all cities will be cities of shalom (Isa. 65:17-25).

Isaiah offers us an audacious vision of a city that will bring an end to neglect, malnutrition, violence, disease, and premature death. There will be no children crying, because they will not be orphaned by either HIV/AIDS or overextended parents on the career treadmill. There will be no expropriated land, because people will be secure in their homes, in a community with neighbors, with food sustainably produced. In this vision our labor is meaningful because we experience a day's good work as joy-filled stewardship of creation. In this vision we inhabit a city of shalom because it is a place of economic stability, care, and generosity. In this vision we indwell a renewed city in a restored creation. Isaiah's vision is of economic viability, ecological sustainability, just resource distribution, and meaningful work. This is a vision of home rooted in nothing less than the very presence of God.

A younger contemporary of Isaiah, a commoner from the village of Moresheth in the Judean foothills southwest of Jerusalem, shared much of Isaiah's divinely inspired vision of shalom. Micah describes Israel's bright future on the far side of the painful consequences of injustice and idolatry. The peoples of the world will flock to Jerusalem to learn the Torah (instruction in right living), and the result will be that "they shall beat their swords into plowshares, and their spears into pruning hooks" (Micah 4:1-4).[3]

---

3. In 6:6-8, Micah summarizes the requirements of right worship and good living: God requires of us mortal humans only that we do justice *(mišpāṭ)*, love kindness *(ḥesed)*, and walk humbly with God. Justice, love, and humility — the markers of shalom.

Weapons of death will be transfigured into tools of life, peaceful garden tools that enhance a household economy and tend the earth. As in the story of Naboth's vineyard, the issue is whether we take and kill or tend and keep. Isaiah and Micah both reach back into some of the oldest and deepest memories of covenantal homemaking with the Creator God.

A similar vision of shalom is found in the Torah. Shalom rings out as what God desires for the earth and earth creatures. For example, Moses calls the people of Israel to a decision by listing the blessings that accompany obedience and the curses that follow from unfaithfulness. If the people keep the commandments of Yahweh and walk in the ways of the LORD, then both cities and fields will flourish, both they and their livestock will be fruitful, both their going out and coming in will be safe. There will be rain in due season, financial security at home, and a fine reputation among the peoples and kingdoms of the world (Deut. 28:1-14).[4] And in the case law it says that, if we keep God's commandments, there will be fruitfulness in the field, nourishment enough and to spare, security from beast and human alike, no fear or violence in the land (Lev. 26:3-6). Shalom in all its many dimensions.

This rich vision of shalom comes together in Psalm 85, a group prayer for deliverance from national adversity, where the psalmist pleads (vv. 8-11):

> Let me hear what God the LORD will speak,
> for he will speak peace to his people,
> to his faithful, to those who turn to him in their hearts.
> Surely his salvation is at hand for those who fear him,
> that his glory may dwell in our land.
> Steadfast love and faithfulness will meet;
> righteousness and peace will kiss each other.
> Faithfulness will spring up from the ground,
> and righteousness will look down from the sky.

Salvation for those who fear Yahweh is at hand. And what does that salvation consist of? Steadfast love *(ḥesed)* and faithfulness *('ĕmûnāh)* will embrace, righteousness *(ṣedāqāh)* and peace *(šālôm)* will kiss. One could not

---

4. The Ten Commandments are set in this context of life-giving shalom. At the end of the Decalogue we are twice reminded that the community should obey the commandments "so that you may live, and that it may go well with you, and that you may live long in the land that you are to possess" (Deut. 5:29, 33).

hope to find four more potent words in Scripture, especially so close together. Steadfast love *(ḥesed)* describes the compassion of the God who heard the groaning of his chosen people in Egypt, remembered his covenant, and acted to relieve their suffering and liberate his people from exile (Exod. 6:2-8). Faithfulness *('ĕmûnāh)* depicts a God who is as reliable and trustworthy as a rock (Ps. 95). Righteousness *(ṣedāqāh)* names the God who desires justice and rightness in all relationships and who delights in children playing in the street (Zech. 8:3-8). And shalom *(šālôm)* is that pregnant Hebrew term that strives to name the ideal world, one that is flourishing in all things and praising God in all ways (Ps. 148). All of these are central attributes of God. All are also crucial marks of God's people in the world God desires. And all are key features of the homemaking and homecoming to which we are called.

The New Testament has no shortage of similar texts: this vision of shalom permeates its pages. For example, Luke begins his Gospel with multiple references to shalom *(eirēnē* in Greek). After Mary has sung the Magnificat, about God's mercy to her and to her people, Zechariah the priest is filled with the Holy Spirit and full of joy at the birth of his baby boy. Praising God for his blessings and thanking God for his mercy, Zechariah exclaims:

> By the tender mercy of our God,
> the dawn from on high will break upon us,
> to give light to those who sit in darkness and in the shadow of death,
> to guide our feet into the way of peace.
>
> (Luke 1:78-79)

God has remembered his covenant with the ancestors and raised up a savior-messiah who will guide the covenant people in the way of shalom — from darkness into light, from death to life. Not surprisingly, at the birth of this baby messiah, the angels declare: "Glory to God in the highest heaven, and on earth peace among those he favors!" (Luke 2:14). On earth, peace. This child shall be a harbinger and bringer of shalom. And when the infant Jesus is brought to the Temple, devout old Simeon, also led by the Spirit, takes him in his aged arms and passionately prays:

> Master, now you are dismissing your servant in peace,
> according to your word;

for my eyes have seen your salvation,
which you have prepared in the presence of all peoples,
a light for revelation to the Gentiles,
and for glory to your people Israel.

(Luke 2:29-32)

Now, says righteous Simeon, I can die in peace.

Luke is not finished with us or with God's vision of shalom. Not much later in his Gospel, he records Jesus' inaugural sermon at the beginning of his public ministry (Luke 4:14-30). Jesus returns to his hometown synagogue in Nazareth, where, filled with the power of the Holy Spirit, he is given the coveted chance to read the lesson from Scripture. Whether he has chosen this text or it is the reading for that day, we do not know. In any case, he reads from Isaiah 61:1-2:

The Spirit of the Lord is upon me,
because he has anointed me
to bring good news to the poor.
He has sent me to proclaim release to the captives,
and recovery of sight to the blind,
to let the oppressed go free,
to proclaim the year of the Lord's favor.

Jesus sits down to comment on the text, as the rabbis did, and it's not surprising that we are told, "The eyes of all in the synagogue were fixed upon him." What will this crazy carpenter-rabbi say about this dynamite text? His first words fall like summer rain on parched ground: "Today this scripture has been fulfilled in your hearing." In other words, Jesus says, God's Spirit is upon me. I am the one anointed to bring good news to the poor, the captive, the blind, the oppressed. I am God's Chosen One, the Messiah, who will, like Moses of old, bring God's people out of exile, an exile that engulfs them in their own land. I, says Jesus, am God's agent of shalom.

It is Jubilee time in Nazareth! Today is the year of the Lord's favor! Today is the day of redemption! Today is the day of release! Today is the day of homecoming! The hometown crowd love the sermon, though some wonder why the rabbi has changed a few things in the text: that reference to sight for the blind, for example, is not in the Isaiah 61 text but was slipped in from Isaiah 42:7; and for some reason Jesus cut the reading short

204

in the middle of verse 2. After the Jubilee reference to the favorable year of the Lord, the Isaiah text actually says: ". . . and the day of the vengeance of our God." But rabbis do that sort of thing. The important point was Jesus' good news to his neighbors that redemptive homecoming is at hand.

The story that follows demonstrates why Jesus dropped the reference to vengeance, and also why he added the reference to the blind and those who needed sight. The Jews in Nazareth thought they had God all figured out. God loved them, not the gentiles. God's salvation was for them, not for people of another race or ethnic group — certainly not for the gentiles who had oppressed them and kept them as exiles in their own land. Jesus deliberately picks a fight with the crowd by referring to two tales that were not exactly favorite bedtime stories for the good folks of Nazareth: the story of Elijah saving the life of a Sidonite widow while Israelite widows died in a famine, and the story of Elisha healing the leprosy of Naaman, a Syrian military man who had oppressed Israelites and taken their children into slavery.

By reminding them of what their very own sacred Scripture teaches, Jesus forcibly insists that God's love and grace and mercy is as wide as the ocean and as high as the sky. God's mercy extends to widows in Zarephath and lepers from Syria — gentiles all. In God's kingdom of shalom there is no place for racism or ethnocentrism. As Luke makes crystal clear, this is precisely the kind of kingdom Jesus comes to inaugurate. If there is to be covenantal homecoming in Jesus, if there is to be a realization of the prophetic vision of a kingdom of shalom, this will be a kingdom as wide as creation and a home suffused with the most radical hospitality.

With Luke's special emphasis on God's mercy and Jesus' compassion — to all manner of outsiders, including slaves of Roman army officers, sonless widows, shunned women, bleeding women, crippled women, banished lepers, despised tax collectors — it is not surprising that Luke ends where he begins. Luke's Jesus, and the God to whom he points, bears witness to shalom. In Luke's final chapter he records the last encounter of the disciples with the resurrected Christ. After the two men met Jesus on the road to Emmaus, some of his disciples had gathered and were pondering that strange story. Jesus suddenly appears to them and greets them: "Peace be with you" (Luke 24:36). God's shalom be with you all. May God's assurance of safety defuse your feelings of fear. May God's blessing of knowledge answer your anxious questions. May God's promise of abiding presence meet your lingering doubt. Luke's *inclusio* of shalom frames his Gospel and its message.[5]

One could argue that the rest of the New Testament is a witness to how the earliest Christian communities struggled with the meaning of this vision of peace in Christ. Jesus reminded Israel of the comprehensive scope and radical inclusivity of God's covenantal homemaking. The covenant that begins with Noah and becomes focused with Abraham was always a covenant for creation-wide homemaking. Covenantal homemaking is always a homemaking of welcome, not one of exclusivity and enclosure for a special people.

No one understood the implications of such a homecoming vision in Christ better than the apostle Paul. In his letter to the Ephesians, Paul paints a stunning picture of shalom. After a reminder that salvation is by grace through faith, Paul speaks directly to the matter of the distinction (and enmity) between Jew and gentile. Gentiles, says Paul, were once "aliens from the commonwealth of Israel and strangers to the covenants of promise, having no hope and without God in the world." He continues:

> But now in Christ Jesus you who once were far off have been brought near by the blood of Christ. For he is our peace; in his flesh he has made both groups into one and has broken down the dividing wall, that is, the hostility between us. He has abolished the law with its commandments and ordinances, that he might create in himself one new humanity in place of the two, thus making peace, and might reconcile both groups to God in one body through the cross, thus putting to death that hostility through it. So he came and proclaimed peace to you who were far off and peace to those who were near; for through him both of us have access in one Spirit to the Father. So then you are no longer strangers and aliens, but you are citizens with the saints and also members of the household of God, built upon the foundation of the apostles and prophets, with Christ Jesus himself as the cornerstone. In him the whole structure is joined together and grows into a holy temple in the Lord; in

---

5. In his second volume, the Acts of the Apostles, Luke includes a succinct summary of the gospel (Acts 10:34-43). In a speech to Cornelius and his clan, Peter declares: "I truly understand that God shows no partiality, but in every nation anyone who fears him and does what is right is acceptable to him. You know the message he sent to the people of Israel, preaching peace by Jesus Christ — he is Lord of all." In short, God's message to his people is this: Jesus is Lord, and this Jesus is God's embodiment of shalom.

whom you also are built together in the Spirit into a dwelling place for God (Eph. 2:12-20).

Jesus the Messiah is shalom incarnate. In his life and death he has broken down the dividing walls of exclusion and enmity between Jew and gentile and has reconciled both groups to God and to each other — one new humanity through the cross. Means and end agree: the goal of peace is achieved by the way of peace. By Christ's blood, freely shed as an innocent victim, God has braided into a single family those who were once divided. Estrangement from God is overcome. Racial and ethnic reconciliation in Christ is made real. Therefore, none are aliens; all are citizens. None are strangers; all are friends. Christ's shalom is for all. In Trinitarian language, Paul affirms that through Christ all have access in the one Spirit to the Father. In the Spirit, through Christ, we have access to the Father.

Mixing metaphors, Paul also speaks of this peacemaking in terms of home construction. Not only are we one new humanity and one body, we are all members of the household of God *(oikeioi tou theou)*. This expansive house has as its firm foundation the good work of apostles and prophets, with none other than Jesus Christ as the cornerstone, the stone without which no sound or true building can be built. Furthermore, in Christ the beams and timbers, the bricks and mortar, are all carefully joined into a single building, a temple set apart for service to God. This house, this one body of Jews and gentiles alike, is the home of God, the place where God is present and people meet God. Homebreakers become homemakers, all because of what Christ has done on the cross. Paul speaks, in Trinitarian fashion, of Christ as the one in whom you all (gentiles) are built together (with the Jews) into a dwelling place of God in the Spirit. The church constitutes the home of God, and this living and breathing home is a home of shalom.[6]

This biblical vision contains within it what we call the virtues of shalom. Before we move on to a discussion of these virtues, three observations about shalom. First, this vision of human flourishing is a vision of a flourishing *community*. This may seem too obvious to mention, but not all visions of the good life are communal. Indeed, modernity gives highest pri-

---

6. For a comprehensive description of shalom in the New Testament, see Willard Swartley, *Covenant of Peace: The Missing Peace in New Testament Theology and Ethics* (Grand Rapids: Eerdmans, 2006).

ority to the autonomous individual as central to the good life.[7] In Scripture, however, shalom aims to describe human community.

In addition, shalom describes humans at peace in *all relationships:* with God, oneself, other people, and the natural world. We tend to limit shalom to our relationships with God or other people, but it is much bigger than that. "Shalom is present," says Nicholas Wolterstorff, "when a person dwells at peace in all his or her relationships: with God, with self, with fellows, with nature."[8] Shalom is both communal and multirelational.

Finally, this vision of human flourishing includes *more than humans.* Indeed, it is, strictly speaking, a vision of the flourishing of all things. As the biblical texts amply indicate, shalom includes wolves and lambs, trees and soil, forests and rivers. It has to do with all kinds of creatures living in right relationships. In summary, shalom is the biblical vision of the creation-wide flourishing of all things. Like a diamond with many facets, shalom is the name for that time and place where all things thrive as God intends. Shalom is that end toward which God's people walk in faith. Walter Brueggemann observes: "The origin and destiny of God's people is to be on the road of *shalom*, which is to live out of joyous memories and toward greater anticipations."[9] We are pilgrims on the way of peace. We are sojourners on the road of shalom. We are homemakers in a world of homelessness, yearning for the great homecoming banquet feast.

The Virtues of Shalom

Discussion of the biblical vision of shalom naturally raises the question of how to bring such a state of universal flourishing into existence, especially

---

7. See Charles Taylor, *Sources of the Self: The Making of the Modern Identity* (Cambridge, MA: Harvard University Press, 1992).

8. Nicholas Wolterstorff, *Educating for Life* (Grand Rapids: Brazos, 2002), p. 101.

9. Walter Brueggemann, *Living Toward a Vision* (Philadelphia: United Church Press, 1982), p. 16. Neal Plantinga captures this well: "The webbing together of God, humans, and all creation in justice, fulfillment, and delight is what the Hebrew prophets call *shalom.* We call it peace, but it means far more than mere peace of mind or a cease-fire between enemies. In the Bible shalom means *universal flourishing, wholeness, and delight* — a rich state of affairs in which natural needs are satisfied and natural gifts are fruitfully employed, a state of affairs that inspires joyful wonder as its Creator and Savior opens doors and welcomes the creatures in whom he delights. Shalom, in other words, is the way things ought to be" (*Not the Way It's Supposed to Be* [Grand Rapids, Eerdmans, 1994], p. 10).

given the sociocultural analysis of the preceding chapter. How do we become agents of shalom in a culture characterized by anthropocentrism, materialism, technicism, and all the other isms mentioned earlier? What kind of people must we be in order to resist the destruction of place, to reject consumption as a way of life, and to oppose the growth-is-always-good mentality of the market? If we long for homecoming in a culture of homelessness, then what are the virtues of homemaking?[10]

If we are to replace patterns of living that produce homelessness, then we will need to be a different kind of people. How we live depends on who we are, and who we are depends on the stories we identify with. Practices are rooted in character, and character is rooted in story. Stanley Hauerwas puts it this way:

> Our character is the result of our sustained attention to the world that gives coherence to our intentionality. Such attention is formed and given content by the stories through which we have learned to form the story of our lives. To be moral persons is to allow stories to be told through us so that our manifold activities gain a coherence that allows us to claim them for our own . . . . Our character is constituted by the rules, metaphors, and stories that are combined to give a design and unity to the variety of things we must and must not do in our lives. If our lives are to be reflective and coherent, our vision must be ordered around dominant metaphors or stories.[11]

Note that Hauerwas offers this depiction of the relationship of ethics, narrative, and character with a sense of considerable generality. The claim is that all human action is shaped in terms of narratively formed character. And this is true because human action, at least if it is self-aware and deliberative, is a matter of human intentionality. In other words, "[w]e do not tell stories simply because they provide us a more colorful way to say what can be said in a different way, but because there is no other way we can ar-

---

10. In asking these questions, we are intentionally pursuing one particular approach to ethics and not others. In asking "What kind of people must we be?" we mean to emphasize virtues rather than duties or consequences. Most scholars adopt one of two basic ethical perspectives: a focus on duties and obligations (deontology) or attention to goods and consequences (teleology). We side with those who argue that attention to the virtues (areteology) is more important than either duties or consequences.

11. Stanley Hauerwas, *Vision and Virtue* (Notre Dame, IN: Fides Publications, 1974), p. 74.

ticulate the richness of intentional activity — that is, behavior that is purposeful but not necessary."[12] There is a "narrative quality" to human experience.[13]

Dwelling in our stories, we relate to "the origins and goals of our lives, as they embody in narrative form specific ways of acting out that relatedness. So in allowing ourselves to adopt and be adopted by a particular story, we are in fact assuming a set of practices which will shape the ways we relate to our world and destiny."[14] The stories we hear — of manifest destiny, of material prosperity, of a crazy carpenter from Nazareth — mold and shape our character. And these grand, meaning-giving stories, as well as the people held up in them as examples or models to follow, are an integral part of the communities in which we live.

Thus a virtue is a narratively formed character trait, an attribute or quality of who we are. And because people are shaped by competing narratives, we find ourselves living in a world of competing understandings of what virtuous living looks like. For example, one strand of folk wisdom says, "Cleanliness is next to godliness." But what is cleanliness? What is a clean home? That depends on what narrative most profoundly shapes that home. Jesus found himself in a lot of trouble over the matter of cleanliness, because he lived out of an understanding of the story of the Jewish covenant that was different from the Pharisees'. An American family shaped by the medically inspired preoccupation with germs and sanitation of the 1950s will have a different idea of cleanliness and defilement than a family that comes from a different part of the world and has been shaped by a different narrative. Or consider greed. While most worldviews throughout history have viewed greed as a vice, modern capitalism has transformed greed from a vice into a virtue. Without self-interested greed, it is argued, the economy would crumble and homeless-

12. Hauerwas, *Truthfulness and Tragedy* (Notre Dame, IN: University of Notre Dame Press, 1977), p. 76.

13. See Stephen Crites's influential essay "The Narrative Quality of Experience," in Stanley Hauerwas and L. Gregory Jones, eds., *Why Narrative? Readings in Narrative Theology* (Grand Rapids: Eerdmans, 1989), pp. 65-88. See also Paul Ricoeur, *Time and Narrative*, vols. 1-3 (Chicago: University of Chicago Press, 1990). Steven Bouma-Prediger unpacks the implications of a virtue ethic rooted in narrative and character formation for ecological ethics in *For the Beauty of the Earth*, ch. 6.

14. Stanley Hauerwas and David Burrell, "From System to Story: An Alternative Pattern for Rationality in Ethics," in *Why Narrative?* p. 186.

ness would be even more widespread than it is. Or consider care. Do we have a responsibility to care for the most vulnerable in our society? Almost everyone would say that trying to form a caring society is a virtuous thing; but the shape that such care might take differs greatly depending on the narrative. If you live out of a narrative in which progress is defined as economic growth at all costs, then caring is giving tax cuts to the rich, doing everything to increase bottom-line profits, and exploiting resources for economic gain today with little attention to ecological consequences tomorrow. Virtues are narratively formed; hence they are never neutral.

Our choices over time steer us in certain directions and color the way we see ourselves and the world. So there is an intimate connection between virtue and vision. As Gilbert Meilaender says, "What duties we perceive — and even what dilemmas — may depend upon what virtues shape our vision of the world."[15] C. S. Lewis captures this point well in *The Magician's Nephew*, Book 6 of *The Chronicles of Narnia*. The creation of Narnia by Aslan looks and feels very different for wicked Uncle Andrew than it does for the children. While the children find it alluring and beautiful and understand the words spoken by the animals, Uncle Andrew shrinks back in fear and hears only barking and howling. Indeed, because of his (evil) character, he misses the whole point and misconstrues the very nature of both Aslan the creator and what is created. As the narrator comments: "For what you see and hear depends a good deal on where you are standing; it also depends on what sort of person you are."[16] Virtues inform vision, and vision shapes action, just as virtues themselves are shaped by habits over time.

In summary, virtues are story-shaped, praiseworthy character traits formed by choices over time that dispose us to act consistent with our most deeply grounded narrative. We know what is truly good and how to live well by looking to people of virtue as role models and by drinking in certain narratives in particular communities. The vision of shalom we meet in the Bible is a vision rooted in the overall narrative of home, homelessness, and homecoming. Shalom is not a principle somehow established as a timeless truth. Rather, shalom is a vision that arises out of a particular way of telling the story of the world, a particular narrative preoccupied

---

15. Gilbert Meilaender, "Virtue in Contemporary Religious Thought," in Richard John Neuhaus, ed., *Virtue — Public and Private* (Grand Rapids: Eerdmans, 1986), p. 9.

16. C. S. Lewis, *The Magician's Nephew* (New York: Macmillan, 1978), p. 125.

with themes of covenantal homemaking. To live in this story gives birth to the virtues of shalom in a community formed by this narrative.

Let's return to our original questions: What kinds of people must we be in order to overcome the deafness and ignorance, denial and indifference that plague our culture? What habitual dispositions must we exhibit to be faithful earthkeepers, the agents of transformation God uses to transfigure the world into a place of shalom? Of the many candidates, we believe that four virtues are most important: peaceableness, justice, compassion, and wisdom.[17] We will not begin to address ecological homelessness and the defilement of our home planet unless we become people who exhibit these traits of character.

Peaceableness

Before we can understand the virtue of peaceableness, we must first ask what peace is. Peace is, minimally speaking and in the usual sense of the term, the absence of hostility and enmity. It is a cease-fire between combatants. More positively, peace denotes concord or harmony in one's relationships. It is, to use the biblical language, righteousness. Peace in this sense is being in right relationships in all of the four ways previously mentioned: right relationships with God, with oneself, with other people, and with our nonhuman neighbors. The "rightness" in these relations is found in the absence of discord and the presence of harmony, a pleasing relationship of the parts with each other.

If this is what peace is, then the virtue of peaceableness is the settled disposition to bring about concord among those in conflict. It is the rare and valuable skill of the consummate mediator who listens carefully to all sides, respects genuine differences, and manages to forge understanding and even agreement among warring factions — whether that is a married couple in crisis, union and management facing off across a picket line, or two countries locked in mortal combat. Peaceableness does not mean an inclination to appease or pacify by ignoring real conflict or sacrificing

---

17. Why, some may ask, these four? In brief, these four are absolutely central to the embodiment of shalom: peaceableness lies at the very center of what shalom is; justice and compassion are essential to the realization of shalom; and the practice of love and compassion require wisdom.

core principles. But it does mean habitually acting in a conciliatory way, seeking by good will to bridge differences and unite antagonists. There can be no experience of home without such a practice of peaceableness.

Peaceableness requires, among other things, honesty. It demands a steadfast refusal to deceive oneself or anyone else, plus a perceptible sincerity of intention and straightforwardness of conduct. The making of peace, in other words, is contingent on truth-telling and transparency. Peaceableness also requires courage, or firmness of resolve and flintiness of spirit in the face of danger. It entails tenacity in the face of opposition and persistence in the face of adversity, because the making of peace is seldom easy or quick.

As the example of Jesus Christ profoundly indicates, peaceableness may require great sacrifice. It may mean personally bearing evil in order to break the cycle of violence. This realization is powerfully evident in the writings and life of Martin Luther King, Jr. For example, in his essay "Nonviolence: The Only Road to Freedom," King says that the creation of a world of shalom "will be accomplished by persons who have the courage to put an end to suffering by willingly suffering themselves rather than inflict suffering on others." And in his famous Christmas Eve (1967) sermon on peace, King declares: "Somehow we must be able to stand up before our most bitter opponents and say: 'We shall match your capacity to inflict suffering by our capacity to endure suffering. We will meet your physical force with soul force. Do to us what you will and we will still love you.'"[18] "Blessed are the peacemakers," Jesus said in one of his famous beatitudes, "for they will be called children of God" (Matt. 5:9). Blessed are those who habitually act in ways that overcome enmity and bring about harmony, even when the cost is high.

The vice opposite to the virtue of peaceableness is contentiousness.[19] It is the disposition to be quarrelsome, belligerent, and disputatious. And

---

18. In James Washington, ed., *A Testament of Hope* (New York: Harper, 1986), pp. 61, 256. This way of nonviolence is also prophetically clear in the writings and life of martyred Salvadoran archbishop Oscar Romero. See, e.g., the collection of essays *The Violence of Love* (Farmington, PA: Plough Publishing House, 1998).

19. Contrary to Aristotle, who argues that every (or almost every) virtue has two associated vices, since a virtue is a kind of mean between two extremes, we claim that the virtues outlined here have only one vice, because they are not means between extremes but intrinsic goods. So one can never get enough peaceableness or justice or compassion or wisdom. There is no vice of excess, only a vice of deficiency.

beyond mere verbal attack, it is the disposition to foment strife and enmity. Like a parasite living on a host, contentiousness feeds on rage and rancor, antipathy and animosity, to fan the fire of discord and accelerate the spiral of violence. The contentious person relishes the dissonant chord and delights in despoiling right relationships. He or she habitually acts to disturb the peace, not in the manner of a righteous prophet disrupting a false "peace," but like a sullen adolescent who is always itching to disrupt life at home, or like an ecological vandal, whose actions foment more destruction.

In a world of ecological homelessness, peaceable people seek long-term, nonviolent solutions for those in the death grip of poverty. Peaceable people expose the emptiness of consumerism and materialism, not with an air of condemnation but in the spirit of conciliation. Peaceable people refuse to stereotype those with whom they disagree in the heated controversy over the local watershed, nor do they belittle those whose views of globalization do not coincide with theirs. Peaceable people cherish what is old and know when to say enough is enough. In a culture of displacement, where feelings of deprivation and alienation are sinking in and hope is fading fast, people of peace are like a healing balm on an open wound. If we are to resist all that conspires to render us homeless on our home planet, and if we are to be earthkeeping homemakers, then we must be makers of peace.

Justice

But the virtue of peaceableness does not, in itself, make for the fullness of shalom. Along with peace and peaceableness, there must be justice. Nicholas Wolterstorff expresses it succinctly: "There can be no shalom without justice. Justice is the ground floor of shalom."[20] Justice is the second virtue of shalom, but what is justice?

Almost every biblical text we have mentioned above includes justice as an integral part of shalom.[21] Psalm 72 is an especially fine example, for it is a prayer for God's blessing on the king. Here we find a rich description of

20. Wolterstorff, *Educating for Shalom* (Grand Rapids: Eerdmans, 2004), p. 23.
21. For an exhaustive listing of biblical texts on justice, see Ron Sider, ed., *Cry Justice: The Bible on Hunger and Poverty* (New York: Paulist, 1980).

justice and the just ruler: justice is what allows the king to rule rightly, for rich and poor alike; justice is what sensitizes the king to those who are weak and needy and thus especially vulnerable to being taken advantage of; justice is what empowers the king to redeem the enslaved from oppression. Liberation from oppression, care for the vulnerable, fairness for all — that is a succinct summary of what justice is.

If justice is a matter of receiving one's due, of enjoying the blessings and the responsibilities of a life directed to shalom, then we could say that justice is enjoying what one has a right to. Since a right is a legitimate claim to some good, a society is just when everyone enjoys the goods to which they have legitimate claim. A society is just when everyone's sustenance rights are respected. A society is just only when it honors legitimate claims to human dignity and respects basic human rights. As Wolterstorff argues, "If persons do not enjoy and possess what is due them, if their rightful claims on others are not acknowledged by those others, then shalom is absent."[22] No justice, no shalom.

So shalom is absent whenever fundamental rights are flouted, whenever basic needs go unmet, whenever legitimate goods are not enjoyed. Liberation from injustice and freedom from oppression are at the very core of shalom. And of special concern in Scripture are the rights of those most vulnerable: the widows, the orphans, and the aliens (or sojourners). These three groups show up often in Old Testament discussions of justice. Again, Wolterstorff says it well:

> What is striking in the Old Testament declarations about justice is the passionate insistence that all members of the community are entitled to a full and secure place in the life of the community. Hence the clanging repetitive reference to orphans, widows, and sojourners. Over and over when justice is spoken of, that trinity is brought into view. For these were the marginal ones in ancient Israeli [sic] society. Justice arrives only when the marginal ones are no longer marginal. (p. 143)

This Old Testament concern for the most vulnerable is also fully present in the life of Jesus. Jesus is very concerned about those on the margins, particularly aware of how the most vulnerable are exploited and mistreated. The modern Western understanding of justice as the free exercise of one's own

---

22. Wolterstorff, *Educating for Shalom*, p. 23.

will, provided only that no harm is done to another, does not remotely resemble this biblical idea of justice.[23]

Justice is about fundamental fairness and respecting the basic rights of other humans. What, then, does a person with a habitual disposition to act justly look like? To put it simply, the just person treats others fairly and, to be more precise, exhibits equity: she treats equals equally and unequals differentially. Note that equity is not the same as equality. Equality implies sameness: one treats everyone, regardless of circumstances, the same. Equity implies different treatment depending on the circumstances, precisely in order to be fair. Equity requires that widows, orphans, and strangers be treated differently.

So we can say that the virtue of justice is the disposition to act equitably; it is habitual fairness. Given that it requires the ability to discern when to treat equals equally and unequals differentially, the virtue of justice requires a kind of practical wisdom.[24] In other words, the virtue of justice assumes an ability to discern when circumstances warrant differential treatment and when people, despite differences, should be treated the same. In terms of the language of rights that we have used above, the just person not only respects people's rights but also knows how rightly to respect one person's rights when faced with the competing rights (and needs) of others.

The fairness at the heart of the virtue of justice, moreover, is fueled by respect. Respect is an understanding of and proper regard for the integrity and well-being of another because of the other's unique character and value. It is a looking back (a re-specting) that acknowledges God-given value. A respectful person neither overlooks you nor looks you over. You are neither part of the scenery nor an object of conquest. In sum, the virtue of justice is the settled disposition to treat others fairly, rooted in wisdom and respect.

The vice contrary to the virtue of justice is injustice. Injustice is the propensity to be partial, to play favorites for no good reason or, more perversely, for personal gain. Injustice is the disposition not to give people their due, and thus it manifests itself in the willingness to violate others'

---

23. For a lucid summary of the main theories of justice in the Western tradition, see Karen Lebacqz, *Six Theories of Justice* (Minneapolis: Augsburg, 1986).

24. In this regard, Aristotle's exposition (in *Nicomachean Ethics,* Book IV, chs. 5, 9-13) on practical wisdom *(phronēsis)* is instructive. Practical wisdom, he argues, involves a number of other intellectual abilities, e.g., deliberation, understanding, and judgment. Judgment is "the right discrimination of the equitable," and those who possess it are called "sympathetic judges" (1143a20).

rights. The parent who always favors the oldest son, for no good reason, over the youngest daughter; the city council that continually looks the other way regarding racist housing practices; the country that steadfastly refuses to acknowledge the legitimate rights of its native peoples — all of these exhibit the vice of injustice. In all these instances, shalom is wounded because the virtue of justice has gone wanting.

In a culture of ecological homelessness, just people fight for the sustenance rights of those who are most vulnerable in our society. Just people acknowledge the unfairness of the consumption patterns of the rich Northern Hemisphere in a world where billions have so little. Just people speak out against the manifest inequities of globalization in a world of ecological wounds and show how current political arrangements fail to respect the rights of all. Just people insist that the good life is much more than the free exercise of one's autonomous will in the consuming pursuit of the bigger and the newer. In a world of perpetual displacements and jarring dislocation, people of justice are like soothing rain on parched earth.

Compassion

But shalom includes more than peaceableness and more than justice. While both are necessary, they are not sufficient. The flourishing that is shalom includes more than the absence of conflict and respecting people's rights. Shalom also includes caring for the needs of others. It includes a special kind of love that we call compassion. Compassion is what happens when love meets suffering, when love meets the broken. One major problem, however, is that the term "love" has been reduced in our culture to a romantic feeling, which itself has been reduced to sex. A shalom vision needs a richer and deeper understanding of love, an understanding rooted in the narrative of Jesus.

While the greatest commandment (found in Matt. 22:36-40; Mark 12:28-31; Luke 10:25-28) is often mentioned as the heart of Jesus' message and the core of Christian ethics, a better candidate is the "new commandment" that Jesus has given us and has lived out himself. In other words, from a Christian perspective, the words and deeds of Jesus are the norm for love as a radical gift.[25] After enacting his love in the washing of his dis-

---

25. For a sophisticated and informed use of this claim in New Testament ethics, see Allen Verhey, *Remembering Jesus* (Grand Rapids: Eerdmans, 2002).

ciples' feet and exhorting his followers to do as he did by washing each other's feet, Jesus declares: "I give you a new commandment, that you love one another. Just as I have loved you, you also should love one another. By this everyone will know that you are my disciples, if you have love for one another" (John 13:34-35). Love as I love, says Jesus — that is, to the point of a cross. And if you love each other the way I love you, people will know you are one of my followers.[26] After the seventh and last of Jesus' "I am's" ("I am the true vine, you are the branches"), Jesus repeats this new commandment: "This is my commandment, that you love one another as I have loved you" (John 15:12). In life and death, in word and deed, Christ is the definition of love, the fulfillment of this new commandment. Thus it is not surprising that, when this kind of love meets the suffering of homelessness and the despoliation of creaturely habitats, it responds with compassion.

Compassion, as its etymology suggests, means to suffer *(pati)* with *(com)* another. Compassion is, as Neal Plantinga succinctly puts it, "the empathetic pity that wants to spare, relieve, or nurture somebody who is suffering."[27] It is one person feeling the pain of another and reaching out to relieve that pain whenever possible. It is no surprise that St. Paul encourages us to rejoice with those who rejoice and weep with those who weep (Rom. 12:15) and to clothe ourselves with compassion *(splanchna oiktirmou)* — literally, the guts of compassion — or, more colloquially, have a heart of mercy (Col. 3:12).

One of the problems with the idea of compassion in our time is that it is so often confused with liberal notions of charity. Housing advocates and environmental activists will often insist that what we need is not more charitable compassion but more justice. Maybe the problem is that compassion has been co-opted in such a way that systems of oppression remain unchallenged. But compassion is too strong a virtue and too integral to a biblically informed way of life to be dismissed. In fact, whenever we read biblical texts about justice, we almost invariably find compassion mentioned in the same breath. While the justice-compassion distinction may seem to make sense of certain modern problems, it is a dichotomy un-

26. It is telling that, in the Greek for this text, all the second-person pronouns are plural, and all the verbs translated "love" in English are from *agapaō,* from which is derived the noun *agapē,* or self-sacrificial love.

27. Cornelius Plantinga, Jr., "Contours of Christian Compassion," *Perspectives* 10, no. 2 (Feb. 1995): 11; see also Allen Verhey, "Suffering and Compassion," *Perspectives* 10, no. 2 (Feb. 1995): 17-18.

known to biblical faith. We might even say that justice is rooted in compassion. The sharing of the pain of another — that is, a *com-passio*, a pain-with — is at the heart of a biblical understanding of a suffering God.[28] And the call to justice is always a matter of recognizing the pain of oppression in the life of another, of sharing the pain in one's own life, and then of bearing the image of the compassionate God by embracing that pain and instituting ways of life that will alleviate that pain.

The problem with justice apart from compassion is that it is too abstract and out of touch: it lacks the immediacy and messiness of real-life relationships forged in pain because it settles for only what people by right have coming to them. As Lewis Smedes reminds us, while compassion "always seeks at least justice because people are deeply hurt when they are denied their rights," compassion also enriches justice by "pushing the common sense of justice beyond itself into the righteousness of the kingdom of God."[29] On the other hand, the problem with compassion apart from justice is that it attends to those floating in the river but does little to stop the numbers of refugees from coming downstream. In short, justice without compassion is too heartless, and compassion without justice is too shortsighted. When compassion and justice each function independently of the other, it results in powerlessness; but together they empower us for reconciliation.

The virtue of compassion is the habitual disposition to suffer with another. The compassionate person perceives the suffering, empathizes with the sufferer, feels sorrow over his suffering, wants to relieve his suffering, and will if possible relieve his suffering.[30] So compassion requires attentiveness. There can be no compassion unless we perceive the suffering of another. And compassion requires a supple imagination. Feeling the pain of another, when the experience may be foreign to you, implies the imaginative ability to walk a mile in another's moccasins. In addition, compassion requires the strength of will to act for the good of the sufferer. Compassion and courage are thus comrades. In short, the virtue of compassion is care rooted in sympathy for the suffering.

We should note that, when love takes on the flesh of compassion, it is directed not only to people but also to all kinds of nonhuman creatures.

28. See Terence Fretheim, *The Suffering of God* (Philadelphia: Fortress, 1984).

29. Lewis Smedes, *Mere Morality* (Grand Rapids: Eerdmans, 1983), pp. 55-56.

30. Plantinga, "Contours of Christian Compassion," p. 11. For an excellent discussion of compassion, see Henri Nouwen, *Compassion: A Reflection on the Christian Life* (New York: Doubleday, 1983).

Volunteers at the local humane society, workers at the city zoo, children on the family farm or at home with a beloved pet — all these display the disposition of compassion, a disposition that is rooted in sympathetic understanding and is evident in actions of care. This disposition of compassion can also be directed toward places such as forest and mountain, river and desert, park and garden and farm. These places of the heart evoke loyalty, affection, and care. As the writings of Wes Jackson, Wendell Berry, and Terry Tempest Williams demonstrate, we sometimes come to love a place so much that we grieve its violation or its loss.[31]

But some environmentalists say that what we need is not compassion but justice. And some advocates for the homeless say that compassionate outreach programs and food banks are all well and good, but that we also need justice that manifests itself in policy analysis and reform. Others try to bring the two together by saying that we need both justice and love. However, rather than this division between justice and compassion, rather than *both* justice *and* compassion, we believe that the world needs *compassionate justice:* that is, compassion-driven politics and a politically involved compassion. We need public policy with an agenda rooted in compassionate justice. Anything less could never be faithful to the One who, when he saw the crowds, "felt compassion for them, for they were distressed and dispirited like sheep without a shepherd" (Mark 9:36).

The absence of compassion is apathy. To lack compassion is to lack feeling *(a-pathos);* not to love in this way is not to care. Therefore, the opposite of compassion is not hatred but indifference, that vice singled out by John the Seer in his rebuke of the church at Laodicea (Rev. 3). To lack the ability to feel with and for another is to be unable to have compassion.

The ecologically apathetic are oblivious to and unconcerned about the havoc wreaked on the earth. They live in no place, since they know no place well enough to really inhabit it. They do not lament the loss of a giant catalpa tree or grieve the destruction of the old parkland meadow. They do not weep for the passing of a time when water was drinkable and air clean. In contrast, Aldo Leopold famously observed: "One of the penalties of an ecological education is that one lives alone in a world of wounds."[32] While

31. See William Vitek and Wes Jackson, eds., *Rooted in the Land* (New Haven: Yale University, 1996); see also Terry Tempest Williams *Refuge: An Unnatural History of Family and Place* (New York: Vintage, 1992).

32. Aldo Leopold, *Sand County Almanac* (New York: Ballantine, 1996), p. 197.

we may question whether we ever live in a world "alone," especially after an ecological education, we need to heed Leopold's warning.

In a world of ecological homelessness, compassionate people reach out to those who suffer from the effects of global warming. Compassionate poeple offer aid to those floating in the stream of homelessness, victims of a market run amuck. Compassionate poeple resist the lure of "upward mobility" by living in a place long enough and well enough to know it and care for its many inhabitants, human and nonhuman, even if this means noticing its wounds and grieving its losses. Compassionate people offer some solace of home and hope to displaced postmodern nomads who are adrift in the flux of shifting identities and shattered dreams. In a poem entitled "The Good Samaritan," Mark Littleton captures the essence of compassion:[33]

> Compassion.
> The stoop of a listening father.
> The touch and wink of a passing nurse.
> The gnarled fingers of a grandmother steadying a swing.
> The clench of a surgeon's teeth as he begins his cut.
> The open hand and pocketbook of a traveling Samaritan.
> The dew of heaven on dry lips.

Wisdom

Peaceableness, justice, and compassion. Shalom would not be shalom without them. But there is something more: wisdom. We can never realize the homecoming of shalom in the day-to-day messiness of our lives without wisdom. We can gain a greater understanding of what wisdom is by distinguishing it from three of its near cousins. First, wisdom is not intelligence or smarts, for people who are very intelligent can be fools. Second, wisdom is not erudition or accumulated knowledge or book learning, for well-read people can be fools. Third, wisdom is not merely technical knowledge or skill or know-how, for technological power without wisdom can be a very destructive thing. Indeed, it is often true that the greater technical knowledge one has, the greater evil one can accomplish. Intelligence, erudition, skill — three good things, but none is wisdom.

33. From Luci Shaw, ed., *A Widening Light* (Wheaton, IL: Harold Shaw Publishers, 1984), p. 72.

Wisdom is the ability to discern paths of shalom in the midst of competing visions and conflicting interests. Such wisdom, at heart, is not an achievement but a gift. Listen to the way Proverbs puts it:

> For the Lord gives wisdom;
> from his mouth come knowledge and understanding;
> he stores up sound wisdom for the upright;
> he is a shield to those who walk blamelessly,
> guarding the paths of justice
> and preserving the way of the faithful ones.
> Then you will understand righteousness and justice
> and equity, every good path. . . .
>
> (Prov. 2:6-7)[34]

Those who are given wisdom are those who "fear the Lord" (Prov. 1:7),[35] those who live their lives in covenant with their Creator, who construct their homes as stewards of the homemaking God. Such people understand righteousness and justice. In their lives of compassionate fidelity, they discover that the ways of wisdom are "pleasantness, and all her paths are peace" (Prov. 3:17).

Wisdom, then, is the ability to discern compassionate paths of justice and peace. But such discernment is rooted most foundationally in being deeply attuned to God's ways with creation. Listen to Proverbs again:

> The Lord by wisdom founded the earth;
> by understanding he established the heavens;
> by his knowledge the deeps broke open,
> and the clouds drop down the dew.
>
> (Prov. 3:19; cf. Ps. 104:24)

Wisdom is depicted as the master craftsman at the Creator's side at the dawn of all things (Prov. 8:22-31). Creation is founded on and suffused with wisdom, and wisdom will not be found apart from a deep, ongoing attentiveness to this creation in all of its dynamic, complex, and wonderful

---

34. The literature on wisdom in the Bible is vast. For starters, see Roland Murphy, *The Tree of Life* (Grand Rapids: Eerdmans, 2002); William P. Brown, *Character in Crisis* (Grand Rapids: Eerdmans, 1996); and Stephen Barton, ed., *Where Shall Wisdom Be Found?* (Edinburgh: T&T Clark, 1999).

35. See also Prov. 9:10; Job 28:28; Psalm 111:10.

interrelatedness. Wisdom will be "at home in the mind of the one who has understanding" (Prov. 14:33), and will direct how such a person, and such a community, will be at home in the world with each other. And this is why Isaiah's messianic king is a man of wisdom and understanding, counsel and might, knowledge and the fear of the Lord (Isa. 11:2). Such a wise king will render righteous judgments for the poor and "decide with equity for the meek of the earth" (Isa. 11:4). No wonder St. Paul refers to Jesus as the wisdom of God (1 Cor. 1:24; cf. Col. 2:3).

The virtue of wisdom, then, is the inclination to make sound and discerning practical judgments, informed by the biblical story and the accumulated experience of the Christian community and aimed at what is truly good. The virtue of wisdom, furthermore, is shot through with an abiding awareness of life's precariousness, an understanding and prizing of the excellences of life, and an unwavering sense of thanksgiving for the sheer giftedness of life. Awareness, appreciation, gratitude — such is the grammar of wisdom.[36]

Therefore, in ecological matters, the wise plan ahead and take the long view; valuing only short-term consequences or returns is the way of foolishness. The ecologically wise exercise restraint and take their time because they are attuned to the cycles and scales of the natural world. And the ecologically wise see everything connected to everything else, and thus they adopt the canoe camper's version of the Golden Rule: treat those downstream as you would have those upstream treat you.

If wisdom is a matter of being attuned to creation and of discerning paths of justice, then foolishness is being profoundly out of touch, the habitual absence of sound judgment or discernment. The fool follows paths of self-interest, destruction, and violence because she knows nothing of justice or compassion. The fool confuses the "goods life" for the good life. Ecologically speaking, foolishness is the disposition to act as if the earth is endlessly exploitable and expendable. Ecological services such as the natural purification of water are invisible to the fool, and ecological costs such as air pollution are mere externalities. By living only for today, the fool acts as though the future doesn't matter. Blind to the future, the fool eats the last seed corn.

In a culture of ecological homelessness, wise people resist the siren song of the false god called More Stuff. Wise people remind a culture infatuated

---

36. For an excellent discussion of gratitude, see Lewis Smedes, *A Pretty Good Person* (San Francisco: Harper and Row, 1990), ch. 1.

with the "world-wide web" that the original and truly important worldwide web is biodiversity. Wise people take into account the consequences of their actions for at least seven generations. They view our home planet as a holy mystery, finite in all its glory, and thus they see "prosperity" for what it truly is — the long-term ruination of God's good earth. In a world of short-term profit and long-term pain, people of wisdom are like a blaze of light on a dark night. If we are to live as redemptive homemakers in this world of eco- logical homelessness, then we must listen to wisdom as she calls out to us from the city gates, public squares, alpine meadows, and prairie grasslands.

There are certainly other virtues central to the biblical vision of sha- lom — for example, humility, contentment, patience. But peaceableness, justice, compassion, and wisdom are at the core: without them it is impos- sible to be people of shalom. What practices do people with these disposi- tions actually engage in? What do such people actually do? Especially with respect to earthkeeping, what do these virtues look like in flesh and blood?

Practices of Earthkeepers

Susan teaches at a liberal arts college and runs an environmental consulting firm. A former U.S. State Department negotiator, she brings the skills of di- plomacy to her work; and because she is a Christian, she also brings her faith to her work. The combination of these two, along with other intangibles of upbringing and experience, means that Susan is a peaceable person. She needed every bit of that character trait when she worked with the watermen of Tangier Island in the Cheasapeake Bay and the environmentalists with whom they clashed, but she pulled off nothing short of a miracle.

In 1998, Susan was on Tangier Island in the middle of the Chesapeake Bay doing research for her doctoral degree from the University of Wiscon- sin, Madison. She was living among a community of fishermen called the "Tangier watermen." But due to pollution, disease, and overharvesting, there was only one fishery left — the blue crab. Consequently, the people of Tangier Island were being pressured by a group of environmentalists, the Chesapeake Bay Foundation (CBF), to change their fishing habits. Meanwhile, the watermen themselves worried about their own economic well-being and the intrusion of outsiders into their way of life.

Tempers flared, emotions ran high on both sides, and an impasse seemed inescapable. Some members of the CBF staff were condescending and acted in disdainful ways toward the people of Tangier Island. Feeling powerless to reverse the decline of their fishery, the watermen showed little respect for those who used the abstract language of environmental science and whose actions might seriously affect their business bottom line. They were suspicious of the CBF, and for good reason.

Susan had immersed herself in the island culture. She lived at the same economic level as the majority of the islanders did, and she dressed according to their conservative standards. She attended worship services and taught Sunday school at the local Methodist church. She helped the women process crabs. Susan genuinely cared about the people and showed respect for their way of life, and thus she quickly won the trust of many of the island people. But it wasn't all a piece of cake. Susan was ostracized by certain members of the island community, and she even received death threats. After falsehoods about an outside speaker had been circulated, the whole process of forging a stewardship covenant came perilously close to blowing up in her face.

But in the end Susan's efforts paid off: she helped to launch a faith-based stewardship initiative, led by the people of Tangier Island, which resulted in a cleaner island and a healthier fishery. Realizing that what all the sides wanted was a healthy Chesapeake Bay fishery, Susan helped the CBF staff appreciate the watermen's faith-based cultural values, and she likewise helped the watermen appreciate the goals of the secular environmentalists. She also enabled the watermen to live into the biblical faith they already professed. Where the CBF had failed, Susan succeeded beyond anyone's wildest imagination.

Susan was successful on Tangier Island for many reasons: her remarkable communication skills, her personal integrity, and her discerning ability to tap into the biblical ethic of stewardship that the watermen already had. But she was successful, above all, because of her uncanny ability to bring about concord among those in conflict. With honesty and courage she broke through the contentious, even violent, debate between antagonistic parties and was able to forge an agreement for the good of both parties and that of Chesapeake Bay as a whole. Susan Drake Emmerich embodies the earthkeeping virtue of peaceableness.

Kent runs a church camp in upstate New York. In the summer he trains staff, deals with emergencies, and pays the bills. He also tells bedtime stories to the many kids who flock to camp, and when he gets a chance he joins in the evening music by playing his mandolin. The rest of the year he runs retreats, raises money, and promotes the camp among neighbors near and far. In his spare time he puts up bat houses, cleans composting toilets, and cultivates an organic garden in unforgiving Adirondack soil. Kent's work is seemingly endless, the job never done.

You sense things are different the moment you arrive at Camp Fowler. Whether it's the sign by the parking area that reads "Future world and local leaders in training here," the bicycles used by the maintenance workers to haul their gear around camp, or the wooden buildings that properly fit their northwoods setting — you sense that this camp has been carefully thought through. Your first impressions are confirmed at the first meal: the menu includes organic and vegetarian items seldom found in typical camp fare, prepared by a woman who pursued a master's degree in home economics so that she could more knowledgeably align the kitchen practices with the core values of the camp. After the meal the campers have a competition to determine which cabin had the least amount of non-compostable food left over (*ort* is the technical term), with all the compostable leftovers going into the bear-proof compost bins near the garden.

This is no ordinary Christian camp. There are certainly many of the usual staples of church camp: morning worship before breakfast, time each day devoted to learning the stories of the Bible, chapel time at night with enthusiastic (if not harmonious) singing. Much of this is led by a local minister who volunteers as chaplain for the week. There are wilderness trips for fishing, sailing, canoeing, and backpacking. Indeed, the Camp Fowler philosophy is similar to many Christian camps: to glorify God, to foster growth in Jesus Christ as Lord, to experience life in a Christian community, and to encourage people to live as disciples of Christ. But what is striking at Camp Fowler is that all of it is suffused with a spirit of shalom. Among the camp's core values are simplicity, hospitality, and community. In recent years its summer-long themes have been peace and justice. And woven through everything is the theme of earthkeeping.

Kent has been at Camp Fowler since 1986, and his imprint more than two decades later is now considerable. Through the years he has intentionally and creatively shaped the place and its practices to reflect the core values of the gospel, not the least of which is the commitment to caring for the earth. But that care is always specific to a particular place. So Kent knows the history of his camp; and while he has learned much from its past, he is not slavishly bound by it. (He has made some mistakes, as he himself will tell you, but he has also learned from them.) Kent also knows his home place well, the nonhuman and human inhabitants. He knows the pileated woodpeckers and barred owls, the tamarack and the golden birch, as well as the director of the library in the local village and the owner of the local paddle shop down the road. Because of his extensive local knowledge, Kent is able to discern the possibilities and the limits of his place. He knows when enough is enough, and thus he resists the pressures to think that bigger is better. Consequently, the camp remains relatively small, of a human and humane scale. In short, Camp Fowler incarnates a kind of wisdom, and this wisdom joins arms with an infectious joy, such that all who come to Camp Fowler — campers, volunteers, staff — catch the spirit of Kent's joyful wisdom and wisdom-filled joy. Kent Busman embodies the earthkeeping virtue of wisdom.

Peaceableness, justice, compassion, and wisdom. Better than a long list of do's and don'ts,[37] Susan and Kent embody the virtues of shalom and illustrate certain practices of earthkeepers in an exemplary way. In a world of ecological homelessness, these friends of the earth — and many others like them — are faithful and hopeful homemakers.

Christians as Aching Visionaries

The Desmond Tutu epigraph at the beginning of the chapter captures well the essence of shalom. The summit of human flourishing, Tutu affirms, is

37. However, if the reader seeks such a list, here are seven simple strategies, taken with permission from the position paper entitled "Globalization, Ethics, and the Earth," written by the Earth and Ethics Working Group of the Theology Commission, Reformed Church in America:

> **Say no.** Don't buy the latest, fastest, biggest. Live simply.
>
> **Tithe.** Give a percentage of your income away — to your church, to Bread for the World, to Church World Service, to missionaries, to the local soup kitchen or homeless shelter.
>
> **Fast.** During Lent or Advent skip a meal or two and use the time to write a letter to your mayor or member of Congress.
>
> **Volunteer.** Work at church or at camp, at the local homeless shelter or nature center, with the local Habitat folks or Greenway group.
>
> **Give.** Go through the clothes closet or toy box or basement and give usable things away.
>
> **Care.** Take care of a pet, a creek, a lake, a forest. Pick up some trash. Recycle. Drive less and walk more.
>
> **Pray.** Pray the Lord's Prayer. Pray the Jesus Prayer. Pray alone, pray with others, pray with the chickadees.

a multifaceted thing: peace and justice, compassion and caring, joy and delight. Shalom is the flourishing of all things created, the reconciliation of all things estranged, and the consummation of all things incomplete. It is heaven on earth. It is the closing scene from *Places in the Heart.*

We who follow Jesus are called to make his vision of shalom real. Richard Mouw puts it this way: "We must share in God's restless yearning for the renewal of the cosmos."[38] So in the Lord's Prayer we pray that God's will be done on earth as it is in heaven. In the doxology we sing that all creatures here below might praise God. In the Apostles' Creed we confess our faith in the resurrection of the dead and life everlasting. And in our everyday living we strive, with God's help, to make this vision incarnate. We yearn for the biblical vision of shalom to be made real. We are, in short, visionaries.

But in a world of ecological homelessness, shalom is often in short supply. It is known as much by its absence as by its presence. And so our yearning is tinged with sadness. We mourn the loss of what could have been. We grieve for what should have been. Thus we are not only visionaries, but aching visionaries. We ache because we painfully realize that the time of shalom, in all its glorious fullness, is not yet here. In his moving meditations on the occasion of the untimely death of his son, Nicholas Wolterstorff speaks of Christians precisely as "aching visionaries." Reflecting on the beatitude "Blessed are those who mourn, for they shall be comforted," he says:

> Who then are the mourners? The mourners are those who have caught a glimpse of God's new day, who ache with all their being for that day's coming, and who break out into tears when confronted with its absence. They are the ones who realize that in God's realm of peace there is no one blind and who ache whenever they see someone unseeing. They are the ones who realize that in God's realm there is no one hungry and who ache whenever they see someone starving. They are the ones who realize that in God's realm there is no one falsely accused and who ache whenever they see someone imprisoned unjustly. They are the ones who realize that in God's realm there is no one who fails to see God and who ache whenever they see someone unbelieving. They are the ones who realize that in God's realm there is no one who suffers oppression and

38. Richard Mouw, *When the Kings Come Marching In* (Grand Rapids: Eerdmans, 1983) p. 65.

who ache whenever they see someone beat down. They are the ones who realize that in God's realm there is no one without dignity and who ache whenever they see someone treated with indignity. They are the ones who realize that in God's realm of peace there is neither death nor tears and who ache whenever they see someone crying tears over death. The mourners are aching visionaries.[39]

We followers of Jesus are called to be aching visionaries. Inspired by God's vision of shalom and mindful of how far the world is from realizing that vision, we yearn for that realm of peace and justice and compassion and wisdom of which the Bible speaks. Especially in a world in ecological crisis, at a time when we are defiling our home planet, we yearn for God's good future of shalom.

39. Nicholas Wolterstorff, *Lament for a Son* (Grand Rapids: Eerdmans, 1987), pp. 85-86.

Wine, Bread, and the Homemaking King

Mark 11–16

What we wanted was as simple as it was elusive. We wanted to be liberated from our oppressors. We wanted the promises to be fulfilled. We wanted to experience the homecoming of the kingdom of God and the destruction of all idolatrous usurpers. We wanted our exile to end. We wanted to come home.

And what we longed for came together in one place and at one time: in the Temple at Passover. No wonder the Romans always sent more troops to Jerusalem during the feast. At Passover we remembered that our God is a God of liberation who had overthrown a violent and oppressive empire before. So nationalist sentiments and liberationist longings were always heightened during the feast. And if what we wanted was homecoming, then it isn't surprising that those longings would find their focus in the Temple. After all, what was the Temple if not the home of God? And wasn't it precisely a return of the presence of God to the Temple that would occasion our liberation? When God comes home again, then we will all be set free. We will be able to go home and live as the chosen people of God ought to live.

So every year at Passover the anticipation ran high. Might this be the year that the divine presence will return? Might this be the year that the kingdom will be restored? Might this be the year of our Jubilee?

Some of us dared to think that maybe, just maybe, this would be the year — because *he* was coming. The one who had been preaching and healing in Galilee for the last few years, the one who seemed to awaken such renewed hope even though he tended to break all the rules. Jesus was coming to Jerusalem for the festival!

I had heard Jesus once during a business trip to the north. He was speaking in parables about seeds and sowers, lamps and mustard bushes

(Mark 4:1-34). I confess that I didn't really understand what he was saying, but there was something in the way that he spoke that made me want to understand. I wanted to know more about this kingdom he was proclaiming.

So when I heard that he was coming to Jerusalem with his disciples and their growing group of followers, I decided that I would join them near Bethany for the last bit of the journey to Jerusalem. When I got there the parade had already begun, and what I saw awakened both hope and fear deep within me. The pilgrims were walking along singing Psalm 118, which was our custom every Passover. But this year there was something different: this year they were laying down leafy branches and their coats as they sang:

> Hosanna!
> Blessed is the one who comes in the name of the Lord!
> Blessed is the coming kingdom of our ancestor David!
> Hosanna in the highest heaven!

I immediately looked around to see if any Roman security forces were nearby. Language about a coming kingdom does not go down very well with the Romans, and this had the look of a reckless and dangerous political demonstration. From the perspective of the Roman occupying forces, a group of oppressed people marching toward the capital city proclaiming that an alternative kingdom is at hand would certainly have the appearance of an insurrection. Things could get violent.

But then I saw that they weren't just talking about a coming kingdom. They actually had a king! There was Jesus in the middle of the crowd, and it was clear that he was the reason for their revolutionary enthusiasm. But, I've got to tell you, he didn't look much like a king. I mean, he was riding a colt. Matter of fact, it was a donkey colt! I wondered aloud to the guy next to me: "What good is a donkey colt for a king about to reclaim his kingdom? The Romans use stallions and chariots in battle. Jesus won't stand a chance." The old man next to me, who had tears in his eyes, immediately replied: "Haven't you read the scriptures? Don't you know that Zechariah said, 'Lo, your king comes to you; triumphant and victorious is he, humble and riding on a donkey, on a colt, the foal of a donkey'?" (Zech. 9:9).

My jaw dropped. When the old man quoted the prophet, I naturally remembered that prophecy. But it had never made any sense to me. How could someone on a donkey win the kingdom? And yet here was Jesus enacting that prophecy before my very eyes. At that point I knew that I was going to follow this crowd, follow Jesus, into Jerusalem just to see what would happen. I'm not saying I was a believer at that point. I'm also not saying I was committed to the kingdom that this unlikely king was bringing. But something deeper and more compelling than mere curiosity made me join this throng on what looked like a very dangerous Passover week in Jerusalem.

We met no resistance when we entered the city. In fact, the Roman guards at the gate kind of chuckled at us as we passed by. I guess a guy on a donkey just didn't seem like much of a security threat, even if he did have a throng of singing pilgrims with him. But I noticed some of the scribes and Pharisees and a few priests looking at us with some disgust — and perhaps fear.

Jesus led the parade directly to the Temple. Nothing new there: that's where these parades always went. A people longing for homecoming were inexorably drawn to the home of God. And as we approached the Temple, I think we were all wondering whether this might be it. Might it be that the presence of God would return to the Temple this week? Was that somehow connected to this donkey-riding king? Might God return from exile and come home, thereby beginning our liberation, our own homecoming?

Well, we would have to wait another day to find out. Today was not the day Jesus was going to do much. Actually, when we got to the Temple, he just kind of walked in, looked around a bit, and walked out. That was it. He didn't seem too impressed with it all. He didn't stop to pray. He just kind of looked the place over and left — rather anticlimactic, if you ask me. There was all this enthusiasm, all this revolutionary fervor out on the road, and it all just dissipated. Jesus left and the crowd dispersed. I went to my cousin's house for the night.

But things started to happen the next morning. I was at the Temple praying when I saw Jesus come in. This time you could tell by the look in his eyes and the way he walked that he'd come with a mission, that something was about to happen. And I could barely keep my heart from racing. Might this be the day we had longed for? Will this prophecy-fulfilling king bring the kingdom? Will the presence of the Holy One again fill this Temple? Might Herod's Temple be blessed and transformed by the glory of the Lord to become the house of God like Solomon's Temple of old?

My excited anticipation was immediately thrown into the deepest confusion by what happened next. Jesus walked over to the tables where people were selling doves so that poor peasants from the countryside could offer their sacrifices, and where people were changing Roman currency into Temple coins. And then he went crazy. He started overturning the tables and yelling at everyone. Money and birds were flying everywhere, people were running all over the place trying to get away from this madman, and then Jesus shouted, "Is it not written, 'My house shall be called a house of prayer for all nations'? But you have made it a den of robbers." And then he left the chaos and walked out of the Temple again.

That night at my cousin's house, we talked about what had happened. All of Jerusalem was talking about this blasphemous attack on the very house of God, the very heart of all Jewish life. My cousin is a servant in the Temple, and he told me that the chief priests had an emergency meeting where they decided that Jesus must die. That didn't surprise me: blasphemy is a crime punishable by death, and Jesus certainly picked the wrong time for his act of blasphemy. All of the hopes of Israel were tied to the Temple. How dare he strip us of that hope?

We talked long into the night about Jesus. I told my cousin what he had said about the Temple being a "den of robbers," and we knew that he was quoting from Jeremiah's sermon against the Temple hundreds of years before (Jer. 7:1-8). But Jeremiah didn't say anything about the Temple being a house of prayer "for all nations." What could that possibly mean? Why would the nations, the *goyim,* ever be allowed into the Temple to pray? It was unheard of. In fact, if unclean gentiles were to enter the Temple, it would be a most terrible defilement. Later in the evening, however, as we were preparing for bed, my cousin blurted out, "Wait a minute! I know where that bit about a house of prayer for all nations is from. It is in the Isaiah scroll, in the same passage where the prophet talks about the eunuchs receiving honor and welcome in the house of God. Just after that the prophet says that the Temple shall be a house of prayer for all people" (Isa. 56:2-8).

For the second time in as many days I had been caught short in my knowledge of Scripture. Twice I had not understood what Jesus was up to because I had forgotten, or perhaps never noticed, what the prophets were talking about. That did not happen a third time. The next day I was back in the Temple. Somehow I knew that Jesus would be back, and I was not disappointed. When I arrived, he was in a debate with the chief priests and scribes, who were challenging him to justify his actions of the previous day. It was the tail end of the conversation, and all I heard him say was that he wouldn't tell them by what authority he acted.

But then he told a parable. I have already mentioned that I liked his parables, and in this one he referred to a passage in Scripture that no one could have missed. "A man planted a vineyard," he began. Any school kid could tell you what the rabbi was alluding to. In his parable Jesus was using the image of a vineyard, just as Isaiah had used that metaphor so many years earlier (Is. 5:1-7). This man planted a vineyard, put a fence around it, dug a pit for the wine press and built a watchtower. This was some vineyard! The similarities to Isaiah's parable were very clear, but there was a difference: Isaiah's vineyard produced wild grapes and poor wine, while the vineyard that Jesus depicted in his parable yielded good fruit and fine wine. The problem was that the owner of the vineyard went away to another country and sent his envoys to obtain his share of the vineyard. But the vineyard tenants refused to give the owner his share; they insulted, beat, and even murdered his envoys.

I was already pondering what Jesus was talking about before he got to the punch line, because I didn't want to get caught short again by something he said. Who was this owner, and where did he go? Well, the vineyard owner in Isaiah's parable is clearly God. Okay, let's say that Jesus is also talking about God here. But where did he go? Was this owner a reference to all the absentee landlords who had been oppressing the land?[40] Maybe, but maybe not. Well, what were we all doing at the Temple this week? Longing for the return of the glory of God to this house! Of course! The owner's leaving shows us that God is in exile. That is, God is in another place, and we are left here to be the tenants of the vineyard. Doesn't the Torah teach us that we are tenants in God's creation, called to tend and keep the earth (Lev. 25:23; Gen. 2:15)? But in Jesus' story, the tenants refuse to be tenants. They act as though it's their vineyard, as though it's only for their own benefit, and they have the total and final control over it. The tenants do violence to the owner's messengers, which is another allusion to Isaiah. We all recognized the pun in the text: the prophet says that God came to the vineyard and expected *mishpat* (justice) but found *mispat* (bloodshed), looked for *tsedeqah* (righteousness) but heard *tse'aqah* (a cry). Likewise, in Jesus' parable the owner of the vineyard looks for righteous dealings from his tenants and a just distribution of the vineyard's proceeds, but what he gets is his servants' shed blood and cries of pain.

40. This would seem to be the clear reference in the parables of the pounds (Luke 19:11-27) and the talents (Matt. 25:14-30).

234

Then came the punch line. Finally the owner sends his son to the tenants, assuming that they would surely respect the son. But no, they see this as an opportunity to be rid of the true heir of the vineyard. So they seize the son, kill him, and throw him out of the vineyard. Murder in the vineyard — the parallels to Naboth and Ahab are unmistakable. The son comes to what is rightfully his; he comes as an envoy of his father to his vineyard home. And he is murdered and thrown out of his rightful home. The consequences for those tenants will be as severe as the judgment on King Ahab in the story of Naboth's vineyard.

Jesus' parable had me spellbound. The implications were so clear. First, he was actually answering the Pharisees' question, "By what authority do you do these things in the Temple?" His answer was: by the authority of the son of the father, and in continuity with the tradition of the prophets of old, who were envoys of the father and were abused and murdered by the Temple leadership. But there was something deeper going on as well. We were longing for the homecoming of our God, and Jesus was telling us that God had sent his envoys home from exile, and that now he had sent his son. God was looking to see whether Israel had tended his vineyard, his good creation, any better than their forefathers had during Isaiah's time. But instead of righteousness and justice, he found bloodshed and the cry of the oppressed. This home, controlled by these stewards, was not a home that would show hospitality to this homecoming God, and thus its stewardship must be given to others.

If the leaders didn't get the connection between this parable and the incident in the Temple the day before, Jesus made it as plain as he could by quoting from the very psalm that the pilgrims were singing. He said: "Have you not read this scripture: 'The stone that the builders rejected has become the cornerstone'?" (Mark 12:10, quoting Ps. 118:22). The son who was rejected will become the cornerstone, not of the restoration of this Temple, which has been rejected, but of a new Temple, a new site of homecoming for the homemaking God. If Jesus' fate hadn't already been sealed when he overturned the tables in the Temple, it was clearly sealed now. You could see it in the faces of the leaders, you could feel it in the crowd, and you could see it in the eyes of Jesus himself.

I stayed as close to Jesus as I could for the next couple of days. He always seemed to be hanging around the Temple, almost as though he were haunting the place or maybe goading the authorities to act. He debated issues of taxation to the emperor, questions of resurrection, details of messianic hope, and he had sharp words for scribes who "devoured widows' houses." He also attacked the Temple financial structure, which had left widows desolate while giving esteem to the rich. And he capped it all off with his most extensive and direct attack on the Temple, in which he specifically described the destruction of this Temple. Sitting on the Mount of Olives, facing the Temple, Jesus gave a long discourse in which he essentially said that God would not come home — at least not here, and not in the way that everyone had thought. Or perhaps when God does come to his "home," he'll do more than turn over a few tables. Perhaps the whole edifice of holy privilege and exclusion will fall!

Throughout these days of teaching and debate in the Temple, I was taken aback by the angry, almost dismissive, tone that Jesus had when responding to his questioners. Except in one instance. A scribe listening to the debate interjected with a question of his own: "Teacher, which is the first commandment of all?" And rather than reply with a question of his own, Jesus simply answered the man by quoting the *shema:* "Hear, O Israel: the Lord our God is one; you shall love the Lord your God with all your heart, and with all your soul, and with all your mind, and with all your strength." And then he added, "The second is this, 'You shall love your neighbor as yourself.' There is no other commandment greater than these" (Mark 12:29-31, quoting Deut. 6:4-5; Lev. 19:18). Before anyone could argue that, while this second commandment was important, it wasn't even one of the Ten Commandments and therefore certainly could not be more important than any of the others, the scribe replied by saying that Jesus was right, that such love for God and neighbor was "more important than all whole burnt offerings and sacrifices."[41]

Everyone was flabbergasted by this comment. How could anyone, let alone a scribe of the Temple, suggest that anything was more important than burnt offerings and sacrifices, especially this week, when everyone was in town to offer such sacrifices and when the Passover lamb was being prepared? But Jesus was clearly impressed with this scribe and replied, "You are not far from the Kingdom of God." Somehow this scribe was zeroing in on something that the rest of us were missing. The homecoming that we longed for was not going to be realized through sacrifice in the Temple, but through our love for God and for our neighbor. Exile ends in love.

I didn't see Jesus again until the fateful events of that Friday morning. I heard that he stayed in Bethany for a couple of days, had dinner at a leper's house, and that a woman anointed him with a costly jar of oint-

---

41. Perhaps this is an allusion to Hosea 6:6 and Micah 6:6-8.

ment. Some said that this was the anointing of a king; others suggested that she anointed him for his death. I think they're both right.

And then there was the meal. Remember, this was Passover week. We all came to Jerusalem and to the Temple to eat the Passover meal, a meal of liberation that reminded us again that our God is a God who will bring his people home. The way the story is told, Jesus took a loaf of bread, blessed it, broke it, gave it to his disciples, and said, "Take, this is my body." Then he took a cup of wine and gave it to his disciples, saying, "This is my blood of the covenant which is poured out for many."[42] Here, in the quiet of an upper room with his closest friends, Jesus made clear what he had been talking about all along. The homecoming of the people of God, the redemption of all of creation, would come about only by way of the Son's suffering. That suffering would be the price God would pay if there was to be a homecoming worthy of the name. If God was to keep covenant with such a covenant-breaking people, then he would have to suffer at the hands of his homebreaking partner.

At that table, almost to make the point all the more poignant and painful, and in the midst of a meal of restored covenant, a betrayal and denial were brewing. One of the twelve friends left the room, and within hours Jesus was arrested and in the custody of the Temple authorities. Another "friend" denied any relationship to Jesus three times before the cock crowed the next morning. And the rest, except for a few women, all fled.

I saw them take Jesus out of the city that morning and — admittedly, from a distance — I saw them put him on that cross. Above his head was an inscription: "King of the Jews." It was then that I believed. I moved from a deeply interested observer of Jesus to become his follower. I know it sounds crazy. Why believe at that point? It would seem that it was all over. The homecoming king is sentenced to the most ultimate form of homelessness, a cursed death on a cross. The one we had hoped would be the redeemer of Israel was now hanging on a Roman cross, banished outside Jerusalem, the very city of shalom.

And yet, as Jesus hung on that cross, as I watched him breathe his last, I knew that he was the Son who had been sent as an envoy of his Father and that we, the tenants of this vineyard, had killed him. And I knew that the kingdom he proclaimed was our only hope of a real homecoming. I knew — don't ask

---

42. It is interesting that the phrase "blood of the covenant" is from Zech. 9:11, the same passage that refers to the coming of a king who will be humble and riding on the foal of a donkey.

me how, I just knew — that the inscription above his head was true. Here was the "King of the Jews" enthroned on a cross. Here was the homemaking king offering up his life and being banished into exile so that our exile could end. Passover, the Exodus from slavery to home, was bound up with death. A lamb had to be sacrificed; the firstborn of the Egyptians had to die on that night (Exod. 11:4-6; 12:29-30). And as I saw Jesus on that cross, I remembered that conversation with the scribe about the greatest commandment: love of God and love of neighbor. That was the path home. And that path could only lead to the cross. If Jesus was to bring us out of our exile, then it would not be through either the violence of revolution or the imposition of an impossible purity. His revolution was a revolution of sacrificial love. No more Egyptians dead in the night. No more annual animal sacrifices. No wonder it was reported that the veil in the Temple split in two when Jesus died!

But there was something else happening on the cross that day. I couldn't have possibly known it then, but I think that somehow I also knew in an intuitive way that Jesus was fighting a battle on the cross. Exile wouldn't end without a battle — we all knew that. But this battle wasn't with Rome, nor even with the Temple authorities. No, this was a battle against the very forces that would always render us homeless. This was a battle with what later we would call the "principalities and powers," with what Jesus would have called the very power of Satan. And it was as if all of creation knew that such a struggle was underway, because from noon to about three o'clock, when Jesus died, the land went dark. The sun refused to shine. But in this battle Jesus was armed only with love. As I look back on it all, I understand why this homemaking king entered Jerusalem on the foal of a donkey, not a chariot and stallion.

I was, of course, deeply sad and still very confused. I knew that this was the home-making king, but I still couldn't see how the kingdom could be established through the finality of the king's death. Then, on the first day of the week, as I was packing my bags to leave Jerusalem, a message came to my cousin's house: Jesus of Nazareth was gone. His tomb was open and the body gone. People were talking about grave robbers, but somehow I knew that wasn't true. Somehow I knew — and it was later confirmed in the community of Jesus' followers — that Jesus had been raised from the dead. The homelessness of the cross and the tomb was being transformed into the homecoming of the resurrected Son. Exile was over, and homecoming was now possible in a deeper and more powerful way than any of us had imagined. I was filled with joy . . . and fear.

Postmodern Homelessness

Amid the post-ironic postulating
And the poet's pilfered rhymes
Meaning feels like it's evaporating
Out of sight and out of mind. . . .

Bruce Cockburn[1]

It used to be that students came to the university in order to get a degree that would be their ticket to a career and a split-level home in the suburbs. They are still coming to the university for a career, but the ticket isn't necessarily to an address in the suburbs anymore. In fact, if the career is good enough, the ticket is more likely an airline ticket, with its concomitant travel awards programs, corporate credit cards, executive lounges, and airport hotels. Welcome to Airworld. Meet Ryan M. Bingham.

Walter Kirn's novel *Up in the Air* is an engaging and evocative entrance into Airworld, that world of planes and airports, "that nation within a nation, with its own language, architecture, mood, and even its own currency — the token economy of airline bonus miles that I've come to value more than dollars."[2] Ryan M. Bingham is a "careers transition counselor" (read: he fires corporate executives) for a large management consulting firm. And he lives in Airworld. He once had an apartment, but that was really only a storage space for him; now he lives in airplanes, airports, and hotels. There

---

1. Bruce Cockburn, "Don't Forget About Delight," from *You've Never Seen Everything* ©2002 Golden Mountain Music Corp.
2. Walter Kirn, *Up in the Air* (New York: Doubleday, 2001), p. 7.

isn't much to Ryan's life. While he has a novel of his own to finish and get published, and there is a new position that he is pursuing at a corporation called Mythtech, his only real passion seems to be to achieve the million-mile mark in his frequent flyer program with Great West Airlines. A million miles! That's an elite club worth joining. In fact, Ryan doesn't want to do anything that will not contribute to that goal.

This novel explores the terrain of what we have been calling the "postmodern nomad." While a real estate agent will solemnly intone to Ryan, "We all need a place to call our own. This is America. This is what we're promised. . . ," Ryan isn't buying it.[3] Not only does Ryan think that home ownership is not in his makeup, he also thinks that trying to find shelter in the ruins of America is little more than a bad joke.

Ryan would likely see an alternative to his kind of nomadism in the restless and rootless character Lester Burnham of the film *American Beauty.*[4] In this film we meet the postmodern nomad stuck in the suburbs, stuck in a loveless and sexless marriage, and stuck in a well-paying yet meaningless job with the utter absence of community or home. The characters all have an address, but their homes are constantly in crisis and near collapse. The movie begins with Lester masturbating in the shower, a fruitless simulacrum of fruit-bearing intimacy. Indeed, Ryan Bingham would find airport hotels less troublesome and disorienting than Lester's suburban "home." Why experience displacement in a place that should be home when you can have a more comfortable displacement in the familiar surroundings of a hotel room that looks like every other one?[5]

This is not to say that all is well in Ryan's life: with this kind of high-flying homelessness comes an incredibly high dose of emptiness. This is a world in which the only suspense left is whether you will land on time and whether the pilots will go on strike. But as we travel thousands of miles with Ryan over a week, we eventually begin to have a sickening realization. Nothing happens. While the novel does have a plot (of sorts), none of the

---

3. Kirn, *Up in the Air,* p. 161.

4. *American Beauty,* directed by Sam Mendes (Dreamworks, 1999).

5. William Leach would suggest that there is not that much to choose from between the master-planned communities in the suburbs "with golf courses and swimming pools, courting millions of affluent Americans 'who move a lot' and want 'instant community'" and the reproduction of the same hotel rooms around the world. Both these homes and these hotel rooms are "utilitarian places to inhabit, leave and recirculate" (*Country of Exiles: The Destruction of Place in American Life* [New York: Vintage, 1999], p. 77).

meetings, none of the goals, none of the sexual encounters, ever really happen. Ryan even misses the moment he crosses the million-mile mark.

But there is something else going on here. Ryan has a hard time remembering things, and for a while he even forgets that he is forgetting: "The mounting memory problems weren't really an issue because there was nothing particularly worth remembering in my life just then and also because I'd developed regular habits."[6] If home is, in the words of Bruce Cockburn, a place of "fond memories" where you can "lie down with a smile," then a homeless existence of sleeping in airports and hotel rooms will necessarily be a life of amnesia.[7] As we have said throughout this book, home is a site of memories. Indeed, home is erected not simply with bricks and mortar but more profoundly with memories of relationships and significant events. To live without such memories is to be deeply homeless.

Memories, however, are rooted in place; at least, any deep and abiding memories are placed. One thing that Ryan certainly lacks is a sense of place. Indeed, the places that we do encounter in Airworld — airport lounges and restaurants, international hotel chains, and so on — are characterized by such a generic sameness that they could literally be anywhere. And if a place could be anywhere, it is, by definition, nowhere. It is a no-place.

But there is another reason why Ryan is placeless. When you live in Airworld, the worst thing that can happen to you (next to crashing, that is) is to be "grounded." Mechanical problems and inclement weather ground airplanes and play havoc with the tight schedules of the Ryan Binghams of the world. Airworld is about being in the air, in transit, on the move. However, for one to have a sense of place requires one to be grounded. As we have seen in Chapter 5, it is precisely a sense of detachment from place, a lack of groundedness, that renders us ecologically homeless.

Walter Kirn does not endorse Ryan's postmodern homelessness. Indeed, the emptiness of Ryan's life, together with his amnesia and the frustration of consistently missed opportunities, are all leading somewhere else. Perhaps even home.[8]

---

6. Kirn, *Up in the Air,* p. 205.

7. From Bruce Cockburn's song, "Joy Will Find a Way," on the album *Joy Will find a Way* ©1975 Golden Mountain Music Corp.

8. Noticing that many people that he meets are experiencing religious conversions, Ryan comments, "All around me God is claiming people. Am I still on his list, or has he skipped me?" (*Up in the Air,* p. 172).

Double Homesickness "Over the Rainbow"

Is Ryan Bingham homesick? On the surface he doesn't seem to have any nostalgic longing to go back home. So, in the sense of nostalgic yearning, no, he doesn't appear to be homesick. But couldn't his very homelessness, his nomadic, plotless wandering itself be an indication that he suffers from a kind of homesickness? There is something about his experience of home that has made him sick — sick of home!

Susan Stanford Friedman identifies, in Dorothy's wanderings in *The Wizard of Oz,* such a double homesickness: "First, she's sick *of* home, her rage surrealistically embodied in the whirling tornado that transports her away from Kansas. Then, she's sick *for* home, pining for the Kansas homestead intensified with each fantastical scene on the journey to Oz. She longs for home — but only after she fulfills her wish to leave it."[9] The path home for Dorothy begins with her longing for a utopian place "somewhere over the rainbow," her traversing the terrain of such a land, finding it wanting, and then being transported back to the home she left by repeating the threefold mantra, "There's no place like home."

The Wizard of Oz could be interpreted as a modernist myth.[10] Homecoming is always possible; one need only say the words. Friedman, however, offers a postmodern reinterpretation of this mantra: while the story displays a double sense of homesickness, Friedman discerns that the magical phrase "there's no place like home" is itself doubly cryptic. "There's no place like home" means *both* "home is *the* best, the ideal, everything that elsewhere is not," *and* "that no place, anywhere, is like home. Nowhere is there a place like home. Home is a never never land of dreams and desire. Home is utopia — a no place, a nowhere, an imaginary space longed for, always already lost in the very formation of the idea of home."[11] In this deconstruction of the mantra we can discern the postmodern shift. Because there is "no place" that can ever really be like home, or because there is no home that one would ever really want to be

9. Susan Stanford Friedman, "Bodies in Motion: A Poetics of Home and Diaspora," *Tulsa Studies in Women's Literature* 23, no. 2 (Fall 2004): 191-92. Roberta Rubenstein also refers to this kind of double homesickness, referring to the Wizard of Oz in *Home Matters: Longing and Belonging, Nostalgia and Mourning in Women's Fiction* (New York: Palgrave, 2001), p. 2.

10. Paul Nathanson, *Over the Rainbow: The Wizard of Oz as a Secular Myth of America* (Albany, NY: State University of New York Press, 1991).

11. Friedman, "Bodies in Motion," p. 192.

"placed" in, Thomas Wolfe's phrase has become a truism of postmodern culture: "You can't go home again."[12]

Home is, in this formulation, an unattainable ideal. But not only that, home is an illusion based on exclusion. Biddy Martin and Chandra Talpade Mohanty put it this way: "'Being home' refers to the place where one lives within familiar, safe, protected boundaries; 'not being home' is a matter of realizing that home was an illusion of coherence and safety based on the exclusion of specific histories of oppression and resistance, the repression of difference within oneself."[13] Dorothy's longing for somewhere "over the rainbow" was born of a desire to break out of the familiar, to transgress the boundaries of home. But in the light of Martin and Mohanty's take on postmodern homelessness, Dorothy's return home comes at the cost of repressing her own difference for the sake of being a good girl who will not dare to dream of life beyond the socioeconomic poverty, gender restrictions, and conservative sameness of a rural home. She certainly won't harbor dreams of leaving the farm in all of its monochromatic boredom for the sake of the technicolor excitement of the city. Dorothy will stay at home from now on because she has come to see that home represents order and safety, while the land of Oz, the land of longing for something more than home, is a land of chaos and threat. Dorothy prefers the homogeneity of Kansas to the disorienting and dangerous heterogeneity of Oz.[14]

But what happens to human longing when it is revealed that home offers an illusion of coherence and safety that can be sustained only if stories of oppression are excluded and difference within the self is repressed? How

12. Thomas Wolfe, *You Can't Go Home Again* (New York: Harper and Row, 1940).

13. Biddy Martin and Chandra Talpade Mohanty, "Feminist Politics: What's Home Got to Do with It?" in Teresa de Lauretis, ed., *Feminist Studies, Critical Studies* (Bloomington, IN: Indiana University Press, 1986), p. 196.

14. While such a postmodern feminist reading has some merit, it seems to miss an important dimension of home that is disclosed in the film. Home is a matter of community, with people who have strengths and weaknesses. Throughout Dorothy's sojourn in Oz she is accompanied by none other than three foundational members of her home community — in all their strengths and weaknesses. She leaves home, but she takes home with her. And her homecoming can only be read as a repressive act of economic and gender oppression from an individualistic perspective that is ignorant of the communal nature of human life and of all experiences of homecoming. Dorothy comes home to be surrounded by the people who love her. It is no wonder that she exclaims with singleness of heart, "There's no place like home! There's no place like home!"

does one relate to the longing for home when the family secrets are revealed? Can one still be nostalgic for a home that was built on the backs of slavery, rape, incest, and violence?[15] Can one still long for homecoming when it is clear that home will be a place of welcome only if we repress our difference for the sake of an imposed order of sameness?[16]

There's another way to put the question. In terms of the plot of *The Wizard of Oz,* it is unthinkable that Dorothy would ever want to sing "somewhere over the rainbow" after her return to Kansas. She's learned her lesson and will not hanker for anything beyond the confines of home again. But what about us? What does this song sound like if it is sung with postmodern cadences? How can we sing of a place beyond the rainbow — where dreams come true, a utopian home beyond the illusions, oppressions, and repressions of the homes we have experienced — if we have lost all hope that home can be anything more than illusion, oppression, and repression? What does "somewhere over the rainbow" sound like in such a context? Consider Tori Amos's take on this classic song.

The singer has returned to the stage for an encore, a solitary woman at the grand piano while the crowd shouts out the names of songs she has not yet performed in the concert. She quietly begins to play and then leans toward the microphone and sings, "Somewhere, over the rainbow . . ." The crowd goes wild.[17] Someone shouts out, "Toto!" But as she continues to sing, a deeply respectful silence falls over the crowd. If you aren't quiet, you won't be able to hear this remarkable performance. Amos's performance of this song of longing for a "dream home" beyond the constrictions of experienced home is immediately arresting. When she gets to the line "and dreams that you dared to dream really do come true," her voice trails off and barely whispers the last word of that phrase — "true." She is likewise

15. Minnie Bruce Pratt recounts (among other things) the sense of homesickness and vertigo that she felt upon more deeply realizing her own family's history of slaveholding and racism. She says: "During the time that I was first feeling all this information, again I lived in a kind of vertigo: a sensation of my body having no fixed place to be: the earth having opened, I was falling through space" ("Identity: Skin Blood Heart," in Emily Bulkin, Minnie Bruce Pratt, and Barbara Smith, *Yours in the Struggle: Three Feminist Perspectives on Anti-Semitism and Racism* [New York: Long Haul Press, 1984], p. 35). The Martin/Mohanty essay, "Feminist Politics," is an extended meditation on Pratt's article.

16. This is a question of specific relevance (and pain) for gays and lesbians who face rejection should they "come out" to their families.

17. Tori Amos, "Somewhere Over the Rainbow — Live," from *Hey Juniper* ©1996 Atlantic Recording Corp.

unable to sing the words "me" and "I." In this performance there is no confidence that dreams could come true, that there might be any kind of homecoming that would resolve the plot tensions of our lives. For Amos, there is no going home. She sings the song as if she is out of breath, all cried out. Her performance is a testimony to the end of dreams and the profound loss of confidence in the hopes of a modernist culture. The pathos of Amos's performance has a sense of pain and homelessness that outstrips the more hopeful longing of Judy Garland's original performance. At heart, this performance questions not just whether the story of homecoming in *The Wizard of Oz* is still believable, but whether the whole narrative of modern culture might have exhausted itself.[18] Postmodern advice to Dorothy might well be to get out of Kansas, but don't expect anything from Oz.

Like Dorothy, a postmodern culture recognizes the Emerald City to be a construct of modernity: we have all seen behind the curtain and know that the Wizard of Oz is a fake and that his shining technology cannot save us. But postmodernism has no mantra of return: there is no going home. Dorothy wishes to "wake up where the clouds are far behind me." And she does. At the end of the movie, she awakens back in the comfort and security of home and kin, and the storm clouds of the tornado are now behind her. Leonard Cohen's postmodern cultural perception is very different in his 1992 song "The Future":

> The blizzard of the world
> has crossed the threshold
> and it has overturned
> the order of the soul.[19]

There is no tornado shelter, there is no "safe place," there is no keeping the storm clouds outside the sanctity of home. This blizzard has "crossed the threshold," the space that serves as a boundary marker between in and out, private and public, belonging and alien, familiar and strange, identity and difference, same and other. It has been transgressed, and all of the various orders of life have been overturned. This culturally disorienting storm has invaded our sense of home, and in doing so it has overturned our very understanding of identity. In the postmodern storm, no storm-free existence is possible.

18. This paragraph is borrowed, in part, from Brian Walsh and Sylvia Keesmaat, *Colossians Remixed: Subverting the Empire* (Downers Grove, IL: InterVarsity, 2004), p. 21.
19. Leonard Cohen, "The Future," from *The Future* ©1992 Sony Music Entertainment.

Why has the blizzard crossed the threshold? Why is the world populated by highflying, groundless people like Ryan Bingham? Why does Dorothy's mantra strike us as an empty illusion of a past era? What else would we expect at the end of a century of ever-increasing mobility and rampant consumerism in which we became more and more aware of the constructed nature of all notions of home? Or we could say, we bought a car, lived in an age of massive migrancy, and recognized that "reality" is nothing more than a primitive method of crowd control that got out of hand. Let's deepen our analysis by reflecting on each of these, in reverse order.

Homeless Home Constructors

When Peter Berger and Thomas Luckman first introduced the notion of social constructions of reality, they described the way such constructions made the world a "home" for people.[20] Humans do not receive the world as their home apart from constructing it as such. "To participate in the society," says Berger, "is to share its 'knowledge,' that is, to co-inhabit its nomos."[21] By describing such knowledge alternately as a "web of meanings," "reality definitions," "symbolic universes," "worldviews," or "plausibility structures," Berger and Luckman's "sociology of knowledge" is getting at the same dynamics of homemaking that we have identified in earlier chapters using the language of worldviews and Bourdieu's notion of *habitus*.

Home is a cultural construct shaped by deeply held beliefs, symbols, and myths. The ordering structure of home is itself rooted in and intentionally reflective of a broader *nomos*, a broader vision of cosmic order that humans necessarily inhabit. The "world-building enterprise," says Berger in *The Sacred Canopy*, is an "ordering, or nomizing activity" (p. 19). Such visions provide us with orientation and a sense of ultimate meaning in the world, and they "shield" us from "the ultimate 'insanity' of . . . anomic terror" (p. 22).

But we are not usually that aware of the constructed nature of our home. The socially constructed order that we inhabit most effectively

20. Peter Berger and Thomas Luckman, *The Social Construction of Knowledge: A Treatise on the Sociology of Knowledge* (Garden City, NY: Doubleday, 1966).
21. Berger, *The Sacred Canopy: Elements of a Sociological Theory of Religion* (Garden City, NY: Doubleday/Anchor, 1967), p. 21.

makes the world a home for us when its constructed character is hidden. The cultural anthropologist Clifford Geertz gets at this when he argues that a worldview best provides a secure home for human activity when it is so internalized that we simply assume that we experience reality the way it truly is, that our picture of the world is "the way things in sheer actuality are."[22] Berger speaks of this in terms of internalization and socialization, but he argues that such a hiding of the constructed nature of our worldview is best accomplished by religion. In religious legitimation the "empirical tenuousness" of the historical institutions that make the world a home for us "is transformed into an overpowering stability as they are understood as but manifestations of the underlying structure of the universe" (Berger, p. 37).

The problem is that, once we become aware of the fact that our sense of being at home in the world is a construal, not a given, the sense of being at home is weakened at best and stripped away from us at worst. The result is a sense of cosmic homelessness. To use Berger's terms, once we notice that the sacred canopy is a cultural product, not a gift of the gods, that canopy can no longer provide ultimate protection because it has lost its sacral legitimacy. And without that protection, "we are submerged," Berger argues, "in a world of disorder, senselessness, and madness" (p. 22). Our well-ordered home gives way to anomie. The experience of the world as our home — in the sense of a place where we belong and know the rules and responsibilities of the house is lost.

But why can't we just live without illusion within our social constructions? Why not just accept the anomie, get used to the disorder? Because the issue isn't just the constructed nature of our worldviews. Beyond acknowledging that our sacred canopy is a cultural product, we have also come to the painful realization that none of our world-making constructions are innocent or benign. Worldviews, plausibility structures, symbolic universes, and sacred canopies — they all appear to have an ineluctable tendency toward ideology.[23] There is something toxic about our constructions.

Not surprisingly, the postmodernist feminist and postcolonial analysts have most powerfully revealed that the constructed home is often (if not

---

22. Clifford Geertz, *The Interpretation of Cultures* (New York: Basic Books, 1973), p. 89.

23. We say "appear" to have such a tendency. Brian Walsh has discussed the relationship of worldview and ideology further in "Transformation: Dynamic Worldview or Repressive Ideology?" *Journal of Education and Christian Belief* 4, no. 2 (Autumn 2000): 101-14.

always) the constricted and oppressive home. Describing a postcolonial "politics of home," Rosemary Marangoly George writes that home "is a pattern of select inclusions and exclusions . . . a way of establishing difference."[24] While the very construction of home necessitates some sort of exclusion, because some must be excluded if others are included, such exclusion must itself be rooted in the establishment of "difference." The outsider must be kept outside because of his or her difference — or otherness — from the sameness and familiarity of what is included in the notion of home. But this also necessitates that the home acts "as an ideological determinant of the subject" (George, p. 2). To be inside, to be included, to be at home requires an obedience to the rules of the household and a conformity to the gender, generational, and power relations of the home.

Moreover, George argues, home construction is more about keeping others on the outside than shaping the identity of those on the inside: "At risk of implying a universal humanism, I will suggest that if any common pattern can be traced in the many versions of home that contemporary cultures provide us, it is one of exclusions. Homes are not about inclusions and wide open arms as much as they are about places carved out of closed doors, closed borders and screening apparatuses" (p. 18).[25]

This is why home constructions are never innocent. As we have seen in our discussion of the meaning of home in Chapter 2, the boundaries of home function both to provide necessary and safe markers of identity for the inhab-

24. Rosemary Marangoly George, *The Politics of Home: Postcolonial Relocations and Twentieth Century Fiction* (Cambridge, UK: Cambridge University Press, 1996), p. 2. See also Linda Hutcheon, *The Politics of Postmodernism* (London and New York: Routledge, 1989), p. 45.

25. Roberta Rubenstein offers an important counterargument to a feminist/postcolonial/postmodern literary criticism in her book *Home Matters* (New York: Palgrave, 2001). Rubenstein summarizes the kind of analysis that we meet in George as follows: "Once domesticity became aligned with confinement and oppression, and once *home* became associated with a politically reactionary backlash against feminism, homesickness went underground, as it were. In this sense, longing for home may be understood as a yearning for recovery or return to the idea of a nurturing, unconditionally accepting place/space that has been repressed in contemporary feminism" (pp. 3-4). Rubenstein counters this kind of feminism by insisting that "belonging is a relational, reciprocal condition that encompasses connection and community: not only being taken care of but taking care" (p. 4). And thus the argument of her analysis of authors such as Barbara Kingsolver, Virginia Woolf, Doris Lessing, Anne Tyler, Toni Morrison, and Julia Alvarez concludes that nostalgia and homesickness are not sentimental and regressive modes of feeling, but rather "both may have compensatory and even liberating dimensions within the frame of the narrative" (p. 5).

itants of home *and* to exclude and even to do violence to those who are outside of the boundary. Boundaries are always ambiguous and often ambivalent, if not malevolent. This is the dimension of the social construction of reality that is emphasized in postmodern thought. From a postmodern perspective, not only is the world socially constructed, we also necessarily erect our constructions in violent ways that invariably oppress the marginal while ideologically legitimating those with the most power. As many African-Americans will powerfully attest, the sacred dream of "life, liberty and the pursuit of happiness" has been for them a brutal nightmare.[26] As many women will painfully declare, the dominant male-centered sacred canopy still disempowers and often abuses them.[27] And as poor people around the world remind us rich folks, our business-as-usual way of life threatens to grind them even further into a despairing life of poverty.[28] If we acknowledge this violence, it forces us to realize that our home is a house of pain.

In summary, one feature of being-at-home is having a sense of order and safety. Home is a place made familiar and secure by the recognition and imposition of order. But the recognition that our order-giving worldview is socially constructed can produce a sense of anomie. Anomie, the loss of meaningful order, thus represents a profound kind of homelessness. The additional realization that one's worldview is violent elicits a sense of complicity and guilt. "If reality is socially constructed, then we have to admit that we have participated (whether actively or by acquiescence) in the construction of what is often a nightmare."[29] And how can we comfortably remain at home there? No wonder Ryan Bingham is groundless, Lester Burnham is masturbating in the shower, and no one can sing "Somewhere over the rainbow" with conviction anymore.

Homelessness, Migrancy, and the Tourist Self

While the postmodern homelessness of the Ryan Binghams and Lester Burnhams may appear to be a malaise reserved for the bored and media-

---

26. See, e.g., Cornel West, *Race Matters* (New York: Random House, 1994).

27. See, e.g., Rosemary Radford Ruether, *Sexism and God-Talk* (Boston: Beacon Press, 1983).

28. See, e.g., Bryant Myers, *Walking with the Poor* (Maryknoll, NY: Orbis, 1999).

29. J. Richard Middleton and Brian J. Walsh, *Truth Is Stranger Than It Used to Be: Biblical Faith in a Postmodern Age* (Downers Grove, IL: InterVarsity, 1995), p. 37.

saturated people of the affluent West, this homelessness is related to a broader geopolitical dynamic of displacement. Indeed, as Angelika Bammer says, "the separation of people from their native culture either through physical dislocation (as refugees, immigrants, exiles, or expatriates) or the colonizing imposition of a foreign culture . . . is one of the most formative experiences of our century."[30] How else are we to consider the thirty million people uprooted during Hitler's regime, the sixty to a hundred million refugees in the world since 1945, the massive migrations of peoples seeking economic security, and the misappropriation of local cultures through imperial colonization and global consumerism? We are all in exile.

Perhaps a more apt metaphor is that of migrancy. Salman Rushdie reflects on this theme in his novels and essays:

> The effect of mass migration has been the creation of radically new types of human being: people who root themselves in ideas rather than places, in memories as much as in material things; people who have been obliged to define themselves — because they are so defined by others — by their otherness; people in whose deepest selves strange fusions occur, unprecedented unions between what they were and where they find themselves. The migrant suspects reality: having experienced several ways of being, he understands their illusory nature.[31]

The experience of migrancy, Rushdie observes, gives one an embodied awareness of the constructed and illusory nature of reality; indeed, he posits the rootless existence of the migrant over against a hopeless nostalgia for roots.[32] For example, contrast a statement by Simone Weil, "To be rooted is perhaps the most important and least recognized need of the hu-

---

30. Angelika Bammer, "Introduction," in Angelika Bammer, ed., *Displacements: Cultural Identities in Question* (Bloomington and Indianapolis: Indiana University Press, 1994), p. xi.

31. Salman Rushdie, *Imaginary Homelands: Essays and Criticism 1981-1991* (London: Granta Books; New York: Viking/Penguin, 1991), pp. 124-25.

32. Indian filmmaker Mira Nair displays some kinship with Ryan Bingham when she observes, "I used to have a joke when people asked me where I live . . . I'd say, 'I live on Air India'" (cited in Susan Stanford Friedman, "Bodies in Motion," p. 197). It is not surprising, then, that her films *Monsoon Wedding, Salaam Bombay,* and *Mississippi Masala* all reflect the global ethnoscape of late modernity — "motion pictures for identities located through repeated dislocations" (Friedman, p. 196).

man soul,"[33] with Rushdie's quip against rootedness: ". . . we pretend we are trees and speak of roots. Look under your feet. You will not find gnarled growths sprouting through the soles. Roots, I sometimes think, are a conservative myth, designed to keep us in our places."[34] The migrant condition, says Rushdie, is an experience of uprooting and disjuncture, and from this experience "can be derived a metaphor for all humanity."[35] Thus Rushdie celebrates "hybridity, impurity, intermingling, the transformation of new and unexpected combinations of human cultures, ideas, politics, movies, songs" (p. 394).[36]

Thus migrancy, rather than exile, is proposed as a more fitting way to describe our condition. Arguing that the postmodern condition is one of migrant rootlessness, Iain Chambers shares Rushdie's suspicion of all talk about roots as masking a conservative and constrictive homemaking agenda: "In the idea of roots and cultural authenticity there lies a fundamental, even fundamentalist, form of identity that invariably entwines with nationalist myths in the creation of an 'imagined community.'"[37] And when one considers the genocidal potential of notions of roots and authenticity, Chambers's concerns are well-founded.[38]

But migrancy comes at a cost. Jamaican cultural critic Stuart Hall has famously noted that "migration is a one way trip. There is no 'home' to go back to."[39] Or, as Chambers has observed, "Cut off from the homelands of tradition, experiencing a constantly challenged identity, the [migrant] stranger is perpetually required to make herself a home in an interminable

---

33. Simone Weil, *The Need for Roots: Prelude to a Declaration of Duties toward Mankind,* trans. A. F. Wills (London: Routledge, Kegan and Paul, 1952), p. 41.

34. Cited by George, *The Politics of Home,* p. 199.

35. Rushdie, *Imaginary Homelands,* p. 394.

36. As Rushdie's friend Bruce Chatwin puts it, "Man is a migratory species" (*The Songlines* [New York: Viking, 1987], p. 178).

37. Iain Chambers, *Migrancy, Culture, Identity* (London and New York: Routledge, 1994), p. 73. Chambers is referring to Benedict Anderson, *Imagined Communities* (London: Verso, 1983).

38. This is why Paul Carter wants to "disarm the genealogical rhetoric of blood, property and frontiers" (*Living in a New Country: History, Traveling and Language* [London: Faber & Faber, 1992], pp. 7-8).

39. Stuart Hall, "Minimal Selves," in L. Appignanesi, ed., *Identity, the Real Me: Postmodernism and the Question of Identity.* ICA Documents 6 (London: ICA, 1987). See also David Morley and Kuan-Hsing Chen, eds., *Stuart Hall: Critical Dialogues in Cultural Studies* (London: Routledge, 1996).

discussion between a scattered historical inheritance and a heterogeneous present" (*Migrancy*, p. 6). A scattered, deconstructed past in which narrative coherence was bought at the expense of suppressed family secrets, violence, and repression can only result in a confused and incoherent present.

It is important to note, however, that postmodern migrancy is not a movement from one fixed site of departure to an anticipated point of arrival. Rather, as Chambers says, "migrancy. . . involves a movement in which neither the points of departure nor those of arrival are immutable or certain. It calls for a dwelling in language, in histories, in identities that are constantly subject to mutation. Always in transit, the promise of homecoming — completing the story, domesticating the detour — becomes an impossibility" (p. 5). Not only are we stripped of any hope of completion, but we also find it impossible to domesticate the detour, to find home-on-the-way, precisely because such domestication will invariably seek to stop, to stay, to dwell, thereby arresting the transit. We all end up dispossessed, displaced, and detached. Always on the move, we have no home to possess or any deeply rooted experience of being placed. No wonder postmodern people are detached, unconnected, and uncommitted.[40]

What is the best metaphor, therefore, to describe postmodern homelessness? Is the postmodern self a *migrant*, always on the move, displaced and without attachments? Or might the metaphor of *vagabond* be more appropriate? This is Zygmunt Bauman's suggestion:

> The vagabond is a pilgrim without a destination; a nomad without an itinerary. The vagabond journeys through an unstructured space; like a wanderer in the desert, who knows only of such trails as are marked with his own footprints, and blown off again by the wind the moment he passes, the vagabond structures the site he happens to occupy at the moment, only to dismantle the structure again as he leaves. Each successive spacing is local and temporary — episodic.[41]

The vagabond lacks both the continuity and direction of the traditional nomad. The vagabond metaphor still conjures up images of roaming hoboes riding the rails, tramps living from hand to mouth in a time of scarcity, or

---

40. For further discussion of the postmodern self, see Middleton and Walsh, *Truth Is Stranger*, ch. 3.

41. Zygmunt Bauman, *Postmodern Ethics* (Oxford and Cambridge, MA: Blackwell, 1993), p. 240.

people with wanderlust backpacking without direction. The postmodern vagabond, however, doesn't travel by train, foot, or gypsy caravan; he is 30,000 feet up in an airplane. The postmodern vagabond quite literally lacks the groundedness of her more traditional counterpart; indeed, she traverses the world of difference in a cocoon of sameness, checking into the same homogeneous hotel room just down the hall from Ryan Bingham.

Thus Bauman suggests another metaphor that is perhaps even more appropriate to the postmodern vagabond — the tourist:

> It is the tourist's aesthetic capacity — his or her curiosity, need of amusement, will and ability to live through novel, pleasurable, and pleasurably novel experiences — which appears to possess a nearly total freedom of spacing the tourist's life-world; the kind of freedom which the vagabond, who depends on the rough realities of the visited places for his livelihood and who may only act to avoid displeasure by escaping, can only dream of. (p. 241)

The tourist's aesthetic capacity is, of course, a consuming capacity that can only be afforded because of the possession of capital. The freedom of the tourist to travel is purchased, and the "volume of freedom depends solely on the ability to pay" (p. 241).

But what does this have to do with migrancy? The migrant populations of forced expulsion we have discussed above are not tourists: their dislocation is not a consumer privilege but an imposed homelessness. So how dare we even compare their experience of migrancy with the postmodern tourist who is happily (or not so happily) consuming the world. Caren Kaplan draws a distinction between going "into literary/linguistic exile with all my cultural baggage intact," and being "cast out of home and language without forethought or permission." And she warns against "a kind of theoretical tourism on the part of the first world critic, where the margin becomes a linguistic or critical vacation, a new poetics of the exotic."[42] We need to be wary of a chic postmodernism that is little more than a voyeurism of the other or that romanticizes migrancy, exile, and homelessness.[43]

---

42. Caren Kaplan, "Deterritorializations: The Rewriting of Home and Exile in Western Feminist Discourse," *Cultural Critique* 6 (Spring 1987): 191.

43. "For people who have been dispossessed and forced to leave for an uncertain destiny, rejected time and again, returned to the sea or to the no man's land of border zones; for

Then again, what else might we expect from a culture of mass consumption that is predicated on mobility? If George Pierson was right when he said that "ours has been the mobile society par excellence" in which "we don't seem to be anchored to place" and "no locality need claim us long," it shouldn't be surprising for us to end up as postmodern tourists.[44]

On the Road to Nowhere

Like most of us, the narrator of Douglas Coupland's book *Life After God* is on the road, but he is coming from nowhere and going nowhere.

> I was in the middle of the three-lane highway in between the speeding lane and the truck lane. My engine was pleasingly silent. I sang loudly and forced myself to listen to my voice: flat and hopefully generic, for I have always tried to speak with a voice that has no regional character — a voice from nowhere. This is because I have never really felt like I was "from" anywhere; home to me, as I have said, is a shared electronic dream of cartoon memories, half-hour sitcoms, and national tragedies. I have always prided myself on my lack of accent — my lack of any discerning regional flavor. I used to think mine was a Pacific Northwest accent, from where I grew up, but then I realized my accent was simply the accent of nowhere — the accent of a person who has no fixed home in their mind.[45]

Not only is the narrator's memory of "home" shaped by the homogenizing forces of a world mediated to him through the screen of a television culture, but he experiences the world he presently inhabits from the vantage point of a hermetically sealed automobile speeding through the countryside on that most nowhere of places, the multilane highway. This person in no-place speaks and sings with "the accent of nowhere."

---

these unwanted expatriated, it seems that all attempts at exalting the achievements of exile are but desperate efforts to quell the crippling sorrow of homelessness and estrangement" (Trinh T. Minh-ha, "Other than myself/my other self," in George Robertson et al., eds., *Travellers' Tales: Narratives of Home and Displacement* [London and New York: Routledge, 1994], p. 12).

44. George W. Pierson, *The Moving American* (New York: Alfred A. Knopf, 1972), p. 29.

45. Douglas Coupland, *Life After God* (New York and London: Pocket Books, 1994), pp. 173-74.

James Howard Kunstler understands Coupland's "nowhere man." In his books *The Geography of Nowhere* and *Home from Nowhere,* Kunstler chronicles the loss of place and loss of identity that has shaped American culture.[46] There is no mystery about why a society that invented the mass production of automobiles, systematically dismantled all forms of public transit (most notably railways and early twentieth-century streetcar lines), and provided mass government subsidies directly to both the automotive industry and the construction of millions of miles of car-friendly roads, would be more heavily dependent on cars than any other country in the world.[47] In the car-crazy culture of America, "one goes somewhere in order to become something. Motion becomes an end in itself, and the mass of equipment needed to support this motion — highways, freeways, fast food huts, lube joints, tract housing — makes every place so bleak that we hate where we came from, hate where we end up, and don't want to pay much attention to what we're passing through."[48] Even more ubiquitous than Airworld, the car culture enables migrancy at a more basic level.

However, the advent of a car-dominated culture is not just the result of mass production, government subsidies, and the suburbanization of America. The mobility of the American people is legendary.[49] There is hardly a

46. James Howard Kunstler, *The Geography of Nowhere: The Rise and Decline of America's Man-Made Landscape* (New York: Simon and Schuster, 1993); see also Kunstler, *Home from Nowhere: Remaking our Everyday World for the 21st Century* (New York: Touchstone, 1996).

47. In ch. 6 of *The Geography of Nowhere,* Kunstler tells the story of how the automotive industry colluded with the oil and rubber companies to buy out and close down railways and streetcar companies across the country in the early twentieth century, and also conspired to secure billions of government dollars to support the ascension of the automobile.

The collusion to shut down the streetcar lines in order to make space for the automobile and its requisite crosstown expressways was brilliantly portrayed in the character of Judge Doom in the movie *Who Framed Roger Rabbit?* Kunstler (in *Geography of Nowhere,* p. 9) recounts this monologue from Doom's plan to sell off the streetcar system of Los Angeles in 1947: "It's a construction plan of epic proportions. They're calling it a freeway! Eight lanes of shimmering cement running from here to Pasadena! I see a place where people get on and off the freeway, off and on, off and on, all day and all night. . . . I see a street of gas stations, inexpensive hotels, restaurants that serve rapidly prepared food, tire salons, automobile dealerships, and wonderful, wonderful billboards as far as the eye can see. My god, it'll be beautiful!"

48. Kunstler, *Home from Nowhere,* p. 60.

49. "US residents stay on the move, census indicates": so ran a headline in the *Chicago Tribune* of Sept. 24, 2003. "America continues to be a country on the move," says Genara Armas. "In the last five years of the twentieth century, close to half the population packed up

nation on earth that can compete with America when it comes to a migrant spirit. Not only is America built on the experience of immigrant peoples, but its very mythology is shaped around the image of the American hero who is "a wandering pilgrim" going forth on a "perpetual quest."[50] From the Atlantic to the Pacific and beyond, America is a nation on the move. Such a sense of mobility has shaped both foreign policy (Manifest Destiny, the Monroe Doctrine, and the more recent National Security Strategy all have a sense of America moving beyond its own boundaries)[51] and approaches to space exploration (President Kennedy's "new frontier").

But in the American experience this sense of the movement of civilizations is rooted in the notion of individual autonomy. And what better technology to enhance this individualism than a car? If the modernist American self is indeed *homo autonomous*, then what better implement for the realization and practice of that autonomy than an *auto*mobile that will transport this mobile self at great speeds over vast terrains in comfort and relative solitude. Not only is the appreciation, knowledge, and care of any particular "place" literally left behind in the exhaust fumes of the automobile, so also do the civic virtues necessary for living together in community evaporate in a car-dominated society.[52] Who needs to develop neighborli-

---

and moved to different homes." According to Census Bureau data from 2000, 45.9 percent of U.S. residents aged 5 and older had moved in the previous five years. This five-year moving rate has stayed at about 46 percent since at least 1970.

50. Lewis H. Lapham, "Who and What Is American?" *Harper's* (Jan. 1992): 46. Loren Wilkinson agrees and offers some helpful comments on the differences between Canadian and American literature with regard to motifs of pilgrimage and homesteading. Referring to comments by Margaret Atwood in her early work *Surviving*, Wilkinson writes: "The guiding myth of Canadian literature, she [Atwood] suggests, is simply survival — first against the rigours of the climate and the landscape; second, against the presence of the mother country from which the ties were never severed, as in the case of the U.S.; third, against the encroaching culture of the more populous United States. The American myth, on the other hand, is that of the frontier: of always pushing forward into new territory." The contrasting symbolic metaphors between Canadian and American literature emerge as house versus horse, Anne of Green Gables versus Huck Finn, and creating a home versus escape from home (Wilkinson, "Pilgrims at Home: The Mutual Challenge of Christendom and Environmental Literature," *Christian Scholar's Review* 32, no. 4 [Summer 2003]: 415-16, n. 4).

51. For a series of important essays reflecting on the "National Security Strategy" see Wes Avram, ed., *Anxious About Empire: Theological Essays on New Global Realities* (Grand Rapids: Brazos Press, 2004).

52. "What happened during the crucial twenty-five years spanning 1893 to 1918, it seems to me, is clear: Americans, given the choice between civilizing their cities through public

ness if one lives in a detached house accessed almost exclusively by the automobile? If one never walks down the block to buy a loaf of bread, then one never notices the new rose bush in Mr. Albert's garden five doors down, nor does one ever meet the single mother and her three kids who live above the local bakery. In fact, with the dominance of the car and the shopping malls that have been built to accommodate its culture, there are hardly any local bakeries to walk to anyway. Civility assumes proximity. We develop civic virtues in the context of societal relationships. But the automobile enhances individuality and reduces proximity to the traffic jam. Civility gives way to road rage.

Civility is a normative idea. We could say, in view of Peter Berger's sociology of knowledge, that whether a people will develop a richly dense culture of civility will depend on whether the construction of the world as home engenders a culture of connectivity and interrelationship in which civility can flourish. A culture of hypermobility has no such structure: an ever-changing, ever-mobile society in which the individual migrates through widely divergent social, cultural, and geographical worlds results in homelessness.

> A world in which everything is in constant motion is a world in which certainties of any kind are hard to come by. Social mobility has its correlate in cognitive and normative mobility. What is truth in one context of the individual's life may be error in another. What was considered right at one stage of the individual's social career becomes wrong in the next. Once more, the anomic threat of these constellations is very powerful indeed.[53]

If mobility engenders anomie, then mobility produces homelessness.

Displaced by our own mobility, worried that if we ever stopped and stayed in one place we would be left behind, and suspicious of any calls to slow down as reactionary at best and anti-American at worst, we are a "country of exiles" who live in what William Leach calls "the landscape of the temporary." This is "the landscape of the improvisational, the landscape of the flexible, or the landscape of the exchangeable and replaceable."

---

works, and using the car to escape the demands of civility, chose the car" (Kunstler, *Home from Nowhere*, p. 43).

53. Peter Berger, Brigitte Berger, and Hansfield Kellner, *The Homeless Mind: Modernization and Consciousness* (New York: Vintage, 1974), p. 184.

It is one occupied by "*expatriates,* accustomed to temporary attachments."[54] There is an expatriate feel to American culture both because America is a land settled by expatriated peoples and because of what appears to be something of an innate restlessness that functions as a prime determinant of the structure of American character.[55]

Why do we embrace such a migratory way of life? Why do we esteem mobility above placedness? Because being migratory and mobile is good for business. Corporate capitalism needs expatriate executives like Ryan Bingham to sign a deal here, play golf with a client there, and show up at a meeting two hundred miles away four hours later. These are the "footloose soldiers" of "history's mightiest cultural and commercial empire" (Leach, p. 65). Production needs a mobile and temporary labor force that will keep the wages low, set worker against worker, and severely undermine labor solidarity (p. 66). And capital needs to be free to invest, disinvest, and reinvest wherever it can reproduce itself at the greatest speed, regardless of place.

Capitalism requires placeless mobility, and what capitalism will offer as compensation for the loss of home and the sacrifice of place is nothing less than freedom. There is a cost to pay, but it is worth the price. There will be ruins in the wake of this mobile capitalism, but something even better will emerge from those ruins, or so claims landscape geographer J. B. Jackson.[56]

Perhaps one might think that "trailer camp" life is an example of mobile American culture at its worst. But Jackson found in the trailer camp something of a symbol of American homemaking. The real significance of mobile homes, he wrote, lay "in a kind of freedom we often undervalue: the freedom from burdensome emotional ties with the environment, freedom from communal responsibilities, freedom from the tyranny of the traditional home and its possessions; the freedom from belonging to a tight-knit social order; and above all, the freedom to move on to somewhere else."[57] Notice that Jackson speaks of "freedom from"

54. William Leach, *Country of Exiles: The Destruction of Place in American Life* (New York: Vintage, 1999), p. 60.

55. Belden C. Lane, *Landscapes of the Sacred: Geography and Narrative in American Spirituality,* expanded ed. (Baltimore and London: The Johns Hopkins University Press, 2002), p. 219.

56. J. B. Jackson, *The Necessity of Ruins* (Amherst: University of Massachusetts Press, 1980).

57. J. B. Jackson, *Discovering the Vernacular Landscape* (New Haven: Yale University Press, 1984), pp. 100-101.

four times and of "freedom to" only once. But if the only "freedom to" that he envisions is the freedom to "move on to somewhere else," it follows that he sees such things as "burdensome emotional ties with the environment," "communal responsibilities," the "tyranny of the traditional home," and any sense of "belonging to tight-knit social order" as constrictions on freedom. And insofar as such ties to a local environment, communal responsibilities, and a sense of tradition and belonging are essential for being at home in the world, then any anthropology rooted in autonomous freedom will by definition render us homeless. Freedom thus defined is a matter of being relieved of the "burdens" of placedness. But we have seen that such freedom isn't so free after all. It comes at a cost: we must sacrifice home.

Scott Russell Sanders isn't buying it. Recognizing that American history does not encourage him "to belong anywhere with a full heart," Sanders has decided to resist the "vagabond wind" that has been blowing throughout American culture and mythology.[58] Whereas all the forces of our culture, and some of the forces of our biology, push us to an itinerant life, Sanders says: "Only by knocking against the golden calf of mobility, which looms so large and shines so brightly, have I come to realize that it is hollow. Like all idols, it distracts us from the true divinity" (Sanders, p. 117). While Ryan Bingham worries about being grounded, Sanders seeks to be a deeply grounded, well-centered inhabitant of place:

> It has taken me half a lifetime of searching to realize that the likeliest path to the ultimate ground leads through my local ground. I mean the land itself, with its creeks and rivers, its weather, seasons, stone outcroppings, and all the plants and animals that share it. I cannot have a spiritual center without having a geographical one; I cannot live a grounded life without being grounded in a *place*. (pp. 120-21)

But what about the reality of a century of expatriates, migrants, and displaced peoples? What about Salman Rushdie's claim that mass migrations have created a new kind of human being, rooted more in ideas than in place? And what about all the constrictions of home, its exclusions and marginalizations — often through violence and bigotry — of other people? Shouldn't Americans be especially sensitive to Rushdie's claim that "to be a

---

58. Scott Russell Sanders, *Staying Put: Making a Home in a Restless World* (Boston: Beacon Press, 1993), p. xv.

migrant is, perhaps, to be the only species of human being free of the shackles of nationalism . . ."?[59] Actually, Sanders replies, America would seem to disprove Rushdie's claim. After all, "who would pretend that a history of migration has immunized the United States against bigotry?" (Sanders, p. 105).[60]

Sanders's disagreements with Rushdie, however, go even deeper than historical debates about the relative benefits of a migrant culture. "I quarrel with Rushdie," he says, "because he articulates as eloquently as anyone the orthodoxy I wish to counter: the belief that movement is inherently good, staying put is bad; that uprooting things brings tolerance, while rootedness breeds intolerance, that imaginary homelands are preferable to geographical ones; that to be modern, enlightened, fully of our time is to be displaced" (p. 106).

Earlier in this chapter we depicted Rushdie's favoring of migrancy as indicative of a postmodern homelessness. And in this section we have seen that what often is attributed to postmodern flux isn't all that dissimilar to the restlessness of an American take on modernist notions of autonomy and mobility. Maybe postmodern homelessness isn't all that radically *post*modern after all. Maybe this kind of homelessness is the cultural fruit of late capitalism, with its penchant for ever-increasing growth of consumer products. Maybe the insatiable desire for "more" is complicit in this preoccupation with mobility, autonomy, migrancy, and difference. Maybe all of this talk of postmodern homelessness is little more than a reflection of the rootlessness of the consuming modernist ego.

Postmodern Migrants or Homeless Consumers?

In his social-psychological study *The Poverty of Affluence*, Paul Wachtel observes that, "in the pursuit of more, in the effort to better ourselves, we

59. Rushdie, *Imaginary Homelands*, p. 124.

60. On this point Sanders can appeal to Edward Said. In his famous essay "Reflections on Exile" (in Russell Ferguson and Cornel West, eds., *Out There: Marginalization and Contemporary Culture* [Cambridge, MA: MIT, 1990]), Said argues that, while "exile, unlike nationalism, is a discontinuous state of being . . . cut off from . . . roots . . . land . . . past," nonetheless the acute temptation of exile is that it gives rise to "an exaggerated sense of group solidarity, and a passionate hostility to outsiders, even those who may in fact be in the same predicament as you" (p. 360). What begins as resentment quickly becomes hostility and bigotry. Add to that a national identity and you have an explosive brew.

must leave behind what we previously had; we must not get 'stuck.'"[61] This is the impetus to mobility of a capitalist culture. Robert Heilbroner observes that "expansion has always been considered inseparable from capitalism," and thus "a 'stationary' nonexpanding capitalism has always been considered either a prelude to its collapse or a betrayal of its historic purpose."[62] No wonder the idea of staying put, being content with one's place, having a deep sense that one has "enough" and needs no more, seems somehow unpatriotic and even crazy in a capitalist society like America. Deborah Tall observes: "To stay in one place for life is often interpreted as being unambitious, unadventurous — a negation of American values. Moving up in the world means moving on."[63] As we argued in our discussion of ecological homelessness in Chapter 5, a capitalist economy depends on a docile population that worships at the cult of the new. Novelty for the sake of novelty is exalted in a culture that identifies itself as "modern." And intrinsic to the cult of the new is "the need to overturn the past and begin again, to disregard all kinds of attachments in the interest of getting the 'new and improved,' whether goods, jobs, entertainment, or places."[64]

A culture fixated on the new, however, is necessarily a throwaway culture. Since attachments are binding, inhibiting freedom, a culture based on migration, money, exploration, and wealth production will have little more than a romantic attachment to place and home. More likely, the capitalist elite will not be able to "take a place seriously because they must be ready at any moment, by the terms of power and wealth in the modern world, to destroy any place."[65]

But what does this kind of capitalism have to do with the postmodern homelessness that we have been discussing throughout this chapter? There

---

61. Paul Wachtel, *The Poverty of Affluence: A Psychological Portrait of the American Way of Life* (Philadelphia: New Society Publishers, 1989), p. 95.

62. Robert Heilbroner, *An Inquiry into the Human Prospect* (New York: Norton, 1974), p. 83. A similar analysis can be found in Daniel Bell, *The Cultural Contradictions of Capitalism*, 2nd ed. (London: Heineman, 1979); see also Bob Goudzwaard, *Capitalism and Progress: A Diagnosis of Western Society*, trans. Josina Van Nuis Zylstra (Grand Rapids: Eerdmans, 1979).

63. Deborah Tall, "Dwelling: Making Peace with Space and Place," in Vitek and Jackson, ed., *Rooted in the Land* (New Haven: Yale University Press, 1996), p. 104.

64. Leach, *Country of Exiles*, p. 13.

65. Wendell Berry, *Sex, Economy, Freedom and Community* (New York: Pantheon, 1992), p. 22.

are three very important points of convergence between the two: they both devalue place, both are preoccupied with boundary crossing, and both esteem choice as the most important expression of human autonomy.

Using "cosmopolitanism" as roughly synonymous with what we have described as globalization, William Leach sees a close relationship between postmodern and postcolonial theory and corporate capitalism.

> Corporate executives, academics and postcolonialists have together brought cosmopolitanism into the mainstream. They seem unified in their views — above all, in their phobia for place. They see place and everything associated with it (memory, the past, tradition) as confining and negatively discriminatory. In every case, they prefer weak fluid boundaries that exclude no one and encourage transgression to the maintenance of old neighborhoods or the protection of established communities, both local and national.[66]

Postmodern tourism and corporate capitalism share a disposable approach to place. What matters is mobility and difference, not stability and familiarity. Mobility — of ideas, people, products or capital — is no respecter of boundaries. The postmodern, boundary-crossing, hybrid migrant is as much a product of global capitalism as are the products that he takes with him on his travels. The deconstructive aversion to boundary fixing is a mirror of global capitalism's "free-trade" agenda that deregulates money markets, tears down barriers to investment, and (selectively) opens borders to the free movement of goods and services.[67]

But what it all comes down to is choice. In both postmodern discourse and global capitalism, boundaries need to be broken down because they inhibit consumer choice. Roger Lundin argues that "the desiring and acquiring self of postmodern cultural theory bears more than a casual resemblance to the unit of consumption at the center of market economies

---

66. Leach, *Country of Exiles*, p. 173.

67. We say that these borders are selectively opened because they are invariably only opened to benefit the most powerful national economies. While the forces of global capitalism want to have open access to African resources and markets, they are consistently resistant to opening Western markets to African products. We wonder whether something akin to this might be going on in much of the talk of alterity and border crossing in postmodern discourse. Who is really crossing the borders in all of this talk, and on whose terms? If the postmodern self is really a voyeuristic tourist of the "other," it seems to us that the "other" is still objectified, marginalized, and commodified.

and democratic societies."[68] Both postmodern tourists and global capitalists want to keep their options open, whether for the identities they will construct in cyberspace or the products they will buy at the mall. Both value choice over loyalty. And both remain deeply homeless because being at home is seen to be a limiting of choices and requires an acknowledgment that we are not autonomous but interdependent and interrelated homemakers.

Walter Truett Anderson succinctly states this often overlooked connection: "Globalism and a postmodern worldview come in the same package; we will not have one without the other."[69] They both emerge at the same historical moment (after 1945), and they both share an anthropology that views humans as units of consumption. And neither is in any significant way a break with the homeless-making autonomy that has characterized modernity. In Chapter 3 we argued that global capitalism is a homeless-making force in the lives of millions upon millions of people in the world. Now we conclude that postmodern homelessness is the unique shape that such homelessness takes in the affluent West and that much postmodern talk of difference, heterogeneity, migrancy, exile, nomadism, marginality, and the like functions to provide ideological legitimacy and comfort to the forces of global consumerism.[70] After all, Ryan Bingham is an agent of corporate capitalism, isn't he?

68. Roger Lundin, *The Culture of Interpretation: Christian Faith and the Postmodern World* (Grand Rapids: Eerdmans, 1993), pp. 73-74.

69. Walter Truett Anderson, *Reality Isn't What It Used to Be* (San Francisco: HarperCollins, 1990), p. 25.

70. For a similar analysis, see Nicholas Boyle, *Who Are We Now? Christian Humanism and the Global Market from Hegel to Heaney* (Edinburgh: T&T Clark, 1998).

Homemaking in Empire

The Epistle to the Colossians

We all just sat there in silence for a while. Tychicus had finished reading Paul's letter to the community, and we just sat there.

Maybe it was that jolt back to the reality of our beloved correspondent — "Remember my chains" — that left us speechless. Or maybe it was more of an awkward silence, not knowing what to say or do. I mean, the whole event had been marked by both excitement and discomfort from the beginning. A letter from Paul to our community — a community that he had never met — was an event of some magnitude. No wonder there was an excitement in the air as the news spread to come to the meeting place that evening! We were a young Christian community, deeply hungry for spiritual direction and teaching, and we longed to learn more about the one we had come to confess as Lord of all creation. A letter from Paul would certainly promise to be rich fare for our hungry souls.

Yet there was a tension in the room as soon as we arrived. You see, not only was Tychicus, the envoy of the apostle and carrier of the letter, there; he also had Onesimus along with him as his co-envoy, a correspondent of the apostle himself. Onesimus, the scandal of the community, the slave who had run away from his master, Philemon (see the Epistle to Philemon). And here he was — sitting in his master's house, where our community was meeting to worship. How could we put together worship in Philemon's house with a living testimony to infidelity sitting in our midst? How could our house church, our attempt to make a home in the kingdom of Jesus, survive such a homebreaking act as a slave running away from his master?

A sense of social embarrassment, even foreboding, had clouded the event. What would Philemon do about Onesimus? How could Onesimus have the nerve to simply walk into Philemon's house in the company of

264

Tychicus? Why wasn't he cowering in fear? Why wasn't he begging for his master's mercy and leniency? How could he just sit there as if somehow his arriving with a letter from Paul would protect him?

Well, whatever was going on in Onesimus's head would have to wait until we heard what Paul had to say to us. Maybe he would even address this vexing problem of slavery in general and Onesimus in particular. You see, underlying the problem of Onesimus were other pressing concerns. We had known from the beginning that following Jesus meant that we confessed a Lord other than Caesar and embraced a way of life counter to the empire. We knew that Christian communities were known for having all things in common, which was breaking down the hierarchy that was at the heart of the *paterfamilias* (see Acts 2:44-47; 4:32-37; 5:1-11). But we weren't sure how far all of this was to go. We found ourselves in constant conversation — and sometimes argument — about whether this meant that the wealthy among us should return lands that they had gained through unjust taxation, whether we should attend the festivals in honor of the imperial household, whether our homes should be adorned with the symbols of the empire, and whether we should do away with the hierarchical social patterns of the empire in our life together. If Paul was going to send Onesimus along with this letter, did it mean he was also going to address those kinds of questions in what he wrote?

As I said, we were all rendered speechless by the end of the letter, and I'm still not sure why. Was it the presence and reference to Onesimus and the issue of slavery that took away our tongues, or was it the sheer power of the whole letter as it was read to us?

First, consider Onesimus. He sat through the whole proceeding looking . . . well, safe. That's it. He looked as if he felt safe, even though we all knew that his was a most precarious predicament. But he didn't seem to have too much anxiety about his situation. Then, at the end of the letter, when Paul actually named Onesimus, he positively beamed! Paul said that Tychicus "is coming with Onesimus, the faithful and beloved brother, who is one of you. They will tell you about everything here."

While Onesimus beamed, you could see jaws dropping all over the place. Onesimus? The runaway slave is faithful? And not only faithful, but he is to be known in our midst not as slave, but as brother?

My hunch is that Paul had a wry smile on his face when he dictated that line. He could probably see all the jaws dropping as he said those words. And he knew full well how he was redefining what faithfulness meant in the kingdom of God as opposed to what fidelity meant in the empire. Rather than allowing us to maintain hierarchical distinctions in our lives, he insisted that this man was neither faithless nor someone who was on the outside of our community because of economic status or a past action. Onesimus, Paul wrote, "is one of you" — a member of the household of faith. It was clear from Paul's very description of Onesimus that this runaway slave was not to be excluded from the household. If we were to take Paul's word on this, then it was clear that there would be wide-ranging implications for our life together.

Yes, people were shocked by this description of Onesimus, which undoubtedly contributed to that awkward silence at the end of the reading. But I like to think that we were quiet for even more profound reasons as well. Some were quiet because their agitation for an otherworldly piety was so directly attacked as unfaithful to the gospel. But most of us were rendered speechless by the sheer audacity of what we had just heard. In a world where the empire pointed to its own economic and agricultural fruitfulness as evidence of the blessings of the gods, Paul told us that the gospel is bearing real fruit throughout the empire and we ourselves were called to a fruitfulness in our lives that was richer and more substantial than anything the empire could offer.

In a world where the image of the emperor was literally everywhere, and where Caesar was taken to be nothing short of divine, Paul proclaimed that Jesus was the image of the invisible God — that Jesus, not Caesar, was Lord of creation, that Jesus was the firstborn of creation and the firstborn from the dead, thereby rendering Caesar's patrilineage irrelevant.

In a world governed by Roman thrones, dominions, rulers, and powers, Paul said that all the thrones, dominions, rulers, and powers are created by and for Jesus Christ. Paul even went so far as to say that the whole cosmos is held together in Christ! The world is an ordered cosmos and a home to us because of Jesus!

And then, in a move that took our breath away, Paul said something that filled us with a fearful joy. In an empire that saw Rome, or sometimes Zeus, or sometimes the emperor himself, as the head of the body politic — that is, the head of the empire itself — Paul turned it all upside down. In an act of subversive imagination, he said that Christ, not Caesar, is the head, and that he is the head not of the imperial body politic, but of the church. Somehow, in Paul's mind, Jesus replaces Caesar as Lord, and the church that subjects itself to Jesus' rule replaces the empire! Neither the imperial household nor the empire itself is the household of the kingdom; rather, the church — represented in our conflicted community gathering in Philemon's house, in the presence of his runaway slave, Onesimus — is the household of the kingdom, the household of the new creation in Christ.

And as if that wasn't enough evidence to have us all convicted of treason, Paul then went to the heart of the empire's pretensions by debunking the very foundation of the *pax Romana*. You all know how Rome keeps the peace, don't you? By putting anyone who would dare to threaten Roman peace on a cross. This is a household erected on violence. But Paul tells us that God reconciled all of creation precisely by making peace through the blood of the cross — the blood of Jesus.

Paul wasn't more than a couple of sentences into his letter by this time, and you could have heard a pin drop for the rest of the reading. He described himself as a servant of this church, this household, and, using a word all of us were familiar with, he said he had received a "stewardship" to make the word of God fully known (Col. 1:25).[71] Like many in our group, he was a steward of a household, and his task was to care for and build up that household so that it could be vital and abundant. This meant that Paul was called to help us to grow up and develop a maturity in our faith so we wouldn't be deceived by empty philosophies from either the heart of the empire or its margins. And if our lives were shaped by the story of Jesus — dead, buried, resurrected, ascended, and coming again — then the story and the lifestyle of the empire would have no hold on us anymore.

It was becoming clear that this story of Jesus was not only the retold and reinterpreted story of Israel but also the story of all of creation and its renewal. The gospel has been proclaimed to every creature under heaven, Paul said at one point. Because of the cross, the cosmos that is held together in Christ is renewed as the household of God.

Later in the letter he called us to put on the new self, "which is being renewed in knowledge according to the image of its creator." This new life in Christ is nothing less than the restoration of our very humanness as we were always called to be: renewed in the image of God, a renewal that would break down all the old barriers, all the imperial constructions of race, religion, class, and economic standing! In this renewal, Paul said, "there is no longer Greek and Jew, circumcised and uncircumcised, bar-

---

71. Translating *oikonomia* as "commission" loses its homemaking overtones.

barian, Scythian, slave and free." This kingdom's renewed household was one of unspeakable inclusion and hospitality.

At this point everyone looked at Onesimus, but he showed no emotion at all. He just sat there looking right at Tychicus as he read. I took a glance at Philemon, though, and noticed a perplexed look on his face.

Then Paul told us what a community rooted in the story of Jesus looks like: compassion, kindness, humility, meekness, and patience. Not exactly the kind of virtues that will help you climb the social and economic ladders of the empire. If we followed the example of Jesus and lived by these virtues, the hierarchical family values of the empire would be fundamentally undermined.

And just as I was wondering how all of this would play out for Onesimus and Philemon, Tychicus was reading that business about forgiveness and bearing with one another, about the love that binds everything together in perfect harmony. I couldn't help wondering what this love would do considering the disharmony in our community, which, of course, was physically embodied by the presence of Onesimus in the room. If we are one body, called to let the peace of Christ rule in our hearts, then how could peace come to the relationship between this slave and his master, between all slaves and all masters?

And if Jesus' words and actions were really to dwell in us richly — and this seemed to be the purpose of Paul's writing to us — then how would that word take up residence in our very dwellings, our households, our economic lives? If we were to teach and admonish one another in wisdom, have a life filled with gratitude and worship, and do everything — in word or deed — in the name of the Lord Jesus in thanksgiving to the Father, then what would wisdom look like in our households? How does our life of gratitude and worship shape our homemaking? And what should Philemon (and the rest of us) do about Onesimus if it's going to be in the name of the Lord Jesus and not the Lord Caesar?

As if anticipating that question — as if he knew that we couldn't bear the tension of listening to his words in the presence of Onesimus, the runaway slave, any longer — Paul then addressed Christian households. Husbands and wives, fathers and children, but most importantly, slaves and masters.[72] At first it sounded as if he was simply reinstating the old hierar-

---

72. The exegesis that follows is dependent on Brian J. Walsh and Sylvia Keesmaat, *Colossians Remixed: Subverting the Empire* (Downers Grove, IL: InterVarsity, 2005), ch. 11.

chies of husbands over wives, fathers over children, and masters over slaves. But I knew enough about Paul to wonder whether this was what was going on. How could the apostle simply reinstitute household violence and oppression after what he had just said about Greeks and Jews, slaves and free? If Christ is "all and in all," then how could he maintain the privileges of the *paterfamilias*?

I was listening very carefully at this point; indeed, we all were. The women, children, and slaves all kind of sat up when Paul addressed them. The very fact that they were addressed and invited to participate in the Christian household was in some ways remarkable. And then there was the way Paul used the word "master" throughout his address to the masters and slaves. "Slaves, obey your masters according to the flesh in everything . . . fearing the Master." "Whatever your task, put yourselves into it, as done for the Master, not for your masters." "Masters, treat your slaves justly and fairly, for you know that you have a Master in heaven." One thing was abundantly clear: masters and slaves together were subject to a Master, and that undermined the ultimate authority of earthly masters.

But there was one other thing that Paul said, and that put the whole relationship between masters and slaves — and particularly Philemon and Onesimus — in a radically different light. At one point Paul said to the slaves: "You know that from the Master you will receive the inheritance as your reward; you serve the messianic Master" (Col. 3:24 [authors' translation]). In an empire where slaves *are* inheritance, that is, they are passed down from father to son, Paul said here that they *receive* an inheritance. What could that mean? Well, for anyone who had been attending to the Hebrew Scripture since their conversion to following this Messiah, the overtones were unmistakable. When in Israel's scriptures did slaves receive an inheritance? In the year of Jubilee, that's when! (see Lev. 25).

Could this mean what it seems to mean? Churches throughout the empire had begun to share all their resources as a response to the idea that, in Jesus, Jubilee has come. Care for the poor, the widows, and orphans was rooted in this interpretation of Jubilee. Paul had just spoken of the centrality of forgiveness in the Christian community and that there was no longer a distinction between slave and free. And now he had evoked the image of Jubilee. If slaves were to receive an inheritance from their true Master, then might not Paul's injunction to masters to treat their slaves "justly and fairly" entail nothing less than their emancipation? And wouldn't this transformation of Christian households serve to undermine the most fundamental hierarchy of the Roman empire?

My mind was racing and I missed a few lines of the epistle until I heard Tychicus drop that bomb of describing Onesimus as a faithful and beloved brother in our midst. Tychicus then ended his reading of the letter with the reference to the apostle's chains. For a few pregnant moments we sat in silence. But then heads started to turn, but not to look at Onesimus. Not even to look at Philemon. No, everyone was looking at me now. I could feel my ears burning and the blood rushing to my face. I must have been beet red.

Paul named me right at the end of his letter: "And say to Archippus, 'See to it that you complete the task that you have received in the Lord.'" People started turning toward me in the silence that followed that statement. Finally Philemon found his voice: "Archippus, my friend, do you have something to tell us?" And I knew that my time had come. My time to take up leadership in the church, my time to take all that I had learned from Scripture, from the stories of Jesus and Paul, and to put that into the service of the community. So I began to interpret Paul's letter for my sisters and brothers in Colossae.

As I began to explain how Paul was subverting the empire for the sake of the kingdom, I noticed that Onesimus was weeping. But they were tears of joy — perhaps even the tears of homecoming.

The Indwelling God
and the Sojourning Community

*God is love, and those who abide in love abide in God, and
God abides in them.*

1 John 4:16

Lord of the starfields, Sower of life,
Heaven and earth are full of your light;
Voice of the nova, Smile of the dew,
All of our yearning only comes home to you.

Bruce Cockburn[1]

"Nobody's home. Everybody's on the move." So writes Julia Keller in an
essay on contemporary American culture.[2] And her remark serves as a
succinct summary of the previous chapter. Observing that people seem to
be moving anywhere, she astutely comments that "anywhere is nowhere,
because infinite possibility of destination is also a kind of hell, a succes-
sion of trap doors depositing us endlessly elsewhere." At the root of this
seeming obsession, she concludes, is "our untethered, free-floating devotion to nowhere. . . . We hover just above surfaces, insisting on the freedom to be off in a jiffy, reveling in our rootlessness." Our technology, furthermore, "enables just this sort of placeless evasion, this driven lack of

---

1. Bruce Cockburn, "Lord of the Starfields," from *In the Falling Dark* ©1976 High Ro-
mance Music.

2. *Chicago Tribune*, June 22, 1999, p. 3.

connection." As a former Microsoft vice president once wrote, computers "liberate us from the 'tyranny of geography.'" This, Keller notes, is "a curious aspiration," and she rhetorically asks: "Could belonging somewhere and having a stake in that somewhere really be all that bad?" Keller concludes by wondering: "Maybe that quiet yearning for a home, a wish long denied, is behind more of the world's darkness than we are ready to admit" (p. 3).

Robert Wuthnow reaches similar conclusions. He argues that in our postmodern times "a traditional spirituality of inhabiting sacred places has given way to a new spirituality of seeking — that people have been losing faith in a metaphysics that can make them feel at home in the universe and that they increasingly negotiate among competing glimpses of the sacred, seeking partial knowledge and practical wisdom."[3] Wuthnow contrasts two spiritualities: a spirituality of *dwelling* that emphasizes habitation and a spirituality of *seeking* that emphasizes negotiation. In the former, "God occupies a definite place in the universe and creates a sacred space in which humans too can dwell," while in the latter "individuals search for sacred moments that reinforce their conviction that the divine exists, but these moments are fleeting" (p. 4).

Underwriting this shift in spirituality from dwelling to seeking are momentous social and cultural changes, the most important of which is that "images of stable dwellings have increasingly been replaced by images of those who have left home: the migrant worker, the exile, the refugee, the drifter, the person who feels alienated or displaced, the person lost in the cosmos, the traveling salesman, the lonesome net surfer, the lonely face in the crowd, the marginal person, the vagrant, the dispossessed or homeless person" (Wuthnow, p. 4). To anyone who has read this far, this list should look very familiar; Wuthnow's analysis more or less mirrors our own. He goes on to conclude that interest in spirituality will not wane but merely take a different form, one that is more seeker-oriented than dwelling-oriented. Wuthnow confesses, however, that "neither of these styles is entirely satisfactory, nor is it enough to argue that individuals must simply find some way to combine both." In his view, "the ancient wisdom that emphasizes the idea of spiritual practices needs to be rediscovered." In other words, we need to recover the practices of prayer, meditation, study

---

3. Robert Wuthnow, "Spirituality in America Since the 1950's," *Theology, News, and Notes* (March 1999), p. 4.

of sacred texts, and sacrificial service. "The point of spiritual practice," Wuthnow emphasizes, "is not to elevate an isolated set of activities over the rest of life but to electrify the spiritual impulse that animates all of life" (pp. 5-6).

We find ourselves in fundamental agreement with Wuthnow's analysis that there has been an important shift in images, and we agree that an interest in spirituality has not waned but will continue to wax. We also agree with Wuthnow that neither of the spiritualities he depicts is satisfactory: what he describes as a "spirituality of dwelling" is too akin to the settled cozy religiosity of 1950s America — white, middle-class, Protestant, safe and secure in the fortress homes of sexism and racism — while what he calls the "spirituality of seeking" could easily devolve into just another individualistic, consumer-driven 1990s form of religion.

What we need is a different image and an alternative way of thinking about Christian faith and spirituality that avoids the pitfalls and problems of both modernity and postmodernity. To achieve this, we propose a recovery of some ancient wisdom of the Christian tradition, including the classic practices that Wuthnow mentions.

If neither a spirituality of "dwelling" nor a spirituality of "seeking" can provide us with a vision and a *habitus* of homecoming, then perhaps the biblical metaphor of *sojourner* can help us negotiate the rough terrain of our dislocated cultural wilderness on the way home. But we can foster a sojourning spirituality only if the world is indeed a place finally hospitable to our homemaking and only if the God to whom our spirituality is directed is a homemaking God. This will require some theological reflection. First, if we long for a spirituality of homecoming in which home is a site of radical hospitality, then we need to reflect on the God of love and the otherness of creation as created and sustained in that love. Second, if we want to engender a homemaking lifestyle and cultural perspective in which home is most fundamentally received as a gift rather than an autonomous achievement, then we need to reflect on the God of grace and the character of creation as a gift. Third, if we want to engage in a homemaking of shalom in the face of a culture of violence, then we need to reflect on the God of goodness and creation as deeply and fundamentally good. On the basis of love, grace, and goodness, reflected in both our understanding of God and of creation, we might be able to find our way to a sojourning spirituality on the way home. However, that kind of sojourning can be sustained only if we are accompanied on that journey by the homecoming God. Indeed, we can find our way home only if we are accompanied by the indwelling God, the God who longs to come home to us.

The God of Love and Creation as Other

New Testament scholar Richard Hays tells the story of walking into his introductory New Testament class and writing on the blackboard in large letters, IT'S ABOUT GOD, STUPID! You wouldn't think that a teacher of Scripture would need to remind his students, many of whom are on the way to ordained ministry, that the Bible is about God. But it is amazing how God can get lost in the busyness and academic rigor of theological studies. And it is also rather disconcerting how God gets lost in much talk about spirituality. Often it seems as though people are talking about some kind of generic spirituality. However, we believe that there is no such thing as generic spirituality. Spirituality is always spirituality of a particular kind, rooted in a particular tradition and in relationship to a particular God or view of God. And if we are looking for a spirituality of homecoming in a culture of dislocation, we need to ask what kind of God, and what kind of a world, would engender such a homecoming.

For example, a God who is understood as living high above this temporal realm in a heavenly home to which he invites forgiven sinners is not a God of creational homemaking. If we embrace a theology rooted in neo-Platonism with a stark dualism between earth and heaven, temporality and eternity, finite and infinite, body and soul, grace and nature, then homecoming can never be in this world. Nor is homecoming simply eschatologically delayed; it is also geographically displaced. Homecoming in such a theology is always somewhere else. Indeed, if home is identified as living eternally with God in a heavenly realm divorced from finite, temporal, bodily, and creational life, then socioeconomic, ecological, and cultural homemaking is irrelevant. In that view, all we need do to fulfill our call to be homemakers is to engage in an evangelism that will show people the way to this heavenly home. How you view God and how you understand the nature and value of creaturely life fundamentally determines how you will engage in homemaking in this world.

So we need to talk about God.[4] And if we begin with God, we must begin with love. As the first epigraph to this chapter (from 1 John 4:16) declares, God is love. The biblical support for this claim is overwhelming. In John's First Epistle, his summary of the character of God succinctly states what is found throughout the New Testament. Matthew records Jesus' words in the Sermon on the Mount: "You have heard that it was said, 'You shall love your neighbor and hate your enemy.' But I say to you, Love your enemies and pray for those who persecute you, so that you may be children of your Father in heaven; for he makes the sun rise on the evil and on the good, and sends rain on the righteous and on the unrighteous" (Matt. 5:43-45). Love everyone, even your enemies, for that is what God does. God spreads his love on all.

In his version of that sermon, Luke includes these lines by Jesus: "But love your enemies, do good, and lend, expecting nothing in return. Your reward will be great, and you will be children of the Most High; for he is kind to the ungrateful and the wicked. Be merciful, just as your Father is merciful" (Luke 6:35-36). Be like God. And what is God like? God is merciful; therefore, be people of mercy.

But it is John who most suggestively presents the notion of a God of love for a theology of home. John emphasizes that when you see Jesus you see God, and what you find in Jesus — in word and deed — is love (John 14:9; 13:1-35). Therefore, says Jesus, "as the Father has loved me, so I have loved you; abide in my love" (John 15:9). Pitch your tent in my love. Build a house and make a home in my love. We can pitch a tent in this love on our sojourning path toward home because Jesus has come from the Father and pitched his tent among us. There is a rich theology of homecoming here that needs to be unpacked.

Reflecting on the relationship between the word of God and the creation of all things, the psalmist says:

4. A brief comment regarding the names for God. We are very aware of the discussion of the problem of naming God, and we concur with the classic Christian tradition that has always asserted that God is ultimately un-nameable. No creature can name God, if by naming God we mean knowing the depth of love that God is. Jean-Luc Marion says: "In other words, among the divine names, none exhausts God or offers the grasp or hold of a comprehension of him." See Jean-Luc Marion, *God Without Being* (Chicago: University of Chicago Press, 1991), p. 106.

For the word of the Lord is upright,
   and all his work is done in faithfulness.
He loves righteousness and justice;
   the earth is full of the steadfast love of the Lord.

By the word of the Lord the heavens were made,
   and all the host by the breath of his mouth.
He gathered the waters of the sea in a bottle;
   he put the deeps in storehouses.

Let all the earth fear the Lord;
   let all the inhabitants of the world stand in awe of him.
For he spoke, and it came to be;
   he commanded, and it stood firm.

(Ps. 33:4-9)

In a move of breathtaking proportions, the psalmist identifies the Torah, the word of the Lord that is upright and calls for righteousness and justice, as nothing less than the word by which the very world was created. The same voice that says, "Hear O Israel: the Lord is our God, the Lord alone" as the foundation of the Torah, is the word that said with majestic and beautiful power, "Let there be. . . ." And because this is a word spoken out of the deep love of the covenantal God, the Creator of all things, the psalmist exclaims, "the earth is full of the steadfast love of the Lord." Creation is literally full of the love of God because creation finds its very origin and sustaining power in that love of God. Replacing the Cartesian *Cogito ergo sum* ("I think, therefore I am"), people of a biblical faith confess, *Sumus amamur, ergo sumus* ("We are loved, therefore we are").

Astonishingly, John takes the psalmist's worldview a radical step further:

In the beginning was the Word, and the Word was with God, and the Word was God. He was in the beginning with God. All things came into being through him, and without him not one thing came into being. What has come into being in him was life, and the life was the light of the world. The light shines in the darkness, and the darkness did not overcome it. (John 1:1-5)

The Word from the beginning — the creative Word that calls all things into being and first said, "Let there be light" — is here identified with nothing less than Jesus Christ. *He* is that Word; *he* was in the beginning with God. But John takes it all so much further when, in a moment of un-paralleled theological audacity, he proclaims that "the Word became flesh and tented among us, and we have seen his glory, the glory as of a father's only son, full of grace and truth" (John 1:14).[5] The Word of God — this creative, calling, engendering, blessing, and powerful Word — takes on flesh. This is a Word of love, and love must be embodied: it must take place somewhere and in some time.

And not only does this Word take on flesh, it tabernacles, or tents, among us. It moves into the neighborhood and makes a home with us. So when Jesus later invites his disciples to "abide" in him and in his love, he is inviting them to a reciprocity of relationship (John 15:7-11). He is, in effect, saying: "I have come to abide with you; I have come to make my home with you. Let's do that together. Come and make your home with me." Love of this kind permeates the Gospels because it characterizes the God to whom Jesus bears witness and the Jesus in whom God is personally present.

It is not surprising, then, that this overarching theme of the love of God is taken up again and again in the rest of the New Testament, whether by the apostle Paul (Rom. 12 or 1 Cor. 13 or Phil. 2) or by James (James 2) or Peter (1 Pet. 3) or John the Seer (Rev. 21–22). Perhaps Paul puts it best in his love letter to the church at Ephesus: "Therefore be imitators of God, as be-loved children, and live in love, as Christ loved us and gave himself up for us, a fragrant offering and sacrifice to God" (Eph. 5:1-2). Live in love, as God exists in love. And this love must be embodied; it must take on flesh. So when he describes the way the Christian community lives out this love, the apostle says that "speaking the truth in love, we must grow up in every way into him who is the head, into Christ" (Eph. 4:15).[6] But the Greek in this text does not actually say that we are "speaking the truth in love." Rather, the text could be translated "truthing in love." Truth is active: it is something we do. And the truth that animates followers of Jesus is a truth embodied in love. The conclusion is clear: if we know anything about God, it is that God is love.[7] And God's love is incarnated in Jesus Christ and ani-

---

5. Where the NRSV translates *eskēnōsen* as "lived," we have more accurately translated it "tented" in order to capture the sojourning nature of this divine homemaking.

6. The Greek reads *alētheuontes de en agapē*.

7. Tutored by Scripture, the Christian tradition concurs with this biblical affirmation. Polycarp and Perpetua, Augustine and Maximus the Confessor, Bernard of Clairvaux and

mates the lives of those who follow Jesus. This love is the very foundation of created life and any possibility of being at home in creation.

In a culture of suspicion and betrayal, this claim is of utmost importance, for there is no antidote to suspicion but trust rooted in love. Summarizing the portrayal of Jesus in the Gospels, Langdon Gilkey says:

> To the amazement of all, the disciples and enemies of Christ alike, the divine power reveals itself in precisely that which is most vulnerable and powerless: self-giving love. Truly here was one of the most radical transformations of values in all historical experience: not the avoidance of suffering, but its willing acceptance in love, became the deepest clue to divinity.[8]

The deepest clue to who God is can be found in Christ the suffering servant. As Jean-Luc Marion suggests, "A properly Christian name of the God who is revealed in Jesus Christ . . . is agape."[9] True power is self-giving love.

But love is not an abstract principle. As we have seen, love is embodied, and any embodiment happens in time and in place. "Once upon a time, there was a king. . . ." Embodied love in time and place always engenders a narrative and is always embraced and experienced in terms of a narrative. "In the beginning was the Word," begins John's narrative. And his narrative is clearly a retelling of an earlier story of the beginning of all things. Narratives, however, especially grand overarching narratives, are problematic in a postmodern culture. It may be true that home is rooted in memory, but we have also reflected on how certain memories legitimate

---

Julian of Norwich, John Calvin and John Wesley, Søren Kierkegaard and Thérèse of Lisieux, Dietrich Bonhoeffer and Mother Teresa of Calcutta. These and many other spiritual and theological masters — Catholic, Orthodox, and Protestant, male and female — speak with one voice: God is love.

8. Langdon Gilkey, *Maker of Heaven and Earth* (Garden City, NY: Doubleday, 1959), p. 217. See also "Creation, Being, and Non-Being," in David Burrell and Bernard McGinn, eds., *God and Creation* (Notre Dame: University of Notre Dame Press, 1990), p. 233, where Gilkey says that it is no surprise that most theologians in this century have questioned the priority of the definition of God as Absolute Being and have, rather, "empathized with Moltmann's effort to understand the divine nature also in terms of the divine suffering present in and revealed through the crucifixion." For an eloquent, profound, and poignant expression of the truth that suffering love is the deepest clue to divinity, see Nicholas Wolterstorff, *Lament for a Son* (Grand Rapids: Eerdmans, 1987).

9. Marion, *God Without Being*, p. 82.

domicide while others are too thin to be able to engender any home-making of substance. Does a narrative of love, the narrative of Jesus, provide an antidote to such understandable postmodern suspicion?

This narrative of God as love and love as gift does provide such an antidote, for it calls into question the view that narratives are always or necessarily violent. As opposed to narratives that provide ideological legitimation for fortresses of exclusion (Amos's strongholds), James Olthuis argues that "narratives are possible, not as grand control devices, but as tales of (broken) love coauthored in community."[10] Against the suspicion of our age, we tell a story of God's suffering love that calls forth a response of trust, without which there is no home. And we strive to embody that love in our homemaking activities for only the kind of suffering love embodied in those who follow Jesus will ever overcome the depth of mistrust found among many in our time. Only authentic self-sacrifice for the good of the other will counter the manipulative counterfeit loves of our culture. Only the excessive love of a free and generous God can move beyond the duty-bound "loves" of exchange. Only, in short, the kind of love found at the very heart of the Christian tradition can address in a healing way the suspicion and pain so pervasive in our age and truly bring us home.

To gain greater insight into this God of love, let's return to Paul's letter to the Ephesians. Writing about how the dividing wall between gentile and Jew is overcome in Christ's sacrifice on the cross, the apostle declares:

> So he came and proclaimed peace to you who were far off and peace to those who were near; for through him both of us have access in one Spirit to the Father. So then you are no longer strangers and aliens, but are citizens with the saints and also members of the household of God, built upon the foundation of the apostles and prophets, with Jesus Christ himself as the cornerstone. In him the whole structure is joined together and grows into a holy temple in the Lord; in whom you also are built together in the Spirit into a dwelling place for God (Eph. 2:17-22).[11]

10. James Olthuis, "Crossing the Threshold: Sojourning Together in the Wild Spaces of Love," in James K. A. Smith and Henry Isaac Venema, eds., *The Hermeneutics of Charity* (Grand Rapids: Brazos, 2004), p. 37.

11. The Greek in v. 22 (*en pneumati*) can be translated either "spiritually" or, better, "in the Spirit."

A Christian ontology of connectedness has its Christological foundation right here. All things are joined together, built together in Christ. Or as the poem of Colossians 1:15-20 loves to repeat, "all things" are created in and for Christ; "all things" are held together in Christ; and "all things" are reconciled through Christ.[12]

Notice two other things from this amazing text. First, Paul frames this language of redemption in terms of homecoming. No longer strangers and aliens; no longer wandering nomads, purposeless tourists; no longer exiles and dispossessed, homeless vagrants. In Christ there is homecoming. In Christ we are citizens, full members with rights and responsibilities, and members of nothing less than the household of God. And if we find our most profound homecoming by entering into the household of God, then we become a holy temple. Our lives are transformed in such a way that we are built together in the Spirit into the very dwelling of God.

But what is the household of God? Pay close attention to this text, and you will notice, second, that the household of God is a triune community of Father, Son, and Spirit. This homecoming that Paul speaks of is consistently "in Christ Jesus." But it is through him that "we have access in one Spirit to the Father," and the home construction project that is under way in the Christian community is a matter of "being built together in the Spirit into a dwelling place for God" (Eph. 2:13-22).

We do not wish to develop here a fully articulated doctrine of the Trinity, but the triune character of God is an important dimension of a biblically conceived theology of home.[13] Christians claim that one God exists eternally in three persons, each person equal in every divine perfection.[14]

12. Brian J. Walsh and Sylvia Keesmaat have reflected further on the Colossian poem in *Colossians Remixed: Subverting the Empire* (Downers Grove, IL: InterVarsity, 2004), ch. 5.

13. In recent years there has been a resurgence of interest in the doctrine of the Trinity. See, e.g., David Cunningham, *These Three Are One* (Oxford: Blackwell, 1998); Colin Gunton, *The Promise of Trinitarian Theology* (Edinburgh: T&T Clark, 1991); David Bentley Hart, *The Beauty of the Infinite* (Grand Rapids: Eerdmans, 2003); Catherine LaCugna, *God for Us: The Trinity and Christian Life* (New York: HarperCollins, 1991); Jürgen Moltmann, *The Trinity and the Kingdom* (San Francisco: Harper and Row, 1981); John Zizioulas, *Being as Communion* (Crestwood, NY: St. Vladimir's Seminary Press, 1985).

14. This understanding of the term "person" in the Christian tradition has a very specific meaning, quite different from that of today. In its classical Christian usage, "person" does not mean what we moderns mean by "person," namely, an individual, an autonomous, self-subsisting center of consciousness. Rather, "person" denotes a distinct but not essen-

These relationships are characterized by mutuality and reciprocity.[15] Hence God is by God's very nature relational: to be God is to be in relationship. And this relationship is a relationship of reciprocal love. The God who is three in one is the God who exists in the mutuality of love.[16]

From the perspective of a theology of home, we could say that God is quintessentially a homemaker because God is a household of mutual love, of mutual dwelling-with, of intimate indwelling. From this perspective, it is not surprising that the world exhibits an ontology of relationship or constitutive relatedness. As Martin Buber once said, "In the beginning is the relation."[17] Relationality is a fundamental characteristic of the world. Being is being-with. Being-in-relation is the nature of things. The household order of creation mirrors the household of God. The divine economy — the divine *oikonomos,* or the ordering of the household of mutual interrelatedness that is God — overflows into the household of creation. Therefore, all existing things are what they distinctively are by virtue of their relationship to other existing things.[18] In ways we do not (and cannot) yet fathom, all existence is coexistence.

Desmond Tutu captures this relational understanding of reality with

---

tially separate way of existing. The Father is the Father only in virtue of the unique relationships with the Son and Spirit. The Son is the Son only in virtue of the unique relationships with the Father and Spirit. The Spirit is the Spirit only in virtue of the unique relationships with the Father and Son.

15. The Greek term *perichōrēsis* is used to describe this relationship. It literally means to make room for (*chorēo*) around or with respect to (*peri*) and thus denotes the mutual indwelling of fully reciprocal love; hence it strives to capture the ontological interdependence and coinherence of the three persons of the Trinity. The Latinate equivalent is "circumincession."

16. The early church claimed that Christ is "the image of the invisible God" (Col. 1:15) and "the exact imprint of God's very being" (Heb. 1:3). They also prayed to Christ and believed him to be their means of salvation. In short, what was said about God was also said about Jesus. Jesus was divine. And yet Jesus and the God to whom he prayed were not identical: there was sameness but also difference. So also with the Spirit, the Advocate whom Jesus promises to send to his followers after he is gone (John 15:26). Those who followed Christ came to regard the Holy Spirit as divine — the power and presence of God. And yet the Spirit is not the same as either the Father or the Son. The upshot of this story is that Christians claim that these three — Father, Son, and Spirit — are one.

17. Martin Buber, *I and Thou,* trans. Walter Kaufmann (New York: Scribner, 1970), p. 69.

18. This theological and ontological claim has been verified again and again in recent years from what we have learned from ecology, string theory, chaos theory, and complexity theory.

respect to human life when he describes the creation story in Genesis: "We are made for companionship and relationship. It is not good for us to be alone. In our African idiom we say: 'A person is a person through other persons.'" This is the meaning of the Nguni term *ubuntu*, which is roughly translated: "My humanity is caught up and inextricably bound up with yours. I am human because I belong."[19] We are who we are by virtue of our relationships with other persons. As Olthuis argues, replacing an ontology of "being" with an ontology of relationship

> . . . is not an encouragement to retrench and build fixed residences in the domesticity of modernity. Neither does it, in postmodern rejection of the modern, need to mean exile in the desert (expulsion and wandering), perpetual homelessness. Rather, we have an invitation to meet and sojourn together in the wild spaces of love as an alternative both to modernist distancing and domination and to postmodern fluidity and fusion. Connection rather than control is the dominant metaphor.[20]

The triune God legitimates neither modernist domination of difference nor postmodern celebration of difference. In this God there is unity amidst diversity. The one is constituted by the many, and the many inhere as one. Thus, as David Cunningham expresses it, "[t]he doctrine of the Trinity calls into question our assumption that the categories of oneness and difference are incommensurable, incompatible, or even necessarily in tension with one another."[21] Why assume that the many must ultimately resolve into the one, or the one is really the many in disguise?

If one of the central issues of our time is how to deal with difference

---

19. Desmond Tutu, *God Has a Dream* (New York: Doubleday, 2004), pp. 25-26. This social understanding of human persons is similar to what is called a social analogy for the Trinity. For one influential statement on this, see Moltmann, *The Trinity and the Kingdom*. For a cogent (short) argument in favor of such an understanding of God as triune, see Cornelius Plantinga, Jr., "Social Trinity and Tritheism," in Ronald Feenstra and Cornelius Plantinga, Jr., eds., *Trinity, Incarnation, and Atonement* (Notre Dame: University of Notre Dame Press, 1989).

20. Olthuis, "Crossing the Threshold," p. 37.

21. Cunningham, *These Three Are One*, p. 8. This is the burden of Colin Gunton's argument in *The One, the Three, and the Many* (Cambridge: Cambridge University Press, 1993): "I have argued that Trinitarian conceptuality enables us to think of our world, in a way made impossible by the traditional choice between Heraclitus and Parmenides, as both, and in different respects, one and many, but also one and many in relation" (p. 7).

282

and otherness, then we have here an important contribution to our understanding. Over against modernity's impulse to colonize all differences (race, gender, nation), the Christian tradition, in its central claim about the nature of God, insists that genuine differences exist and certain differences are good. Homemaking need not be seen as homogenizing — the eradication of all difference. We can be who we are (clan, ethnic group, nation) without necessarily eradicating all who are other. And over against the postmodern impulse to celebrate every difference (textual reading, moral perspective, way of life), this claim about the nature of God calls into question any difference that violently excludes. This Christian understanding of the triune God helps us conceive of homemaking as both the shaping of identity and the embrace of difference. The household of God sheds light on how we might move beyond current views of difference and make our own households places of homemaking.

When we speak about the relationship of God to the world, we often set God's transcendence or otherness in opposition to God's immanence or presence. It is as though the more present God is in the world, the less "other" God is believed to be; inversely, the more transcendent God is perceived to be, the less immanent. However, in the classical Christian tradition at its best, these two attributes are in harmony. Indeed, as Aquinas argues, the one entails the other because God can be supremely present to creation only if God is supremely other, that is, not limited by finite existence.[22] Or, in the words of Gerard Manley Hopkins:

> . . . God is so deeply present to everything that it would be impossible for him, but for his infinity, not to be identified with them, or from the other side, impossible but for his infinity so to be present to them. This is oddly expressed, I see; I mean a being so intimately present as God is to other things would be identified with them were it not for God's infinity, or were it not for God's infinity he could not be so intimately present to a thing.[23]

Commenting on Hopkins, Loren Wilkinson says: "Rather than the greatness of God being understood as distancing Creator from Creation, God's greatness is here seen to enable a deeper intimacy of Creator and Cre-

---

22. Aquinas, *Summa Theologiae*, I.8.1 and I.11.4.

23. Gerard Manley Hopkins, *Sermons and Writings*, ed. Christopher Devlin (London: Oxford University Press, 1959), p. 128.

ation."[24] Intimacy only if greatness; presence only if infinity. God is distinct from creation and thus able to be intimately related to creation, lovingly upholding and sustaining all things.[25]

The biblical word for this relationship is covenant. The covenantal God is not content with a relationship with creation from a distance. The divine household of the triune God creates in order to include the created other in this household. God makes covenant, that is to say, enters into a marriage relationship of homemaking, with all of creation through the creature who images this God. This is a relationship of deepest intimacy. The image of the bride and bridegroom that comes up throughout Scripture uses nothing less than a sexual metaphor to help convey this intimacy: we are called to know God as a wife "knows" her husband.[26] Such covenantal intimacy with the God of love engenders a deep spirituality of hospitable homemaking.

Therefore, God and creation are neither one and the same (pantheism) nor unrelated to each other (deism). Nor is it true that the more immanent God is, the less transcendent God has to be. Rather, the Christian tradition insists that God indwells creation and creation is God's dwelling place. Indeed, creation is a cosmic sanctuary, a holy temple, where God resides and abides and rules. Richard Middleton persuasively shows that the Bible envisions the cosmos as God's sanctuary, with all creatures invited to sing praise to the indwelling Creator.[27] God indwells that which is genuinely other, without subsuming or overwhelming it. Such is the nature of things in a world intimately indwelt by a God who is love.

24. Loren Wilkinson, "The New Story of Creation: A Trinitarian Perspective," *Crux* 30, no. 4 (Dec. 1994): 32.

25. In traditional language, the Father creates the world through the Son and in the Holy Spirit. Creation is from God (Father), through God (Son), and in God (Spirit). Indeed, not just creating but also sustaining and redeeming the world involve all three persons of the Trinity. The whole divine economy is enacted by the whole Trinity, though particular persons are seen to have specific tasks. So, for example, John Calvin says that "[i]t is the Spirit who, everywhere diffused, sustains all things, causes them to grow, and quickens them in heaven and in earth" (*Institutes*, 1.13.14).

26. Indeed, the Hebrew word for knowing, 'yada, carries with it the notion of sexual intercourse.

27. J. Richard Middleton, *The Liberating Image: The Imago Dei in Genesis 1* (Grand Rapids: Brazos, 2005), pp. 77ff. See also John Stackhouse, ed., *What Does It Mean to Be Saved?* (Grand Rapids: Baker Academic, 2002).

The God of Grace and Creation as Gift

Central to the Christian understanding of creation is the claim that creation is the sheer gift of a gracious creator. That is, God did not have to create any world at all, and God was not obligated or forced to create this particular world. Creation is both ontologically and existentially contingent.[28] Creation need not be. Creation exists only because of God's gracious decision.[29] And God is able freely to intend and effect action because God is the epitome of self-giving love. Based on our exegesis of Psalm 33 above, we could say that "God's love is not only at the root of the divine decision to create the world (*why* God created) but also describes the most fundamental character of reality (*what* God created). Creation is wrought by the extravagant generosity of God's love."[30] Indeed, the Christian confession of God as triune affirms that God is a perichoretic family of love — a community of mutually indwelling love characterized by overflowing generosity.

The generosity of God's love in calling creation to be is an important feature of any adequate response to postmodern homelessness. In an age of cynicism and suspicion, when all is seen as a covert bid for power by competing self-interests, the only truly credible witness will be flesh-and-blood nonmanipulative regard for others. Dietrich Bonhoeffer is one example of a powerful response to Nietzsche's presumption that all Christian claims to truth are but disguised attempts to control and dominate, because Bonhoeffer, in deed as well as in word, powerfully railed against cheap grace and testified to the way of the cross. Anthony Thiselton puts it this way: "It is as if Bonhoeffer said to Nietzsche from his Nazi prison: 'But not all Christians are as you suggest. For even if you are right about 'religion' as a human construct, authentic Christian faith lies in identification with the Christ who neither sought power by manipulation, nor was 'weak' in the sense of being bland, conformist, or world-denying.'"[31]

---

28. Robert Russell, "Cosmology, Creation, and Contingency," in Ted Peters, ed., *Cosmos as Creation* (Nashville: Abingdon, 1989), p. 195.

29. For a more extended presentation of this notion of decision, see Steven Bouma-Prediger, "Creation as the Home of God: The Doctrine of Creation in the Theology of Jürgen Moltmann," in *Calvin Theological Journal* 32, no. 1 (Apr. 1997): 72-90.

30. J. Richard Middleton and Brian Walsh, *Truth Is Stranger Than It Used to Be* (Downers Grove: InterVarsity, 1995), p. 149.

31. Anthony Thiselton, *Interpreting God and the Postmodern Self* (Grand Rapids: Eerdmans, 1995), p. 23. The *locus classicus* for Bonhoeffer's treatment of "cheap grace" is *The Cost*

Thiselton states it well: "A love in which a self genuinely *gives* itself to the Other *in the interests of the Other* dissolves the acids of suspicion and deception" (p. 160). Any hope that the Christian message of shalom will rouse the attention of homeless nomads depends on our resisting the temptation to use God and others for our own advancement. As Marion reminds us, "Love is not spoken, in the end it is made."[32]

The confession of creation as gift reveals a world that need not be but comes to be and continues to be because of God's extravagant grace. The power that moves the cosmos is the same Love who freely tented among us, rendering it possible to forge a hope that fully confronts the sharp and bent edges of reality while bearing witness to God's good future of shalom.

The theme of creation as gift also addresses the postmodern view of the self as malleable and homeless nomad — for two reasons. First, a phenomenology of gift and giftedness reveals that, when one is given a gift, the appropriate response is gratitude to the giver and care for the gift.[33] This implies a human identity: We are *homo gratus*, the grateful human. Olthuis observes: "This gift *of* love is also a gift *for* love" since "the gift is simultaneously a call. It is the birth of human agency as response-ability for the gift."[34] He continues:

> The process of receiving identity is at the same time a process of constituting one's identity in relation to others. A self is born not only in and through receiving (love), but equally, reciprocally in and through giving (love) to others. The two sides belong inextricably together. In this understanding of identity and agency, not as self-creation or self-certification but as a received empowerment, a call to live out and fulfill, it remains important to talk (in contrast to postmodernism) of a core self of continuity, coherence, and agency. (pp. 34-35)

We find our true selves not in endless permutations of fashionable identities but in responding to God's bountiful and gracious provisions with humble gratitude and joyful care. We care for all God's creatures because it is a fitting

---

of Discipleship (New York: Macmillan, 1963), ch. 1. See also Bonhoeffer, *Letters and Papers from Prison* (New York: Macmillan, 1971).

32. Marion, *God Without Being,* pp. 106-107.

33. We realize that there is very large discussion about "the gift." See, e.g., Alan Schrift, *The Logic of the Gift* (New York: Routledge, 1997), and from a theological perspective, Steven Webb, *The Gifting God* (New York: Oxford, 1996). We do not intend to enter this debate; rather, we merely affirm our view that the gift is not reducible without remainder to calculative exchange.

34. Olthuis, "Crossing the Threshold," p. 34.

response to God's providential care for us. We are grateful because God is gracious. Grace begets gratitude, and gratitude care. Furthermore, we express that gratitude and exercise that care on this blue-green earth. We are placed creatures in a garden "just east of Eden" (Gen. 2:8). The Amish writer Robert Riall expresses it this way: "To be human is to be a local creature. Man was not made to be a restless wanderer through the world."[35] We humans from the humus are not independent, isolated, autonomous selves, but rather located persons-in-community, including our biotic community. We are bound up not only with God and other humans but also with the plants and animals, oceans and mountains, of this exquisitely complex and beautiful planet.

By affirming that we are persons-in-relationship who are at home on Planet Earth, gifted and called to respond to God's provisioning grace with gratitude and care, the confession of creation as gift challenges the modern self-image of the human as autonomous rational individual and also calls into question the postmodern image of humanity as hopelessly unstable and isolated. If in modernity we have the heroic self and in postmodernity we have the resigned self, our acknowledgment of creation as gift makes it possible to posit the *responsive* and *responsible* self: gratefully loving God and faithfully serving the neighbor in need.

This affirmation of the God of grace and creation as gift also speaks to our deafness to the earth's creatures and our despoliation of creation. For the giftedness of creation, as the Bible reminds us, includes the conviction that all creatures exist to praise the God who indwells our common cosmic home. For example, Psalm 148 calls on all created things to praise God: the angels and hosts of heaven, the sun and moon and stars, fire and hail, snow and frost, water and wind, mountains and hills, fruit trees, wild animals, creeping things, kings and princes and rulers, women and men. All creatures are invited to sing a symphony of praise to the God of unsurpassing glory.[36]

---

35. Elmo Stoll and Robert Riall, *Strangers and Pilgrims: Why We Live Simply* (Aylmer, ON, and LaGrange, IN: Pathway Publishers, 2003), p. 35. Riall goes on (also p. 35) to say: "Adam was placed in Eden, no other place, of all possible spots on the planet. Scripture is quite specific about its location. Adam became a settled Edenite, if you will. He was never a cosmopolitan." And so "Adam's local horizon was not extensive enough to be measured by country, or state, or even by county. His world was so intensive that it could be measured by trees — which trees were for him, which were not, and where each was. Adam was created for an intensely local horizon."

36. Similar examples of the praise offered to God by nonhuman creatures are found in Isaiah 42–44, 55, and in many other psalms, e.g., Psalms 96 and 98.

Albert Borgmann refers to this speaking nonhuman other as "eloquent reality" and reminds us that it "speaks in its own right and in many voices."[37] Creation is eloquent, if only we have the ears to hear. Creation as gift calls us to acknowledge the ways we have muffled the voices of our neighbors, both human and nonhuman, and challenges us to listen for the groaning of creation so that we might work for its redemptive flourishing.

Moreover, creation as gift implies not only that creation is eloquent, but also that the astonishing number of nonhuman creatures are valuable regardless of their usefulness to us. In the effusiveness of divine grace, God has created and continues to create and sustain a profusion of beings whose value extends beyond their human usefulness. Psalm 104, for example, speaks not only of all things as being created by God, but speaks of the world as a cosmos in which all creatures — wild asses, cedars of Lebanon, storks, marmots, young lions — depend on God for their existence and their flourishing. And these creatures are valuable not only because of their usefulness to humans — some are, indeed, essential to us — but because they are valuable to each other (e.g., the cedars are valuable as places for birds to nest and the mountains are valuable as places of refuge and rest for the wild goats). Most importantly, they are valuable simply because God made them out of the abundance of his love. We live in a world of radical relationality, and all value in the world is realized and experienced in terms of that relationality. In brief, usefulness to humans is only one of several values nonhuman creatures have.[38] God is a generous giver of what evokes joy and delight.[39] God is not miserly but open-

37. Albert Borgmann, *Crossing the Postmodern Divide* (Chicago: University of Chicago Press, 1992), p. 119. Borgmann perceptively comments: "Postmodern criticism gets arrested prematurely, however, when, having considered critically the modern arrogation of reality, it accepts naively the legacy of that arrogance, namely, the disappearance of reality. Worse, postmodern criticism gets caught in dogmatism when it restricts the postmodern conversation to humanity and dismisses without further thought the possibility of eloquent things. The postmodern theorists have discredited ethnocentrism and logocentrism so zealously that they have failed to see their own anthropocentrism. Why reject a priori the very possibility that things may speak to us in their own right?" (p. 117).

38. Holmes Rolston, III, *Environmental Ethics* (Philadelphia: Temple University Press, 1988), ch. 1. John Calvin speaks of creation as "this magnificent theatre of heaven and earth, crammed with innumerable miracles" — valuable for its own sake as well as for its provisions to humans. See *Institutes*, 2.6.1; 3.10.2; cf. 1.6.2; 1.14.20. For an excellent book-length exposition of Calvin's view of nature, see Susan Schreiner, *The Theatre of His Glory* (Grand Rapids: Baker, 1991).

39. This theme of delight is developed in Bouma-Prediger, "Creation as the Home of

288

handed in creating a world both bountiful and beautiful. The Christian doctrine of creation has no room for any anthropocentric utilitarianism that finds nonhuman creatures valuable only insofar as they serve human needs.

In summary, by affirming that creation is eloquent and valuable beyond human usefulness, the confession of creation as gift repudiates both modern views of "nature" as a mere mute resource to be pillaged and postmodern re-enchantments of "Nature" as divine. Insofar as both modernity and postmodernity are characterized by an unbridled (though unacknowledged) anthropocentrism, recognition of creation as gift makes it possible to embrace a theocentrism in which one properly acknowledges both the eloquence of reality and the grace of its Creator and thus overcomes our creational autism by attending to "the dearest freshness deep down things."[40] That attention to the eloquence and gift character of creation engenders a homemaking of gratitude.

The God of Goodness and Creation as Good

One of the distinguishing features of Christian theology is the belief that creation is essentially good. The fall is contingent, not necessary: evil is a perversion of God's intentions for creation. Evil is all too real, but it is an alien intruder that has no legitimate place in God's good creation. Thus, for example, neither a Manichean cosmology, in which evil is seen as a cosmic principle or power equal to good, nor a Babylonian cosmogony, in which creation is the product of a violent battle, accurately conveys the way things are. Nor are either of those worldviews conducive to a homemaking vision of life. In the biblical view, God wages no war in creating, but rather speaks creation into existence. There is in this vision of life no primordial conflict among the gods. Rather, "the Scriptures begin with the effortless, joyous calling forth of creation by a sovereign Creator who enters into a relationship of intimacy with his creatures."[41]

This means that a biblical worldview will grant no ontological standing or priority to evil or violence. Indeed, violence is seen, in this worldview,

---

God." See also Wolterstorff, *Until Justice and Peace Embrace* (Grand Rapids: Eerdmans, 1983), ch. 7.

40. Part of a line from Gerard Manley Hopkins's poem "God's Grandeur."
41. Middleton and Walsh, *Truth Is Stranger*, p. 153.

as an illegitimate alien intruder into God's good creation. In contrast to an ontology of violence, then, the Scriptures begin with an ontology of peace.[42]

God is good; indeed, God is overflowing Goodness. And therefore creation is good. Violence is not originary; peace is primordial.

These claims are extremely significant given the postmodern suspicion of all stories as necessarily manipulative and a view of reality as inherently violent. The affirmation of a good God and a good creation, in opposition to the assumption that chaos is primary, is truly good news. For those who believe that violence is woven into the warp and woof of reality, there is no hope that the future will ever be substantially better than the present. In contrast, the assertion that evil is real but not ontologically necessary implies that a good God can and will overcome evil in the future. Good will triumph in the end. Pedro Trigo observes:

> God creates out of free will, out of love. God creates out of the divine word of benediction. What exists, then, is blessed, good, primordially good, only good, transcendentally good: not only good in principle, for the creative word of blessing resounds everlastingly.[43]

So we acknowledge the violence, but we remember the God who is good. Evil is powerfully real, but goodness is primordial.

By confessing the goodness of creation, we reject any modern notion of perfectibility while also refusing to accept the postmodern presumption that violence will always have the last word. If in modernity there is creation without the fall (and hence little need for redemption) and in postmodernity there is the fall without creation (and hence little hope of redemption), then embracing creation as the good gift of a good and gracious God makes it possible — indeed, shows that it is necessary — to hold creation and fall together (with redemption) in a grand story that tells how the Homemaker of heaven and earth willingly absorbs evil in order to restore a broken home and make of it a place of homecoming. Home is primordial. Homelessness is an alien intruder. Homecoming is the longing that is deepest in the human heart, indeed, in all of creation.

This claim about creation as good also speaks to our self-understanding.

---

42. Middleton and Walsh, p. 153.
43. Pedro Trigo, *Creation and History* (Maryknoll, NY: Orbis, 1991), p. 87.

One implication of the goodness of creation is that finitude is good. Human finitude in particular is not evil, not something to be escaped. We have a penchant for forgetting this central feature of our existence. Indeed, we have a deep desire to avoid looking our finitude, especially our mortality, straight in the face. For to acknowledge the temporally limited nature of our existence raises the question of whether death is the end of life or whether there is Someone who is sufficiently able and willing to preserve our life beyond biological death and in whom we can rest in spite of our fear and anxiety. Not surprisingly, Scripture often speaks of human finitude. For example, Psalm 8, which refers to humans as having been created a little lower than God and crowned with glory and honor, also reminds us that humans are finite.[44]

But we are not merely finite; we are faulted. Though they are often confused, those two are not the same. Finitude is a good feature of human existence: it is simply how God made us, a feature of our humanity to joyfully accept. But faultedness is not God's intention: the brokenness we know in ourselves and all around us is something we acknowledge with regret and seek, with God's grace, to overcome.

This feature of human existence is also powerfully depicted in Scripture. The *locus classicus,* of course, is Genesis 3, where Adam and Eve, doubting that God is really trustworthy and afraid that God is keeping the best to himself, desire to transcend their creaturely finitude and become like God in knowing good and evil. They succumb to believing that their home was based on an economics of scarcity rather than the divine economics of extravagance. Fearing that there would not be enough, or that it would not be good enough, anxious about whether God was truly a generous provider, they attempt to secure their own future. But in this attempt to gain for themselves what only God can provide, they fail to trust in God, they experience alienation, and they become homebreakers. A home of trust and loyalty devolves into a site of fear and anxiety. Their relationship with God is broken, they become estranged from each other, they lose touch with their own true selves, and they are alienated from the earth. In these four ways they, and we, are homeless. The Bible confirms what we

44. The finitude of humanity is also powerfully portrayed in the book of Job. In the deluge of questions put by God from the whirlwind (chs. 38–41), Job is, among other things, forcibly reminded of his finitude. Job has not commanded the morning or entered the storehouses of the snow or provided prey for the ravens. He does not know when the mountain goats give birth or who let the wild asses go free. That the hawk soars and the eagle mounts up is not Job's doing. Job's power and knowledge are finite. He is creature, not Creator.

know in our hearts: the world and our own lives are not the way they are supposed to be.[45]

By affirming that we are finite and faulted creatures, the confession of creation as good unmasks the pretensions of modernity, which would like us to believe in the godlike capabilities of human power (technology) and ingenuity (creativity). It also provides an awareness of *nomos* when we are facing the abyss of postmodern anomie. If the modern self is an epistemic homeboy, confident in what he knows and that he knows, and the postmodern self is an epistemic nomad, aware only that no one can really know anything, then the acknowledgment of creation as good implies that we are epistemic sojourners. We are on a journey seeking truth and the Truthful One, aware that such truth is catholic, that is, known only according to the whole *(kata holos)* and not from merely our limited perspective, and known always partially and provisionally this side of the eschatological fulfillment of all things when God will be all and in all. Because we are both situated and sinful, our claims to truth must be put forward with genuine humility and self-critical honesty. But we live in a good world that is indwelt by a good God, whose grace hounds our guilt and in whose loving embrace we can rest when facing our own mortality.[46]

Finally, the theme of creation as good addresses our deafness to the degradation of the earth. That creation is good means not only that goodness is more primordial than evil and that finitude is good; it also means that creaturely difference is good and that harmony need not be purchased at the price of dominating the other. Difference is built into creation itself. As is evident in the Genesis 1 creation story, through God's "let there be's" the earth brings forth living creatures of every kind: birds, fish, animals both domestic and wild, flying and creeping things, even sea monsters. Because of God's wise creative activity, the diverse kinds of creatures fit together into a harmonious whole. John Milbank says:

> Christianity, however, recognises no original violence. It construes the infinite not as chaos, but as a harmonic peace which is yet beyond the circumscribing power of any totalizing reason. Peace no longer depends

45. Two books that illuminate the phenomenon of sin very clearly are Ted Peters, *Sin* (Grand Rapids: Eerdmans, 1995), and Cornelius Plantinga, Jr., *Not the Way It's Supposed to Be* (Grand Rapids: Eerdmans, 1995).

46. Middleton and Walsh discuss the shape of a sojourning epistemology in *Truth Is Stranger*, p. 171.

upon the reduction to the self-identical, but is the *sociality* of harmonious difference.[47]

As any basic biology course will confirm, the world certainly knows radical difference, including predation, parasites, and pathogens. But nature red in tooth and claw notwithstanding, biology and theology concur in affirming that creation is a place of flourishing fittedness.

Furthermore, God calls us to serve and protect the garden that is the earth, our home — and to do so for its own sake (Gen. 2:15). We are to offer homemaking hospitality to the other, including the nonhuman other, in a way that gives evidence of genuine openness, receptivity, and attentiveness.[48] Rather than blindly or knowingly seeking to dominate, we are to exercise the kind of stewardly care that befits us as God's image-bearing representatives.[49] Care, not wanton disregard or ignorant misuse, should characterize our way of life.[50] And as many attest, we need the wild otherness of wild places to foster our own sense of humility and joy.[51] In other words, our serving and protecting the earth and its creatures is fostered by spending time in places where our own sense of control is diminished and our sense of dependence is magnified. We need both the domesticity of home and to be "at home" in places of wildness, without the urge to domesticate the wilderness.

In summary, the confession of creation as good rejects both the modern project of technological control and the postmodernism that finds dif-

---

47. John Milbank, *Theology and Social Theory* (Oxford: Basil Blackwell, 1990), p. 5. As Middleton and Walsh put it (*Truth Is Stranger*, p. 154): "This [ontology of peace] is not, however, the peace of an imposed homogeneity. That would be violence all over again. Rather, the biblical worldview perceives in the world a wonderful variety of different *kinds* of creatures living together in fundamental harmony. . . . There is, therefore, a *sociality* of difference."

48. See, e.g., Merold Westphal's suggestive essay, "Existentialism and Environmental Ethics," in Edwin Squiers, ed., *The Environmental Crisis* (Mancelona, MI: AuSable, 1982). For another attempt to spell out virtues such as these, see Bouma-Prediger, *For the Beauty of the Earth*, ch. 6.

49. See, especially, Middleton, *The Liberating Image*; see also Douglas John Hall, *Imaging God* (Grand Rapids: Eerdmans, 1986).

50. For example, in *Caring for Creation* (New Haven: Yale University Press, 1994), leading ecological philosopher Max Oelschlaeger advocates this term as the centerpiece of his "ecumenical approach to the environmental crisis."

51. Many classic wilderness writers make this claim, e.g., Henry David Thoreau and John Muir. For a recent defense, see Bill McKibben, *The Comforting Whirlwind* (Grand Rapids: Eerdmans, 1994), ch. 4.

ference necessarily inimical to authentic community. If in modernity the fearful flight from otherness leads to the hubris of ecological degradation and in postmodernity the recognition of otherness occasions despair concerning our earthly home, reflection on creation as good and God as good prompts not despair but faith and the kind of joyful keeping of creation that is fitting of creatures grateful for God's good and gracious provisions.

Christ-Followers as Sojourners

"The church of God that sojourns at Smyrna to the church of God that sojourns at Philomelium, and to all those of the holy and Catholic Church who sojourn in every place: may mercy, peace, and love be multiplied from God the Father and our Lord Jesus Christ."[52] So begins *The Martrydom of Saint Polycarp,* the oldest account outside the New Testament of the martyrdom of a Christian for his faith, in this case probably in February of AD 156. The church that sojourns. It is a powerful image, but its meaning is often lost on us today. What or who are sojourners? What does it mean to sojourn? Because we believe this is the best image or most apt metaphor to describe the church in our age of displacement, let's explore what it means and does not mean to be a sojourner.

Perhaps the best place to start is with Erazim Kohác's perceptive comparison of the plowman, the wayfarer, and the pilgrim. The plowman is "a dweller on the land and a tiller of the good earth, deeply rooted in the land of his ancestors, tending it with calloused hands and passing it on to his descendents."[53] A farmer, the plowman is an eternal dweller, always at home. His roots have sunk deep; he has achieved his home. The plowman clings to his particular place. Indeed, he thinks of home as a place — his place.

The wayfarer or wanderer is the opposite of the plowman or dweller. In Kohác's words: "Dwellers are strong in sinking roots, wayfarers in traveling light. Dwellers seek to stay with their love. Wayfarers know the task vain and cut their anchor rope before time and tide can drag them down" (p. 38). The wayfarer is an eternal nomad, a wanderer who is never at

---

52. "Martyrdom of Polycarp," in Cyril Richardson, ed., *Early Christian Fathers* (New York: Macmillan, 1970), p. 149.

53. Erazim Kohác, "Of Dwelling and Wayfaring: A Quest for Metaphors," in Leroy Rouner, ed., *The Longing for Home* (Notre Dame: University of Notre Dame, 1996), p. 32.

home. He has not sunk down any roots, if he has roots at all, because the goal is to travel light. He has not achieved home, for there is no home, and the wayfarer seeks none. The wayfarer clings to no place because he is indifferent to all places; indeed, he thinks of home as no place.

In contrast to both the plowman and the wayfarer there is the pilgrim. The pilgrim "is not a wayfarer in the classic sense" for "the wayfarer has no home, both by choice and by definition, and seeks none." Pilgrims, however, "bear the dream of homeland in their hearts, weeping by the rivers of Babylon as they remember Zion," and thus they are "clearly dwellers, not wayfarers." Their "basic posture is one of dwelling, of becoming incarnate in a time and a place, though life has called them to the life of the wayfarer" (p. 44). But the pilgrim is not a dweller the way the plowman is, for the pilgrim is not (yet) at home. Like the wayfarer, the pilgrim "accepts life on the road," but without the wayfarer's characteristic indifference to place. Indeed, the pilgrim has the "the ploughman's love for the land, though without the ploughman's clinging" (p. 45). In his clearest statement, Kohác says:

> The pilgrim's basic posture is one of dwelling, of reaching out to the land and all the particularity of incarnation in love and labor, yet with the wayfarer's awareness that home can find only transient instantiations on this earth. Home is not a place; it is a posture, willing to be at home, whose forms in this life are never final and forever. Like the wayfarer the pilgrim can never arrive, but for a different reason. The wayfarer cannot arrive because he is unwilling to risk the commitment of incarnation. The pilgrim can never arrive because he has given of himself to too many places and left too much of himself behind at each move. (p. 45)

For Kohác, the pilgrim is neither farmer nor nomad, but exile. Neither an eternal dweller nor an eternal wanderer, but a dweller called to another place. Neither always at home nor never at home, but at home on the move. The pilgrim has roots and sinks them deep in a particular place; but if necessary, she moves to another place and sinks roots there. Thus, while she never fully achieves home, the pilgrim is a homemaker. The pilgrim neither clings to her place nor is indifferent to all places, but loves her place without clinging to it. In contrast to the dwelling plowman and the wayfaring wanderer, the pilgrim is a wayfaring dweller.[54]

54. The literature on the pilgrim *(viator, peregrinus)* in human history, and especially in the Christian past, is quite large. One important place to start is Gerhardt Ladner, "*Homo*

With his term "pilgrim," Koháč comes very close to describing what we mean by "sojourner."[55] The Christian sojourner is a dweller, but all dwelling this side of God's good future fully realized is provisional and incomplete. The sojourner sinks roots in a particular place, makes a home, dwells, but she always knows that she could be called elsewhere, to sink roots there, to make a home, and to dwell. The sojourner neither clings to her particular place, like the plowman, nor is indifferent to all places, like the wayfarer or postmodern nomad. The sojourner loves her place but without clinging to it.

We can love a place because creation is good and we are called to dwelling. We can dwell in a place because we know we are accompanied by the indwelling God. But the pilgrim knows that there is a "not yet" character to this indwelling. We are all still sojourning toward that final homecoming, and thus we are not to erect any home this side of the eschaton as a fortress of finality. All homes are provisional. Commenting on Augustine's understanding of himself as a pilgrim, Gilbert Meilaender notes that being a pilgrim requires mastering "the art of loving this world without clinging to it."[56] None us, not even Augustine, achieve such mastery, but being a sojourner is well encapsulated by thinking of it in these terms: the art of lov-

---

Viator: Medieval Ideas on Alienation and Order," *Speculum* 42, no. 2 (Apr. 1967): 233-29. The classic twentieth-century book on the pilgrim or sojourner is Gabriel Marcel, *Homo Viator* (Chicago: Regnery, 1951), whose telling subtitle is *Introduction to a Metaphysic of Hope.*

55. We prefer the term "sojourner" to the notion of pilgrim for several reasons. See Sharon Daloz Parks, "Home and Pilgrimage: Comparison Metaphors for Personal and Social Transformation," *Soundings* 72, nos. 2-3 (Summer/Fall 1989): 297-315. Parks points out how terms such as "pilgrim" can become limited in meaning. That is, terms such as "pilgrim" — which conveys detachment rather than connection, journeying over against homesteading — can become identified as predominantly or exclusively male. What we need, she argues, are "metaphors of detachment *and* connection, pilgrims *and* homemakers, journeying *and* homesteading" (p. 301). With our use of "sojourner," we are attempting to do just that: combine the best of pilgrim and homemaker into one potent image.

A second reason for using "sojourner" rather than "pilgrim" has to do with the associations of the latter with "the Pilgrims," who immigrated to the United States. "Sojourner" is a stranger term, less well known, and for that reason, once explained, less likely to be misunderstood.

Third, the term "sojourner" is more biblical than the term "pilgrim." Indeed, "sojourner" has a rich biblical resonance — in both testaments.

56. Gilbert Meilaender, "(Re)reading Augustine's Confessions," *The Cresset* (Christmas/ Epiphany 1996): 11. Prompted by his own move from Ohio to Indiana, Meilaender offers a number of insightful reflections on place, time, and home in "Creatures of Place and Time: Reflections on Moving," *First Things* (Apr. 1997): 17-23.

ing this world, of deeply caring for it and making a welcoming home in it, but without grasping at our provisional home as if it were our final home.

So the sojourner is a homemaker, but a homemaker who is potentially on the move. And the homeland for which the sojourner yearns is not some other world, but this world redeemed and transfigured. The contrast is not ontological but eschatological. Because the kingdom of God is not yet realized in its fullness, the sojourner yearns for its consummation. And that is why Christian sojourners are aching visionaries who bear witness to and work for a future of shalom. None of the categories of displacement that we elucidated at the beginning of Chapter 2 fit Christian sojourners: we are not immigrants or refugees, exiles or migrants, tourists or postmodern no-mads. If we understand ourselves properly, then in contrast to all of them we are, in a real sense, at home. But this being at home is a posture, a way of being in the world. It is a journeying homemaking characterized by all the things revealed by that phenomenology: permanence, dwelling, memory, rest, hospitality, inhabitation, orientation, and belonging.

If the sojourner image is a potent way to capture the Christian way of being in our postmodern world, our age of exile and dislocation, what are the marks of Christian sojourners and a sojourning church? In addition to a concern for housing rights and an economy of care, the virtues of shalom and the practices that mark us as earthkeepers, here are three characteristics of a sojourning people. Christian sojourners are, first of all, people of the Book, who, second, love one another, and, third, enter-tain angels: those three characteristics can be summarized as memory, community, and hospitality.

Christian sojourners are people of the Book. Their lives are shaped by the stories from the Bible and its grand Story — from the joyous homemak-ing of the Creator through the costly homemaking of Jesus to the glorious homecoming of God, the great reconciler and recycler. We wayfaring dwell-ers find our identity and direction in God's grand Story, and thus we are peo-ple of *memory.* We remember the grand story and all the little stories that are part of it, the sad stories as well as the happy stories. We especially strive to remember the stories we find uncomfortable or wish weren't there. As Elie Wiesel reminds us, the great temptation is to forget. And as Wendell Berry insists, inhabiting a place and sustaining a proper home economics is impos-sible without an adequate memory of the people and other inhabitants of that place. Or, as the Old Testament expresses it again and again, without memory the people perish. Without memory we don't know who we are or where home is or what home looks like. There can be no sojourning home-making without memory.[57]

But to say we are people of memory is not merely to say we remember the past. Merold Westphal puts it this way: "Historical memory is utterly in-dispensable to the Christian life, but it is inseparably linked to the present and future tenses of faith."[58] As some Christians hear liturgically pro-claimed during the celebration of Holy Communion, this is "a feast of re-membrance, communion, and hope." Or, as many Christians reply in their Eucharist liturgy: "Christ has died! Christ is risen! Christ is coming again!" This implies that the remembering characteristic of a sojourning people is not merely a recollection of past facts, but "a matter of recalling or repre-senting to consciousness something that may be forgotten through inatten-tion. Here memory is not the ability to answer questions but the openness to having our lives (trans)formed by what we attend to." In other words, "Christian memory is a moral rather than an intellectual virtue" (p. 11). Without such memory, the dense moral culture of home is impossible. Re-membering our grand Story is a way of allowing ourselves to be addressed by it and by the God who authored it. Thus the challenge of remembering, of paying attention to the familiar so that it strikes us afresh, is "the assign-ment to make the self-sacrificial love of Christ the paradigm for our own lives" and to recall that the comfort of the gospel "is not to be basked in but built on" (p. 11). As Westphal reminds us, Christian memory is "dangerous memory, dangerous to the 'tranquilized everydayness' of Christians in need of awakening and dangerous to the established order . . . when it confronts Christians whom memory has awakened" (p. 11). We remember our in-spired grand Story (sacred Scripture) and communal memory (living tradi-tion) in order to allow them to shape our present lives.

As we have stated before, however, this raises the question, Which memories will be retrieved? How exactly will the biblical story be retold? Which traditions will be normative for the life of the community? It should be clear that our own retelling of the biblical story draws on certain traditions in emphasizing the themes of home, homelessness, and home-coming. While the Bible is not often interpreted in this way, we are con-

---

57. One excellent example of how memory and remembering function in Christian ethics can be found in Allen Verhey, *Remembering Jesus: Christian Community, Scripture, and the Moral Life* (Grand Rapids: Eerdmans, 2002).

58. Merold Westphal, "Lest We Forget," *Perspectives* 11, no. 2 (Feb. 1996): 10.

vinced that ours is not only a faithful reading of the biblical story but one crucial for the times in which we live.

Christian sojourners love one another. The second feature of sojourning Christians is *community*. The God whom Christians worship and serve is a community of love — a family of interpenetrating, exuberant, excessive, overflowing love. Jean Vanier says: "More and more people are becoming conscious that our God is not a powerful lord telling us to obey or be punished but our God is *family*. Our God is three persons in love with each other; our God is communion."[59] And this God who is communion calls us to be in communion, that is, calls us to be a community of love. We do not sojourn solo; we do so with others who, like us, have been called to dwell in the world as homemakers.

Many in the Christian tradition remind us of this central feature of our life together as sojourners. In his opening greeting to the churches, the writer of the *Martyrdom of Polycarp* explicitly mentions mercy, peace, and love; and it is evident in his account that devotion to Jesus as Lord and love of God and the church animated Polycarp's life. In the spirit of simplicity and humility for which he was renowned, Francis of Assisi simply says, after quoting Matthew 5:44: "And let him show his love for the other by his deeds."[60] Countless others, women and men, have set their course by the light of love, the costly homemaking love of Christ.

Dietrich Bonhoeffer, living in a Christian community while teaching at the underground seminary in Finkenwalde, Germany, in the late 1930s, speaks wisely about the love necessary for such a community, its promise as well as its perils: "He who loves his dream of community more than the Christian community itself becomes a destroyer of the latter, even though his personal intentions may be ever so honest and earnest and sacrificial."[61] Ideological idealism, in other words, easily runs roughshod over the real people who make up the community. In a similar vein, Søren Kierkegaard exposes what he calls "the egocentric service of the good" and argues that true love prompts service to God and neighbor for their own

---

59. Jean Vanier, *From Brokenness to Community* (New York: Paulist, 1992), p. 35.

60. *Francis and Clare: The Complete Works* (Ramsey, NJ: Paulist, 1982), p. 30. See also John Michael Talbot, *The Lessons of St. Francis* (New York: Penguin, 1997). This echoes the admonitions of the elder Zosima in Dostoevsky's *The Brothers Karamazov*, who again and again encourages Alexei (and others) to engage in "active love." See *The Brothers Karamazov* (San Francisco: North Point Press, 1990), pp. 56-58, 285, 319, 362.

61. Dietrich Bonhoeffer, *Life Together* (New York: Harper and Row, 1954), p. 27.

sake.[62] This is so important for Bonhoeffer that he concludes: "The existence of any Christian life together depends on whether it succeeds at the right time in bringing out the ability to distinguish between a human ideal and God's reality, between spiritual and human community."[63] The art of loving this world without clinging to it is impossible without this kind of self-transcending love. Without a self-forgetful or disinterested love, the community we seek cannot happen.[64]

Vanier speaks of Christian community as a community of bonding, caring, and mission, whose most fundamental feature is love, manifested in reconciliation and forgiveness.[65] All humans, says Vanier, desire communion, to love and be loved, but all are also wounded and fearful. All have erected walls of exclusion. Only love, ultimately the love of God, can break down the fortresses of fear and allow us to "journey home, a journey towards becoming what we really are, towards finding our deepest identity and gradually opening ourselves to others."[66] Only in love can we arrive home, "where we are safe . . . a place of communion . . . a place where we can be ourselves and welcome the reality of our beauty and our pain."[67] Our beauty and our pain.

For Henri Nouwen, the Christian life is a journey from the house of fear to the house of love. As Jesus indicates in John 15, the house of love is a place of intimacy, fecundity, and ecstasy. But Nouwen describes our time as an age of homelessness: "Probably no word better summarizes the suffering of our time than the word 'homeless.' It reveals one of our deepest and most painful conditions, the condition of not having a sense of belonging, of not having a place where we can feel safe, cared for, protected, and loved."[68] In contrast, Jesus offers us a home: "In my father's house there are many dwelling places," and "Abide in me as I abide in you" (John 14:2; 15:4). This home is a "place or space where we do not have to be afraid but can let go of our defenses and be free, free from worries, free from tensions, free from pressures. . . . Home is where we can rest and be

---

62. Søren Kierkegaard, *Purity of Heart Is to Will One Thing* (New York: Harper and Row, 1956), ch. 6.

63. Bonhoeffer, *Life Together*, p. 37.

64. Merold Westphal refers to this kind of love as useless self-transcendence. See *God, Guilt, and Death* (Bloomington, IN: Indiana University Press, 1984), ch. 8.

65. Vanier, *From Brokenness to Community*, ch. 2.

66. Vanier, *Our Journey Home* (Maryknoll, NY: Orbis, 1997), p. 133.

67. *Our Journey Home*, p. xi.

68. Henri Nouwen, *Lifesigns* (New York: Doubleday, 1986), p. 28.

healed."[69] Whatever else the sojourning Christian community is (and there are many kinds and shapes and sizes), it is an embodiment, frail and fragile to be sure, of the love of God in Christ.

Christian sojourners entertain angels. *Hospitality* is the third marker of the sojourning Christian community. We find hospitality prominent in the Old Testament. The Israelites were called to be hospitable, especially to the widows, orphans, and strangers in their midst. There are two reasons given for why they should be a people of hospitality. First, the strangers to whom they offered hospitality could be messengers of God and, second, since they were recipients of God's hospitality during their liberation from bondage in Egypt and while they wandered in the wilderness, they should be a people who provide hospitality to the sojourners in their midst (Gen. 18–19; Lev. 19:33-34; Deut. 10:19). This last argument is most important: the Israelites were to imitate God's own hospitality.

In the New Testament, Jesus exercised hospitality to a most unlikely band of outcasts, rejects, and misfits. Indeed, "Christianity continues and intensifies the call to practice hospitality to the needy stranger, for Christ is present in the impoverished alien and hospitality to the poor is required of all who would enter the Reign of God."[70] The parable of the sheep and goats is perhaps the most famous text in this regard. When the righteous ask the king when it was that they saw him a stranger and welcomed him, the king replies, "Just as you did it to one of the least of these who are members of my family, you did it to me" (Matt. 25:40). Whenever we care for the needy, we show hospitality to Christ himself. Throughout the New Testament we find similar stories and admonitions concerning hospitality, especially to be practiced toward those most vulnerable. The apostle Paul enjoins us to "extend hospitality to strangers" (Rom. 12:13). Peter encourages us to "be hospitable to one another without complaining" (1 Pet. 4:9). And the author of Hebrews says: "Let mutual love continue. Do not neglect to show hospitality to strangers, for by doing that some have entertained angels without knowing it" (Heb. 13:1-2). So important is hospitality to the Christian life, Smith and Carvill conclude, that "the practice of hospitality lies close to the center of a Christian's life before God."[71]

69. Nouwen, *Lifesigns*, p. 27.

70. Patrick McCormick, "The Good Sojourner: Third World Tourism and the Call of Hospitality," *Journal of the Society of Christian Ethics* 24, no. 1 (2004): 91.

71. David Smith and Barbara Carvill, *The Gift of the Stranger* (Grand Rapids: Eerdmans, 2000), p. 85.

But what exactly is hospitality? The term is often misunderstood. For many it connotes "tea parties, bland conversation, and a general atmosphere of coziness."[72] In point of fact, Christian hospitality is quite different. To the early church, hospitality meant "transcending social and ethnic difference by sharing meals, homes, and worship with persons of different backgrounds."[73] Indeed, the early church was known for including the poorest and neediest — those who could not return the favor. And so for the church today, hospitality means recognizing the stranger (of whatever kind) in our midst. This implies not only respecting the humanity and dignity of the stranger, but also acknowledging our common vulnerability and shared suffering.[74] Patrick McCormick puts it well: "More than simply providing for the basic needs of the poor, hospitality is an opening of one's household to others, a welcoming of guests into one's home, and an invitation to share a meal. When we offer hospitality to someone, we recognize them as a companion, a colleague, a friend. The offer of hospitality transforms the stranger into a neighbor."[75] Practically speaking, hospitality can take many forms, though almost always it would seem to imply sharing a common meal.

In his moving meditation on the story of the Emmaus travelers, Henri Nouwen provides a winsome description of Christian hospitality: "The two traveling friends invite, indeed, press the stranger to stay with them. 'Be our guest,' they say. They want to be his hosts. They invite the stranger to lay aside his strangeness and become a friend to them. That's what true hospitality is all about, to offer a safe place, where the stranger can become a friend."[76]

Memory, community, and hospitality. Christian sojourners are people of the Book who love one another and entertain angels. Without biblical memory, generous community, and sacrificial hospitality, no authentic Christian community can exist.

72. Henri Nouwen, *Reaching Out* (New York: Image Books, 1975), p. 66.

73. Christine Pohl, *Making Room: Recovering Hospitality as a Christian Tradition* (Grand Rapids: Eerdmans, 1999), p. 5.

74. As Christine Pohl notes, this is especially evident in the writings of John Calvin. That all human beings are made in the image of God is absolutely central for Calvin, and the basis of our respect for all people, even the stranger. See *Making Room*, pp. 64-67.

75. McCormick, "The Good Sojourner," p. 94.

76. Henri Nouwen, *With Burning Hearts* (Maryknoll: Orbis, 1995), pp. 59-60.

Homeward Bound

All of us are on a journey. But the stories we tell of our earthly pilgrimages are not all the same. Many today describe their journey as one of perpetual homelessness. Suspicious of all claims to truth, restless and anxious about the future, fearfully aware that we are despoiling our earthly home, many of us feel awhirl in the postmodern world. The home we remember is at best a happy memory, and the home we hope for is a fading dream. In the words of Simon and Garfunkel, postmodern nomads, despite claims that there are no homes, find their hearts longing to be:

> Homeward bound, I wish I was,
> Homeward bound.
> Home — where my thought's escaping.
> Home — where my music's playing.
> Home — where my love lies waiting, silently for me.

We long for that familiar place where we belong, where we will be loved, where the home we dream of may just be real. Like Simon and Garfunkel, in the last line of the last verse, we wayfarers sing, "I need someone to comfort me."[77]

The second epigraph at the beginning of this chapter contains words from another wayfaring song. Like Simon and Garfunkel, Bruce Cockburn sings of yearning for home, but this home is the Lord of the starfields and the Sower of life. After his confession of praise to the creating-sustaining God of the Bible, he prays in a powerful refrain: "O Love that fires the sun, keep me burning." The central claim of the Christian faith is that the love that fires the sun is our true home. In a culture of incredulity toward grand narratives, of rootlessness and isolation, of deafness to the groaning of creation — to such a culture these are words of healing and shalom. The Christian story redemptively addresses the hopes and fears of suspicious postmodern nomads living homeless on an increasingly uninhabitable earth. The Christian community at its faithful best embodies love and grace and hope for those dazed and disoriented in a culture of dislocation.

Christians, too, are on a journey. We also yearn for home. But our tale of home-seeking is a story of a sojourning people at home in creation because

---

77. Simon and Garfunkel, "Homeward Bound," from *Parsley, Sage, Rosemary, and Thyme* ©1966 Columbia Records.

of a good God who gives them sustenance for the journey and who comes in person to comfort them. The Love that lies waiting for us, to hear Christians tell it, is that fierce Love who fires the sun and that self-emptying Love who pitched his tent among us. Our Redeemer is our Creator. We are not yet at home, and so we, like our forebears, walk by faith and not by sight. But the day is coming when God's glory will fill heaven and earth, when all tears save those of joy will disappear, and when our mourning will turn to dancing. We will experience a heaven-on-earth homecoming of comfort and belonging and delight. Shalom will prevail, and our yearning hearts will find their home in the heart of God. Such a story is good news indeed.

The Great Homecoming

Revelation 21–22

It all began with joy.
And it all will end with joy.

God had once upon a time made a home —
    a place of dwelling
    of belonging
    of communion.

Out of the extravagance of love,
    from God's overabundant generosity,
God laid the cornerstones of the home
    that is the heavens and the earth
and filled it with creatures great and small.

Only to have his blessed homemaking
become a cursed homebreaking.
To have violence displace peace,
    hate supplant love,
    death overcome life,
because Adam and the daughters and sons of Adam
    failed to trust God,
    went their own way,
    broke relationship.

You know the story.
You humans live the story.
You know it all too painfully well.

And so do we.
So does God.

But also know this.
Open your eyes and ears to what I now have to tell you.
Rivet your imagination on what is beyond imagining,
for my story speaks of God's great good future,
    when all is set right,
    when all is as it should be,
    when shalom is made fully real.
The great homecoming.

John the Seer,
alone on the island of Patmos he was,
when I came to him,
one of the seven angels.

There John was given a vision,
a Spirit-inspired vision,
of what life is now like for us
and what life will some day be like for all.

John gazed upon a new heaven and a new earth —
a panorama of a renewed heavenly earth,
or was it an earthly heaven?
He wasn't quite sure.
Whatever it was
    it took his breath away,
    it left him gaping wide-eyed in wonder.

The sea —
symbolic of the realm of chaos,
home to the blasphemous beast,
place of constant threat and foreboding —
was no more.

And the new Jerusalem —
the holy city of God,

the place of justice and peace,
the home of shalom —
like a beautiful bride adorned for her husband
descended to earth.

And then a Voice from the throne spoke,
from somewhere inside the city,
thundering and yet winsome,
ear-splitting and yet soothing:
    "Behold, the home of God is among you humans.
    I will pitch my tent with you mortals,
    and you will be my people,
    and I in person will be with you.
    And I will wipe every tear from your sorrowful eyes,
    and death will be no more,
    and mourning and crying and pain will be no more,
    for the former things have passed away."

I remembered the Spirit pitching his tent with the Israelites
in the wilderness,
and the very Word pitching his tent among humans,
in flesh and blood.
It seemed to be God's way with a wayward world —
to make his home with the homeless.
John remembered too.
And he ached for that day
when death and mourning, crying and pain would be no more.
I could feel his yearning, though he spoke not a word.

And then the Voice spoke again:
    "Behold, I am making all things new!
    These words are trustworthy and true!
    For I am the Alpha and the Omega,
    the Beginning and the End,
    the All-Embracing One.
    To the thirsty I give the water of life.
    To those who conquer with love,
    I will be their God and they my children.

But to those who refuse my love,
who reject my grace,
who renounce my homemaking,
their place will be the burning lake of homelessness."

"All things renewed? Could it be?
Not all new things but all things new —
renewed, refurbished, renovated.
Is it possible?"
I could read John's mind.
He hadn't yet mustered the strength to speak,
but his mind was racing.

In the power of the Spirit,
I carried John up to a great, high mountain,
for an even better view of what lay before him.
Then I showed John the bride of the Lamb —
the slain Lamb who reigns as Lord.
From there I showed him the holy city Jerusalem,
coming down out of heaven from God.
It brought tears to his eyes — tears of joy they were —
and I think it was a healing balm for his hurting heart.
He stood on tiptoes, straining to see it all,
then fell to his knees, wide-eyed and speechless.

This bride, the new Jerusalem, glowed
with the radiance of incomparable jewels —
rare jasper, fine crystal —
    luminous,
    brilliant,
    clear.
This city of shalom exuded the weight of God's glory.

How to describe this city? I'm not sure one can.
John tried to describe it, and so will I.

The city had around it a high wall with twelve gates,
    three on each of its four sides,

    each gate named for an Israelite tribe.
The foundations of the wall were rock-solid,
    for each had been poured
    by the faithful work of the twelve apostles.
I took out my gold measuring stick, sure and true,
    to fix the dimensions of this city,
and, as I expected, it was a cube — a symbol of perfection.

The walls were built of jasper.
The streets paved with gold.
The foundations were adorned with precious jewels
    well known in the world of Adam,
each one representing one of the tribes of Israel:
    jasper, deep red like the crest of a pileated woodpecker;
    sapphire, dark blue like the sky straight above on a cloudless day;
    agate, whiteish-grey with flecks of dark green like a galactic nebula;
    emerald, light green like bracken fern fiddleheads;
    onyx, thin bands of white on black like a longfin bannerfish;
    carnelian, reddish-brown like rich earthy soil;
    chrysolite, light green like fresh olives;
    beryl, translucent blue-green like Mediterranean Sea water;
    topaz, transparent yellow-red like fine white wine;
    chyrsoprase, deep green like unripe apples;
    jacinth, brownish red like vermilion rock;
    amethyst, pale pink-purple like a newly blooming lilac.
This was a city jeweled with the mineral wealth of the world,
aglow with the stones found on the breastplate of Aaron the high priest,
and beautiful beyond all measure.

My friend John searched for the Temple, but did not find it.
By the look on his face he asked me why there was no house for God,
and I replied that there was no temple in this perfect city
because the Lord God the Almighty and the victorious Lamb —
they themselves were the temple.
In this heaven-on-earth city, God was everywhere immediately present.
All creation was now God's home.

And so this city had no need of sun or moon to shine on it,
for the very glory of God was its light.
Its lamp was the Lamb, the One who was slain,
and by that light walked the nations —
    all peoples
    all ethnic groups
    all kings and queens
    all presidents and prime ministers
bringing their cultural treasures —
the best they had to offer —
through the never-shut gates of the city.
As Isaiah foretold long ago,
all peoples from all nations were bringing into this city
the glory and honor of the nations —
    from Midian and Sheba and Tarshish,
    from Antioch and Alexandria and Athens,
    from Corinth and Laodicea and Rome,
    from Washington and Beijing and Moscow,
    from Tokyo and London and Paris,
    from Rio and Nairobi and New Delhi.
People of every tribe and tongue,
carrying their treasures into the radiant city.
The true wealth of nations flowed like a cavernous mountain stream
into the holy city.

This was a most unusual city.
    A city of unparalleled beauty.
    A city of hospitality for all.
    A city of safety.
    A city of shalom.
Our dwelling place and God's home.

John had not said a word.
Rendered speechless by the onslaught of sights and sounds,
he merely drank it all in, dazzled and dazed.

Just when it seemed he could take no more,
I showed John the river of the water of life,

bright as crystal, cascading from the throne of God and the Lamb
right smack-dab through the middle of the city.
On both sides of this life-giving river grew the tree of life
producing twelve kinds of fruit, one for each month,
sustenance the year around.
And the leaves of this tree were for the healing of the nations.
No more trees felled for battering rams
to lay siege to medieval cities.
No more trees cut for sailing masts
to power colonial warships.
No more trees pulped for propaganda
to fuel the fires of ethnic cleansing.
This tree is for life.
This tree is for the healing of the nations.
This tree is for shalom.

At the sight of this river and this tree
John finally found the words and strength to speak.
"Amen. So be it!
That on this heavenly earth the curse will be no more!
That the weight of inherited sorrow will be lifted!
That the taint of sin will be washed clean by the blood of the Lamb!
Amen. So be it!
That we will see God face to face!
That we will have God's name on our foreheads!
That the Lord God himself will be our light!
Amen. So be it!
That as God intended from the beginning,
we will reign with God forever and ever!"

These words, said I, are trustworthy and true.
You can depend on them and on the One who speaks them.

It all began with joy.
And it all will end with joy.

God once upon a time made a home —
a place of dwelling

of belonging
of communion.

Out of the extravagance of love,
    from God's overabundant generosity,
God laid the cornerstones of the home
    that is the heavens and the earth
and filled it with creatures great and small.

And God the great homemaker will make all things new.
Open your eyes and ears to this mind-boggling vision.
Rivet your imagination on God's great good future,
    when all is set right,
    when all is as it should be,
    when shalom is made fully real.

The great homecoming.

Amen. So be it!

Redemptive Homecoming

Home . . . hard to know what it is if you've never had one
Home . . . I don't know what it is, but I know I'm going
Home . . . that's where the hurt is.

U2[1]

How come history takes such a long, long time
When you're waiting for a miracle?

Bruce Cockburn[2]

The forces of domicide continue unabated. As we complete this book, thousands have died over the question of homeland in the Middle East, where Israel, Hamas, and Hezbollah have been in violent combat. Many thousands grieve. And it is all in the name of home! Israel fights to secure her homeland in the midst of enemies who are committed to her destruction. Hamas takes up the Palestinian cause of a right to return to homelands that have been expropriated by Israel. Hezbollah joins the battle in solidarity with the Palestinians and in ideological hatred of Israel. Home is always a contested space. And that strife always seems rooted in conflicting memories and antithetical stories.

In the name of homeland security, the United States and its allies are

---

1. U2, "Walk On," from *All You Can't Leave Behind* ©2000 Universal International Music.
2. Bruce Cockburn, "Waiting for a Miracle," from *Waiting for a Miracle* ©1987 Golden Mountain Music.

occupying the homelands of the Iraqi and Afghani peoples. Again, thousands die and many thousands mourn, and homes are broken all around the region. War is bad news for homemaking. And it is not just the homes of the combatants, civilians, and their families that are devastated. The Persian Gulf runs black with pollution, as the hostilities and burning oil fields destroy the habitats of birds, fish, and ocean plants.

Down in the valley, Kenny is still in his squat with his brothers; Kenneth, meanwhile, has to look at his blackberry to figure out which city he will have to call home tomorrow evening. Kenny's friends on the waiting list for subsidized housing are no closer to being housed than they were a year ago. And while Kenneth's financial situation is better than ever (war is good for business), things are getting more and more tense in his marriage. It seems that Julie wants to stay in one place a little longer and is refusing to travel with her husband as much.

Ours is an age of displacement. And the realities of socioeconomic, ecological, and cultural homelessness seem to only intensify as the twenty-first century gets on its feet. Homelessness seems to be an intractable problem, and once we begin to glimpse the scope, complexity, and interrelatedness of the crises of homelessness in all of its forms, it is difficult to live in hope. Scott Russell Sanders writes of the crisis of hope in the lives of his children and his students.

> Suppose your daughter is engaged to be married and she asks whether you think she ought to have children, given the sorry state of the world. Suppose your son is starting college and he asks what you think he should study, or why he should study at all, when the future looks so bleak. Or suppose you are a teacher and one student after another comes to ask you how to deal with despair. What would you tell them?
>
> My children and my students have put those questions to me — haltingly, earnestly — and I feel I owe them an answer. They are not asking for assurances of pie in the sky, for magic pills or guardian angels, for stories ending happily ever after, but for real and present reasons to face the future with confidence.[3]

Most of us, we suspect, have felt the bite of such questions and the weight of obligation to provide real and present reasons for hope. Sanders writes

3. Scott Russell Sanders, *Hunting for Hope* (Boston: Beacon, 1998), p. 1.

about young people who worry not just about their own private futures but also "about the future of our whole motley species, our fellow creatures, and the planet." We could say that they are anxious because of the various kinds of homelessness we have described in these pages. But their question is pointed and real: Is there any real hope? If so, why and what and how? Sanders continues:

> The young people who put their disturbing questions to me have had an ecological education, and a political one as well. They know we are in trouble. Everywhere they look they see ruined landscapes and ravaged communities and broken people. So they are asking me if I believe we have the resources for healing the wounds, for mending the breaks. They are asking me if I live in hope.[4]

Everywhere we look we see ruined landscapes and ravaged communities and broken people. In a home-breaking world, are there resources to heal the wounds and mend the breaks? In their song "Walk On," U2 put it this way: "Home . . . hard to know what it is if you've never had one/Home . . . I can't say what it is but I know I'm going/Home . . . that's where the hurt is." In the face of intractable homelessness, is there any way home? Is homecoming possible if we've never had a deep experience of home?

Hope, Home, and Imagination

Not without imagination. If all we can see is what lies before our eyes, if all we can perceive is the devastating reality of domicide, then a homecoming hope will always be elusive. Hope requires a vision that goes "just beyond the range of normal sight."[5] We need to go beyond normal sight because, "the trouble with normal," says Bruce Cockburn, "is it always gets worse."[6] Walter Brueggemann has argued that "the key pathology of our time, which seduces us all, is the reduction of the imagination so that we are too numbed, satiated and co-opted to do serious imaginative

---

4. Sanders, *Hunting for Hope*, p. 2.

5. Bruce Cockburn, "Hills of Morning," from *Dancing in the Dragon's Jaws* ©1979 Golden Mountain Music.

6. Bruce Cockburn, "Trouble with Normal," from *Trouble with Normal* ©1983 Golden Mountain Music.

work."[7] There is something about life in urban homogeneity that strips us of imagination. There is something about being anonymous consumers that leaves us unable to imagine life otherwise. And there is something about all of this that renders us numb, as emotionally disconnected from our own placelessness as we are from the homelessness of others.

Hope requires liberated imaginations. Phylis Novak knows this from the lives of street kids in Toronto. Some of the very same young people we described in Chapter 3 above have found their way to Sketch, a ministry that Phylis directs.[8] At Sketch, street-involved kids are given watercolors and acrylic and oil paints — and the freedom to create. They can pick up a guitar, a video camera, or they have the freedom to hang out in a recording studio. There is even a kitchen for kids to try out new recipes. In the context of a safe environment and supportive mentoring and apprenticeships, young people tell their stories and dream their dreams. Sketch creates a physical, emotional, and communal space for creativity. And in the awakening of imaginations that happens in that space, street-involved and homeless youth find a way to imagine alternatives to both the dominant society that has not worked for them and the dead end of life on the street.

Captive imaginations cannot conceive of life outside the constrictions of normalcy. Bruce Cockburn suggests that it is the artist's calling to see otherwise, to be able to see through the lies,[9] the reifications, the false sense of normality that will leave us numb, "paralyzed in the face of it all,"[10] with a sense of resignation before the inevitable. This is why imagination is an essential feature of hope: no imagination, no hope.[11]

---

7. Walter Brueggemann, *Interpretation and Obedience* (Minneapolis: Fortress, 1991), p. 199.

8. See the Sketch website at http://www.sketch.ca/.

9. See his song "People See Through You," from *World of Wonders* ©1985 Golden Mountain Music.

10. A line from Cockburn's song "Gavin's Woodpile," from *In the Falling Dark* ©1976 Golden Mountain Music. In a recent interview, Cockburn describes his art in relationship to political and economic forces this way: "State powers are interested in keeping us numb and asleep. We need to stay awake. Part of my job is to help people stay awake — and to help myself stay awake — by looking at these situations and writing songs about them. It's up to the listeners what they want to do about it, but I need to be a witness." Greg King, "In a Dangerous Time," *The Sun* (June 2004), accessed online at: http://cockburnproject.net/front.html.

11. Hope is, in brief, confident expectation of future good. The hopeful person does three things: she imagines some good future, she believes that a good future is possible, and she longs for that good future to become real. Thus hope combines imagination, faith, and

However, artists do not create hope; rather, they bear witness to hope. Cockburn writes that he has "seen the flame of hope among the hopeless/ And that was truly the biggest heartbreak of all/That was the straw that broke me open."[12] Hopelessness is acquiescence to the empire, the powers of normalcy, and it is a luxury that only those who take their comfort from the empire can afford. The homeless, who are victimized by the empire, cannot afford such a luxury.

Such a "flame of hope among the hopeless" is nowhere more powerfully voiced than in Cockburn's song "Santiago Dawn."[13] Recounting revolutionary opposition to the Pinochet regime in Chile, ten years after the CIA-supported overthrow of Salvadore Allende's elected government on September 11, 1973, Cockburn sings:

At the crack of dawn the first door goes down
Snapped off a makeshift frame
In a matter of minutes the first rock flies
Barricades burst into flame

First mass rings through the smoke and gas
Day flowers out of the night
Creatures of the dark in disarray
Fall before the morning light

Bells of rage — bells of hope
As the ten-year night wears down
Sisters and brothers are coming home
To see the Santiago dawn

Santiago sunrise
See them marching home
See them rising like grass through cement
In the Santiago dawn

---

desire. For a perceptive and lucid exposition of hope, see Lewis Smedes, *Standing on the Promises: Keeping Hope Alive for a Tomorrow We Cannot Control* (Nashville: Thomas Nelson, 1998).

12. "Last Night of the World," from *Breakfast in New Orleans, Dinner in Timbuktu* ©1999 Golden Mountain Music.

13. "Santiago Dawn," from *World of Wonders* ©1985 Golden Mountain Music.

In this Isaiah-like vision of homecoming, dawn is possible, the ten-year night can be dispelled by a dawn of new beginnings, and darkness can be "dead and gone," because homecoming is an ineluctable force in human life. Creatures of the dark, agents of domicide, the violent forces of homelessness are in disarray and "fall before the morning light."[14] But note which bells are ringing, calling the people home in the face of the forces of homelessness: "First mass rings through the smoke and gas/Day flowers out of the night/Creatures of the dark in disarray/Fall before the morning light." These "bells of rage — bells of hope," these bells of homecoming, are the bells of the mass. There is the possibility of a homecoming resurrection only because of the sacrifice of Jesus that is recounted and celebrated in the mass. The very ringing of these bells constitutes a call to a subversive story of liberation, a eucharistic narrative of day flowing out of the night.

The vision that animates hope amid hopelessness should not be confused with optimism. When asked to explain how he kept going during the decades of despair prior to the liberation of the Czech Republic from a repressive communism, Václav Havel replied: "I am not an optimist. . . . I am a person of hope. . . . I cannot imagine that I would strive for anything if I did not carry hope in me."[15] Elsewhere, Havel put it this way: "Hope is not prognostication. It is an orientation of the spirit, an orientation of the heart; it transcends the world that is immediately experienced, and is anchored somewhere beyond its horizons. . . . Hope is definitely not the same thing as optimism."[16] As Sanders observes, "Havel's actions make clear that he is not saying that our hope should be *invested* elsewhere, in heaven or a utopian future, but that it *comes from* elsewhere, to encourage and strengthen us for good works here."[17] Like optimism, hope is for this world: in that sense, hope is *this*-worldly. But unlike optimism, the source of hope does not derive from this world: its source lies beyond.

More exactly, optimism is generally based on a modernist faith in progress, while hope is rooted in faith in God. As N. T. Wright argues, optimism is based on "a belief in Progress," born of the Enlightenment, which claims that "the world is getting better and better" because of our "indus-

---

14. To catch the Isaiah-like overtones, see Isaiah 40–55 and 60:4-22. On Second Isaiah as a vision of homecoming, see Walter Brueggemann, *Hopeful Imagination: Prophetic Voices in Exile* (Philadelphia: Fortress, 1986), ch. 5.

15. Quoted in Smedes, *Standing on the Promises*, p. 30.

16. Václav Havel, *Disturbing the Peace* (New York: Alfred Knopf, 1990), p. 181.

17. Sanders, *Hunting for Hope*, p. 27.

trial progress" and "technological innovation." Such progress, some believe, will produce "a world in which old evils will be left behind," to which Wright remarks, "Try telling that to a Holocaust survivor, a Tutsi refugee, a Honduran peasant." Such belief in a perfectible world flies in the face of the facts of history. In contrast to optimism, says Wright, hope has to do "not with steady progress, but with a belief that the world is God's world and that God has continuing plans for it."[18] Indwelling all things and renewing creation as home for creature and Creator alike, we have seen, is at the heart of those plans.

But how can we live in such hope? Sanders provides an articulate and compelling answer to his questioning students. We can live in hope, he believes, because the "leaping up in expectation" that is hope is anchored in many things: wildness, bodiliness, family, fidelity, skill, simplicity, beauty, and ultimately God.[19] In short, there are certain features of our common human experience that ground our hope. Built into the created order are signs of God's good and loving presence. As N. T. Wright affirms, the signs of hope "are not the evidences of an evolution from lower to higher forms of life, or from one ethical or political system to another, but the signs built into the created order itself: music, the birth of a baby, the appearance of spring flowers, grass growing through concrete, the irrepressibility of human love." Thus, he concludes, "some parts of our world simply point beyond themselves and say, "Look! Despite all, there is hope."[20] This sacramental universe is one basis of hope.

Wendell Berry gets at the same thing when he says that "authentic underpinnings of hope" can still be found in the very dynamics of nature. "Though we have caused the earth to be seriously diseased," he continues, "it is not yet without health. The earth we have before us now is still abounding and beautiful." And so Berry concludes, "The health of nature is the primary ground of hope — if we can find the humility and wisdom to accept nature as our teacher."[21]

18. N. T. Wright, *The Millennium Myth* (Louisville: Westminster/John Knox, 1999), p. 39.

19. Sanders, *Hunting for Hope*, chs. 4, 5, 7, 8, 9, 11, 12, 13.

20. Wright, *The Millennium Myth*, pp. 39-40.

21. Wendell Berry, *Sex, Economy, Freedom and Community* (New York and San Francisco: Pantheon, 1993), p. 11. Bill McKibben refers to the health of nature in the face of the human threat as "nature's grace" in his wonderful book, *Hope, Human and Wild* (Boston: Little, Brown and Company, 1995), p. 15.

But this brings us back to imagination. One can see the health of nature as a ground of hope only if one has eyes to see. One can see how this world of wonders points beyond itself only if one views the world sacramentally. Indeed, one can live in hope only if that hope is anchored somewhere beyond the horizons of present reality, beyond the range of normal sight. Hope for homecoming can be sustained only by an imagination that is rooted in memories that go deeper than the present homelessness and a vision that can see beyond the ubiquitous forces of domicide.

At the beginning of his novel *Remembering*, Wendell Berry offers a poem/prayer addressed to the "Heavenly Muse, Spirit who brooded on/ The world and raised it shapely out of nothing." To the Spirit who helped give birth to a creational home, Berry prays, "Touch my lips and burn away/All dross of speech, so that I keep in mind/The truth and end to which my words now move/In hope." Berry longs, in this novel and in all of his writings, to engender a hope in the midst of "worldly body broken." And so he prays: "Rule my sight by vision of the parts/Rejoined. And in my exile's journey far/From home, be with me, so I may return." A vision of the parts rejoined. A vision of the restoration of what has been torn asunder. A vision of an exilic journey coming home. Here is an imagination that engenders hope, an imagination of homecoming.

At the heart of the Christian gospel is the message that we all are homeless, but that there is a home in which our yearning hearts can and will find rest. That home is creation redeemed and transfigured, a place of grace that is inhabited by an indwelling God of unfathomable love. The Christian gospel, in other words, is a grand story of redemptive homecoming that is at the same time grateful homemaking. There is no better biblical story to capture this good news than the one in Luke 15:11-32. Listen again, perhaps for the first time, to that story of homecoming and homemaking.[22]

The Homemaking Father

I couldn't believe it. I just couldn't believe it. None of us could believe it. It was unthinkable . . . impossible. In our village no one had ever made such

---

22. This retelling of the parable of the prodigal son is indebted to the insights of Kenneth Bailey in *The Cross and the Prodigal: Luke 15 Through the Eyes of Middle Eastern Peasants*, 2nd ed. (Downers Grove, IL: InterVarsity, 2005).

a request before: "Give me the share of the property that will belong to me." Those were his very words. Carefully chosen words, they were. He slyly avoided using the word "inheritance"; that would imply family responsibility. But taking his share of the family responsibility was the farthest thing from his mind. This boy wasn't interested in building his father's house. He, in truth, was a homewrecker, not a homebuilder.

The shame of it all! We were all shamed by the request Jacob made to his father. The entire household was embarrassed by this self-centered request from this ungrateful son. What was most shocking and disturbing was that, with his impertinent request, the boy proclaimed his desire for his father to die. It was a death wish, this request. "Father, I wish you were dead" — that was what he was really saying. What kind of family raises such a child? What kind of son says that about his father? The pride of him, and the shame for us. Unthinkable.

We all wondered what our master would do. Some of us bet that he would do what every other village father would do: put this mutinous kid in his place, discipline him in no uncertain terms, or maybe even disown him. But our master, Jacob's father, did as his son requested. With a wounded heart, or so it seemed to me, he divided his property between his stay-at-home older son and this rebellious younger son. Our master gave Jacob one third of his assets. One third of the houses. One third of the land. One third of the animals. He gave him what the Torah requires for the younger son's inheritance, and in only a few days Jacob had converted it all to cash. You can guess what he got for it all — the sheep, the goats, the land. He was forced to sell cheap because it was a buyer's market. But sell he did, even under those circumstances. Well, this was quite a blow to the farm. To lose one-third of its wealth in such a short time was a staggering loss. How would we recover? How could we?

All of us in the village knew that this broken relationship between Jacob and his father should have been healed. There should have been reconciliation, but for that to happen, there had to be a go-between. And we all knew this mediator should have been the older son, Levi. For duty's sake, he should have intervened to bring his father and younger brother together. Even if he disliked his brother, he should have been the mediator for the sake of his father. But for some reason he did nothing; for some reason he did not want a reconciliation. We then realized that he, too, had a strained relationship with his father. The family was more broken than we thought. And Levi, I discovered, had a dark wish of his own. He hoped that

Jacob would get what was coming to him and would never return home. "Get lost," Levi said, "and if you die, so be it." Because of what Jacob had done, Levi no longer considered Jacob his brother.

Once he had traded his inheritance for cash, Jacob set off. No farewell parties, no well-wishing from family and friends, no one pleading with him to stay. He just wandered off all by himself, which apparently is what he wanted. Be his own boss. Do his own thing. I spied him leaving early that morning as the sun was breaking over the horizon, hot and dry. I wondered how he would survive. His real inheritance was his clan; his social security was his family. That was where he belonged, because he was accepted there and was safe there. Did he really know what he was doing? I feared for him. Where was home if not here? But most of the other servants said, "Good riddance!" After what he had done, it wasn't surprising they reacted that way. But I worried. People don't trust vagabonds. It's dangerous out there. Where will he find home?

And oh, the risk he took! I saw him head off in the direction of the land of the gentiles. We all knew what that meant. Any Jew who lost his inheritance among the gentiles would not be welcome back home. If he tried to return home, he would be cut off. Banned. Excommunicated. He would have burned his bridges. He would be homeless.

That day I noticed my master's face. It was frozen in pain. It was lined with grief. I knew he suffered. He was estranged from both his sons. His home was broken.

From what I later learned, Jacob traveled into a far country, a long way from his own people. And he squandered his money among the unclean gentiles. Spendthrift that he was, Jacob scattered all his money like seed thrown on the ground. No surprise, really: we all knew he was a fool. Among these people he threw big parties, dished out expensive gifts, and built a reputation for generosity. He bought esteem and companionship. He gained status. He was living, so he thought, the good life.

But when he had squandered everything, had spent his last dime, a severe famine descended on the land like a blanket of dread, and Jacob was in need. He thought briefly about returning home, but that was impossible. He would have to face his scornful brother and live forever indebted to him. And he would have to face the entire village and the near certainty of being cut off from them, forever an exile mocked and taunted by the community itself. This was too much to bear. He wasn't that desperate. He still had his pride.

Jacob's life was getting very difficult. His money was gone, and his so-called friends had vanished. He pawned his outer coat, his family ring, and his shoes for money to buy some food to feed his empty gut. Around him people were stealing food, beggars were multiplying faster than cockroaches, and some old people were dying of starvation. The famine was brutal. He tried begging, but he was a foreigner and no one gave him anything. So Jacob tried to get work at a prominent local farm. In fact, he begged for work — said he'd do anything for a meager meal. Knowing that Jacob was a Jew (and that Jews detested pigs), and wanting to get rid of this foreign beggar, the gentile farmer offered him a job he was sure Jacob would refuse — feeding pigs. To the man's great surprise, Jacob took the job and went out to the field to feed the pigs. This good Jewish boy was in an unclean land among unclean people feeding unclean animals. It didn't get any worse than that.

But it did get worse. Jacob got so famished and so desperate that he longed to eat the very slop the pigs ate. Jacob had gone off the bottom rung of the Jewish social ladder. He was off the charts and couldn't get any lower. He had descended to live like the garbage-eating swine, craving their slop but unable to eat it because his stomach simply couldn't take it. Oh, to be a pig, he thought, able to fill my belly with food.

One day Jacob hit bottom. He was so starved that his hunger overcame his shame. So he resolved to go home. Even the servants back home, he reasoned, had it better than he did. They weren't working with pigs and wishing they could share the slop. Even the servants on the farm back home had enough bread to eat, with some to spare. Others had food, while he was hungry. It was as simple as that. He would go to where the food was.

So he hatched a plan. He knew he would be cut off from both family and community if he returned without the money. That was the long-established custom: restoration was impossible until he paid his debts. But what could he do to earn money? He couldn't ask to be taken back as a son; he had forfeited that honor. Nor could he ask to be taken in as a slave; slaves didn't make any money. But he could earn money as a skilled craftsman. That's the ticket! he thought. He would try to persuade his father to hire him as a craftsman's apprentice, and then he would use that money to eventually pay off his debts. The problem was all about money, wasn't it? So Jacob carefully crafted a speech designed to convince his father to give him another chance. Using the words of Pharaoh to Moses before the last of the Egyptian plagues, Jacob would say: "Father, I have sinned against heaven and before you." And then he added his request: "I am no longer worthy to be called your son; treat me like one of your skilled laborers."

This plan, he thought, was perfect. This would allow him to live in the nearby village with the other skilled workers rather than at home with his angry older brother. This would allow him to make up for the money he lost without having to ask for anyone's help. This would allow him to put all his problems behind him without really asking for forgiveness. If only he could convince his father to trust him one more time.

And so Jacob set off. As he approached his hometown, he was famished and exhausted; he had been walking for days. And his anxiety increased as he anticipated a gauntlet of rejection from the villagers. He expected that he'd have to endure the ceremony of excommunication. He was certain he'd have to sit outside his family home, maybe for a very long time, until being summoned by his father. He was beginning to doubt whether this plan of his would work and whether he was willing to pay the price.

But what Jacob saw as he approached his hometown he could not believe. His eyes were deceiving him, he thought. This was an illusion. We saw it, too, those of us working on the edge of town that dreary day, and didn't believe it either. Nothing like this had ever happened before. This was incredible! But our eyes were not deceived. There was the master, Jacob's father, running — in fact, racing — toward Jacob as fast as his aged legs could carry him. In our town, no man his age, certainly not the master, runs anywhere. It's undignified. And among my clan, the head of the household goes out to no one: that, too, is unbecoming. People come to him. On top of that, my master had hitched up his robe in order to run better, thus showing his legs. This was most humiliating and shameful!

The only explanation I could think of for such public humiliation was that this running father was filled with compassion for his homeless son. And so it was that when the running father met his stunned son, he embraced him and kissed him again and again. Somehow, my master had a hunch that his long-lost son was returning home, and fearing the ridicule and rejection his son would face from the villagers as he entered town, he was filled with compassion. So he violated all the social conventions, and he ran out to greet him to save him from the scorn and rejection. It was an unprecedented homecoming for a son who was thought lost and most likely dead.

What happened next exceeded our already astonished imaginations. Jacob, finally freeing himself from his father's bear hug, fell down at his feet and began the speech he had memorized while walking those many miles home: "Father, I have sinned against heaven and before you. I am no longer worthy to be called your son." But he could not finish. For, through his tears, he finally saw what his pride had so long blinded him from seeing: his father's suffering and his father's great love. The young man's scheme dried up like a drop of sweat in the desert, and genuine remorse filled his aching heart. Overwhelmed by the outpouring of his father's love, Jacob abandoned his plan and simply threw himself at the mercy of his father. At long last he acknowledged being lost and he accepted being found.

By then, most of the town was gawking in amazement. The master's house servants, friends of mine, had finally caught up with him, and as they were catching their breath, he told them, "Bring out the best robe, and put it on him, and put a ring on his finger and shoes on his feet." So Simon ran back to the main house and got the most elegant and beautiful robe and put it on Jacob. Meanwhile, Samuel ran back and fetched the family signet ring and a pair of fancy shoes and put those on Jacob as well. It was very clear to us that this lost boy was no outcast, no untrustworthy servant, no slave. He was a son — a beloved son. And because his father had accepted him, so did we. He was home. Home at last.

Then the master told us to stop work and start the party. Kill the fatted calf, cook that prime veal, break out the best wine, and celebrate, the master told us, "because this son of mine was dead and is alive; he was lost and is found." So party we did. It was glorious. A fitting end to a most unusual day. Except for one thing: I noticed that Jacob's older brother, Levi, wasn't there. Why wasn't he at the party? But I already knew the answer. After a while I noticed that Levi's father was also missing.

I set out for the field where Levi had been supervising field workers earlier in the day. On the path to the field, quite near the house, I came upon Levi and his father locked in a heated argument. Levi had apparently heard the music and singing and started toward the house. He had asked one of the young boys who were milling around near the house what was going on. He didn't remember any party planned for this night.

"Your brother has appeared," the boy blurted out, "and your father has killed the fatted calf, because he has received him with shalom." The boys then excitedly told Levi the whole story as they had heard it from the villagers.

"My brother?" Levi spit out loud. What brother would that be? He had no brother. He had assumed — he had hoped — his father's younger son was dead. But somehow he had showed up again? How could that be? Impossible! "And the fatted calf has been slaughtered?" he repeated aloud to himself. Butchering the fatted calf meant a great celebration was in the making. For this? Impossible! And worst of all, "My father has reconciled with this scoundrel of a son? Is eating with him? How can there be shalom?" he murmured under his breath. Impossible!

"Where are my rights!"? I heard Levi exclaim to his father as I stood silently along the path. "For all these years I have worked like a slave for you. I have been faithful. I have never disobeyed your command. And yet you have never given me even a scrawny young goat so that I might party with my friends. This is not fair!" He paused briefly to catch his breath, veins bulging from his neck, anger reddening his ears, his black eyes glaring at his father.

"But when this son of yours comes back, the one who squandered your property with prostitutes, you kill the fatted calf for him? This is not right! I refuse to go in!" He screamed it with all the passion in him. The partygoers inside the main house heard it over the music and singing. Some of them came outside to see what all the ruckus was about. What would happen now? This was a most serious personal insult to the guests, and especially to the father, because all male family members of the host were expected at a party to greet all the guests, and the oldest son was expected to serve as headwaiter. Now this full-blown dispute was in full view of the entire village. There could be no private rebuke for this public insult.

We waited to see how the father would respond, expecting the usual. For this flagrant public rebellion the older son would be promptly and severely punished. But I wasn't so sure. I had seen the agony on my master's face when Jacob left home. I had witnessed the most unusual events earlier this day. I had watched in amazement as this running father greeted his lost son and embraced him with compassion. I was now present for this confrontation with his older son, and it did not escape me that this father who had taken the initiative to meet his younger son had now gone out to meet his older son. Twice in one day he had violated established social customs by going out to meet an estranged family member. What would happen this time?

We watched, in shock, as this father, already humiliated by having to leave his guests in the house, now further humiliated himself by publicly pleading with his petulant son to come in to the party. This father, already enduring the shame of a public dispute, entreated his older son to be reconciled — to him and to his brother. This father, out of the depths of his deep love, beseeched his son to participate in his offer of shalom. In response to his son's anger, envy, and pride, the father firmly but gently spoke: "My dear son, you are always with me, and all that is mine is yours. We *had* to celebrate and rejoice, because this brother of yours was dead and has come to life; he was lost and has been found." Once again, we couldn't believe our eyes and ears. Grace, pure grace, for both rebellious sons. Then the final question: would the older son accept it? Would he, like his younger brother, acknowledge being lost and accept being found?

I am old now, but I remember that day like it was yesterday. Every detail of those scenes is clearly etched in my mind's eye, and I remember each spoken word. I will never forget the running, compassionate father and his two lost sons. I will never forget the depth of this father's love or the breadth of his mercy. As long as I live, I will never forget this gracious homemaker. From isolation to intimacy, from stranger to family member, from exile to home.

Bibliography

1. The Nature of Home

Abbey, Edward. *The Journey Home*. New York: Plume, 1991.

Abram, David. *The Spell of the Sensuous: Perception and Language in a More-than-Human World*. New York: Vintage, 1996.

Agnew, John, and James Duncan, eds. *The Power of Place: Bringing Together Geographic and Sociological Imaginations*. Boston: Unwin Hyman, 1989.

Altman, Irwin, and Carol Werner, eds. *Home Environments*. New York: Plenum, 1985.

Bakken, Peter. *Finding the Center of the World*. North Liberty, IA: Harvest Books, 2003.

Berger, Peter. *The Sacred Canopy*. Garden City, NY: Anchor Books, 1967.

Berry, Wendell. *Another Turn of the Crank*. Washington, DC: Counterpoint, 1995.

———. *Home Economics*. New York: North Point, 1987.

———. *Jayber Crow*. Washington, DC: Counterpoint, 2000.

———. *Remembering*. San Francisco: North Point, 1988.

———. *Sabbaths*. San Francisco: North Point, 1987.

Bonner, Barbara, ed. *Sacred Ground: Writings about Home*. Minneapolis: Milkweed, 1996.

Bouma-Prediger, Steven, and Brian Walsh. "Education for Homelessness or Home-making: The Christian College in a Postmodern Culture." *Christian Scholar's Review* 32, no. 3 (Spring 2003): 281-95.

———. "Response: If It Ain't Broke, Don't Fix It: A Reply to Robin Klay and John Lunn." *Christian Scholar's Review* 33, no. 4 (Summer 2004): 443-50.

Buechner, Frederick. *The Longing for Home*. San Francisco: HarperCollins, 1996.

Casey, Edward. *The Fate of Place: A Philosophical History*. Berkeley: University of California Press, 1997.

———. *Getting Back Into Place: Toward a Renewed Understanding of the Place-World*. Bloomington, IN: Indiana University Press, 1993.

Chapman, Tony, and Jenny Hockey, eds. *Ideal Homes? Social Change and Domestic Life*. London and New York: Routledge, 1992.

Bibliography

Douglas, Mary. *Purity and Danger.* London: Routledge and Kegan Paul, 1966.

Duncan, James, and David Ley, eds. *Place/Culture/Representation.* London: Routledge, 1993.

Durning, Alan. *This Place on Earth: Home and the Practice of Permanence.* Seattle: Sasquatch Books, 1996.

Eliade, Mircea. *The Sacred and the Profane.* New York: Harcourt, Brace and World, 1959.

Erickson, Joyce Quiring. "On Being at Home." *Cross Currents* 43, no. 2 (Summer 1993): 235-46.

Feld, Steven, and Keith Basso, eds. *Senses of Place.* Santa Fe, NM: School of American Research Press, 1996.

Fiffer, Steve, and Sharon Sloan, eds. *Home: American Writers Remember Rooms of Their Own.* New York: Vintage, 1995.

Heidegger, Martin. *Basic Writings.* Edited by David Krell. New York: Harper & Row, 1977.

Hiss, Tony. *The Experience of Place.* New York: Vintage, 1990.

Illich, Ivan. "Dwelling." *Co-evolution Quarterly* 41 (Spring 1984).

Jackson, John Brinckerhoff. *Discovering the Vernacular Landscape.* New Haven, CT: Yale University Press, 1984.

———. *The Necessity of Ruins.* Amherst: University of Massachusetts Press, 1980.

———. *A Sense of Place, A Sense of Time.* New Haven, CT: Yale University Press, 1994.

Jackson, Wes. *Becoming Native to This Place.* Washington, DC: Counterpoint, 1996.

Keillor, Garrison. *Leaving Home.* New York: Penguin, 1997.

Kingsolver, Barbara. *Animal Dreams.* New York: HarperCollins, 1990.

Kron, Joan. *Home-Psych: The Social Psychology of Home and Decoration.* New York: Potter, 1983.

Lane, Belden. *Landscapes of the Sacred: Geography and Narrative in American Spirituality.* New York: Paulist, 1988.

———. *The Solace of Fierce Landscapes: Exploring Desert and Mountain Spirituality.* New York: Oxford University Press, 1998.

Pearlman, Mickey, ed. *A Place Called Home: Twenty Writing Women Remember.* New York: St. Martin's, 1997.

Rapoport, Amos. *House Form and Culture.* Englewood Cliffs, NJ: Prentice-Hall, 1969.

Relph, E. *Place and Placelessness.* London: Pion, 1976.

Rouner, Leroy. *To Be at Home.* Boston: Beacon, 1991.

———. *The Longing for Home.* Notre Dame: University of Notre Dame Press, 1996.

Rybczynski, Witold. *Home: A Short History of an Idea.* New York: Penguin, 1987.

Said, Edward, "Reflections on Exile." In *Out There: Marginalization and Contemporary Cultures,* edited by Russell Ferguson et al. Cambridge, MA: MIT Press, 1990.

Saile, David. "The Ritual Establishment of Home." In *Home Environments,* edited by I. Altman and C. Werner. New York: Plenum, 1985.

Sanders, Scott Russell. *Hunting for Hope.* Boston: Beacon, 1998.

———. *Staying Put: Making a Home in a Restless World.* Boston: Beacon, 1993.

Tall, Deborah. "Dwelling: Making Peace with Space and Place." In *Rooted in the Land,* edited by William Vitek and Wes Jackson. New Haven: Yale University Press, 1996.

Tournier, Paul. *A Place for You.* New York: Harper and Row, 1968.

Tuan, Yi-Fu. *Space and Place.* Minneapolis: University of Minnesota Press, 1977.

————. *Topophilia: A Study of Environmental Perception, Attitudes, and Values.* New York: Columbia University Press, 1990.

Turner, Victor. *The Ritual Process.* Chicago: Aldine Publishing Co., 1969.

Vitek, William, and Wes Jackson, eds. *Rooted in the Land: Essays on Community and Place.* New Haven: Yale University Press, 1996.

Walsh, Mary. *"Moving to Nowhere": Children's Stories of Homelessness.* New York: Auburn House, 1992.

Weil, Simone. *The Need for Roots.* London: Routledge and Kegan Paul, 1952.

Westerhoff, Caroline. *Good Fences: The Boundaries of Hospitality.* Boston: Cowley, 1999.

Wiesel, Elie. "Longing for Home." In *The Longing for Home,* edited by Leroy S. Rouner. Notre Dame: University of Notre Dame Press, 1996.

Williams, Terry Tempest. *Refuge: The Unnatural History of Family and Place.* New York: Vintage, 1991.

Winquist, Charles. *Homecoming: Interpretation, Transformation and Individuation.* AAR Studies in Religion 18. Missoula, MT: Scholars Press, 1978.

2. Economics, Housing, and Homemaking

Alston, Phillip. "Hardship in the Midst of Plenty." In *The Progress of Nations 1998 — Industrialized Countries: Commentary.* Geneva: UNICEF, 1998.

Applebaum, Richard. "The Affordability Gap." *Society* 26 (May-June 1989).

Bell, Daniel. *The Cultural Contradictions of Capitalism.* 2nd ed. London: Heineman, 1979.

Berger, Thomas. *Northern Frontier/Northern Homeland: Report of the Mackenzie Valley Pipeline Inquiry.* Ottawa: Supply and Services Canada, 1977.

Boyle, Nicholas. *Where Are We Now? Christian Humanism and the Global Market: From Hegel to Heaney.* Edinburgh: T&T Clark, 1998.

Burt, Martha, et al. *Helping America's Homeless.* Washington, DC: The Urban Institute, 2001.

Caton, Carol L. M., ed. *Homeless in America.* New York: Oxford University Press, 1990.

Daly, Gerald. *Homeless: Policies, Strategies and Lives on the Street.* London: Routledge, 1996.

Daly, Herman, and John Cobb. *For the Common Good: Redirecting the Economy Toward Community, the Environment, and a Sustainable Future.* Boston: Beacon, 1989.

Davidson, Alexander. *A Home of One's Own: Housing Policy in Sweden and New Zealand from the 1840s to the 1990s.* Stockholm: Almqvist & Wiksell International, 1994.

Bibliography

Della Costa, John. "Outsourcing, Downsizing, Mergers and Cutbacks: Folks Are Living with a Creeping Sense of Homelessness." *Catholic New Times* (May 3, 1998).

Dovey, Kimberly. "Home and Homelessness." In *Home Environments,* edited by I. Altman and C. Werner. New York: Plenum, 1985.

Engelstad, Diane, and John Bird, eds. *Nation to Nation: Aboriginal Sovereignty and the Future of Canada.* Toronto: Anansi Press, 1992.

Esber, George S., Jr. "Designing Apache Homes with Apaches." In *Anthropological Praxis: Translating Knowledge into Action,* edited by Robert M. Wuff and Shirley J. Fiske. Boulder and London: Westview Press, 1987.

Franco, Robert, and Simeamativa Mageo Aga. "From Houses without Walls to Vertical Villages: Samoan Housing Transformations." In *Home in the Islands: Housing and Social Change in the Pacific.* Honolulu: University of Hawaii Press, 1997.

Fuller, Millard. *A Simple, Decent Place to Live: The Building Realization of Habitat for Humanity.* Dallas: Word, 1995.

Giamo, B., and J. Grunberg, *Beyond Homelessness: Frames of Reference.* Iowa City, IA: University of Iowa Press, 1992.

Glasser, Irene. *Homelessness in Global Perspective.* New York: Macmillan, 1994.

Gornik, Mark R. *To Live in Peace: Biblical Faith and the Inner City.* Grand Rapids: Eerdmans, 2002.

Goudzwaard, Bob. *Aid for the Overdeveloped West.* Toronto: Wedge Publishing, 1975.

———. *Capitalism and Progress: A Diagnosis of Western Society.* Translated by Josina Van Nuis Zylstra. Grand Rapids: Eerdmans, 1979.

———. "Globalization, Exclusion, Enslavement." *Reformed World* 46, no. 3 (September 1996).

———. *Globalization and the Kingdom of God.* Grand Rapids: Baker, 2001.

Goudzwaard, Bob, and Leo Andringa. *Globalization and Christian Hope.* Toronto: Public Justice Resource Centre, 2003.

Goudzwaard, Bob, and Harry de Lange. *Beyond Poverty and Affluence: Toward an Economy of Care.* Grand Rapids: Eerdmans, 1995.

Hall, Peter. *Cities of Tomorrow.* Oxford: Blackwell, 1988.

Hallowell, A. Irving. "Ojibwa Ontology, Behavior and World View." In *Culture in History,* edited by S. Diamond. New York: Columbia University Press, 1960.

Harries, Karsten. *The Ethical Function of Architecture.* Cambridge, MA: MIT Press, 1998.

Hawken, Paul, Amory Lovins, and L. Hunter Lovins. *Natural Capitalism.* Boston: Little, Brown and Co., 1999.

Hepworth, Mike. "Privacy, Security and Respectability: The Ideal Victorian Home." In *Ideal Homes? Social Change and Domestic Life,* edited by Tony Chapman and Jenny Hockey. London: Routledge, 1999.

Jacobsen, Eric O. *Sidewalks in the Kingdom: New Urbanism and Christian Faith.* Grand Rapids: Brazos Press, 2003.

Jencks, Christopher. *The Homeless.* Cambridge, MA: Harvard University Press, 1994.

Joint Center for Housing Studies. *The State of the Nation's Housing, 2003*. Boston: Harvard University Press, 2003.

Kane, Hal. *The Hour of Departure: Forces that Create Refugees and Migrants.* Worldwatch Paper 125. Washington, DC: Worldwatch Institute, 1995.

Klein, Naomi. *No Logo: Taking Aim at the Brand Bullies.* Toronto: Random House, 2000.

Korton, David. *When Corporations Rule the World.* 2nd edition. Bloomfield, CT: Kumarian, 2001.

Layton, Jack. *Homelessness: The Making and Unmaking of a Crisis.* Toronto: Penguin, 2000.

Loring, Ed. "Housing Comes First." *The Other Side* (May/June 2002): 32-33.

Macpherson, Cluny. "A Samoan Solution to the Limitations of Urban Housing in New Zealand." In *Home in the Islands: Housing and Social Change in the Pacific,* edited by Jan Rensel and Margaret Rodman. Honolulu: University of Hawaii Press, 1997.

Mayor's Homelessness Taskforce. *Taking Responsibility for Homelessness: An Action Plan for Toronto.* Toronto: Municipal Government, 1999. [Also known as the "Golden Report," after Anne Golden, its chief author.]

McKay, Stan. "Calling Creation into Our Family." In *Nation to Nation: Aboriginal Sovereignty and the Future of Canada,* edited by Diane Engelstad and John Bird. Toronto: Anansi Press, 1992.

McQuaig, Linda. *The Culture of Impotence: Selling the Myth of Powerlessness in the Global Economy.* Toronto: Penguin, 1999.

Modell, Judith. "(Not) In My Back Yard: Housing the Homeless in Hawaii." In *Home in the Islands: Housing and Social Change in the Pacific,* edited by Jan Rensel and Margaret Rodman. Honolulu: University of Hawaii Press, 1997.

Naugle, David K. *Worldview: The History of a Concept.* Grand Rapids: Eerdmans, 2002.

Olthuis, James H. "On Worldviews." *Christian Scholar's Review* 14, no. 2 (1985).

Orr, David. *The Nature of Design: Ecology, Culture and Human Intention.* New York: Oxford University Press, 2002.

Overholt, Thomas W., and J. Baird Callicott. *Clothed in Fur and Other Tales: An Introduction to an Ojibwa World View.* Washington, DC: University Press of America, 1982.

Paul, Greg. *God in the Alley: Being and Seeing Jesus in a Broken World.* Colorado Springs: WaterBrook Press, 2004.

Porteous, J. Douglas, and Sandra Smith. *Domicide: The Global Destruction of Home.* Montreal and Kingston: McGill-Queen's University Press, 2001.

Rensel, Jan, and Margaret Rodman, eds. *Home in the Islands: Housing and Social Change in the Pacific.* Honolulu: University of Hawaii Press, 1997.

Riciutti, Anthony. "The Economics of the Way: Jubilee Practice Among the Early Christians According to the Acts of the Apostles." M.Phil.F. thesis, Institute for Christian Studies, Toronto, 2001.

Rossi, Peter. *Down and Out in America: The Origins of Homelessness.* Chicago: University of Chicago Press, 1989.

Ruddick, Susan. *Young and Homeless in Hollywood: Mapping Social Identities*. New York: Routledge, 1996.

Saegert, Susan. "The Role of Housing in the Experience of Dwelling." In *Home Environments*, edited by I. Altman and C. Werner. New York: Plenum Books, 1985.

Sassen, Saskia. *Globalization and Its Discontents: Essays on the New Mobility of People and Money*. New York: New Press, 1998.

Scott, James C. *Seeing Like a State: How Certain Schemes to Improve the Human Condition Have Failed*. New Haven: Yale University Press, 1998.

Sewell, John. *Houses and Homes: Housing for Canadians*. Toronto: Lorimer, 1994.

Shkilnyk, Anastasia M. *A Poison Stronger than Love: The Destruction of an Ojibwa Community*. New Haven: Yale University Press, 1985.

Sider, Ron. *Just Generosity: A New Vision for Overcoming Poverty in America*. Grand Rapids: Baker, 1999.

Sine, Tom. *Mustard Seed Versus McWorld: Reinventing Life and Faith for the Future*. Grand Rapids: Baker, 1999.

State of Emergency Declaration: An Urgent Call for Emergency Humanitarian Relief and Prevention Measures. Toronto Disaster Relief Committee, 1998.

Stiglitz, Joseph. *Globalization and Its Discontents*. New York: W. W. Norton, 2002.

Timmer, Doug, Stanley Eitzen, and Kathryn Talley. *Paths to Homelessness: Extreme Poverty and the Urban Crisis*. Boulder, CO: Westview, 1994.

The Toronto Report Card on Homelessness 2003. Toronto: Municipal Government, 2003.

Vandezande, Gerald. *Justice, Not Just Us: Faith Perspectives and National Priorities*. Toronto: Public Justice Resource Centre, 1999.

Wallace, Iain. "Globalization: Discourse of Destiny or Denial?" *Christian Scholar's Review* 31, no. 4 (Summer 2002).

Wallis, Jim. *God's Politics*. New York: HarperCollins, 2005.

Walzer, Michael. *Interpretation and Social Criticism*. Cambridge, MA: Harvard University Press, 1987.

Ward, Jim. *Organizing for the Homeless*. Ottawa: Canada Council on Social Development, 1989.

Webber, Marlene. *Street Kids: The Tragedy of Canada's Runaways*. Toronto: University of Toronto Press, 1991.

Young, David, Grant Ingram, and Lise Swartz, *Cry of the Eagle: Encounters with a Cree Healer*. Toronto: University of Toronto Press, 1989.

3. Ecology, the Home Planet, and Earthkeeping

Andruss, Van, Christopher Plant, Judith Plant, and Eleanor Wright, eds. *Home! A Bioregional Reader*. Philadelphia: New Society, 1990.

Barnhill, David Landis, ed. *At Home on the Earth: Becoming Native to Our Place*. Berkeley: University of California Press, 1999.

Beatley, Timothy, and Kristy Manning. *The Ecology of Place: Planning for Environment, Economy, and Community.* Washington, DC: Island Press, 1997.

Berry, Thomas. *The Dream of the Earth.* San Francisco: Sierra Club, 1988.

Berry, Wendell. *Citizenship Papers.* Washington, DC: Shoemaker & Hoard, 2003.

———. *The Gift of Good Land.* New York: North Point Press, 1981.

———. *Sex, Economy, Freedom and Community.* New York: Pantheon, 1993.

———. *The Unsettling of America: Culture and Agriculture.* San Francisco: Sierra Club, 1977.

Bouma-Prediger, Steven. *For the Beauty of the Earth: A Christian Vision for Creation Care.* Grand Rapids: Baker Academic, 2001.

———. "Poor and Oppressed Unite." In *Handbook of U.S. Theologies of Liberation,* edited by Miguel de la Torre. St. Louis: Chalice, 2004.

Brown, Lester. *Eco-Economy: Building an Economy for the Earth.* New York: W. W. Norton, 2001.

Brueggemann, Walter. *Living Toward a Vision.* Philadelphia: United Church Press, 1982.

Bratton, Susan Power. *Six Billion and More: Human Population Regulation and Christian Ethics.* Louisville: Westminster/John Knox, 1992.

Caplan, Robert. *The Ends of the Earth: A Journey to the Frontiers of Anarchy.* New York: Random House, 1996.

Costanza, Robert, et al. "The Value of the World's Ecosystem Services and Natural Capital." *Nature* (May 15, 1997).

Daily, Gretchen, ed. *Nature's Services: Societal Dependence on Natural Ecosystems.* Washington, DC: Island Press, 1997.

Daily, Gretchen, and Katherine Ellison. *The New Economy of Nature: The Quest to Make Conservation Profitable.* Washington, DC: Island Press, 2002.

DeGraaf, John, David Wann, and Thomas Naylor. *Affluenza: The All-Consuming Epidemic.* San Francisco: Berrett-Koehler, 2001.

DeWitt, Calvin. "Biogeographic and Trophic Restructuring of the Biosphere: The State of the Earth under Human Domination. *Christian Scholars' Review* 32, no. 4 (Summer 2003).

———, ed. *The Environment and the Christian: What Can We Learn from the New Testament?* Grand Rapids: Baker, 1991.

Dillard, Annie. *Pilgrim at Tinker Creek.* New York: Perennial Classics, 1998.

Dunlap, Riley, George Gallup, Jr., and Alex Gallup. *Health of the Planet.* Princeton, NJ: George Gallup International Institute, 1993.

Durning, Alan. *How Much Is Enough? The Consumer Society and the Future of the Earth.* New York: W. W. Norton, 1992.

Flavin, Christopher. "The Legacy of Rio." *State of the World 1997.* New York: W. W. Norton, 1997.

Grandberg-Michaelson, Wesley. *Ecology and Life.* Waco: Word, 1988.

Hansen, James, et al. "Surface Temperature Analysis: If There's Global Warming, Why Am I Freezing My Buns Off?" NASA Goddard Institute for Space Studies: available at www.giss.nasa.gov/data/update/gistemp/Januaries.

Hauerwas, Stanley. *Character and the Christian Life*. San Antonio, TX: Trinity University, 1985.

————. *Truthfulness and Tragedy*. Notre Dame: University of Notre Dame Press, 1977.

————. *Vision and Virtue*. Notre Dame: Fides Publications, 1974.

Hauerwas, Stanley, and L. Gregory Jones, eds. *Why Narrative? Readings in Narrative Theology*. Grand Rapids: Eerdmans, 1989.

Hertsgaard, Mark. *Earth Odyssey: Around the World in Search of Our Environmental Future*. New York: Broadway Books, 1998.

Jacobson, Jodi. *Environmental Refugees: A Yardstick of Habitability*. Worldwatch Paper 86. Washington, DC: Worldwatch Institute, 1988.

Kaplan, Robert. "The Coming Anarchy." *Atlantic Monthly* (February 1994).

————. *The Ends of the Earth: A Journey to the Frontiers of Anarchy*. New York: Vintage, 1996.

Kelly, Kevin, ed. *The Home Planet*. Reading, MA: Addison-Wesley, 1988.

Kingsolver, Barbara. *Small Wonder*. New York: HarperCollins, 2002.

Kohac, Erazim. *The Embers and the Stars: A Philosophical Inquiry into the Moral Sense of Nature*. Chicago: University of Chicago Press, 1984.

Lebacqz, Karen. *Six Theories of Justice*. Minneapolis: Augsburg, 1986.

Leopold, Aldo. *Sand County Almanac*. New York: Ballantine, 1966.

Lewis, C. S. *The Magician's Nephew*. New York: Macmillan, 1978.

Lynas, Mark. *High Tide: The Truth about Our Climate Crisis*. New York: Picador, 2004.

McDonough, William, and Michael Braungart. *Cradle to Cradle: Remaking the Way We Make Things*. New York: North Point, 2002.

McFague, Sallie. *The Body of God: An Ecological Theology*. Minneapolis: Fortress, 1993.

McKibben, Bill. *The Comforting Whirlwind*. Grand Rapids: Eerdmans, 1994.

————. *The End of Nature*. New York: Doubleday, 1989.

————. *Hope, Human and Wild*. Boston: Little, Brown, 1995.

McNeill, J. R. *Something New Under the Sun: An Environmental History of the Twentieth Century World*. New York: W. W. Norton, 2000.

Meilaender, Gilbert. *The Theory and Practice of Virtue*. Notre Dame: University of Notre Dame Press, 1984.

————. "Virtue in Contemporary Religious Thought." In *Virtue — Public and Private*, edited by Richard John Neuhaus. Grand Rapids: Eerdmans, 1986.

Menzel, Peter. *Material World: A Global Family Portrait*. San Francisco: Sierra Club, 1994.

Nash, James. *Loving Nature: Ecological Integrity and Christian Responsibility*. Nashville: Abingdon, 1991.

Nevel, Bernard, and Richard Wright. *Environmental Science*. 8th edition. Upper Saddle River, NJ: Prentice Hall, 2002.

Nisbet, E. G. *Leaving Eden: To Protect and Manage the Earth*. Cambridge, UK: Cambridge University Press, 1991.

Nuland, Sherwin. *How We Die*. New York: Vintage, 1993.

Oelschlaeger, Max. *Caring for Creation*. New Haven: Yale University Press, 1994.

Orr, David. *Earth in Mind: On Education, Environment, and the Human Prospect.* Washington, DC: Island Press, 1994.

―――. *Ecological Literacy: Education and the Transition to a Postmodern World.* Albany: SUNY Press, 1992.

Pimm, Stuart. *The World According to Pimm: A Scientist Audits the Earth.* New York: McGraw-Hill, 2001.

Plantinga, Cornelius, Jr. *Not the Way It's Supposed to Be.* Grand Rapids: Eerdmans, 1994.

Postman, Neil. *Technopoly: The Surrender of Culture to Technology.* New York: Vintage, 1993.

Ricoeur, Paul. *Time and Narrative,* vols. 1-3. Chicago: University of Chicago Press, 1990.

Rolston, Holmes, III. *Conserving Natural Value.* New York: Columbia University Press, 1994.

―――. *Environmental Ethics.* Philadelphia: Temple University Press, 1988.

Ryan, John, and Alan Durning. *Stuff: The Secret Lives of Everyday Things.* Seattle: Northwest Environment Watch, 1997.

Santmire, H. Paul. *Nature Reborn: The Ecological and Cosmic Promise of Christian Theology.* Minneapolis: Fortress, 2000.

―――. "Partnership with Nature According to the Scriptures, Beyond the Theology of Stewardship." *Christian Scholar's Review* 32, no. 4 (Summer 2003).

―――. *The Travail of Nature: The Ambiguous Ecological Promise of Christian Theology.* Philadelphia: Fortress, 1985.

Sheldon, Joseph, and David Foster. "What Knowledge Is Required for Responsible Stewardship of Creation?" *Christian Scholar's Review* 32, no. 4 (Summer 2003).

Smedes, Lewis. *Choices: Making Right Decisions in a Complex World.* San Francisco: Harper and Row, 1986.

―――. *A Pretty Good Person.* San Francisco: Harper and Row, 1990.

Speth, James. *Red Sky at Morning: America and the Crisis of the Global Environment.* New Haven: Yale University Press, 2004.

Vitousek, Peter, et al. "Human Domination of Earth's Ecosystems." *Science* 277 (1997).

Wackernagel, Mathis, and William Rees. *Our Ecological Footprint.* Gabriola Island, BC: New Society, 1996.

Walsh, Brian J., Marianne Karsh, and Nik Ansell. "Trees, Forestry and the Responsiveness of Creation." *Cross Currents* 44, no. 2 (Summer 1994).

Westphal, Merold. "Existentialism and Environmental Ethics." In *The Environmental Crisis,* edited by Edwin Squiers. Mancelona, MI: AuSable, 1982.

Westra, Laura. *The Principle of Integrity: An Environmental Proposal for Ethics.* Lanham, MD: Rowman and Littlefield, 1994.

Wilkinson, Loren. "Pilgrims at Home: The Mutual Challenge of Christendom and Environmental Literature." *Christian Scholar's Review* 32, no. 4 (Summer 2003).

Williams, George. *Wilderness and Paradise in Christian Thought.* New York: Harper and Brothers, 1962.

Wilson, Edward. *Biophilia.* Cambridge, MA: Harvard University Press, 1984.

Wirzba, Norman. *The Paradise of God: Renewing Religion in an Ecological Age*. Oxford: Oxford University Press, 2003.

Wirzba, Norman, ed. *The Art of the Commonplace: The Agrarian Essays of Wendell Berry*. Washington, DC: Counterpoint, 2002.

Wolterstorff, Nicholas. *Educating for Life*. Grand Rapids: Brazos, 2002.

———. *Educating for Shalom*. Grand Rapids: Eerdmans, 2004.

World Development Report 2003. Washington, DC: World Bank, 2003.

4. Postmodernity, Identity, and Sojourning

Anderson, Benedict. *Imagined Communities*. London: Verso, 1983.

Anderson, Walter Truett. *Reality Isn't What It Used to Be*. San Francisco: HarperCollins, 1990.

———, ed. *The Truth about Truth: De-confusing and Re-constructing the Postmodern World*. New York: Putnam, 1995.

Avram, Wes, ed. *Anxious about Empire: Theological Essays on New Global Realities*. Grand Rapids: Brazos Press, 2004.

Bammer, Angelika, ed. *Displacements: Cultural Identities in Question*. Bloomington, IN: Indiana University Press, 1994.

Bauman, Zygmunt. *Modernity and Ambivalence*. Ithaca: Cornell University Press, 1991.

———. *Postmodern Ethics*. Oxford: Blackwell, 1993.

Bellah, Robert, et al. *Habits of the Heart: Individualism and Commitment in American Life*. Berkeley: University of California Press, 1985.

Berger, John. *And Our Faces, My Heart, Brief as Photos*. New York: Vintage, 1991.

Berger, Peter, Brigitte Berger, and Hansfield Kellner. *The Homeless Mind*. New York: Vintage, 1974.

Berger, Peter, and Thomas Luckman. *The Social Construction of Knowledge: A Treatise on the Sociology of Knowledge*. Garden City, NY: Doubleday, 1966.

Berman, Marshall. *All That Is Solid Melts Into Air*. New York: Simon and Schuster, 1982.

Bernstein, Richard. *The New Constellation: The Ethical-Political Horizons of Modernity/ Postmodernity*. Cambridge, MA: MIT Press, 1992.

Borgmann, Albert. *Crossing the Postmodern Divide*. Chicago: University of Chicago Press, 1992.

———. *Power Failure: Christianity and the Culture of Technology*. Grand Rapids: Brazos, 2003.

Bourdieu, Pierre. *Outline of a Theory of Practice*. Cambridge, UK: Cambridge University Press, 1977.

Bourdieu, Pierre, and Loic J. D. Wacquant. *An Invitation to Reflexive Sociology*. Chicago: University of Chicago Press, 1992.

Bulkin, Emily, Minnie Bruce Pratt, and Barbara Smith. *Yours in the Struggle: Three Feminist Perspectives on Anti-Semitism and Racism*. New York: Long Haul Press, 1984.

Caputo, John. *Against Ethics.* Bloomington, IN: Indiana University Press, 1993.

————. *Radical Hermeneutics: Repetition, Deconstruction, and the Hermeneutic Project.* Bloomington, IN: Indiana University Press, 1987.

Carter, Paul. *Living in a New Country: History, Traveling and Language.* London: Faber & Faber, 1992.

Chambers, Iain. *Migrancy, Culture, Identity.* London: Routledge, 1994.

Chatwin, Bruce. *The Songlines.* New York: Viking, 1987.

Clapp, Rodney. *Border Crossings: Christian Trespasses on Popular Culture and Public Affairs.* Grand Rapids: Brazos Press, 2000.

Coupland, Douglas. *Life After God.* New York and London: Pocket Books, 1994.

Friedman, Susan Stanford. "Bodies in Motion: A Poetics of Home and Diaspora." *Tulsa Studies in Women's Literature* 23, no. 2 (Fall 2004).

Gare, Arran. *Postmodernism and the Environmental Crisis.* London: Routledge, 1995.

Gass, William. "The Philosophical Significance of Exile" (interview with Nuruddin Farah, Han Vladislave, and Jorge Edwards). In *Literature in Exile,* edited by John Gladd. Durham, NC: Duke University Press, 1990.

Geertz, Clifford. *The Interpretation of Cultures.* New York: Basic Books, 1973.

George, Rosemary. *The Politics of Home: Postcolonial Relocations and Twentieth-Century Fiction.* Cambridge, UK: Cambridge University Press, 1996.

Gergen, Kenneth. *The Saturated Self: Dilemmas of Identity in Contemporary Life.* San Francisco: HarperCollins, 1991.

Giroux, Henri. *Border Crossings: Cultural Workers and the Politics of Education.* London: Routledge, 1992.

Grenz, Stanley. *A Primer on Postmodernism.* Grand Rapids: Eerdmans, 1996.

Griffioen, Sander, and Richard Mouw. *Pluralisms and Horizons: An Essay in Christian Public Philosophy.* Grand Rapids: Eerdmans, 1993.

Hall, Stuart. "Minimal Selves." In *Identity, the Real Me: Postmodernism and the Question of Identity,* edited by L. Appigananesi. London: ICA, 1987.

Harvey, David. *The Condition of Postmodernity: An Inquiry into the Origins of Cultural Change.* Oxford: Basil Blackwell, 1989.

Hauerwas, Stanley. "The Christian Difference: Or Surviving Postmodernism." In *Anabaptists and Postmodernity,* edited by Susan and Gerald Biesecker-Mast. Telford, PA: Pandora Press, 2000.

Haughton, Rosemary. "Hospitality: Home as the Integration of Privacy and Community." In *The Longing for Home,* edited by Leroy Rouner. Notre Dame, IN: University of Notre Dame Press, 1996.

Havel, Václav. *Living in Truth.* London: Faber and Faber, 1986.

Heilbroner, Robert. *An Inquiry into the Human Prospect.* New York: W. W. Norton, 1974.

Hutcheon, Linda. *The Politics of Postmodernism.* London: Routledge, 1989.

Kaplan, Caren. "Deterritorializations: The Rewriting of Home and Exile in Western Feminist Discourse." *Cultural Critique* 6 (Spring 1987).

Kirn, Walter. *Up in the Air.* New York: Doubleday, 2001.

Kunstler, James Howard. *The Geography of Nowhere: The Rise and Decline of America's Man-Made Landscape.* New York: Simon and Schuster, 1993.

———. *Home from Nowhere: Remaking Our Everyday World for the 21st Century.* New York: Simon and Schuster, 1996.

Lakeland, Paul. *Postmodernity: Christian Identity in a Fragmented Age.* Minneapolis: Fortress, 1997.

Lapham, Lewis H. "Who and What Is American?" *Harper's* (January 1992).

Leach, William. *Country of Exiles: The Destruction of Place in American Life.* New York: Pantheon, 1999.

———. *Land of Desire: Merchants, Power, and the Rise of a New American Culture.* New York: Vintage, 1993.

Levinas, Emmanuel. *Totality and Infinity.* Pittsburgh: Duquesne University Press, 1969.

Ley, David. "Modernism, Postmodernism and the Struggle for Place." In *The Power of Place: Bringing Together Geographical and Sociological Imaginations,* edited by John A. Agnew and James S. Duncan. Boston: Unwin Hyman, 1989.

Lifton, Robert Jay. *The Protean Self.* New York: Basic Books, 1993.

Lundin, Roger. *The Culture of Interpretation: Christian Faith and the Postmodern World.* Grand Rapids: Eerdmans, 1993.

Lyon, David. *Postmodernity.* Minneapolis: University of Minnesota Press, 1994.

MacIntyre, Alasdair. *After Virtue: A Study in Moral Theory.* Notre Dame: University of Notre Dame Press, 1984.

Martin, Biddy, and Chandra Talpade Mohanty. "Feminist Politics: What's Home Got to Do with It?" In *Feminist Studies, Critical Studies,* edited by Teresa de Lauretis. Bloomington, IN: Indiana University Press, 1986.

McKibben, Bill. *The Age of Missing Information.* New York: Plume, 1992.

Middleton, J. Richard, and Brian J. Walsh. *Truth Is Stranger Than It Used to Be: Biblical Faith in a Postmodern Age.* Downers Grove: InterVarsity, 1995.

Minh-ha, Trinh T. "Other than myself/my other self." In *Travellers' Tales: Narratives of Home and Displacement,* edited by George Robertson et al. London and New York: Routledge, 1994.

Morley, David, and Kuan-Hsing Chen, eds. *Stuart Hall: Critical Dialogues in Cultural Studies.* London: Routledge, 1996.

Myers, David. *The American Paradox: Spiritual Hunger in an Age of Plenty.* New Haven: Yale University Press, 2000.

———. *The Pursuit of Happiness: Who Is Happy and Why.* New York: William Morrow, 1992.

Nathanson, Paul. *Over the Rainbow: The Wizard of Oz as a Secular Myth of America.* Albany: SUNY, 1991.

Norris, Christopher. *What's Wrong with Postmodernism.* Baltimore: Johns Hopkins University Press, 1990.

Olthuis, James. "A Cold and Comfortless Hermeneutic or a Warm and Trembling Hermeneutic: A Conversation with John Caputo," *Christian Scholar's Review* 19:4 (June 1990).

———. "Crossing the Threshold: Sojourning Together in the Wild Spaces of Love." In *A Hermeneutics of Charity*, edited by James K. A. Smith and Henry Isaac Venema. Grand Rapids: Brazos, 2004.

———, ed. *Knowing Other-Wise: Philosophy at the Threshold of Spirituality*. New York: Fordham University Press, 1997.

Pierson, George W. *The Moving American*. New York: Alfred A. Knopf, 1972.

Postman, Neil. *Technopoly: The Surrender of Culture to Technology*. New York: Vintage, 1993.

Rabinow, Paul, ed. *The Foucault Reader*. New York: Pantheon, 1984.

Rifkin, Jeremy. *Time Wars: The Primary Conflict in Human History*. New York: Touchstone Books, 1987.

Robertson, George, et al., eds. *Travellers' Tales: Narratives of Home and Displacement*. London: Routledge, 1994.

Rubenstein, Roberta. *Home Matters: Longing and Belonging, Nostalgia and Mourning in Women's Fiction*. New York: Palgrave, 2001.

Rushdie, Salman. *Imaginary Homelands: Essays and Criticism 1981-1991*. London: Granta Books/New York: Viking/Penguin, 1991.

Said, Edward. "Reflections on Exile." In *Out There: Marginalization and Contemporary Cultures*, edited by R. Ferguson, M. Gever, Trinh T. Minh-ha, and Cornel West. Cambridge, MA: MIT Press, 1990.

Sibley, David. *Geographies of Exclusion: Society and Difference in the West*. London: Routledge, 1995.

Smith, Christian. *Moral, Believing Animals: Human Personhood and Culture*. Oxford: Oxford University Press, 2003.

Statton, Henry. *Wittgenstein and Derrida*. Lincoln, NE: University of Nebraska Press, 1984.

Taylor, Charles. *Sources of the Self: The Making of the Modern Identity*. Cambridge, MA: Harvard University Press, 1989.

Taylor, Mark McLain. "Vodou Resistance/Vodou Hope: Forging a Postmodernism that Liberates." In *Liberation Theologies, Postmodernity and the Americas*, edited by David Batstone et al. New York: Routledge, 1997.

Wachtel, Paul. *The Poverty of Affluence: A Psychological Portrait of the American Way of Life*. Philadelphia: New Society, 1989.

West, Cornel. *Race Matters*. New York: Random House, 1994.

Westphal, Merold. *God, Guilt, and Death*. Bloomington, IN: Indiana University Press, 1984.

———. "Placing Postmodernism." *Christian Scholar's Review* 20, no. 2 (December 1990).

———. "Positive Postmodernism as Radical Hermeneutics." In *The Very Idea of Radical Hermeneutics*, edited by Roy Martinez. Atlantic Highlands, NJ: Humanities Press, 1997.

———. "Postmodernism and Religious Reflection." *International Journal of the Philosophy of Religion* 38 (December 1995).

————, ed. *Postmodern Philosophy and Christian Thought*. Bloomington, IN: Indiana University Press, 1999.

Wolfe, Thomas. *You Can't Go Home Again*. New York: Harper and Row, 1940.

Wuthnow, Robert. "Spirituality in America Since the 1950's." *Theology, News, and Notes* (March 1999).

Wyschogrod, Edith. "Dwellers, Migrants, Nomads: Home in the Age of the Refugee." In *The Longing for Home*, edited by Leroy Rouner. Notre Dame, IN: University of Notre Dame Press, 1996.

5. Theology of Home

Anderson, Bernhard. *From Creation to New Creation*. Philadelphia: Fortress, 1994.

Anker, Roy. *Catching Light*. Grand Rapids: Eerdmans, 2005.

Bailey, Kenneth. *The Cross and the Prodigal: Luke 15 Through the Eyes of Middle Eastern Peasants*. 2nd edition. Downers Grove: InterVarsity, 2005.

Barton, Stephen, ed. *Where Shall Wisdom Be Found?* Edinburgh: T&T Clark, 1999.

Bass, Dorothy, ed. *Practicing Our Faith: A Way of Life for a Searching People*. San Francisco: Jossey-Bass, 1997.

Birch, Bruce. *Let Justice Roll Down: The Old Testament, Ethics, and Christian Life*. Louisville: Westminster/John Knox, 1991.

Boff, Leonardo. *Cry of the Earth, Cry of the Poor*. Maryknoll, NY: Orbis, 1997.

Bonhoeffer, Dietrich. *The Cost of Discipleship*. New York: Macmillan, 1963.

————. *Letters and Papers from Prison*. New York: Macmillan, 1971.

————. *Life Together*. New York: Harper and Row, 1954.

Bouma-Prediger, Steven. "Yearning for Home: The Christian Doctrine of Creation in a Postmodern Age." In *Postmodern Philosophy and Christian Thought*, edited by Merold Westphal. Bloomington, IN: Indiana University Press, 1999.

Brown, William P. *Character in Crisis*. Grand Rapids: Eerdmans, 1996.

————. *The Ethos of the Cosmos: The Genesis of Moral Imagination in the Bible*. Grand Rapids: Eerdmans, 1999.

Brueggemann, Walter. *Cadences of Home*. Louisville: Westminster/John Knox, 1997.

————. *A Commentary on Jeremiah: Exile and Homecoming*. Grand Rapids: Eerdmans, 1998.

————. *Hopeful Imagination: Prophetic Voices in Exile*. Philadelphia: Fortress, 1986.

————. *Ichabod Toward Home: The Journey of God's Glory*. Grand Rapids: Eerdmans, 2002.

————. *Interpretation and Obedience: From Faithful Reading to Faithful Living*. Minneapolis: Fortress Press, 1991.

————. *Isaiah 40–66*. Louisville: Westminster/John Knox, 1998.

————. *The Land: Place as Gift, Promise, and Challenge in Biblical Faith*. Philadelphia: Fortress, 1977.

————. *Old Testament Theology: Essays on Structure, Theme, and Text.* Philadelphia: Fortress, 1992.

————. *The Prophetic Imagination.* Philadelphia: Fortress, 1978.

————. "Reflections on Biblical Understandings of Property." In *A Social Reading of the Old Testament.* Minneapolis: Fortress, 1994.

————. *A Social Reading of the Old Testament.* Minneapolis: Fortress, 1994.

————. *Texts Under Negotiation: The Bible and Postmodern Imagination.* Minneapolis: Fortress, 1993.

Buber, Martin. *I and Thou.* New York: Scribner, 1970.

Cunningham, David. *These Three Are One.* Oxford: Blackwell, 1998.

Dostoevsky, Fyodor. *The Brothers Karamazov.* San Francisco: North Point Press, 1990.

Dyrness, William. *The Earth Is the Lord's: A Theology of American Culture.* Maryknoll: Orbis, 1997.

Elliott, John. *A Home for the Homeless: A Sociological Exegesis of 1 Peter, Its Situation and Strategy.* Philadelphia: Fortress, 1981.

Finger, Thomas. *Self, Earth, and Society: Alienation and Trinitarian Transformation.* Downers Grove: InterVarsity, 1997.

Gilkey, Langdon. "Creation, Being, and Non-Being." In *God and Creation,* edited by David Burrell and Bernard McGinn. Notre Dame, IN: University of Notre Dame Press, 1990.

————. *Maker of Heaven and Earth.* Garden City, NY: Doubleday, 1959.

————. *Naming the Whirlwind: The Renewal of God-Language.* Indianapolis and New York: Bobbs-Merrill, 1969.

"Globalization, Ethics, and the Earth," a position paper of the Earth and Ethics Working Group of the Commission on Theology of the Reformed Church in America.

Gorringe, Timothy J. *A Theology of the Built Environment: Justice, Empowerment, Redemption.* Cambridge, UK: Cambridge University Press, 2002.

Gundry-Volf, Judith, and Miroslav Volf. *A Spacious Heart: Essays on Identity and Belonging.* Harrisburg, PA: Trinity Press International, 1997.

Gunton, Colin. *The One, the Three, and the Many: God, Creation, and the Culture of Modernity.* Cambridge, UK: Cambridge University Press, 1993.

————. *The Promise of Trinitarian Theology.* Edinburgh: T&T Clark, 1991.

Gustafson, James. *Ethics from a Theocentric Perspective.* Chicago: University of Chicago Press, 1981.

Hall, Douglas John. *Imaging God: Dominion As Stewardship.* Grand Rapids: Eerdmans, 1986.

Hanson, Paul. *The People Called: The Growth of Community in the Bible.* San Francisco: Harper and Row, 1986.

Hart, David Bentley. *The Beauty of the Infinite.* Grand Rapids: Eerdmans, 2003.

Havel, Václav. *Disturbing the Peace.* New York: Alfred Knopf, 1990.

Hess, Carol Lakey. *Caretakers of Our Common House.* Nashville: Abingdon, 1997.

Hiebert, Theodore. *The Yahwist's Landscape: Nature and Religion in Early Israel.* New York: Oxford, 1996.

Hill, Craig. *In God's Time.* Grand Rapids: Eerdmans, 2002.

Hopkins, Gerard Manley. *Sermons and Writings.* Edited by Christopher Devlin. London: Oxford University Press, 1959.

Keesmaat, Sylvia. "Colossians, Book of." In *Dictionary for Theological Interpretation of the Bible,* edited by Craig Bartholomew. Grand Rapids: Baker, 2005.

————. "Sabbath and Jubilee: Radical Alternatives for Being Human." In Canadian Ecumenical Jubilee Initiative, *Making a New Beginning: Biblical Reflections on Jubilee.* Toronto: CEJI, 1998.

King, Martin Luther, Jr. *A Testament of Hope.* Edited by James Washington. New York: Harper & Row, 1986.

Kinsler, Ross and Gloria. *The Biblical Jubilee and the Struggle for Life.* Maryknoll, NY: Orbis, 1999.

Kohác, Erazim. "Of Dwelling and Wayfaring: A Quest for Metaphors." In *The Longing for Home,* edited by Leroy Rouner. Notre Dame, IN: University of Notre Dame, 1996.

LaCugna, Catherine Mowry. *God For Us: The Trinity and Christian Life.* San Francisco: HarperCollins, 1991.

Ladner, Gerhardt. "*Homo Viator:* Medieval Ideas on Alienation and Order." *Speculum* 42, no. 2 (April 1967).

Limouris, Gennadios, ed. *Justice, Peace, and the Integrity of Creation: Insights from Orthodoxy.* Geneva: WCC, 1990.

Lowery, Richard. *Sabbath and Jubilee.* St. Louis: Chalice, 2000.

Marcel, Gabriel. *Homo Viator.* Chicago: Regnery, 1951.

Marion, Jean-Luc. *God Without Being.* Chicago: University of Chicago Press, 1991.

McCormick, Patrick. "The Good Sojourner: Third World Tourism and the Call of Hospitality." *Journal of the Society of Christian Ethics* 24, no. 1 (2004).

Meeks, Douglas. *God the Economist: The Doctrine of God and Political Economy.* Minneapolis: Fortress, 1989.

Meilaender, Gilbert. "Creatures of Place and Time: Reflections on Moving." *First Things* (April 1997).

————. "(Re)reading Augustine's Confessions." *The Cresset* (Christmas/Epiphany 1996).

Middleton, J. Richard. *The Liberating Image: The Imago Dei in Genesis 1.* Grand Rapids: Brazos, 2005.

Milbank, John. *Theology and Social Theory: Beyond Secular Reason.* Oxford: Basil Blackwell, 1990.

Morgan, James. "Memory, Land, and Pilgrimage." *Religious Education* 87, no. 4 (Fall 1992).

Moltmann, Jürgen. *The Coming of God: Christian Eschatology.* Minneapolis: Fortress, 1996.

———. *God in Creation: A New Theology of Creation and the Spirit of God.* San Francisco: Harper and Row, 1985.

———. "Shekinah: The Home of the Homeless God." In *The Longing for Home,* edited by Leroy Rouner. Notre Dame, IN: University of Notre Dame Press, 1996.

———. *The Spirit of Life: A Universal Affirmation.* Minneapolis: Fortress, 1992.

———. *The Trinity and the Kingdom.* San Francisco: Harper and Row, 1981.

Mouw, Richard. *When the Kings Come Marching In.* Grand Rapids: Eerdmans, 1983.

Murphy, Roland. *The Tree of Life.* Grand Rapids: Eerdmans, 2002.

Myers, Bryant. *Walking with the Poor.* Maryknoll, NY: Orbis, 1999.

Nouwen, Henri. *Compassion: A Reflection on the Christian Life.* New York: Doubleday, 1983.

———. *Lifesigns: Intimacy, Fecundity, and Ecstasy in Christian Perspective.* New York: Doubleday, 1986.

———. *Reaching Out.* New York: Image Books, 1975.

———. *The Return of the Prodigal: A Story of Homecoming.* New York: Doubleday, 1994.

———. *With Burning Hearts: A Meditation on the Eucharistic Life.* Maryknoll, NY: Orbis, 1995.

Parks, Sharon Daloz. "Home and Pilgrimage: Comparison Metaphors for Personal and Social Transformation." *Soundings* 72, nos. 2-3 (Summer/Fall 1989).

Peters, Ted. *Sin: Radical Evil in Soul and Society.* Grand Rapids: Eerdmans, 1995.

Plantinga, Cornelius, Jr. "Contours of Christian Compassion." *Perspectives* 10, no. 2 (February 1995).

———. "Social Trinity and Tritheism." In *Trinity, Incarnation, and Atonement,* edited by Ronald Feenstra and Cornelius Plantinga, Jr. Notre Dame, IN: University of Notre Dame Press, 1989.

Pohl, Christine. *Making Room: Recovering Hospitality as a Christian Tradition.* Grand Rapids: Eerdmans, 1999.

Purcell, Michael. "Homelessness as a Theological Motif: Emmanuel Levinas and the Significance of the Home." *The Scottish Journal of Religious Studies* 15, no. 2 (Autumn 1994).

Rasmussen, Larry. *Earth Community, Earth Ethics.* Maryknoll, NY: Orbis, 1996.

Richardson, Cyril, ed. *Early Christian Fathers.* New York: Macmillan, 1970.

Ricoeur, Paul. *Symbolism of Evil.* Boston: Beacon, 1967.

Romero, Oscar. *The Violence of Love.* Farmington, PA: Plough Publishing House, 1998.

Rossing, Barbara. *The Rapture Exposed.* Boulder, CO: Westview, 2004.

Ruether, Rosemary Radford. *Sexism and God-Talk.* Boston: Beacon Press, 1983.

Russell, Robert. "Cosmology, Creation, and Contingency." In *Cosmos as Creation,* edited by Ted Peters. Nashville: Abingdon, 1989.

Schreiner, Susan. *The Theatre of His Glory: Nature and the Natural Order in the Thought of John Calvin.* Grand Rapids: Baker, 1991.

Schrift, Alan, ed. *The Logic of the Gift: Toward an Ethic of Generosity.* New York: Routledge, 1997.

Shaw, Luci, ed. *A Widening Light*. Wheaton, IL: Harold Shaw Publishers, 1984.

Sider, Ron, ed. *Cry Justice: The Bible on Hunger and Poverty*. New York: Paulist, 1980.

Smedes, Lewis. *Mere Morality*. Grand Rapids: Eerdmans, 1983.

———. *Standing on the Promises: Keeping Hope Alive for a Tomorrow We Cannot Control*. Nashville: Thomas Nelson, 1998.

Smith, Daniel. *The Religion of the Landless*. San Francisco: Harper & Row, 1989.

Smith, David, and Barbara Carvill. *The Gift of the Stranger: Faith, Hospitality, and Foreign Language Learning*. Grand Rapids: Eerdmans, 2000.

Stoll, Elmo, and Robert Riall. *Strangers and Pilgrims: Why We Live Simply*. Aylmer, ON, and LaGrange, IN: Pathway Publishers, 2003.

Thiselton, Anthony. *Interpreting God and the Postmodern Self: On Meaning, Manipulation and Promise*. Grand Rapids: Eerdmans, 1995.

Tracy, David. *On Naming the Present: God, Hermeneutics, and Church*. Maryknoll, NY: Orbis, 1994.

———. *Plurality and Ambiguity: Hermeneutics, Religion, Hope*. San Francisco: Harper and Row, 1987.

Trigo, Pedro. *Creation and History*. Maryknoll: Orbis, 1991.

Tutu, Desmond. *God Has a Dream*. New York: Doubleday, 2004.

Vanier, Jean. *Community and Growth*. New York: Paulist, 1989.

———. *From Brokenness to Community*. New York: Paulist, 1992.

———. *Our Journey Home: Recovering a Common Humanity Beyond Our Differences*. Maryknoll, NY: Orbis, 1996.

Verhey, Allen. *Remembering Jesus: Christian Community, Scripture, and the Moral Life*. Grand Rapids: Eerdmans, 2002.

———. "Suffering and Compassion." *Perspectives* 10, no. 2 (February 1995).

Volf, Miroslav. *Exclusion and Embrace: A Theological Exploration of Identity, Otherness, and Reconciliation*. Nashville: Abingdon, 1996.

Walsh, Brian J. "'At Home in the Darkness, But Hungry for Dawn' — Global Homelessness and a Passion for Homecoming in the Music of Bruce Cockburn." *Cultural Encounters* 1, no. 2 (Summer 2005).

———. "Homemaking in Exile: Homelessness, Postmodernity and Theological Reflection." In *Reminding: Renewing the Mind in Learning*, edited by Doug Blomberg and Ian Lambert. Sydney, Australia: Centre for the Study of Australian Christianity, 1998.

———. "One Day I Shall Be Home: Homecoming Lyrics by Canadian Bruce Cockburn." *Christianity and the Arts* 7, no. 1 (Winter 2000).

———. "Reimaging Biblical Authority." *Christian Scholar's Review* 26, no. 2 (Winter 1996).

———. *Subversive Christianity: Imaging God in a Dangerous Time*. Seattle: Alta Vista College Press, 1994.

———. "Transformation: Dynamic Worldview or Repressive Ideology?" *Journal of Education and Christian Belief* 4, no. 2 (Autumn 2000).

Walsh, Brian J., and J. Richard Middleton. *The Transforming Vision*. Downers Grove: InterVarsity, 1984.

Walsh, Brian J., and Sylvia C. Keesmaat. *Colossians Remixed: Subverting the Empire*. Downers Grove, IL: InterVarsity, 2004.

Webb, Stephen. *The Gifting God: A Trinitarian Ethics of Excess*. New York: Oxford University Press, 1996.

Welker, Michael. *Creation and Reality*. Minneapolis: Fortress, 1999.

Westphal, Merold. "Lest We Forget." *Perspectives* 11, no. 2 (February 1996).

———. *Overcoming Onto-Theology: Toward a Postmodern Christian Faith*. New York: Fordham University Press, 2001.

Wilkinson, Loren. "The New Story of Creation: A Trinitarian Perspective." *Crux* 30, no. 4 (December 1994).

Wolff, Hans Walter. *Anthropology of the Old Testament*. Philadelphia: Fortress, 1981.

Wolterstorff, Nicholas. *Lament for a Son*. Grand Rapids: Eerdmans, 1987.

———. *Until Justice and Peace Embrace*. Grand Rapids: Eerdmans, 1983.

Wright, N. T. *Jesus and the Victory of God*. Minneapolis: Fortress, 1996.

———. *The Millennium Myth*. Louisville: Westminster/John Knox, 1999.

———. *The New Testament and the People of God*. Minneapolis: Fortress, 1992.

Zizioulas, John. *Being As Communion*. Crestwood, NY: St. Vladimir's Seminary Press, 1985.

Author Index

Subject Index

Aboriginal peoples. *See* Indigenous peoples

Agribusiness, 9-12. *See also* Agriculture

Agriculture, 17. *See also* Agribusiness

American Beauty, 240

"American Dream," 108

Amnesia, 7-14, 19, 130, 153, 187n.68, 241. *See also* Memory

Amos, Tori, 244-45

Animals: as part of creation, 129, 287-89, 292-94; compassion for, 219

Anthropocentrism, 15n.22, 288n.37, 209, 289. *See also* Ecological crisis (causes of): anthropocentrism

Architecture, 113-19, 122; as expressions of values, 134-36; meaning of, 131-34; and modernity, 131-32; uniformity of, 131, 131n.29. *See also* City planning; Housing

Automobiles (and mobility), 254-57

Borders, 45-54, 96n.27, 164n.7, 248, 262. *See also* Boundaries

Boundaries, 41, 45, 46-55, 58, 60-62, 65, 248-49; ambiguity of, 45, 49-51, 53, 249; and construction of home, 243, 248; dynamism of, 54; and exclusion, 46-47, 49-51, 53-55, 248-49, 110-11, 110n.57, 243; and hospitality, 52-55, 60; and hybridity/border-crossing,

48-49, 262; and identity, 51-55; and Jesus, 191-93; and modernity, 48; necessity of, 46; and order, 53; and security, 51-53. *See also* Borders

Bush, George H. W. (housing legislation), 89, 101n.38. *See also* Neoconservative agenda

Bush, George W. (agenda of), 150. *See also* Neoconservative agenda

Capitalism, 48, 60, 102-3, 106n.48; and "domicide," 110n.58; and ecological crisis, 165n.10, 175-77, 182; and postmodern homelessness, 258, 260-63; and virtue, 210-11. *See also* "Domicide"; Globalization; Neoconservative agenda

Catholic Worker Movement, 60. *See also* Dorothy Day

Church: and empire, 264-70; as home of God, 207; and Jubilee practices, 27; as sojourning community, 294, 297-302

City planning, 136. *See also* Architecture; Housing

Climate change, 161-62, 164, 178. *See also* Ecological crisis

Cockburn, Bruce, 59, 67, 94-95, 239, 241, 271, 303, 313, 315-17

Cohen, Leonard, 245-46

351

27, 33, 36-37, 74-75, 207, 237, 264, 291, 305, 315

Homecoming, 9-11, 64-66, 128; biblical vision of, 12-28, 30, 34, 119-20, 153, 155-56, 191-95, 200, 203-8, 230-38, 280, 290, 304-12; and God, 274-75; hope for, 315-19; and housing, 129-30; as literary theme, 9-11; and pilgrimage, 296-97; and Prodigal Son parable, 319-26; spirituality of, 273-74; in *The Wizard of Oz*, 242-45

HomeComing (coalition), 147n.63

Homemaking: 53, 56-67, 153-57; as activity of the Creator, 14-16, 29-37, 273, 297, 304; as activity of empire, 18-19; as activity of human beings, 16; as activity of Jesus, 23-27, 191, 238, 297; as aspect of the covenant with Israel, 16-18, 206; 211-12; as divine attribute, 274-75, 277n.5, 279, 282-84, 320-26; and ecological concerns, 15n.22, 167, 199; economics of, 112, 141-45, 151-52; and hospitality, 293; and inhabitation, 62; and memory, 9, 11, 13-14, 297; relationship to home, 125-26, 139-40; spirituality of, 273-74; as ultimate hope, 27; virtues of, 208-9; and war, 313-14; as way of life, 273, 297-302; and worship, 268

Homelessness: biblical understanding of, 12-28, 118, 298; and boundaries, 46, 50-53; in Canada, 98-100; of the crucifixion, 237-38; as cultural crisis, 145-52; culture of, 7-12; as displacement, 4-7; ecological, 40, 158-89; and empire, 153-57; in Hawaii, 58; and hope, 315-20; and housing, 41-42, 125; and mobility, 57; postmodern, 40, 239-63, 272, 285-86, 300, 302-3, 314-15; and powerlessness, 146; socioeconomic, 40, 76-93, 112, 145-52; spiritual, 40; as spiritual crisis, 141; types of, 40-45; through loss of community, 138; in the U.S., 89n.10, 97-98,

100-101; and worldview, 125, 129, 137, 139. *See also* Displacement: culture of; Homelessness industry; Housing

Homelessness industry, 104

Homesickness, 11, 61-64; postmodern, 242-49

"Homeward Bound," 302-3. *See also* Simon and Garfunkel

Hope, 188-89, 199, 221, 286, 290, 303, 314-20; postmodernity's loss of, 244-45, 290

Hospitality, 20, 52-55, 60-61, 66, 82, 112, 140, 205, 268, 293, 297, 301-2; as practice of Israel, 301; as practice of Jesus, 301. *See also* Neighborliness

Household (early Christian), 268-70. *See also* Church

Housing, 51n.28, 94, 125-26; affordable, 87-89, 91-92, 93n.28, 96n.26, 97-101, 105, 108, 110-11, 147; as commodity, 127; and homes, 126-28, 130-32, 139-40, 151-52; as human right, 126-27, 140, 144-51; and indigenous people, 122-25, 129-32, 137-39; public, 133, 139-40, 147; and public policy (Canada), 89, 98-100, 104; and public policy (Sweden and New Zealand), 108n.52; and public policy (U.S.), 89, 97-98, 100-101; standardization of, 140; and worldviews, 125-40

Humanity: as creature, 14-15; finitude of, 290-91; as image of God, 31-33; postmodern understanding of, 287; reconciliation of, 207; sinfulness of, 291

Identity, 41, 45-46, 51-52, 54, 58-59, 62, 64, 124, 129-30, 132-34, 146n.62, 190-91, 248-49, 251, 255, 283, 286

Idolatry, 13-14, 16, 19, 57n.33, 141, 153, 201, 259; of economism, 141n.47

Imagination, 33, 111-12, 138, 177, 219, 266, 306, 312, 315-16, 320

Immigration, 42, 45, 82-83, 250, 256, 297

Scripture Index